Getting Answers to Your Questions

A Middle-Level Educator's Guide to Program Evaluation

Getting Answers to Your Questions

A Middle-Level Educator's Guide to Program Evaluation

Brenda Guenther LeTendre, Richard P. Lipka

Christopher-Gordon Publishers, Inc.
Norwood, Massachusetts

Credits

Christopher-Gordon Publishers, Inc.
1502 Providence Highway, Suite 12
Norwood, MA 02062
(800) 934-8322

Printed in the United States of America

10 9 8 7 6 5 4 3 2 1   03 02 01 00 99

Library of Congress Catalogue Number: 99-72585
ISBN: 0-926842-94-3

Brief Contents

Long Contents

CHAPTER 10 Solution-Seeking Questions 299

Acknowledgements

The genesis of a book such as this springs from many sources. Throughout the years, we have had the privilege of working with many remarkable educators who have helped us hone our thinking about question asking and question answering. In particular, we wish to thank the principals and teachers working with middle-level youngsters who have both challenged our ideas and shown us the way. They always required that we stay grounded in the real world of middle schools.

Special thanks also goes to Henry M. Levin, director of Stanford University's Accelerated Schools National Center, and Joan Solomon at the Missouri Department of Elementary and Secondary Education for sharing their ideas with us and giving us the opportunity to work closely with teachers and principals in Accelerated Schools across the United States. This work in the real world of schools helped us to refine the ideas you will encounter in this book.

Finally, we wish to thank Janice Cooke, a middle school educator in New Jersey, who not only took part of her much-deserved summer "vacation" to read the rough draft of this book, but also provided us with invaluable suggestions about ways to make the book more teacher-friendly.

Dedication

To my husband, Dana LeTendre, who not only opened the doors of opportunity for me personally and professionally, but also acts each day as a friendly critic of my ideas.

—Brenda LeTendre

To my wife, Nancy Lipka, whose creeds and deeds as a public school teacher keep the flame of public education burning brightly.

—Richard Lipka

To all middle-level educators in schools across North America who, day in and day out, strive to do "right by the kids."

Preface

Why We Wrote This Book

- Is the new hands-on math program working?
- Should we adopt a 10-block schedule?
- How can we reduce the number of fights in the cafeteria?
- What evidence do we have to answer critics who want to dismantle our service learning curriculum?

Each school day, middle school educators pose questions such as these as they strive to "do right by the kids." Individually or in teams, educators work to solve problems—problems that run the gamut from the simple (How can we get more students to participate in intramural basketball?) to the complex (How can we increase the reading ability of our students?).

Our experience in working in schools tells us that teachers and principals are very good at asking questions. However, they are not always able to get the answers they need. Why? First, they sometimes *do not know how* to get the answers. They simply lack the skills for collecting meaningful data, analyzing and interpreting that data, and then making decisions based on their findings.

Second, they *lack the time* needed to gather answers to their questions. Too often, middle school educators face problems that won't wait. They must find solutions fast.

Finally, many times educators simply *are not willing to dig* for the answers they need. They already "know" the appropriate solution. To them, investigation is just a waste of time. Unfortunately, they often find out too late that their "solutions" really don't work and they must go back to square one.

With this book, we hope to remove these three barriers to answer-seeking. First, this book will give you the tools you need to get your questions answered. We will show you, through numerous examples, how to use the techniques of program evaluation to find answers to your questions, from the simple to complex.

Second, while none of us can manufacture time, we will provide you with suggestions on how you can "capture" time by using information to help you work more effectively and efficiently.

Finally, we will show you how to use program evaluation techniques to make sure that you select solutions that truly solve your problems.

Who Should Read This Book?

We wrote this book especially for teachers and principals working in middle schools. But given our emphasis on broad collaboration, we expect that it will interest any adult engaged in the quest to improve teaching and schools. Support staff, central office administrators, school board members and parents can also profit from reading this book.

As we finish the manuscript for this book, we have already begun work on two similar books—one for high school educators and one for those in elementary schools. Both books will draw on the same core concepts and processes we present in this book. However, we will tailor each book to the particular issues and realities faced by educators working in high schools and elementary schools. In this way, we hope to make the techniques of question-asking and question-answering accessible to all educators.

How Can This Book Help You?

This book can help you:

- Demonstrate to yourself and others what you have accomplished.

- Find solutions that address the core reasons and *really* solve the problem.

- Guide you in improving your teaching and your school so that you "do right by the kids."

But It's All Unrealistic!

Some who flip through this book may say we're dealing in fantasy. No teacher will get this involved in evaluating innovations. But we're *not* talking about fantasy. Indeed, we know hundreds of teachers who are, at this moment, intimately involved in gathering, analyzing, and interpreting data with the ultimate goal of finding solutions and making better decisions to improve their classrooms and schools.

For example, in every school across the state of Missouri, teachers and administrators work together as part of the state's Comprehensive School Improvement Process, to gather, analyze and interpret data, all in an effort to improve the quality of education for their students. Similarly, the over 20,000 teachers working in Accelerated Schools nationwide are engaged in improving their classrooms and schools by using evaluation techniques to take stock, determine what worked, and solve problems.

The list of examples can go on for pages. One thing we've learned in the last decade of school reform is that *good* schools don't just happen. Schools are good because the adults in them decide to collaborate in systematically solving problems, and then take action based on their findings.

A Prime Belief

A prime belief permeates this book: teachers, principals, and even students should, indeed must, collaborate in seeking answers to the questions they face daily. The days of the be-all, know-all principal who can single-handedly solve all school problems are over. Likewise, teachers can no longer act as Lone Rangers, coming each day into their classrooms, closing the doors, and teaching *their* children, oblivious to the rest of the school.

We've all heard the African proverb—"It takes a whole village to raise a child." We also believe it takes the *whole* school to educate a child. For this reason, many of the examples we use in this book show groups of educators, a team or even a whole faculty, working together to pose and answer questions.

Despite this belief, we also know that a teacher may find herself alone, a single voice seeking change among those who steadfastly cling to the status quo. Even though you may have to go it alone, take heart. You, too, will find this book helpful. It will provide you with the knowledge and skills you need to lead the way in changing your *own* classroom. Perhaps your colleagues will take notice and your efforts in your own classroom will plant the seeds of change within the entire school.

A Gentle Warning

As you read the upcoming chapters, much of the material will sound familiar and instantly make sense. However, you may occasionally bump into concepts and terms that, at first, seem intimidating simply because you think you should already know this stuff but don't. In our experience, few graduate programs, and even fewer undergraduate programs, cover all the information we discuss in this book. You'll find that as you encounter example after example of the concepts in action, your understanding will grow and your uneasiness will pass.

How We Organized This Book

We have organized this book keeping in mind the realities of an educator's busy life. The introduction lays a foundation, defining the three categories of questions that you, as a middle school educator, will most likely want answered as you work to educate students. It also includes an explanation of the key concepts of program evaluation. Chapters 1 through 6 walk you through the six steps in conducting an evaluation, while chapter 7 gives solid advice about clearly communicating the results of your evaluation to a variety of audiences including parents and school boards.

In the remaining chapters, we explore in greater depth each of the three categories of questions educators want answered. Chapter 8 focuses on getting answers to *Taking-Stock Questions*. These questions ask: *"Where are we now?"*. This chapter not only shows you how to pose questions that really do get at the "here and now," but also provides you with techniques for collecting meaningful data. Chapter 8 concludes with two case studies, one showing how a team of middle school educators used program evaluation methods to take stock of their current situation and the other demonstrating how an individual teacher took stock in her own classroom.

Chapter 9 concentrates on getting answers to *Effectiveness Questions*. These questions ask—*"Did our solution work?"*. This chapter demonstrates how you can use the techniques of program evaluation to determine if your solutions, big or small, actually worked. Chapter 9 also includes two case studies demonstrating how program evaluation methods can guide both individual teachers and teams of educators in improving their teaching practice and schools.

Chapter 10 features techniques for getting answers to *Solution-Seeking Questions*. These questions ask—*"What is our problem and how should we solve it?"*. This chapter guides you through the crucial first step in solving any difficulty—defining your problem. It also provides you with suggestions on how to search for and ultimately decide on, solutions that will really work. Chapter 10 concludes with a case study illustrating how a group of middle school practitioners used these evaluation skills to achieve success in their school. This chapter also shows how one teacher used the techniques to solve a problem she faced in her own classroom. The epilogue rounds out the book by summarizing its key points.

We have tried to make this book especially "friendly," providing you with clear explanations and readily accessible information. We hope you'll find the following features especially helpful:

- At the end of each chapter, we provide a summary of the major concepts and advice given in the chapter. This way you can easily go back and refresh your memory about key information.

- We also give an annotated list at the end of each chapter of print resources and Websites that you can consult for more information. We provide the address for our own Web page where you'll find hot links to all the recommended Websites, along with links to the publishers of the books we recommend. Given the rapid pace of change on the Internet, we will update our Web page regularly to keep our list of recommendations current.

- Finally, some of the examples in this book describe special program or teaching strategies that may pique your curiosity. We've marked these real-world interventions with an ✳. You'll find more information about these programs in the appendix.

A Final Word

In this day of increased accountability, coupled with demands that innovative practices be research-based, we feel that this book fills a crucial need. Whether you are trying to improve the teaching practices in your own classroom, or trying to reform your entire school, you will find this book a practical guide to getting your questions answered. Questions that can lead to a better education for all students.

Introduction

Intro.1—The Real World Calls for Judgments

Situation 1

"That's simply not true!" Beverly, a middle school educator, fumed as she looked at the newspaper article. The headline read: "Area Middle Schools Shortchanging Students." She quickly scanned the article and found that the reporter had obtained the latest state assessment scores for the community's three middle schools. In math and science, students at all three schools, including Beverly's, ranked below the state average. "We are, too, doing a good job! I know our kids are doing better than these state tests show," she muttered to herself, vowing to raise the issue at the next meeting of the School Improvement Committee.

Situation 2

"Look, this block scheduling we've been using for the past two years appears to be the answer to our problems," explained Murray, a middle school teacher, to his fellow teachers during a School Improvement Committee meeting. "But I'm getting lots of grumbling from our high school colleagues. They say we just jumped on the fad bandwagon and our kids are suffering. The high school teachers believe our kids simply won't be ready for the rigors of high school courses. How can we prove to them that block scheduling is working and our kids will *indeed* be ready?"

Situation 3

"I don't want to have to do that again," Joan complained to the principal's secretary as she walked out of the vice-principal's office where she left four very angry 7th grade girls. "That's the second time today I've had to break up a shouting match between girls during passing period. Is it me or does it seem that this kind of thing is happening all the time? We need to do something to stop this!"

Beverly, Murray and Joan need answers. Like middle school educators everywhere, they face situations daily that require them to get answers to difficult questions. In Situation 1, Beverly and her colleagues need to *take stock* of their school, answering the questions: "Where are we *now*?" and "How *healthy* is our

1

school?". In Situation 2, Murray and his fellow middle school educators need to *determine the effectiveness* of block scheduling. They need to ask and honestly answer the tough questions: Is it really working and should we continue using it? Finally, in Situation 3, Joan also needs to ask questions and get answers, but her questions have a different purpose—to *find a solution* to a problem.

These three types of questions—taking stock questions, effectiveness questions, and solution-seeking questions—form the structure for this book. Chapters 8, 9 and 10 deal specifically with practical strategies you can use to get answers to these types of questions. In this introduction, along with chapters 1 through 6, we lay the foundation. We begin by discussing the differences between research and evaluation. We then move on to give an overview of the six-step process you can use to get answers to your questions.

Intro.2—*First Cousins:* Research and Program Evaluation

In education, whenever we are faced with questions that need answers, we often turn to two broad processes for getting answers:

1. We conduct some research or
2. We perform an evaluation of a program.

Actually, research and program evaluation are first cousins. Both research and program evaluation collect, analyze and interpret data, and draw conclusions. Indeed, researchers and evaluators may employ many of the same techniques in collecting and analyzing data. But the *cousins* of research and program evaluation part company when it comes to purpose. Researchers seek to explain, describe, or determine the effectiveness of an intervention. Program evaluators go one step further. Not only do they seek to explain, describe, and determine effectiveness, *evaluators also judge the worth or merit of the intervention.* In addition to questions like *Did it work?*, program evaluators also answer questions about value like *"It is worth continuing?"* and *"Is it worth doing?"*.

> Clarification: We wish to make clear that the focus of this book is on *program* evaluation. It does not address the evaluation of students for the purpose of assigning grades or the evaluation of teachers to decide merit pay, tenure, or continued employment. However, you should know that researchers and program evaluators might use student grades or teacher performance evaluations to decide whether or not a particular innovation is working. For example, a researcher might use student grades in writing as a means of determining if the Bay Area Writing Program✳ is indeed effective in teaching students how to write.

Intro.3—A Closer Look at Research

Now that we have differentiated between the two broad processes of getting answers, research versus program evaluation, let's examine each one more closely. We will begin with research.

As educators we are quick to banter around the question, *"Do you have any research to back this up?"* But just what do we mean by research? To our students, doing research means a trip to the library or a ride on the World Wide Web to find various sources that speak to a topic. This is not what we mean by research. Nor do we see research as simply a review of literature to collect detailed descriptions of what XYZ Middle School did to solve its students' reading problems.

When we say *research,* we mean something more. We mean something rigorous that provides answers to questions about schools and learning. Researchers, whether they live in middle school classrooms or universities, engage in systematic inquiry designed to find out what works, how it works, and why it works. They concentrate on answering the following types of questions:

- What's going on here?
- Did it work?
- How does it work?
- Why did this work or why didn't this work?

By answering these questions, researchers hope to describe, provide evidence, discover causes, discern predictive patterns, and, finally, generate knowledge that can explain phenomena across similar situations and locations. They observe using systematic methods, seeking to produce valid conclusions justified by credible evidence. Finally, they strive to conduct studies that other researchers can replicate and obtain similar results. They want results that can withstand the scrutiny of other researchers.

Intro.4—Issue Box

Action Research

"A rose by any other name is still a rose."
—W. Shakespeare

"A program evaluator known as an action researcher is still a program evaluator."
—LeTendre and Lipka

In recent years, a new category of inquiry has emerged—action research. Two characteristics set action research apart from the more traditional types of research. The first distinguishing characteristic concerns *who* does the research. Traditional researchers tend to reside in universities or educational research laboratories. Research is their main job. On the other hand, action researchers tend to be practicing teachers and administrators. Their main job is to educate youngsters. They conduct research to help inform their practice so they can do a better job of educating youngsters.

The second distinguishing characteristic of action research centers around *purpose.* Traditional researchers seek knowledge as a means of explaining how and why something works. They wish to create theory that can be generalized to many situations and locations. In contrast, action researchers examine their *own* classrooms and schools in order to inform their *own* practice, not somebody else's practice.

Given our previous distinction between research and program evaluation, we contend that action researchers are really engaging in program evaluation and *not* research. Yes, they often use the methods employed by researchers to gather, analyze and interpret data, but they go the next step. Action researchers use their findings to judge the *worth or value* of an intervention. In addition to the question *"Did it work?"*, action researchers, like program evaluators, also answer questions about value: *"It is worth continuing?"* and *"Is it worth doing?"*. Furthermore, they use their findings to make decisions about how they can improve their teaching and their schools.

Intro.5—A Closer Look at Program Evaluation

You'll remember earlier in the chapter we called program evaluation a *first cousin* of research. Like researchers, program evaluators systematically collect, analyze and interpret data, but program evaluators go one step further. Not only do program evaluators seek to explain, describe, and determine the effectiveness of an intervention, they also use a wide array of research methods to judge the quality, worth and usefulness of an intervention. In evaluation, educators make *judgments* and then use these judgments to guide their decisions about how to spend money, assign resources, and educate youngsters.

As program evaluators, middle school educators concentrate on the following questions:

- How good is this?
- Is this worth doing?
- Did it work?
- Is it worth continuing?
- How can we make this better?

To gain a better understanding of what we mean by program evaluation, let's examine our three situations with Beverly, Murray, and Joan through the lenses of program evaluation.

In Situation 1, Beverly is incensed that the local newspaper portrays her school as "shortchanging students." Not only does she want to "tell it like it really is" by describing the current state of her school, but she also wants to assess the health of her school. Just how well does her school stack up against established standards of excellence? When Beverly and her colleagues *take stock* of their school in light of established standards, they have crossed the line from research to evaluation. They are now judging the worthiness, the goodness of their school. They must begin with a thorough and accurate picture of the school, and then they can move to the next step of improving their school.

Evaluation definitely plays a role in Situation 2. Murray and his fellow middle school educators want to prove to the high school faculty that the new schedule works and the middle school kids will indeed be ready for the rigors of high school. Not only will Murray and his colleagues need to honestly answer the question, *"Is it working?"*, but they need to be ready for a series of value questions. Implicit behind the comments of the high school faculty members is the question, *"Is block scheduling really worth doing?"*. Furthermore, if Murray and his colleagues do find that block scheduling is working, they must also ask, *"How can we make it better?"*. Both of these questions require that Murray and his fellow educators *make judgments* about the worthiness of block scheduling.

In Situation 3, Joan *seeks a solution* to the excessive name-calling that occurs during the passing periods. At first, evaluation only hovers on the horizon in this situation. Joan and her colleagues begin by describing what is going on, discovering patterns and determining causes. However, once Joan and her colleagues determine the core causes of the name-calling, they will build an action plan to address these underlying causes. After they implement their solution, they will ask—*"Did it work? Is this intervention worth continuing? How can we fine-tune this intervention?"*. With these judgment questions, evaluation enters the scene.

As you can see, program evaluation has a direct role in answering questions that take stock of a current situation, as well as questions that determine effectiveness and make judgments about the worthiness of an intervention. Furthermore, program evaluation eventually comes into play when educators seek solutions. Once educators implement an action plan designed to solve a problem, they must ask "Did it work? If so, is it worth continuing?"

Intro.6—The Flavors of Program Evaluation

Program evaluation comes in three sets or *flavors:*

- Informal and formal evaluation
- Formative and summative evaluation
- Internal and external evaluations

All these flavors can play an important role in helping you get your questions answered.

Intro.7—Informal and Formal Evaluation

The first two flavors of program evaluation have to do with *how structured and systematic* the evaluation process is. Informal evaluation, just as its name implies, takes a less methodical and rigorous approach. Formal evaluation, on the other hand, requires that evaluators carefully specify beforehand, and along each step of the way, the procedures they will follow in collecting, analyzing and interpreting data. Furthermore, during a formal evaluation, evaluators strive for as much objectivity as humanly possible.

Judging the quality of ice cream might serve as a good example to distinguish between informal and formal evaluation. Let's say that the owners of Cool

Licks, a local ice cream shop, want to determine how well their ice cream stacks up against the ice cream sold by a nationally-franchised store located near the interstate highway. One day, the owners of Cool Licks visit the competition and each orders a scoop of vanilla ice cream. "I like ours better," says one owner. "Yea, I agree," concurs the other, "Ours has more of a vanilla taste." They leave convinced that their ice cream is superior.

These two owners have definitely engaged in evaluation, but this is what we call *informal evaluation*. They walked into the store and simply tasted the ice cream. They made no attempt to establish beforehand the criteria they would use to judge the quality of their competition's ice cream. Furthermore, each owner probably had in mind a different, implicit set of standards for judging the quality of the ice cream. Finally, the owners made no attempt to obtain *accurate, unbiased* information. As owners of a competing ice cream shop, they most likely possessed from the start a bias *against* the franchised product which made it impossible for them to gather accurate, objective data about their competitor's ice cream.

In contrast to informal evaluation, *formal evaluation* is

- Planned
- Systematic
- Objective

In a formal evaluation, someone actually draws up a full-blown evaluation plan on paper *before* the evaluation even begins. During the planning stages of a project, evaluators will often design how they will judge the worthiness of an intervention even *before* the program itself gets implemented. Furthermore, in a formal evaluation, educators systematically define beforehand the judgment criteria they will use, and then take an equally systematic approach in collecting, analyzing, and interpreting data. Finally, formal evaluators strive to conduct the evaluation in an objective manner, keeping things as free of bias as humanly possible. They seek to use judgment methods that will withstand the scrutiny of skeptics and supporters alike.

Let's return to our ice cream shop owners for a look at formal evaluation. To conduct a formal evaluation comparing their vanilla ice cream to that of their competitor, the owners would *begin by generating the general questions they want answered* by the evaluation. These questions can be as broad as, *"How does our vanilla ice cream stack up against that of our competitor?"*.

Next, before collecting any data, they *systematically define how they will judge* the quality of the ice cream. They might consult the Food and Drug Administration's standards that define the various grades of ice cream from basic to premium. They can then begin building a set of judgment criteria, ranging from the amount of butterfat and vanilla flavoring in the ice cream to the actual feel of the ice cream on the tongue. Some of these criteria will rely on data objectively analyzed (such as the amount of butterfat) while some will rely on the subjective assessments of trained tasters (such as the feel of the ice cream in the mouth).

Once they have established their judgment criteria, the owners then *lay out a written evaluation that draws on the best practices of product evaluation*. This written plan specifies what data they will need, what methods will be used to collect and analyze the data, and who will do these tasks. They also determine a time line for completing all the evaluation duties. To make sure they have covered all their bases, the owners show the evaluation plan to a panel of expert food product evaluators and incorporate their suggestions. This formal evaluation plan then guides the collection, analysis, and interpretation of the data. Finally, the owners of Cool Licks examine the data and apply the preestablished criteria of "ice cream goodness" to judge how well their ice cream stacks up against that of their competitor.

Intro.8—Informal and Formal Evaluation in Action

So what does all this about informal and formal evaluation mean for our middle school educators Beverly, Murray, and Joan who all need answers to their questions? Let's look at Beverly's situation. In Situation 1, Beverly reads the newspaper article criticizing area middle schools and she quickly declares, "That's simply not true! We are, too, doing a good job! I know our kids are doing better than these state tests show." At this point, Beverly has made an *informal evaluation*. She bases her judgment on her own private criteria of school goodness and relies on her own perceptions, rather than any systematic examination, in making her judgment about her school. However, if she's really serious about refuting the newspaper's claim that her school is "shortchanging students," she needs to engage in a *formal evaluation*, where she and her colleagues first systematically define the judgment criteria and then use equally systematic, non-biased methods to collect, analyze and interpret information. Only then can her judgments of her school's goodness withstand the scrutiny of skeptics and newspaper reporters.

Intro.9—No Matter What Flavor, Define Judgment Criteria Beforehand

Before we proceed to the other flavors of evaluation, we want to alert you to a particular bias that we, as authors, hold about informal and formal evaluation. Every day we, as educators, constantly evaluate what we and others are doing. However, most of our evaluations fall into the informal category. For the most part, our judgments are private and idiosyncratic. We don't suggest that educators stop doing informal evaluations. Indeed, we're not sure it's even possible for a humans to stop making informal judgments. These judgments help us to survive.

But we do suggest that you use the processes of *formal* evaluation more frequently whenever you face decisions about how to improve your classroom practice or your school. We ask that you become more systematic and deliberate in your evaluations, that you systematically define your judgment criteria *before* you judge and that you systematically collect, analyze and interpret the information that you use to make your judgments. Formal evaluation can range from simply taking five minutes to jot down an evaluation plan before you try out a new teaching strategy to working with a group of colleagues over a month's time to draw up a full-blown evaluation plan that you will submit with a grant proposal.

Intro.10—Formative and Summative Evaluation

Now that we have revealed our bias towards formal evaluation, let's move to the second set of evaluation flavors. This pair of flavors revolves around the *timing* of the evaluation, at what point during implementation you conduct the evaluation. *Formative evaluation* occurs *during* implementation and seeks to provide information that will tell you whether you are on the right track or need to make slight adjustments. For example, a chef making a pot of soup will begin (implement) the soup and as it cooks, she will periodically taste the broth and adjust the seasonings accordingly. This periodic tasting is formative evaluation. In contrast, *summative evaluation* occurs *at the end* of the implementation and seeks primarily to provide information about the effectiveness, usefulness, and worth of the intervention. Using the soup example, the chef serves the soup and asks the diners, "How is it? Do you like it?". Their answers constitute a summative evaluation of the soup.

Unfortunately, many educators (and policy makers in state houses and Washington D.C.) focus solely on summative evaluation. They want only to taste the soup at the end and care little about tasting and adjusting the seasonings as the soup cooks. We strongly advise you to engage in both formative *and* summative evaluation as you implement any new strategy, whether it is something you try in your own classroom or it is something your entire school implements. You need to periodically check your progress and make adjustments. Only through these formative evaluations can you ensure that your intervention will have a reasonable chance of success. Otherwise, you might find that you have to toss out an entire batch of educational "soup" at the end, just because you failed to add a pinch of "salt" while it was cooking.

Situation 2 facing Murray illustrates the need for both formative and summative evaluation. Implementing block scheduling at a middle school is no easy feat. Indeed, for successful implementation, faculties often spend up to one year in preparation before switching to a block schedule. Obviously, during the implementation of block scheduling, Murray and his fellow middle school colleagues informally evaluated how well the new schedule worked. You can bet that talk in the teachers' lounge during the first few months of the block schedule centered around what was going right and wrong. Furthermore, some of these formative evaluations led to adjustments that improved the implementation. But unfortunately, this informal formative evaluation was just that, informal. The staff simply had not built into their implementation plan any systematic way of gathering feedback from students, parents, and staff—feedback that could help them fine-tune their implementation of the block schedule. In hindsight, Murray now realizes that formative evaluation, done in a systematic formal way, would have made sense.

Now, after using the block schedule for two years, he and his middle school colleagues face a skeptical high school faculty that demands to know if the block scheduling is indeed working. Murray also suspects that the school board, parents, and patrons also want to know the effectiveness and worth of the new schedule. At this point, Murray and his fellow teachers turn to summative evaluation to answer the tough questions like: *"Does it work?"* and *"Is it worth continuing?"*. Once again, a systematic, formal summative evaluation makes sense.

Intro.11—Internal and External Evaluation

The final set of evaluation flavors focuses on *who* conducts the evaluation. An *internal evaluation* relies on people in-house to conduct the evaluation. Often, these internal evaluators are also the implementors. For example, let's say your team has started using graphic organizers to help students learn and retain information. Before you begin using graphic organizers with your students, your team agrees on the outcomes you hope to accomplish by using this instructional strategy. Furthermore, you also delineate what you would accept as evidence that graphic organizers do indeed help your students learn and retain facts and concepts. You design an evaluation plan and your team systematically collects, analyzes, and interprets the data. You then make a judgment, based on the evidence, about whether or not graphic organizers work and are worth continuing to use.

In contrast, an *external evaluation* uses people other than the implementors to conduct the evaluation. In fact, external evaluators are outsiders who have *no* stake in whether or not the intervention works or has value. External evaluators are impartial observers who systematically collect, analyze, and interpret data, and use preestablished criteria to make judgments.

Intro.12—Advantages of Conducting an Internal Evaluation

Let's return to the owners of Cool Licks to illustrate the pros and cons of both internal evaluation and external evaluation. If the ice cream shop owners decide to do the evaluation themselves then they will be doing an *internal* evaluation. Some advantages of doing an internal evaluation include:

- Doing the evaluation themselves, the Cool Licks owners will incur *few out-of-pocket expenses* since they will use in-house resources.

- As owners of Cool Licks, they *possess an intimate knowledge* of the ice cream business in general and the Cool Licks shop in particular. When it comes to data collection, they know what's both feasible and relevant to collect.

- Since they *hold a deep understanding* of the ice cream business, the Cool Licks owners might see connections and patterns in the data that less knowledgeable external evaluators might miss.

- Finally, the Cool Licks owners' *familiarity with the context* of their shop and products may allow them to offer recommendations that are more workable and relevant than an outsider might propose. For example, knowing that vanilla is the "flagship" flavor in their community, the owners might focus their recommendations more on improving that flavor than improving the quality of the more esoteric flavors such as bubble gum and gooseberry.

Intro.13—Disadvantages of Conducting an Internal Evaluation

On the other hand, there are two distinct disadvantages to using an internal evaluator rather than someone external who has little or no stake in the outcome of the evaluation.

First, internal evaluators have a stake in the outcome of the evaluation and *may inadvertently skew the results towards success.* If the Cool Licks owners desperately want their ice cream to beat out the competitor's brand, they may judge

Cool Licks as the best when the data says otherwise. This tendency towards bias calls into question the credibility of their findings and judgment.

Second, internal evaluators may be so close to a project that they *cannot see the big picture*. The owners of Cool Licks know a lot about the detailed workings of their ice cream shop, but may lack the ability to pull back and discern critical, overarching patterns that only those with dispassionate objectivity might see.

Intro.14—Advantages of an External Evaluation

As with most things in life, there are pros and cons to using external evaluators as well. If the ice cream shop owners decide to go with an external evaluator they can expect to reap the following benefits:

- An independent *external evaluator can bring a measure of objectivity and credibility* to the evaluation. He or she does not have a vested interested in whether Cool Licks gets the "best" rating. Therefore, the likelihood of rendering a dispassionate, fair judgment increases. [You might be thinking that because the Cool Licks owners hired the evaluator, such a monetary arrangement might unconsciously sway the evaluator to think more favorably of the Cool Licks vanilla ice cream. Yes, such a bias might occur. However, competent, professional evaluators can build safeguards into an evaluation plan that minimize the effects of such biases.]

- An external evaluator, whose continued employment is not on the line, is *often more willing than an internal evaluator to be the bearer of bad news*. An external evaluator can tell it like it is, mincing no words should the Cool Licks vanilla lose the taste-off.

- An external evaluator *brings a level of expertise in conducting evaluations* that an in-house evaluator may not possess. The Cool Licks owners would be the first ones to admit that they know how to make ice cream, however, they have only a cursory knowledge of how to conduct a systematic, credible product evaluation.

- Finally, external evaluators "*can bring with them a fresh, outside perspective. Unlike the internal evaluator, they see both the forest and the trees, often detecting unwarranted assumptions that are accepted by insiders*" (Worthen, Sanders, and Fitzpatrick, 1997, p. 204). The Cool Licks owners may assume that only the quality of the ice cream counts with customers. In reality, convenience, such as a drive thru window, outweighs quality, making the national franchise's brand more appealing. An insightful external evaluator would more likely spot this erroneous assumption than the owners themselves.

Intro.15—Disadvantages of an External Evaluation

There are three distinct disadvantages in using an external evaluator. First, like premium quality ice cream, *competent external evaluators cost money*. Not only would the ice cream owners have to pay a fee for the external evaluator's time and expertise, they would also have to cover any expenses associated with data collection and analysis. Such expenses can often result in an expensive bill.

Second, external evaluators *often experience some degree of delay as they try to understand the project.* The Cool Licks owners may find that an external evaluator takes weeks, rather than days, gathering the data simply because she doesn't know the first thing about the ice cream business.

Finally, *finding a competent external evaluator may prove difficult.* Section Intro.18 offers some advice on selecting a competent external evaluator.

> Epilogue: The owners of Cool Licks, the local ice cream shop, decided to commission a formal, external evaluation of their vanilla ice cream. The verdict: Cool Licks ice cream coldly smacked the competition!

Intro.16—Internal and External Evaluation in Action

Let's leave the world of vanilla ice cream and return to Murray and his colleagues at the middle school as they work to design an evaluation of the school's block scheduling. Murray's situation once again provides a good example of when to use internal evaluators and when to use external evaluators. During the first year of using the block schedule, Murray and his fellow staff members could have easily acted as internal evaluators systematically collecting, analyzing, and interpreting data to fine-tune the implementation of the block schedule. Now that two years have passed and the new schedule is fully in place, the situation calls for a summative evaluation. Murray and his fellow staff members could elect to conduct the summative evaluation. However, if they produce a report praising block scheduling, the skeptical high school teachers could easily cry foul. "Of course, you see it working," they might say. "You want it to work. You only collected data that would show what you believe. You're biased and your report is only self-serving." The high school teachers would have a legitimate point because Murray and his colleagues *do* have a stake in the evaluation.

To assuage these misgivings about biased internal evaluators, Murray and his colleagues should turn to outside evaluators to pass judgment about the effectiveness and worth of block scheduling. These evaluators should possess the knowledge and skills needed to conduct a formal evaluation, and at the same time, have no stake in the outcome of the evaluation. Where can they go for these impartial, competent evaluators? The local university might have such folks in the education and business departments. The state department of education often maintains a list of evaluators available for hire. Murray and his colleagues might be tempted to use an evaluator from the district's central office. This is fine, as long as the district's evaluator can maintain an acceptable level of impartiality.

Intro.17—Issue Box

When You Should *Not* Conduct Your Own Evaluation

As you recall, one of the "flavors" of evaluation is external evaluation, where people other than the program's implementors conduct the evaluation. Using an external evaluator can be expensive since most competent external evaluators conduct evaluations "for hire." Despite the added expense of using an external evaluator, sometimes you really should employ an impartial evaluator. But when? The following questions can help you decide.

If you answer Yes to 4 out of the 7 following questions, you should consider employing a competent external evaluator to conduct the evaluation of your program.

1. Has the district/state spent a *substantial* amount of money implementing this program? (As a rule of thumb, we classify costs exceeding $100,000 as substantial.)

2. Is the whole world watching? Is a wide audience that goes beyond your district interested in the results of the evaluation? For example, several school districts around the country recently experimented with using private contractors to run local elementary schools in hopes of dramatically improving poor performing schools. The results of these evaluations will not only guide the actions of the contracting district, but will also influence the actions of other school boards around the country. For this reason, using an external evaluator to evaluate such ventures would be prudent.

3. Do you have hopes of disseminating your program to schools across the state or country?

4. Are the stakes so high that an internal evaluator might either consciously or unconsciously bias the evaluation results towards obtaining a particular judgment?

5. Are the decision-makers who will use the evaluation results to decide the fate of the intervention already convinced of the program's worthlessness and, thus, would require "hard, objective evidence" to change their minds?

6. Will the skeptics about the program's effectiveness more readily accept the findings of an impartial observer over those of an in-house evaluator?

7. Does the evaluation require specialized knowledge and skills that available in-house evaluators do not possess?

If you answered yes to 4 or more of the above questions, you should seriously consider commissioning an external evaluation of your project. However, you should know that an external evaluator costs money and may be difficult to find.

Intro.18—Issue Box

Hiring an External Evaluator

Hiring an external evaluator has many similarities with hiring a new teacher for your building. You want to find out enough information about the qualifications and competencies of the person *before* hiring, so that you can make a reasonable assessment as to whether or not the person can do the job.

First, review the potential evaluator's track record in conducting evaluations. Talk with previous clients to see if they were satisfied with the evaluator's work. You should ask to see copies of evaluation reports the person has written. (Keep in mind that an evaluator may have conducted an evaluation whose final report must remain confidential because of stipulations in the contract.) Does the evaluator have experience in conducting an evaluation similar to yours? However, you shouldn't automatically dismiss potential evaluators just because they haven't done similar evaluations. Ask yourself, "Has the person conducted credible evaluations?".

Second, review the academic preparation of the potential evaluator. Has the person taken graduate courses that focus specifically on doing *educational* evaluations? We aren't saying that you should rule out someone whose training and experience in evaluation are outside the field of education. However, in our experience, someone who knows the culture of schools often does a more accurate job.

Finally, consider the potential evaluator's "people" skills. Will you feel comfortable working with this person? Will your colleagues, the students, the parents, the administrators, the school board also feel comfortable working with the person?

Once you settle on a competent external evaluator, involve this person early in the proposal writing stage of the project *before* implementation begins. This early involvement will help give the project evaluation a proactive rather than reactive stance. The external evaluator can help you identify the individuals or groups who, by attitude or skill, have the potential to be supporters of, or detractors from your project. You can then use this information to help design project activities that not only build on the foundation of support, but also minimize or eliminate potential concerns. Early involvement of an external evaluator can also increase the potential for collecting systematic, continuous data which is useful for both formative and summative judgments.

Finally, an external evaluator can act as the project's "conscience." As a detached party, an external evaluator can ask *"Why?", "What if?", and "How come?"* when others within the project may be reluctant to ask.

Intro.19—Chapter Highlights

Major Concepts

☞ As they strive to improve their classrooms and schools, middle school educators across the nation want answers to questions that:

1. Take stock of the current situation

2. Determine the effectiveness of an intervention

3. Seek solutions to problems

☞ Research and program evaluation are "first cousins," often using similar methods. Program evaluators go one step further. They *also* judge the worth or value of an intervention.

☞ Informal evaluation takes a casual approach, while formal evaluation requires a systematic, rigorous and objective plan for collecting, analyzing and interpreting data.

☞ Formative evaluation occurs *during* implementation and seeks to provide educators with information they can use to make mid-course corrections. In contrast, summative evaluation occurs *at the end* of implementation and seeks to judge the effectiveness, usefulness, and merit of the intervention.

☞ Internal evaluation relies on in-house people to conduct the evaluation, while external evaluation uses people other than the implementors to conduct the evaluation.

Advice

√ Use the processes of formal evaluation whenever you face decisions about how to improve your classroom practice or your school.

√ Become more systematic and deliberate in your evaluations, even if that means simply taking five minutes to jot down an evaluation plan before you try out a new teaching strategy with your students.

√ Consider using an external evaluator if 4 out of the following 7 conditions exist:

1. The district/state has spent more than $100,000 implementing the program.

2. A wide audience that goes beyond your district will show interest in the results of your evaluation.

3. You wish to disseminate your program to schools across the state or country.

4. The stakes are so high that an internal evaluator might either consciously or unconsciously bias the evaluation results towards making a particular judgment.

5. School decision-makers who will use the evaluation results to decide the fate of the intervention are already convinced of the program's worthlessness and, thus, require "hard, objective evidence" to change their minds.

6.   Skeptics will question the findings of an in-house evaluator they see as biased.

7.   The evaluation will require specialized knowledge and skills that in-house evaluators do not possess.

√ If you decide to use an external evaluator you should:

• Evaluate the potential evaluator's track record in conducting evaluations.

• Review the academic preparation of the potential evaluator.

• Consider the potential evaluator's "people" skills.

√ Once you settle on a competent external evaluator, involve this person during the proposal writing stage of the project *before* implementation begins.

Intro.20—The Road Ahead

Chapters 1 through 6 continue to lay the foundation, giving detailed information on how to conduct your own evaluations. Chapter 7 will discuss ways you can share your findings, while chapters 8, 9, and 10 will go even deeper into the specifics of answering questions that take stock, determine effectiveness, and seek solutions.

Intro.21—Resources

Print Resources

Brainard, E. A. (1996). *A hands-on guide to school program evaluation*. Bloomington, IN: Phi Delta Kappa Educational Foundation.

Packs into 70 pages a good overview of program evaluation. Quickly walks through a 10-step process for planning and conducting an evaluation. Gives the reader enough information to get started. A good "starter" book for teachers and administrators alike.

Fink, A. & Kosecoff, J. (1978). *An evaluation primer*. Thousand Oaks, CA: Sage.

A gem of a book despite the 1978 copyright date. Advice on planning and conducting school-based evaluations still solid. Very user-friendly. Assumes little prior knowledge on the part of an intelligent reader. Packed into 90 pages in an 8½ x 11 format with welcomed use of white space. Gives a good overview of key concepts concerning program evaluation.

Fitz-Gibbon, C. T. and Morris, L. L. (1978). *How to design a program evaluation*. Thousand Oaks, CA: Sage.

Everything you want to know about designing a program evaluation (both formative and summative). Written clearly with illustrative case studies sprinkled throughout. Drawback: small text font can strain the veteran educator's eyes. Has two decision trees that walk you toward the appropriate design for your particular evaluation. One decision tree deals with situations where you have the luxury of collecting data *before* the program has started, while the other decision tree provides guidance when you find that you must collect data *after* the program has started.

Glanz, J. (1998). *Action research: An educational leader's guide to school improvement.* Norwood, MA: Christopher-Gordon Publishers, Inc.

An excellent companion piece to our book. Covers some of the same topics we do but at times in more depth and with a slant more towards research. Grew out of the author's experience in teaching a graduate course on educational research. Deals with both research and program evaluation, with the purpose of creating reflective practitioners. Ably guides the educator through the research process from identifying what to study, selecting a research design, collecting data and, finally, analyzing and interpreting data. Hits that happy medium between too much and too little information. Includes periodic exercises (with answers provided) so that you can check your understanding of concepts.

Herman, J. L. & Winters, L. (1992). *Tracking your school's success: A guide to sensible evaluation.* Newbury Park, CA: Corwin Press.

HIGHLY RECOMMENDED. Written for practitioners (both teachers and administrators) interested in whole school improvement. Focuses on providing educators with the guidance and tools to answer the following questions:

- How are we doing?
- How can we improve?
- How can we share our successes?

The end of each chapter includes an annotated list of suggested readings.

King, J. A., Morris, L. L., & Fitz-Gibbon, C. T. (1987). *How to assess program implementation.* Thousand Oaks, CA: Sage Publications.

Focuses specifically on how you can judge whether or not the intervention/ strategy you're evaluating was implemented in the way you intended. Covers each step from the initial planning for the assessment to summarizing, analyzing, and reporting your data. The appendix includes over 100 questions you can use to guide your assessment of program implementation.

McMillan, J. H. & Schumacher, S. (1997). *Research in education : A conceptual introduction (4th ed.).* New York: Longman.

Should be part of every district's professional library. A good overall reference on reading and doing educational research. Filled with very readable school-based examples, along with excerpts from published research studies. Excellent glossary of research terms.

Patten, M. L. (1997). *Understanding research methods: An overview of the essentials.* Los Angeles: Pyrczak Publishing.

An easy-to-understand, stripped-down version of the Macmillan and Schumacher book. In 127 pages, covers the basics of research design, ethics, reviewing the literature, sampling, measurement instruments, and statistical analyses. When you need only a spoonful of research methods, this is the book to consult.

Sanders, J. R. (1992). *Evaluating school programs: The program evaluation guide for schools.* Newbury Park, CA: Corwin Press.

Can serve as a short (70 pages) companion to this book. Written for the novice evaluator as the first in the six-book series, *The Program Evaluation Guides for Schools.* Covers some of the same topics as our book, but not in depth. Includes a case study used throughout the book to illustrate various steps in the evaluation process.

Schmuck, R. A. (1997). *Practical action research for change*. Arlington Heights, IL: IRI Skylight Training and Publishing, Inc.

Excellent resource that guides educators through the action research process. Provides a good grounding in the differences between traditional research and action research. Includes numerous case studies that show K–12 educators (as individuals, teams, and even entire faculties) engaged in various action research efforts. Chapter 4 discusses the advantages and disadvantages of using various methods to collect data through questionnaires, interviews, observations, and reviewing documents. Throughout, asks the reader to reflect and apply the concepts. Would serve as an excellent companion to our book, *Getting Answers to Your Questions*.

Stringer, E. T. (1996). *Action research: A handbook for practitioners*. Thousand Oaks, CA: Sage Publications.

A highly readable handbook designed for educators wanting to jump into the realm of action research, a "sibling" of evaluation.

Worthen, B. R., Sanders, J. R., & Fitzpatrick, J. L. (1997). *Program evaluation: Alternative approaches and practical guidelines*. (2nd ed.). White Plains, NY: Longman.

Provides a complete and easy-to-understand discussion of all phases of educational evaluation from planning to reporting. Highly recommended as *The Joy of Cooking* for the evaluation field.

Internet Resources

The World Wide Web (also known as the Internet) represents one of the great leaps forward in putting information at the fingertips of educators everywhere. With a few keystrokes and clicks of your mouse, you can wander through huge virtual libraries. Unfortunately, the vastness of the Web can often overwhelm and intimidate us. Furthermore, the Web changes daily (indeed even hourly). One day you can access your favorite Web site and the next day the address has changed. Therefore, to make things easier, we recommend that you visit our Web page at :

http://www.pittstate.edu/edsc/ssls/letendre.html

At this address, you will find all the Web sites we recommend at the end of each chapter. With a simple click of your mouse, you can go straight to the recommended sites. Furthermore, we will regularly verify each of the sites we recommend as well as add others. This way we can keep our recommended resource list on the cutting edge.

Department of Education
http://www.ed.gov
Serves as an excellent gateway to all the Web sites maintained by the U.S. Department of Education.

Department of Education Publications
http://www.ed.gov/pubs/OR/ConsumerGuides/webpage.html
Connects to *Using the Internet: World Wide Web Pages Featuring Education*, an article designed to give the novice Web user a sense of the Internet's power. Includes links to many sites educators will find valuable.

ERIC/Clearinghouse on Assessment and Evaluation
http://ericae.net/
EXCELLENT resources on all topics associated with conducting program evaluation. Selected topics (all with hot links to relevant sites) include action research, achievement data, alternative assessment, fairness in testing, goals and standards, instructional and program evaluation, organizations, pedagogy in educational measurement (much how-to stuff here), qualitative research, statistics, test descriptions, test reviews, and tests on-line.

Mettetal, Gwynn
http://www.iusb.edu/~gmetteta/
Takes you to Professor Mettetal's Web page at Indiana University South Bend where you'll find links to action research Web sites. Also includes a handy piece titled *How to report statistics, a quick guide.*

National Middle School Association (NMSA)
http://www.nmsa.org
Gateway site that connects to a myriad of resources surrounding middle school issues. Connects to home page of the National Middle School Association which also includes hotlinks to other Web sites categorized under government, libraries and museums, organizations, K–12 teacher resources, networks, and NMSA's affiliate organizations.

National Education Library
http://www.aspensys.com/eric/
Takes you to the National Education Library's ERIC (Educational Resources Information Center). A slick site funded by the U. S. Department of Education where you can search the ERIC database and connect with other system-wide ERIC resources such as the Clearinghouses and Adjunct Clearinghouses. You'll find the site for The Clearinghouse on Assessment and Evaluation most useful since it provides information on educational assessment.

Widener University/Wolfgram Memorial Library
http://www.science.widener.edu/~withers/pyramid.htm
Provides a tutorial on search strategies and, in particular, includes a section on evaluating web resources to decide which are credible.

> Note: Accessing Web sites requires that you type the address or URL *exactly*. Even one small misplaced letter or symbol will produce the message "URL not found." Also, you may find that sometimes a very long address will fail to take you to the site you want. You may even get a message that says: "The requested URL is not found on this server." We suggest that you try removing a portion of the address and try again. For example, the above address for Gwynn Mettetal's personal Web page is http://www.iusb.edu/~gmetteta/. Shorten the address to the main server's address http://www.iusb.edu/. This will take you to the homepage of her university, and then you can use the buttons there to find her personal Web page.

CHAPTER 1

Doing Evaluations

Step 1—Pose Questions

1.1—Know About Research, Know HOW to Do Evaluation

Our belief is this: Middle school educators need to know about research and they need to know *how to do* program evaluation. Rarely, do they wish to generate knowledge simply to satisfy curiosity. Like researchers, they may want answers to such questions as:

- What's going on here?
- Did it work?
- How does it work?
- Why did this work or why didn't this work?

But middle school educators don't stop there. They frequently take the next step and use this information to make judgments about a strategy's worth or merit. They become program evaluators. Furthermore, middle school teachers and principals use these judgments to inform their practice. Thus, during their professional careers, middle school educators, like yourself, will act more often as evaluators than researchers.

1.2—A Recipe for Doing Evaluations

In the introduction, we laid the foundation and discussed the various flavors of program evaluation. Now let's talk about how you can actually *get* the answers to your questions. Conducting a credible evaluation of any strategy within your classroom or school requires that you follow these six steps:

1. Pose questions.
2. Establish judgment criteria.
3. Make a plan.
4. Gather data.
5. Analyze data.
6. Interpret the results of your analysis.

In the remainder of this chapter, we will discuss Step 1 of program evaluation: Pose questions. In chapters 2 through 6, we will walk through the rest of the evaluation process, providing guidance and examples each step of the way. Later, in chapters 8, 9, and 10, we will provide even more detail about how you can use this same 6-step process to answer questions that take stock, determine the effectiveness of an intervention, and seek solutions.

1.3—Step 1: Pose Questions—What Do I Want to Know?

In Step 1, you need to pose the questions that will guide your investigation. What is it you *want* to know? Frequently, this question translates to "What is it you *need* to know?" It is our experience that we rarely live in the best of all possible worlds and we often have to settle for what we need rather than what we want.

At the outset, the questions you pose will most likely fall within the three categories we mentioned in the introduction. These questions should:

- take stock,
- determine effectiveness, or
- seek solutions.

Some *taking stock* questions that can get your evaluation off to a good start include:

- *Where are we NOW?*
- *How "healthy" is our school?*
- *How do we stack up against the standards?*

If you want to *determine the effectiveness* of a strategy, you can simply ask:

- *Did it work?*
- *Did we achieve what we set out to accomplish?*
- *Did it make a difference?*

Finally, if your purpose is to *find a solution* to a problem, you can begin by simply asking:

- *What's going on here?*
- *What's causing the problem?*

Once you have posed these overarching questions, you frequently need to break them down into more manageable subquestions. For example, if your overarching question is "Did it work?", you might also want to answer additional questions like: *"How can we make this better?", "Why did it work?",* or *"Why didn't it work?".* Chapters 8, 9, and 10 will illustrate in more detail how these subquestions can emerge.

Finally, you should realize that rarely in a program evaluation will you anticipate all the pertinent questions you want to answer about the strategy you are evaluating. You absolutely need to pose some questions *before* you begin. However, you should also remain flexible and open to additional questions that might emerge *during* the evaluation itself. Don't ignore these questions just because you didn't pose them during this crucial Step 1. But a word of caution—Pose new, important questions and get them answered, but don't lose your focus.

1.4—Who Should Pose Questions?

"None of us is as smart as all of us." People often cite this statement when they speak of the power of shared problem-solving and shared decision making. We suggest that this same sentiment applies when you pose the questions that will guide your evaluation. Rarely should only one person do this. You should seek input from a variety of quarters. This way you can build ownership among important groups for the evaluation itself, as well as ensure that the evaluation answers the right questions. One important group that should have input in posing questions includes *those who will use the results* of your evaluation to make decisions about the fate of the program. These decision makers can range from you, as an individual teacher, to policymakers such as your local school board. You should ask them—*"What information do you need to help you make your decision about continuing the program?"*.

A second important group that should have some say about the questions that will guide your evaluation includes *those who are affected by the intervention, either directly or indirectly.* For example, let's say that this school year, you and your team members have incorporated a Socratic Seminar✶ into your instructional program for students. At the end of the school year, you will make a decision as to whether or not you will retain this innovation in your plans for next year's students. As the teachers implementing the Socratic Seminar, you should play a primary role in posing the questions that will guide your evaluation. Indeed, in this example, you are not only affected by the implementation, but you will also decide whether or not to continue using the Socratic Seminar.

But, as teachers, you are not the only ones affected by the use of the Socratic Seminar. Your students are also directly touched by its use and they, like you, should have a say in the questions that will guide your evaluation. You should also seek suggestions about evaluation questions from those who are indirectly influenced by the strategy. This group may include the parents of your students, fellow teachers who might want to adopt the Socratic Seminar, and administrators who may allocate resources to continue the implementation of your innovation. In order to help pose a comprehensive array of evaluation questions, you should ask these folks—*"What do we want to know that will help us make a decision as to whether or not we should continue using the Socratic Seminar in our classes?"*.

Finally, you should review your intentions for implementing the program in the first place. *What did you hope to accomplish? What do you need to find out so that you can tell whether or not you actually achieved what you intended?*

As you can see, the questions that will guide your evaluation can, and should, come from many people—from students, parents, community members, policymakers, funding sources, and of course from you and your colleagues. The key is to seek input on the evaluation questions from a variety of sources. If the scope of the strategy or program you are evaluating does not extend beyond your own classroom, you may need to consult only a handful of stakeholders. However, if the scope of the strategy or program has far-reaching implications, you should broaden the base of people who will give you input about the questions that will guide your evaluation.

1.5—Chapter Highlights

Major Concepts

☞ Credible program evaluations follow 6 steps:

1. Pose questions
2. Establish judgment criteria
3. Make a plan
4. Gather data
5. Analyze data
6. Interpret the results of your analysis.

☞ In Step 1 you need to pose the questions that will guide your investigation.

☞ Your initial questions might include questions that:

Take stock
      Where are we now?
      How "healthy" is our school?
      How do we stack up against the standards?
Determine the effectiveness
      Does it work?
      Did we achieve what we set out to accomplish?
      Did it make a difference?
Find a solution
      What's going on here?
      What's causing the problem?

☞ The people who will use the results of your evaluation to make decisions about the fate of your program should help pose the evaluation questions.

☞ The people affected by the program, either directly or indirectly, should help in posing the questions that will guide your evaluation.

☞ The evaluation questions should also flow from the original intentions of the implementors.

Advice

√ In Step 1, pose the general questions that will guide your evaluation like— *"What do I want to know?"* and *"What do I need to know?"*

√ Next, break your initial general questions into more manageable subquestions.

√ *During* the evaluation itself, stay flexible and open to additional questions that might arise.

√ Always stay focused. Refrain from posing too many questions that may satisfy your curiosity, but will take you off track during an evaluation.

√ As you pose the questions that will guide your evaluation, seek input from the decision makers who will use the results to decide the fate of your program. You should ask—"What do you need to know to help you make your decision about continuing this program?".

√ Also solicit guiding questions from those people who are affected by the intervention, either directly or indirectly. You should ask them—"What do we want to know that will help us make a decision as to whether or not we should continue using the program?".

√ Finally, review the original intentions of the program implementors by asking—"What do we need to find out so that we can tell whether or not we actually achieved what we intended?".

1.6—The Road Ahead

Step 1—Pose Questions, gets the evaluation process rolling. In the next chapter, we tackle Step 2 where you explicitly establish beforehand the judgment criteria you will use to judge the worthiness of the program or strategy. In Step 2 you answer the question—*"On what basis, will I judge the worth of the program?"*.

1.7—Murray Does Step 1

Figure 1.1   Evaluation Process Step 1

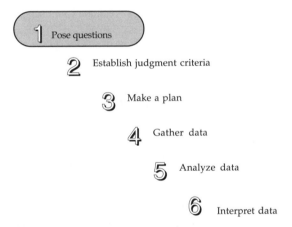

1 Pose questions

2 Establish judgment criteria

3 Make a plan

4 Gather data

5 Analyze data

6 Interpret data

Let's now apply our suggestions for *Step 1: Pose questions* to the situation faced by Murray and his colleagues at Strivinghigher Middle School as they confront a high school faculty skeptical about the effectiveness of the middle school's block schedule. Recently, at a meeting of the School Improvement Committee, Murray raised his concern about all the negative talk coming from the high school teachers concerning the middle school's use of block scheduling. "Many say our kids aren't ready for the rigors of high school," he reported.

During the same meeting the principal also told the committee that she too has been hearing lots of skepticism from the high school folks. Just the other day at the monthly secondary principals' meeting, the high school principal approached her about concerns his staff were voicing. And, this morning, the superintendent called her saying that several board members and prominent parents were asking, "Does this block scheduling really work? Is it worth all the effort and money?"

"I think it's time we conduct an evaluation to see just how effective the block schedule is," Murray suggests. All members of the committee agree and they begin posing questions they want answered by the evaluation. Their initial questions attempt to determine the effectiveness of block scheduling:

- "Does it work?"
- "Are we achieving what we set out to accomplish when we began using the block schedule two years ago?"
- "Has it made a positive difference in student learning?"

The principal chimes in with the board member's question:

- "Is it worth all the effort and money?"

Murray and his colleagues decide they also want some additional questions answered to help them fine tune their implementation of block scheduling. They want to know:

- "How can we make this better?"
- "What's going smoothly?"
- "What's not going so smoothly?"

Within 15 minutes the School Committee realizes that they need to enlist some outside help. "We can't do this on our own," says Murray. "We just don't have enough time. Plus, if we do it ourselves, our critics will just say we simply stacked the deck."

"I agree," another committee member says. "We need to find a credible, skilled, outside person to help us."

"And this person needs to work cheap," the principal quickly adds, "The budget's tight and we can spend no more than $500 on an outside evaluator."

Just as the group was about to decide to drop the idea, Murray suggests that perhaps someone at the local university might be able to help for only a small fee or perhaps even at no cost. "I'll call Professor Alwayshelpful," Murray volunteers, "She was my advisor when I worked on my master's degree."

By the end of the meeting, the committee has generated several sets of questions to guide their evaluation but they know they need more input. The decision to continue or terminate the middle school's block schedule goes beyond Murray and his colleagues. The school board may have the final say in the matter. For this reason, Murray and the other members of the School Improvement Committee decide to consult with several others, asking them:

- "What questions do you need answered to help you decide if block scheduling is working or not?"

Later that week, Murray and his colleagues talk to the superintendent, some board members, a handful of parents whose children attend the middle school, some middle school students, the high school principal, and various high school teachers, particularly those who express the most skepticism about the value of block scheduling.

Surprisingly, Murray and his colleagues find that all these people basically want to know the answers to the same questions that they initially posed:

- "Does it work?"
- "Are we achieving what we set out to accomplish when we began using the block schedule?"
- "Has it made a positive difference in student learning?"

However, the high school faculty members add another dimension. They also want to know:

- "Does the block schedule adequately prepare the middle school students for the rigors of high school?"

During the week, Murray calls Professor Alwayshelpful who says she'll see if any of her students in the doctoral seminar on program evaluation might be interested in doing the project for special investigations credit. Ph.D. students Yolanda and Stan leap at the chance and tell Murray they'll be at the next School Improvement Committee Meeting. They want to get involved early in the planning stage of the evaluation.

Now that Murray and his fellow middle school teachers have compiled a beginning list of questions to guide the evaluation of block scheduling, they need to move to Step 2. In Step 2, they will establish the criteria they will use to judge the effectiveness of the strategy.

1.8—Resources

Print Resources

References recommended in earlier chapters are preceded by an "★". The number of ★'s indicates the number of previous recommendations.

★Brainard, E. A. (1996). *A hands-on guide to school program evaluation.* Bloomington, IN: Phi Delta Kappa Educational Foundation.

A good, 70-page overview of program evaluation that quickly walks through a 10-step process for planning and conducting an evaluation. Includes an

11-point check list for choosing an appropriate focus for your evaluation (p. 14) that you will find valuable as you pose the questions that will guide your evaluation.

*Fink, A. & Kosecoff, J. (1978). *An evaluation primer.* Thousand Oaks, CA: Sage Publications.

A gem of a book despite the 1978 copyright date. Chapter 2 focuses on formulating credible evaluation questions. Provides examples throughout.

*Herman, J. L. & Winters, L. (1992). *Tracking your school's success: A guide to sensible evaluation.* Newbury Park, CA: Corwin Press.

HIGHLY RECOMMENDED. Written for practitioners (both teachers and administrators) interested in whole school improvement. Chapter 2 provides pointers, as well as examples, of useful questions that can guide your evaluation. Entire book focuses on providing educators with the tools they need to answer the questions:

- How are we doing?
- How can we improve?
- How can we share our successes?

*King, J. A., Morris, L. L., & Fitz-Gibbon, C. T. (1987). *How to assess program implementation.* Thousand Oaks, CA: Sage Publications.

Appendix includes over 100 questions that can get your juices flowing as you pose questions to assess how the program your evaluating was actually implemented.

Internet Resources

NOTE: You can easily access the Websites we recommend below by simply going to our Web page located at

http://www.pittstate.edu/edsc/ssls/letendre.html

From our Web page, a simple click of your mouse will take you straight to the selected Website. We regularly verify these sites and add others that we find worthy of our recommendation.

Center for Applied Research and Educational Improvement (AREI)
http://carei.coled.umn.edu/
Connects to an excellent site that includes a research and resources section organized around various innovative practices including block scheduling. For example, gives a comprehensive literature review on block scheduling, with links to relevant Websites, publications, ERIC abstracts, how-to guides, and other useful references on block scheduling.

Council of Chief State School Officers
http://www.ccsso.org/
Serves as a gateway to Websites sponsored by state departments of education in all 50 states. Has a searchable database and a hot button link to a section called "Resources" filled with examples of program evaluations. Also a great resource for questions that can guide your evaluation.

National Middle School Association (NMSA)
http://www.nmsa.org
Gateway site that connects to a myriad of sources regarding middle school issues. You'll find the on-line article entitled *NMSA Research #11: Evaluating the Effectiveness of Programs* especially helpful.

CHAPTER 2

Doing Evaluations

Step 2—Establish Judgement Criteria

2.1—On What Basis Will I Judge the Worth of the Program?

No matter whether you pose your questions to take stock, determine the effectiveness of a strategy, or seek solutions, you and your colleagues eventually ask yourselves:

- Is this worth doing?
- Is this worth continuing?

2.2—Just Do It Up-Front!

Step 2 requires that you determine *up-front* the criteria you will use to make these judgments. Why do this up-front? Why not wait until we get all the data collected to decide how we want to judge the program? The first reason has to do with the difficulty we humans have in separating feelings from facts. All the stakeholders associated with a program already have in their minds some sort of criteria that they will use to judge the worthiness or value of any program. Indeed, they may already have arrived at a judgment and are simply collecting data to confirm that judgment. However, such criteria are often implicit and rarely well-defined. Furthermore, if stakeholders actually define such criteria, they tend to do so at the end of an evaluation, when their emotions are so mixed with the facts that they can barely tell one from the other. Under such emotional situations, we, as humans, tend to make snap judgments based on gut feelings rather than data. To avoid the trap of snap, emotion-laden judgments, program evaluators explicitly state the criteria they will use to judge the worthiness of a program *before* they gather any data.

Another primary reason why you should define your judgment criteria up-front is that, frequently, these yardsticks will dictate the kinds of data you will need to collect. For example, if your criteria for judging the effectiveness of the Drop Everything and Read (D.E.A.R.)✳ program is, "Our students will read 20% more fiction books during the semester," you know you will need to collect data that show the number of fiction books read by students the semester before the implementation of the D.E.A.R. program, as well as the number of books they read during the semester of implementation. Thus, both the questions posed in Step 1 and the criteria defined in Step 2 will guide your evaluation.

2.3—Elements of Judgment Criteria

Two elements make up the judgment criteria you will use to judge the value or worth of your program:

1. The *criteria* or components that you will examine
2. The *standards* or specific levels of performance you wish to attain

Criteria define specifically what aspects of a performance you will examine. For example, if we were evaluating the effects of a hands-on algebra course on students' mathematical understanding, we might examine the following criteria as part of our evaluation of the overall success of the course:

1. Accuracy in problem-solving
2. Clarity in explaining how a problem was solved
3. Application of learning to novel situation
4. Ability to distinguish between relevant and irrelevant information in a problem

But criteria only tell us what to examine. They don't tell *how* to judge the quality of the performance. This is where standards come into play. Standards specify the quality level we wish to achieve.

Continuing with our example of evaluating the effects of a hands-on algebra course, we now define the quality level we want for each of the four criteria:

CRITERIA	STANDARD
1. Accuracy in problem-solving	1. Over 80% of the students will make no, or only minor, computational errors on a series of performance tests designed to gauge their understanding of algebraic concepts.
2. Clarity in explaining how a problem was solved	2. Over 80% of the students will be able to orally explain how they solved a problem, showing each step of their thought processes.
3. Application of learning to novel situation.	3. When presented with a real-world situation requiring the use of algebraic problem-solving, over 80% of the students will accurately solve the problem.
4. Ability to distinguish between relevant and irrelevant	4. When presented with a "messy" mathematical situation, over 80% of information in a problem the students will accurately indicate which pieces of information they need to solve the problem.

2.4—Examples of Judgment Criteria

What might judgment criteria look like? Below are some examples:

- "Our students will read 20% more fiction books during the semester."
- "Our students will show a statistically significant difference between their pretest and post test scores on the state mathematics performance assessment."
- "Over 75% of the parents of our students will converse with their middle school children about the importance of doing well in school."
- "Over 80% of the teachers in our school will indicate they use performance assessments regularly in their classrooms."

All the above examples serve as a yardstick by which you can measure the worth of a project or strategy. Each includes both the specific program component we will examine and the level of quality we wish to attain. For some of the above judgment criteria, you can easily gather the evidence you need to make your judgment, while for others, the job requires more sophisticated data collection methods and analysis.

2.5—Cast Your Net Wide When Defining Judgment Criteria

In defining the criteria and standards you will use to judge the worth of your intervention, you should follow the same techniques suggested in Step 1 to generate your evaluation questions. You should cast your net wide, asking a variety of people—"On what basis should we judge the value of this program?". If this opening question doesn't produce much response, you might probe with questions such as:

- "What evidence will prove to you that the program worked?"
- "How would we know for sure that the program failed?"
- "How will you judge whether or not we should continue using the program?"

The following techniques will ensure that you get a breadth of ideas concerning the criteria and standards you will use to judge the worthiness of the program under examination. Plus, by asking various people to help define the judgment criteria, you build interest in your evaluation itself and assure that you use the right yardstick in measuring the merit of the program.

- Seek judgment criteria *from stakeholders*. You should canvass each group of stakeholders who are directly or indirectly influenced by the program under examination. Worthen, Sanders and Fitzpatrick (1997) suggest that stakeholders for a school-wide intervention include:
    1. Policymakers (such as board members)
    2. Administrators (within your building and at the district office)
    3. Practitioners (this includes you and your colleagues who are implementing the strategy)

4.   Primary consumers (such as students who directly benefit from the innovation)

5.   Secondary consumers (such as parents and patrons who are affected by what happens to primary consumers)

- Gather judgment criteria by *reviewing the purpose of the strategy.*   Every intervention, large or small, has a purpose. That purpose is either implied, or formally laid out in writing. For example, if your school has a Teacher Advisory Program,✳ when you first implemented the program you hoped it would result in some particular outcomes. These expected outcomes, whether implicit or explicit, can help establish the criteria and standards you will use at the end of the project to judge the project's worth or merit.

- Garner judgment criteria by *examining research literature.*   A quick surf of the educational databases on the World Wide Web will usually produce information about programs similar to the one you are examining. Sometimes, you'll even find articles that deal with the exact same program you have implemented. A swift perusal of this literature will often give you ideas about judgment criteria and standards you might use in evaluating your own program.

- Draw judgment criteria from *checklists, standards, guidelines.*   Numerous educational associations, accreditation agencies, and even the department of education in your own state have developed a multitude of checklists, standards, and guidelines that you might find useful in establishing the criteria that you can use to judge the worth of your program. Section 2.10 Resources includes a partial listing of criteria and standards established by various national bodies.

- Collect judgment criteria by *consulting with experts.*   We have found it extremely helpful to get input from independent experts. Often these folks can provide a perspective that we haven't thought about simply because we are too close to the program. You usually can find independent experts working at local colleges or universities, in your state department of education, or at an educational service center serving your area.

2.6—Issue Box

"Achieving" is Different from "Doing"

Many "so-called" evaluations we have seen submitted as end-of-grant reports simply list all the activities the implementors did. These "evaluations" really do not answer the central questions of evaluation:
- Is it worthwhile?
- Did it work?
- Should we continue it?

These reports are really status reports and not evaluations. Simply giving a month-by-month listing of all activities does not give any indication that these activities actually accomplished your goal and made a difference. It's one thing to hold an open-house for grandparents as part of a effort to increase family involvement in education, and still another thing entirely to show that the open house actually resulted in increasing the learning of youngsters within your school.

2.7—Chapter Highlights

Major Concepts

☞ As you evaluate strategies in your classroom or school, you will eventually make some judgment where you will ask yourself:

- Is this worth doing?
- Is this worth continuing?

☞ Step 2 requires that you determine *up-front* the criteria and standards you will use to make these judgments.

☞ Setting judgment criteria up-front helps to:

Avoid snap judgments based on gut feelings
Define the kinds of data you will need to collect

☞ The judgment criteria includes both:

The *criteria* or components that you will examine
The *standards* or specific levels of performance you wish to attain

Advice

√ Seek judgment criteria *from stakeholders.*
√ Gather judgment criteria by *reviewing the purpose of the strategy.*
√ Garner judgment criteria by *examining research literature.*
√ Draw judgment criteria from *checklists, standards, guidelines.*
√ Collect judgment criteria by *consulting with experts.*

2.8—The Road Ahead

Thus far in Steps 1 and 2 in the evaluation process, we have worked to focus our evaluation. We've posed the questions that will guide evaluation and we have specified the criteria and standards we will use eventually to judge the worth or value of our intervention. In the next chapter we will use these questions and judgment criteria to lay out a plan on how we can gather, analyze and interpret the information we need.

2.9—Murray Does Step 2

Figure 2.1   Evaluation Process Step 2

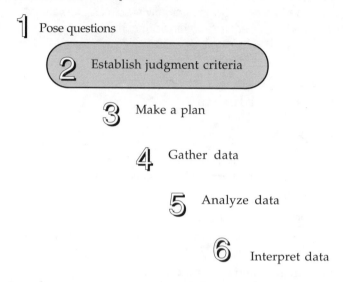

1 Pose questions

2 Establish judgment criteria

3 Make a plan

4 Gather data

5 Analyze data

6 Interpret data

In Step 1, Murray and his fellow middle school teachers compiled the questions that will guide the evaluation of block scheduling. Basically, they want to know if block scheduling is accomplishing what they hoped when they first implemented it two years ago. Plus, they want to find out ways to fine-tune its implementation. Finally, the high school teachers want to know if the middle school students are being adequately prepared for the rigors of high school.

Now, in Step 2, they need to make explicit the criteria and standards they will use to judge the effectiveness of the block schedule. As in Step 1, Murray and his colleagues consult a variety of sources to gather ideas about appropriate judgment criteria. They begin by asking the stakeholders:

- On what basis should we judge the value of block scheduling?
- What types of information would help you judge whether or not block scheduling is good for our students?

Members of Murray's committee talk with policy makers (board members), administrators (the high school principal and the superintendent), practitioners (their fellow middle school educators), primary consumers (middle school students), and secondary consumers (high school faculty members and parents of middle school students). Murray also reviews the original proposal the middle school faculty presented to the school board when they asked for approval to begin the block schedule.

But Murray and his group don't stop there. They also want input from sources *outside* the school district to augment the thoughts of staff, patrons, and students within the district concerning the criteria for judging the worth of the block schedule. This is where graduate students Yolanda and Stan take the lead. They begin by searching the Internet, looking for research on block schedules. They check ERIC on-line and do a general search on the HotBot search engine using the Boolean phrase *"middle school"* and *"block schedule."* To their amazement, they find over 250,000 hits, most consisting of Web pages representing middle schools using block scheduling. Yolanda and Stan then add and *research* to narrow the field to 216 hits. After spending about six hours scanning the most relevant articles, they pick up several items to include in the list of judgment criteria.

Working with three very computer-literate students, Murray, too, has gone on the Internet. He and the students discover a handful of lists detailing the standards that all good middle schools should meet. Murray decides to share these with the Committee.

Finally, Murray calls two professors at the local university. Both professors specialize in issues relating to the middle school level and one has had considerable experience conducting large-scale program evaluations. Murray explains what he is doing and one professor quickly suggests some relevant criteria Murray might use. The other professor wants a bit more time; she wants to ask the students in her Program Evaluation course to brainstorm germane criteria.

Murray and his colleagues synthesize all the suggestions they received and run a draft of the judgment criteria by several other members of the faculty and various decision-makers at central office. This process results in the following eight benchmarks they will use to gauge the worth of their middle school's block schedule.

Benchmark 1:   Students on the block schedule will master a higher percentage of items on the state criterion-referenced assessment in reading comprehension, mathematical problem-solving, science knowledge, and expository writing proficiency than similar students not on a block schedule.

Benchmark 2:   Students on the block schedule will have a higher attendance rate than similar students not on a block schedule.

Benchmark 3:   Students on the block schedule will show more engagement during academic classes than similar students not on a block schedule.

Benchmark 4:   Students on the block schedule will choose to complete more academically challenging projects than similar students not on a block schedule.

Benchmark 5:   Students on the block schedule will show a more positive attitude towards school in general than similar students not on a block schedule.

Benchmark 6:   Students on the block schedule will show a greater sense of self-efficacy than similar students not on a block schedule.

Benchmark 7:   Students on the block schedule will demonstrate a greater willingness to take responsibility for their own learning than similar students not on a block schedule.

Benchmark 8:   Students on the block schedule will demonstrate greater perseverance when faced with a difficult learning task than similar students not on a block schedule.

The School Improvement Committee expands their list of previously generated evaluation questions to include the following questions that stem from the eight benchmarks:

- Did students improve in reading comprehension, math problem-solving, science knowledge, and expository writing?
- Did students achieve higher attendance rate?
- Do students show more engagement in class?
- Do students choose more academically challenging projects?
- Do students show a more positive attitude?
- Do students show more willingness to take responsibility?
- Do students show more perseverance?
- Do students exhibit greater self-efficacy?

Now, Murray is ready for Step 3, where he and his colleagues will actually lay out a plan for conducting the evaluation of the middle school's use of block scheduling.

2.10—Resources

Print Resources

References recommended in earlier chapters have an * by them. The number of *'s indicates the number of previous recommendations.

Borders, L. D. & Drury, S. M. (1993). *Counseling programs: A guide to evaluation.* Newbury Park, CA: Corwin Press.

Part of the series entitled: *The Program Evaluation Guides for Schools*, edited by Richard M. Jaeger (1992) and published by Corwin Press. Includes a list of standards and indicators for effective school counseling programs gleaned from extensive literature review. Standards can apply across all grade levels. Lists each standard and then suggests a data collection method for gathering information about that standard. Also includes six vignettes illustrating how to evaluate various aspects of a school's counseling program. Provides a list of references on quality school counseling evaluation and needs assessment.

Bright, G. W., Uprichard, A. E., & Jetton, J. H. (1993). *Mathematics programs: A guide to evaluation*. Newbury Park, CA: Corwin Press.

Part of the series entitled: *The Program Evaluation Guides for Schools*, edited by Richard M. Jaeger (1992) and published by Corwin Press. Gives a list of standards and indicators for effective school mathematics programs, drawn from the National Council of Teachers of Mathematics' Curriculum and Evaluation Standards for School Mathematics (1989) and the Professional Standards for Teaching Mathematics (1991), both available from the NCTM located in Reston, VA. Lists each standard and then suggests a data collection method for gathering information about that standard. Also includes six vignettes showing how to evaluate various aspects of mathematics programs. Provides a good list of references on mathematics education.

Leithwood, K. & Aitken, R. (1995). *Making schools smarter: A system for monitoring school and district progress*. Thousand Oaks, CA: Corwin Press.

Provides excellent lists of criteria that you might use to judge the quality of your school or district. Includes judgment criteria dealing with the following areas: mission, goals, organizational culture, strategic planning, management, leadership, instructional services, decision-making, policies, procedures, and school-community relations at both the district and school levels. Also suggest various indicators that you could use to judge whether or not your school or district meets these criteria. Finally, provides sample surveys that you could use to collect the data you need to make your judgments.

O'Sullivan, R. G. & Tennant, C. V. (1993). *Programs for at-risk students: A guide to evaluation*. Newbury Park, CA: Corwin Press.

Part of the series entitled: *The Program Evaluation Guides for Schools*, edited by Richard M. Jaeger (1992) and published by Corwin Press. Gives a list of standards and indicators of quality for the evaluation of programs for at-risk students, gleaned from evaluations of programs within Georgia public schools. Lists each standard and then suggests a data collection method for gathering information about that standard. Includes six vignettes showing how to evaluate various aspects of programs for at-risk students. Also provides copies of the data collection forms for each vignette and a good set of references on selecting and constructing measurement instruments.

Olson, M. W. & Miller, S. D. (1993). *Reading and language arts programs: A guide to evaluation*. Newbury Park, CA: Corwin Press.

Part of the series entitled: *The Program Evaluation Guides for Schools*, edited by Richard M. Jaeger (1992) and published by Corwin Press. Provides a list, applicable to all grade levels, of standards and indicators of effective school reading and language arts programs derived from an extensive review of the literature covering the last 10 years. Lists each standard and then suggests a data collection method for gathering information about that standard. Includes six vignettes showing how to evaluate various aspects of a school's reading and language arts program. Also includes a list of books and articles describing high quality reading and language arts programs.

Schurr, S. L. (1992). *How to evaluate your middle school: A practitioner's guide for an informal program evaluation.* Columbus, OH: National Middle School Association.

A must for middle-level educators wanting to know if their programs fit the needs of their students. Provides over 25 survey and observation instruments based on the characteristics of exemplary middle schools.

Vallecorsa, A. L, deBettencourt, L U., & Garis, E. (1993). *Special education programs: A guide to evaluation.* Newbury Park, CA: Corwin Press.

One more in the series entitled: *The Program Evaluation Guides for Schools,* edited by Richard M. Jaeger (1992) and published by Corwin Press. Provides a list of generic standards and indicators for effective special education programs drawn from an extensive literature review by the authors. Lists each standard and then suggests a data collection method for gathering information about that standard. Also illustrates how to evaluate various aspects of special education programs through six vignettes, often including actual copies the various data collection instruments used. Provides a list of references focusing on special education programming and evaluation.

Wiggins, Grant. (1998). *Educative assessment: designing assessments to inform and improve student performance.* San Francisco: Jossey-Bass Inc., Publishers.

Chapter 5 in this book provides a 34-page gold mine of possible judgment criteria for evaluators. Covers, in both depth and breadth, the range of current standards and criteria educators use to assess the knowledge, skills and values students have learned.

Internet Resources

NOTE: You can easily access the Websites we recommend below by simply going to our Web page located at
http://www.pittstate.edu/edsc/ssls/letendre.html
From our Web page, a simple click of your mouse will take you straight to the selected Website. We regularly verify these sites and add others that we find worthy of our recommendation.

Council of Chief State School Officers
http://www.ccsso.org/
Looking for judgment criteria based on the standards set by your state department of education? This Web address will take you there. Shows a map of the United States and by simply clicking on your state, connects to your state department's Web site where you can find the learning outcomes and accreditation standards established by your state. If you want to get further ideas on judgment criteria, click on the other states as well.

Eisenhower National Clearinghower for Mathematics and Science Education
http://www.enc.org/
A click on the "Ideas" button connects to a section on Standards and Frameworks. Includes links to full text versions of math and science standards estab-

lished by various groups such as the National Council of Teachers of Mathematics, the National Academy of Sciences, and the American Association for the Advancement of Science. Also links to several state curriculum standards in math and science (As of August, 1998, includes FL, KS, CO, ID, AL, MS, MT, ND, OH, PA, TN, and VT).

Library-In-The-Sky
http://www.nwrel.org/sky2/
Maintained by the Northwest Regional Educational Laboratory, one of 10 regional labs funded by the U. S. Department of Education. A search using "standards" yields a bevy (just under 100) of links to standards by content area. Also includes many state standards.

Math Forum
http://forum.swarthmore.edu/
Maintained by Swarthmore College, this site's search engine will yield links to Websites that deal with math standards. Also includes links to content standards in other subject areas as well.

National Center on Educational Outcomes
http://www.coled.umn.edu/NCEO/
Provides information and links to various on-line publications and Websites dealing with outcomes and indicators for monitoring educational results for students, especially students with disabilities. Includes a searchable database that can yield possible judgment criteria for your evaluations.

National Center for Research on Evaluation, Standards, and Student Testing (CRESST)
http://cresst96.cse.ucla.edu/index.htm
Takes you to the Website of the National Center for Research on Evaluation, Standards, and Student Testing (CRESST) which conducts research on important topics related to K-12 educational testing. Funded by the U. S. Department of Education. Allows you to search on keywords within the site's database which includes reports and newsletters on standards that can guide your thinking as you establish the judgment criteria for your evaluations.

North Central Regional Educational Laboratory
http://www.ncrel.org
Connects to the North Central Regional Educational Laboratory, one of 10 regional agencies funded by the federal government to support states and schools. Provides resources that can help you establish the judgment criteria for your evaluation. Also links to the other nine regional labs. To find the lab serving your area, simply click on "Other Regional Educational Laboratories." A map of the United States will appear and you simply click on your region and go directly to the Website of the lab.

CHAPTER 3

Doing Evaluations

Step 3—Make a Plan

3.1—How Do I Proceed?

Now that you have the questions that will guide your evaluation and the criteria and standards you will use to judge the worth of the innovation you are evaluating, you are ready to make a plan for getting your questions answered. Essentially, you want to sketch out *who* will collect *what* data, by *when,* using *what methods.* You will also want to plan *how to analyze* the data you gather. Finally, you will want to very briefly outline the structure of your final *evaluation report.*

We find that building a matrix like the one on page 40 in Figure 3.1 is the easiest way to develop an evaluation plan. In column A, you simply list each of the evaluation questions you posed in Step 1. Now, using common sense mixed with your knowledge of good program evaluation techniques, you build the rest of the matrix, planning how you will gather and analyze the information you need. If you are conducting a modest, informal evaluation of a new strategy you implemented in your own classroom, you can simply sketch in the matrix to provide a rough guide for your evaluation. Figure 3.6 on page 56 gives an example of one middle school teacher's rough guide for evaluating her use of math journals in her classes. If, however, you are undertaking a more complex, formal evaluation like the one Murray and his colleagues are designing to evaluate their school's use of block scheduling, you should flesh out each cell of the matrix more thoroughly. At the end of this chapter, we show Murray's more detailed evaluation plan.

3.2—Column B: What Information Do You Need?

Let's now look more closely at each column of our evaluation planning matrix. Column B requires that you identify the information you will need to answer each evaluation question. For example, if the evaluation question is *"Did the after-school homework center improve home-school relations?",* you need to list in Column B all the information necessary to answer this question. In this case, you want opinions of teachers, students and family members *before* and *after* the implementation of the homework center. You want to canvass those who use the homework center and those who do not use the homework center. You also want some evidence concerning the number of positive contacts between parents and teachers.

Figure 3.1   Evaluation Planning Matrix

A Evaluation Question	B Information needed?	C Using what method?	D Who will collect?	E By When?	F How analyze?
Did the homework center improve home-school relations?	A. Opinions of those who DO use the homework center	Interview 5 randomly selected parents and students	Vice-principal	May 15	Vice-principal, summary for each question by June 1
		Survey completed by all students who attend center	Homework Center staff	May 1	Volunteer students in homework center, tallies and %'s for each question by May 15
	B. Opinions of those who DO NOT use the homework center	Interview 10 randomly selected parents and students	Counselor	May 15	Counselor, summary for each question by June 1
		Survey completed by all students who *do not* attend the center	Advisory teachers Teacher Advisory Co-ordinator	May 5	Students in the 7th Grade Gold Team, tallies and %'s for each question by May 22
	C. Opinions of staff • Administrators • Counselors • Teachers who work in the homework center • General staff	Interview principal, vice-principal, counselors, and teachers who work in the homework center	Students in Journalism Club	May 15	Journalism Club Students, summary for each question by June 1
		Survey completed by all teachers	Vice-principal	May 5	PTA volunteers, tallies and %'s for each question by May 22
	D. Number of positive contacts between home and school.	Review of "Notes Home" forms for current 8th graders over past 2 school years and current year	Counselor, students in Zoo Team	May 15	Counselor students in Zoo Team, tallies and line graph by June 1

As you complete Column B, you want to keep in mind two important things:

1. Who will want to know about the findings of your evaluation?
2. What evidence will these audiences deem credible?

Murray's task of demonstrating to the high school faculty that the middle school's block scheduling does not jeopardize the students' readiness for high school aptly shows the importance of these two factors. If Murray and his colleagues only collect opinions from middle school students asking them, *"In your opinion, do you think the middle school's block schedule is preparing you for success at high school?"*, they're in trouble. As far as the high school teachers are concerned, middle school students, who have yet to experience firsthand the realities of high school, cannot generate credible data for this question.

3.3—Column C: What Data Collection Methods will You Use?

Column C asks that you designate the data collection methods you will use. This column probably requires the most careful thinking of any piece of your evaluation planning matrix. Indeed, university professors teach semester-long courses on methods of research and evaluation that deal exclusively with the issues you must address in Column C. Rather than giving a detailed course on data collection methods at this point, we will provide only a brief overview of the various ways you can use to gather credible data. Later in chapter 4, we will discuss these methods more thoroughly. Furthermore, in chapters 8, 9, and 10, we give additional descriptions of the various data collection methods you can use to answer questions that take stock, determine effectiveness, and seek solutions.

We do, however, want to take time now to distinguish between the two broad categories of data that you can collect. Essentially, data come in two forms: numbers and words. Number data are called *quantitative data*. These are data we get by counting things, events, or people. We can quantify or measure the data in some way. Furthermore, we can add, subtract, multiply, divide, find averages, and calculate ratios with quantitative data. (More on this when we discuss ways to analyze data.) Some examples of quantitative data include:

• The number of books read by students during a semester

• The number of hours that students volunteered at the local homeless shelter

• The average student scores on the state mathematics assessment subtest on problem-solving

• The average amount of money spent by teachers from their own pocket on science supplies.

Word data is called *qualitative data*. We can collect these data by asking, watching, or reviewing documents. Rather than simply count things, events, or people, we record our data in the form of words. Some examples of qualitative data include:

• Student comments about how much they enjoyed reading various books during the semester

• Comments made by clients at the local homeless shelter concerning their interactions with student volunteers

- Teacher judgments as to how well students can use problem-solving skills in mathematics

- Explanations given by various administrators as to why they budget little money for science supplies.

In contrast to quantitative data, we cannot add, subtract, multiply, divide, find averages, or calculate ratios with qualitative/word data. We can, however, report percentages. For example, you could report that 76% of the parents surveyed said that they "often" talk with their child about school matters during the weekend.

```
┌──────────────────────────────────────────────────────┐
│                         FYI                            │
│                                                        │
│ Strange as it may sound, the word "data" is plural.    │
│ Thus, re-searchers and evaluators say: "The data       │
│ show . . ." "The data are . . ."The singular form is   │
│ "datum" which you infrequently see or hear since we    │
│ rarely collect just ONE piece of information.          │
└──────────────────────────────────────────────────────┘
```

Now that we have distinguished between quantitative and qualitative data, let's talk more about planning how you will actually collect your data. Fleshing out Column C on our planning matrix requires that you:

1. Consider the design of your evaluation

2. Attempt to corroborate your evidence

3. Find ways to collect data in a simple and reliable manner.

3.4—The Design of Your Evaluation

Let's examine each of these tasks separately. First, you need to consider the design of your evaluation. While, entire college courses focus on evaluation design, we will give only an overview. At the end of this chapter we list several resources you can consult for more thorough discussions of evaluation designs.

Program evaluators draw from two schools of thought when they put together a plan for conducting an evaluation. First, they rely on the *designs used by researchers*. These experimental and non-experimental research designs seek to describe, establish causation, or discover a relationship between two or more variables. A familiar research design is the classic experiment where we randomly create two groups. (See Figure 3.2) Keeping all things constant, one group (the experimental group) receives the special intervention, while the other group (the comparison group) doesn't receive it. Afterwards, we take measurements (perhaps a test of algebraic concepts) and compare the results. If the experimental group outperforms the comparison group, we can logically conclude that the intervention caused the difference.

Another familiar research design is a time-series study that uses only one group of subjects. In this design, we measure a variable, such as students' reading ability, several times *before* the intervention and then again several times *after*. (See Figure 3.3.) We then compare the baseline measures with the posttests to determine if the intervention produced an alteration in the pre-intervention trend.

Figure 3.2   Experimental-Comparison Group Research Design

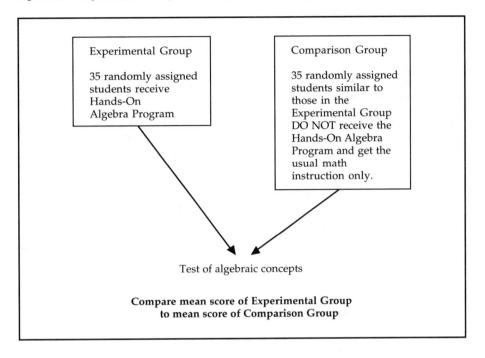

Figure 3.3   Times Series Design

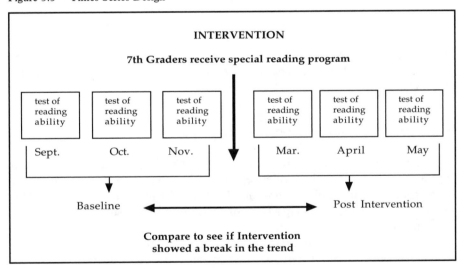

If we see a break in the pre-intervention pattern, then we can conclude that the intervention made a difference.

Numerous other research designs exist that you can adapt to meet the purposes of evaluation. Chapter 9 deals with answering effectiveness questions and explains in more detail several research designs you'll find useful. Furthermore, at the end of this chapter, we list several resources that give a thorough explanation of these various research designs.

3.5—Evaluation Approaches

When developing their evaluation plans, program evaluators not only draw on the designs used by researchers, they also consult the various approaches found in the evaluation literature. Worthen, Sanders, and Fitzpatrick (1997) describe six distinctive approaches that you can follow when conducting an evaluation. These approaches include the following:

1. The *objectives-oriented* evaluation approach judges how well the program has met the original objectives specified in a project's proposal.

2. The *management-oriented* evaluation approach strives to answer the questions decision-makers need to render a judgment about the program.

3. The *consumer-oriented* approach mirrors the evaluations found in the magazine *Consumer Reports* and seeks to provide educators with the information they need to make wise purchases and adoptions.

4. The *expertise-oriented* approach employs outside experts who use a set of externally established criteria and standards to judge the quality of a program or even an entire school.

5. The *adversary-oriented* approach requires that evaluators delineate the strengths and weaknesses of a program or present both sides of a controversial issue much like lawyers do in a trial.

6. The *naturalistic and participant-oriented* evaluation approaches focus on getting into the "trenches" and seek to fulfill the information needs of all stakeholders in the program, not just the decision-makers.

In chapter 8, our example involving Beverly takes the expertise-based approach to evaluation, while in chapter 9 we illustrate the use of the objectives-oriented approach. For a complete (and very readable) description of all six approaches, please consult Worthen, Sanders, and Fitzpatrick (1997) listed in Section 3. 21—Resources.

3.6—Corroborating the Evidence

In many ways, a program evaluator and a trial attorney work in similar fashion. The attorney seeks credible evidence that will help a jury make a decision concerning a defendant's guilt or innocence. Likewise, the program evaluator amasses credible evidence that will help a body of decision-makers make a decision about the value or merit of a program.

Furthermore, both program evaluators and trial attorneys also seek evidence that will corroborate tentative conclusions. One piece of evidence is rarely enough to convict in a court of law. The same is true in an evaluation. The program evaluator may form a tentative conclusion based on one piece of evidence, but she can not seal that conclusion until she gets other evidence that corroborates or confirms her conclusion. She needs *several* pieces of evidence that all point towards the same conclusion.

This need for multiple pieces of evidence is especially true when you collect qualitative data, such as the opinions and statements you might glean from talking with people. Program evaluators call this process of using multiple sources of data triangulation.* Essentially, you draw your conclusions from data collected from a variety of sources using a variety of data collection methods. (See Figure 3.4.)

Triangulation is particularly important when you collect and analyze qualitative/word data, the kind of data you often get from asking people questions on surveys. Just as a police detective builds a case against a particular suspect using multiple pieces of evidence, the program evaluator logically derives a conclusion from *multiple* pieces of information. A conclusion drawn from just one piece of evidence lacks impact, while an inference deduced from several pieces of evidence carries more weight.

Figure 3.4   What Triangulation Looks Like

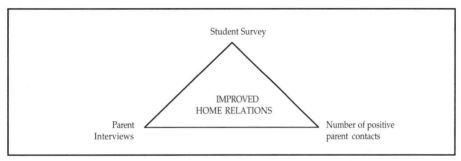

You might find the matrix in Figure 3.5 helpful as you plan how you will gather qualitative data to answer each of your evaluation questions. This matrix is called a Cross-Walk of Qualitative Data Collection Methods and helps to ensure that you gather sufficient evidence to form credible conclusions. For each question, you should try to collect qualitative data from a least two different sources using at least two different collection methods. Thus, you should have at least two "X's" in each row of the Cross-Walk matrix. At the end of this section we will show how Murray and his colleagues used the Cross-Walk of Qualitative Data Collection Methods in planning their evaluation of their school's block schedule.

3.7—Data Collection: Keep it Simple

As you plan how to collect your data, you should keep two things in mind:

1. Keep it simple.
2. Keep it reliable.

As you plan your evaluation, remember to K.I.S.S. your efforts. That means **K**eep **I**t **S**imple, **S**weetheart!! Keeping it simple means relying on existing data when you can and collecting new data only when you must. Too often educators forget about the wealth of data that already exists. Remember all those forms you filled out and turned in to the office? Someone tabulated them and the information lies somewhere in a file. Or what about the parent/community surveys you had to conduct as part of your state accreditation process? All this information can serve as data to help you evaluate your programs.

---

* First described in the book *Unobtrusive measures* (1965). by Webb, E. J., Campbell, D. T., Schwartz, R. D. and Sechrest, L. Chicago: University of Chicago Press.

Figure 3.5   Cross-Walk of Qualitiative Data Collection Methods

Evaluation Questions	Reviewing		Observing		Asking										
	Documents	Artifacts	Structured	Unstructured	Written Questionnaire					Interview					
					Teachers	Non-cert.	Principal	Families	Students	Teachers	Non-cert.	Principal	Families	Students	

The best places to look for existing data include the principal's office, student cumulative files, and the district office. In particular, the district-level administrators who handle state and federal grants, such as Title I and special education, will have reams of data that you might find helpful. You can also find valuable existing data in teachers' classrooms. Portfolios of student work and student grades are just two examples.

Even though you will rely on existing data first, often you will also want to collect new data. Again, common sense and practicality should direct your efforts. Making a plan using the Evaluation Planning Matrix (Figure 3.1) and the Cross-Walk of Qualitative Data Collection Methods (Figure 3. 5) will keep your data collection work focused and efficient. For example, if you have several evaluation questions that you can answer by observing classrooms, you don't want to conduct a separate observation for each evaluation question. Rather you want to consolidate and conduct only *one* observation, gathering *all* the observation data you need at one time. This saves time and effort. Chapters 8, 9, and 10 will provide several examples of how you can keep your data collection efficient and practical.

3.8—Data Collection: Keep it Reliable

Not only do you wish to keep your data collection efforts simple, you also want to collect information in a reliable manner. This means you must be as systematic and impartial in collecting data as humanly possible. We really can't ever eliminate bias, but we should definitely try to minimize it.

Bias can creep into an evaluation in many ways. Let's give a few illustrations. First, bias can occur in *how you collect the data.* Perhaps the IQ test you used to collect data about children's academic potential is biased against students who come from poverty homes and thus systematically underestimated their intelligence.

Second, bias can occur in *how you select your subjects.* Perhaps the group of students you selected to receive the experimental Hands-On Equations algebra✴ instruction were better math students from the outset and would have known more than the students in the comparison group (those who did not get the Hands-On Equations algebra instruction) no matter what instructional strategy you used.

Finally, *your own beliefs* can skew your data collection. Because *you* believe the program works, you collect data that slants the results towards showing success. For example, if Murray and his colleagues interview and survey only those students, parents, and teachers who have shown support for block scheduling, they will lose credibility in the eyes of critics and neutrals alike. If Murray and his colleagues make no effort to give a balanced view of block scheduling, supporters and critics alike will discount the results.

How can you minimize bias during data collection?

- Assume the role of a friendly critic, a devil's advocate, as you plan and conduct your evaluation. Continually ask yourself, *"Will this look credible in the eyes of our audience?".*

- Strive to collect your data from different sources (i.e., teachers, administrators, parents) using different methods (i.e., review of documents, interviews with parents, classroom observations).

- Consult with a neutral, third party to check whether or not your plans for data collection and analysis seem objective and minimize systematic bias.

- Finally, provide a balanced view of the program you are evaluating. Make sure that as you collect data you examine both sides of the issues, allowing both the pros and cons to emerge.

3.9—Reviewing, Observing, and Asking

Program evaluators (and researchers as well) use three basic methods to collect data:

1. They *review* documents or artifacts.

2. They *ask* people for facts or opinions.

3. They *observe* situations.

Program evaluators often gather useful data by *reviewing* documents and artifacts. Documents might include grant proposals, cumulative records, budget expenditures, or newspaper articles. *The American College Dictionary* (1963) defines artifact as "any object made by man [or woman] with a view to subsequent use." To a program evaluator, artifacts include photos, audio and video tapes, student-made displays, art works, and a myriad of other things that you can hold in your hands and review. Educators often overlook the usefulness of reviewing student-made artifacts when they evaluate the effectiveness and worth of a project. In chapter 8, we will examine how to get answers to questions that take stock. In that chapter, we will give a detailed illustration of how you can collect valuable data by reviewing documents and artifacts that your school routinely produces.

Program evaluators also gather data by *asking*. They generally do so by interviewing people or sending out a written survey. Either way, the evaluators hope to get information that will help answer the evaluation questions. In chapter 9, Effectiveness Questions, we will discuss more thoroughly how you can use interviews and surveys to gather data.

Not only do program evaluators review and ask, they also *observe*. Sometimes they observe using a structured format designed to examine particular behaviors. A teacher-made or standardized test of knowledge or skills is really a kind of structured observation.

Other observations involve tallying the behaviors you see. For example, let's say you have decided to try shifting your teaching behavior from being "a sage on the stage" to more of a "guide on the side." You roughly sketch out an evaluation plan. Your primary evaluation question is this: "Did I really change my teaching behavior so that the students talk more than I do?" To check this out, you decide to videotape several lessons *before* you alter your teaching behavior and then videotape several other lessons *after* you change your behavior. In the privacy of your own living room, you view the tapes and use Flanders' Interaction Analysis★ observation form to chart how much talking you do versus the students.

At other times, a program evaluator may want to look for some behaviors in particular, but will not use a structured form. For example, a middle school in

---

★ Flanders' Interaction Analysis [explained in Flanders, N. A. (1970). *Analyzing teaching behavior.* Reading, MA: Addison-Wesley.] is one of many structured observation forms you can use to record classroom events.

the Midwest found that student behavior in the cafeteria deteriorated so much that nearly every day several shouting matches occurred and on some days students actually exchanged blows. In an effort to figure out what was going on, two teachers observed during each lunch period throughout one week. One teacher always recorded "things that went right," while the other teacher documented "things that went wrong." Later, these teachers and their colleagues analyzed these observations and found that certain behavior patterns emerged. They then used this information to craft an action plan to improve the lunch room situation.

Finally, program evaluators may observe in a totally non-structured way, simply scripting everything that goes on in a particular situation. Later, they will see if any particular patterns emerge. Careful observation can yield valuable data that you can use to answer your questions. Unfortunately, educators generally overlook the power and practicality of observational data. Later in chapter 10, where we deal with answering questions that seek solutions, we will discover just how valuable observations can be.

3.10—Column C: Using What Method?

Let's now return to the Evaluation Planning Matrix in Figure 3.1. We embarked on this discussion about types of data, evaluation designs, and data collection methods so that we could fill in Column C: Using What Method? of the Evaluation Planning Matrix. Figure 3.1 shows this column completed. We now move to Column D where you must delineate *who* will collect the data.

3.11—Column D: Who Will Collect the Data?

Thus far in planning your evaluation, you have designated your evaluation questions, specified the information you need to answer those questions, and delineated how you will collect the information. Now in Column D, you need to designate *who* will collect each set of data. People to collect data may include:

- Yourself

- Students*

- Clerical staff within the school

- Support staff such as the counselor, the school psychologist, the nurse, or teacher assistants

- Parent or community volunteers

- An impartial third party [For example, these folks can come from elsewhere in the district or from a local college or university. Sometimes you might even have to hire someone to collect your data.]

---

*Encouraging students to design and conduct evaluations of school or community programs provides students with a real-world experience that requires them to apply their critical thinking, communication, and mathematical skills.

Filling out Column D requires that you consider who are the most logical people to collect the data. When making this determination, you should consider the following:

- *Who has easy access to the data you need?*   If you need information about disciplinary referrals to the principal's office, a clerk in that office might be the best person to collect such data.

- *Who has the necessary skills to collect the data?*   Collecting data successfully, particularly through interviewing or observing, requires skill and practice. You may need to provide training for those who will collect your data or find someone who already possesses these skills.

- *Who will others see as an unbiased, objective data collector?*   In cases where the person who collects data can either consciously or unconsciously skew the results, you might want to use impartial, third parties to collect your data. You might want to review our discussion in Section Intro.17 on page 11 giving the pros and cons of using an outside evaluator.

- Finally, in some evaluations you need to consider *who can be trusted to keep the information confidential.*   Sometimes people don't feel comfortable telling "the truth as they know it," unless they believe that what they say will not be used against them. Not only will you want to ensure confidentiality, but you will also want respondents to trust the data collector and feel comfortable "telling it like it is."

3.12—Issue Box

Rights of Human Subjects

As your evaluation becomes more and more formal and external, you must become increasingly concerned about the code of ethics that researchers and evaluators have established when dealing with humans as subjects. At the very least, as you formalize your evaluation, you need to consider the issues of informed consent and privacy as discussed below. We also suggest that you check with the district office to make sure you comply with your district's research and evaluation policies.

You can find an excellent discussion of the right of human subjects in *Designing and Conducting Research: Inquiry in Education and Social Science* written by Drew, Hardman, and Hart and published by Allyn and Bacon (1996).

As a middle school educator who will conduct formal evaluations, you should keep the following rights in mind as you collect data for your evaluations:

- You should *obtain informed consent* from those who will provide information *before* you interview or survey them. Informed consent means that you explain in general what kind of information you want from them and how you will use this information. Also you must tell people that they may refuse to participate and no harm will come to them. For example, if you ask students to complete a survey about their feelings concerning the relationship between their parents and the school, they must not receive any punishment if they refuse to complete the survey. Also, you must let people know that they can withdraw their consent at any time during an interview or survey, without any negative consequences happening to them.

- You must also *protect people's rights to privacy* by insuring their confidentiality. While conducting the evaluation, you should keep the information you gather confidential. You might even want to label interview sheets and other data collection forms with identification numbers rather than names. In the evaluation report you should not use names unless you have the person's permission to do so. For example, let's say you interview the superintendent and you want to include one of her quotes in the final report. You must get her permission to do so. If she does not give her permission, you have two choices: you can leave out the quote or use the quote but attribute it by writing: "one staff member said . . .".

3.13—Column E: When Will You Collect the Data?

In Column E you indicate the schedule you will follow in collecting the information you need to answer the evaluation questions. We suggest that when building the schedule, you consult with those who will help collect data, asking them just how much time they will need to get the information you want. Once you and your colleagues have devised a feasible schedule, make it even more feasible by including some extra days to cover the unexpected delays that always arise. If you are conducting an evaluation that takes several months to collect the data, you should set intermediate deadlines so you can make mid-course corrections to your timeline. The key in setting any schedule is to keep it reasonable and then monitor your progress against your timeline.

3.14—Column F: How Will You Analyze the Data?

In Column F of the Evaluation Planning Matrix, you sketch out your plans for analyzing the data you collect. You need to designate *who* will analyze the data, *how* they will analyze the data, and *when* you expect them to complete the analysis. As with data collection, those who analyze the data may include:

- Yourself
- Clerical staff within your school

- Students*

- Support staff such as the counselor, the school psychologist, the nurse, or teacher assistants

- Parent or community volunteers

- An impartial third party, a volunteer, or someone you hire for the task

When deciding whom you should ask to analyze the data, you should consider the following:

- *Who has the time to do the analysis?*   Be realistic and try not to unduly overburden any one person with all the data analysis. Spread the task around. However, do realize that whoever does the data analysis will have to spend a considerable amount of time wallowing in the data to generate credible conclusions. Good data analysis is not a superficial, once-over-lightly activity. You need to *know* your results and stay open to patterns that may emerge.

- *Who has the necessary skills to analyze the data?*   Some data analysis, like reporting tallies and calculating averages, requires only rudimentary mathematical skills, while other types of data analysis demand more sophistication. Please remember that you can easily teach students and adults how to do various simple statistical analyses. Furthermore, should you need some statistical analysis that goes beyond your own skills, we're sure that someone at your local university will be happy to provide some guidance.

- *Who will be able to render an unbiased, objective analysis of the data?*   Just as bias can distort an evaluation during data collection, it can easily skew the analysis of the data. This is particularly true, if stakeholders (those who will be directly affected by the outcome of the evaluation) do all of the analyses. Bias begins to creep into the data analysis whenever you stray from the admonishment that Dragnet's Joe Friday always gave: "Just the facts, ma'am. Just the facts." Too often when we evaluate a program that is near and dear to our hearts, we see what we want to see and sometimes even see what is not there. We give the data an unwarranted positive spin. Because they have a vested interest in showing the success of block scheduling, Murray and this colleagues will have to be particularly careful that they don't compromise their objectivity.

How can you minimize bias during the data analysis stage?

1. Assume the role of a friendly critic, a devil's advocate, as you analyze the data. Continually ask yourself, *"Am I seeing only what I want to see?"* and *"Will this look credible in the eyes of our audience?"*.

2. Require that you have at least three pieces of evidence supporting each conclusion you draw from your data.

3. Ask someone, with no vested interest in the outcome of the evaluation, to review your conclusions, answering the question. *"Are the conclusions in our report justified from the evidence presented?"*

---

*Using students to analyze data requires them to apply their critical thinking, communication, and mathematical skills to solve a real-world need.

4. Finally, provide a balanced view of the program you are evaluating by reporting both the positive and negative findings. Consciously search for pros and cons.

3.15—Planning How to Analyze Your Data

In fleshing out Column F of the Evaluation Planning Matrix, not only do you want to designate *who* will analyze the data, but also *how* they will analyze the data. At this point you don't have to go into detail, but you should have a general idea of how you want to analyze your data. Your planning should consider these three steps in data analysis:

1. How you will organize your data.
2. How you will describe your data.
3. How you will draw statistical inferences from your data, should you choose to do so.

In this chapter, we will give only a brief overview of the various data analysis methods you might want to use. Later in chapter 5 when we discuss Step 5: Analyze Data, we will provide a more thorough discussion of data analysis. In chapters 8 and 9 we'll actually apply these analytical techniques to several real-world examples.

In analyzing data, you must first *organize* the data into some understandable form so that you can summarize and describe them. This process might include such activities as:

• Tallying how many people answered YES to question 6 on the survey about parents' relationship with the school
• Listing all the comments made by students in response to the question, "What do you like best about going to the Homework Center?"
• Entering into a spreadsheet all the scores students made on a reading pretest and posttest, or recording the number of disciplinary referrals for fighting made during the last 5 years

The next step requires that you decide how you want to *describe* your results. For some data, such as the number of people who answered YES to question 6, you might simply want percentages. For comments given during interviews or on surveys, you might want the statements sorted into categories with tallies for each type of comment. Or in addition to a tally, you might want a simple listing of the comments themselves by category or a synthesis giving the gist of what people said. In chapters 9 and 10, we will show various ways to organize and describe qualitative/word data.

With quantitative/number data, such as student test scores, you might want to report some sort of average and give a sense about the range of scores. We suggest that as you plan your statistical analysis, ask yourself, "What sort of descriptive statistics will make sense to my audience?". It may be that a school board member might more readily comprehend a range than a standard deviation. When we get to Step 5: Analyze Data in chapter 5, we will discuss more fully the options available for describing quantitative data.

In some evaluations you may want to go beyond simply describing your data; you may want to use it to show that using a particular innovation actually *caused* students to learn more than a conventional teaching strategy. To show causation you need to employ inferential statistics that help you answer the question, *"Did it make a significant difference?"*. With qualitative data, you may want to utilize other statistical methods to ascertain whether or not people prefer one choice over another, whether or not a correlation exists between variables, or if a significant difference exists among the median scores of various groups.

Using inferential statistics requires a certain level of sophistication. Later in chapter 5 under Step 5: Analyze Data, we will briefly explain some of the more common procedures used in inferential statistics. At the end of chapter 5, we list several highly readable statistical texts that you can consult for more information.

Once you decide how you will analyze your data, you can complete Column F and your Evaluation Planning Matrix is now finished and can serve as a blue print for your data collection efforts.

Getting Kids Involved!

Throughout this book, we recommend that you involve your students in conducting program evaluations. We've found a wonderful Website that can help you do just that:

http://www.ups.edu/community/tofu

This address connects to the "Tools for Understanding" site maintained by The University of Puget Sound in Washington. The site's Resource Guide for Extending Mathematical Understanding in Secondary Schools includes high-quality resources and ideas for involving your students in collecting, organizing, analyzing, and presenting data. It provides *complete* lesson plans, all with down-loadable student worksheets, that you can use to teach your students how to identify and clarify problems; collect, organize, and analyze real-world data; and clearly communicate their results either orally or in writing. Both the "Math Concepts" and "Integrated Lessons" sections contain lessons that integrate math problem-solving, computer technology, and communication skills around real-world situations that middle school students will find intriguing.

3.16—ALWAYS Make a Plan

Using the Evaluation Planning Matrix to plan a formal evaluation is a must if you want to remain focused and avoid wasting time, energy, and money. Indeed, the more ambitious and formal the evaluation, the more imperative it is that you complete a written Evaluation Planning Matrix. Not only do formal evaluations profit from this advance planning, but even modest, informal evaluations benefit from planning. Figure 3.6 is an example of an evaluation plan that Mary Smith quickly jotted down one day during her planning period. While Mary's plan is not as detailed as our plan for evaluating one middle school's Homework Center, it does provide direction for Mary's evaluation of her students' use of math journals✻. Our advice is this: *Always create a plan BEFORE you conduct an evaluation,* even if that plan is a quickly sketched out plan on scratch paper. A plan will keep you on track and help you efficiently carry out your evaluation.

3.17—Final Considerations

Before you finalize your Evaluation Planning Matrix, you need to take two other things into consideration.

First, you need to *review the judgment criteria that you established in Step 2.* Does your evaluation plan stipulate that you will collect <u>all</u> the data you will need when you apply the judgment criteria established in Step 2?

For example, let's say that this past semester you began using Howard Gardner's concept of multiple intelligences✻ in designing science activities for your students. Now, at the end of the semester, you want to evaluate the value of these new learning activities. In roughing out an evaluation plan, you stipulated the following as one of the criteria that you will use to judge the success or failure of these new science activities: "Student understanding of habitats will increase."

As you look over your Evaluation Planning Matrix, you find that nowhere have you included any assessment of your students' understanding of habitats. So you quickly add an additional evaluation question under column A: "How much did students increase their understanding of environmental science concepts?" You then fill in the remaining columns B through F of the matrix to make sure you gather all the data you will need.

Second, if you plan to write a report of your evaluation for others, *you need to consider what the final report will look like* and ask yourself the following questions:

- Who will read the final report?

- What will they want to know?

- Does your Evaluation Planning Matrix include plans for collecting the information that these audiences will want?

- What major headings will you incorporate in your evaluation report?

- Does your Evaluation Planning Matrix include plans for collecting the information you will need to write each of the sections in your report?

3.18—Chapter Highlights

Major Concepts

☞ Step 3: Make a Plan provides you with the essential road map that will keep you focused whether you conduct a formal or informal evaluation.

☞ Number data are called quantitative data, while data in the form of words are called qualitative data.

Figure 3.6   Mary Smith's Plan for Evaluating the Use of Math Journals in Her A.M. Block Classes

A Evaluation Questions	B Information Needed	C Using What Method	D Who Will Collect	E By When	F Analyze How/Who/When?
① Do students learn math concepts better by using math journals?	Some demonstration of student understanding comparing A.M. classes (who used journals) and P.M. classes (who didn't)	• Weekly quizzes • Student-written explanations of concepts • Student questionnaire	Me Me Me	Mar. 15 Mar. 17 Mar. 22	Mean scores Me by Mar. 22 Mean score using rubric Me by Mar. 22 Tallies & %'s Me by Mar. 25 (Maybe kids can do this)
② Do students improve their problem-solving thinking by using math journals?	Some demo of student problem-solving comparing A.M. and P.M. classes	• Scores on ITBS math problem-solving section • Scores on math problem-solving section on state assessment • Student questionnaire	Me from counselor Me from counselor Me	April 15 April 15 Mar. 22	Mean scores Me by May 1 Mean scores Me by May 1 Tallies & %'s Me (or kids) by Mar. 25

☞ Program evaluators draw from two schools of thought when they put together a plan for conducting an evaluation: research designs and evaluation approaches.

☞ The classic experiment uses two randomly created groups. The researcher/evaluator keeps all things constant except that one group (the experimental group) receives the special intervention, while the other group (the comparison group) doesn't. If the experimental group outperforms the comparison group, we can logically conclude that the intervention caused the difference.

☞ A time-series study uses only one group of subjects who get measured several times *before* the intervention and then again several times *after*. If we see a break in the pre-intervention pattern, then we can conclude that the intervention made a difference.

☞ Triangulation involves using multiple sources to draw conclusions.

☞ Bias can creep into an evaluation in the way you collect the data, select your subjects, and let your own beliefs cloud your objectivity.

☞ Program evaluators (and researchers as well) use three basic methods to collect data:

1. They *review* documents or artifacts

2. They *ask* people for facts or opinions

3. They *observe* situations

Advice

√ Consider involving students in collecting and analyzing data.

√ Always create a plan *before* you conduct an evaluation even if that plan is a quickly sketched out plan on scratch paper.

√ Use the Evaluation Planning Matrix which requires you to specify:

• Your evaluation questions (Column A)

• What information you will need (Column B)

• What methods you will use to collect the information (Column C)

• Who will collect the information (Column D)

• By what date will you have the information collected (Column E)

• How will you analyze the information (Column F)

√ As you plan how to collect your data, keep two things in mind:

1. Keep it simple.

2. Keep it reliable.

√ Honor the rights of human subjects to informed consent and privacy.

√ Review the judgment criteria that you established in Step 2 and make sure your evaluation plan stipulates collecting *all* the data you will need to render your judgments.

√ Finally, consider what the final evaluation report will look like and make sure your Planning Matrix include plans for collecting the information that your audiences will want.

3.19—The Road Ahead

Thus far, you have posed your evaluation questions, established your criteria for judging the success or failure of the program you are examining, and have laid out a plan of how you will collect the data you need to make your judgment. In the next chapter, we get into the nitty-gritty of *how* you collect the information you need.

3.20—Murray Does Step 3

Figure 3.7   Evaluation Process Step 3

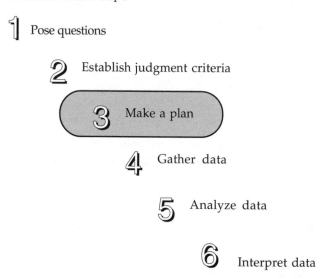

1 Pose questions

2 Establish judgment criteria

3 Make a plan

4 Gather data

5 Analyze data

6 Interpret data

Up to this point, Murray and his colleagues have decided on both the questions that will guide the evaluation and the criteria and standards they will use to judge the effectiveness of block scheduling. Now, Murray and his colleagues, with the help of graduate students Yolanda and Stan, sketch out an evaluation plan.

"Whew! We're finally finished," Murray exclaimed as the committee gathered up their belongings after completing the Evaluation Planning Matrix shown in Figure 3.8.

"Well, you know we're only just beginning," replied Yolanda, one of the graduate students from the university who had volunteered to help with the school's evaluation of the block schedule.

"But it's a good beginning," Stan, another graduate student volunteer, added. "All this good thinking will keep us focused in the months ahead. It seems like a lot but it's do-able, especially since, Murray, you and your colleagues, will collect the formative evaluation information."

"I'm especially glad we did that Cross-Walk," Murray said. "It really pointed out some glaring holes in our data collection plans."

Because much of the data Murray and his colleagues will collect is qualitative/word data from surveys and inter-views, they double checked their plan to make sure they will collect enough data to form credible conclusions. Using a Cross-Walk of Qualitative Data Collection Methods (Figure 3.9), they made sure they included plans to collect data from a least two different sources using at least two different collection methods. This way they can *triangulate* their conclusions using data from a variety of sources.

After completing the Cross-Walk, they found some holes in their plan. They went back and made sure they had two X's in each row of the Cross-Walk.

Once they sketched out the Evaluation Planning Matrix, Murray and his team went back to the judgment criteria they established in Step 2, making sure that their evaluation plan stipulated collecting all the data they will need to apply the criteria and standards.

Finally, Murray and his colleagues (again working with Yolanda and Stan) brainstormed the major sections they want to include in the final evaluation report Yolanda and Stan will present to the school board in July. They decided on the following table of contents:

Executive Summary
Description of Strivinghigher Middle School's Block
    Schedule
Evaluation Questions
Description of the Middle School Student Population
    Demographics
    Achievement
Methodology
Results
Conclusions and Recommendations

After generating a list of the possible sections of the final evaluation report, they discovered they had not included any plans to collect data that describe the demographics of the middle school's student population. They added this feature and Yolanda and Stan volunteered to put the Planning Matrix on the computer and make copies for everyone.

"When can we share this plan with the central office folks?" Murray asks.

"How about next Wednesday?" Yolanda suggests.

"Sounds good to me," Murray and Stan reply.

"I'll call and get us an appointment after 3:30 with the Director of Secondary Education," Murray says. "She really needs to review all this before any data collection begins."

Figure 3.8   Evaluation Planning Matrix Developed by Murray and his Colleagues

A Evaluation Question	B Information needed?	C Using what method?	D Who will collect?	E By When?	F How analyze?
1. Did students improve in reading comprehension?	For current 8th graders at Strivinghigher Middle School & comparison school & mastered % on state reading assessment since in 3rd grade	Review of state assessment printouts	Yolanda	June	Plot on line graph % mastered over time to see if a break in the trend for Strivinghigher students, Yolanda by July t-test comparing mean change scores for Strivinghigher students and comparison students, Oct. to May, Yolanda by July
2. Did students improve in math problem-solving?	For current 8th graders at Strivinghigher Middle School & comparison school % mastered on state math assessment since in 3rd grade	Review of state assessment printouts	Yolanda	June	Plot on line graph % mastered over time to see if a break in the trend for Strivinghigher students, Yolanda by July t-test comparing mean change scores for Strivinghigher students and comparison students, Oct. to July, Yolanda by July
3. Did students improve in science knowledge?	For current 8th graders at Strivinghigher Middle School & comparison school % mastered on state science assessment since in 3rd grade	Review of state assessment printouts	Yolanda	June	Plot on line graph % mastered over time to see if a break in the trend for Strivinghigher students, Yolanda by July t-test comparing mean change scores for Strivinghigher students and comparison students, Yolanda by July
4. Did students improve in expository writing?	For current 8th graders at Strivinghigher Middle School & comparison school % mastered on state writing assessment since in 3rd grade	Review of state assessment printouts	Yolanda	June	Plot on line graph % mastered over time to see if a break in the trend for Strivinghigher students, Yolanda by July t-test comparing mean change scores for Strivinghigher students and comparison students, Yolanda by July

A Evaluation question	B Information needed?	C Using what method?	D Who will collect?	E By When?	F How analyze?
5. Did students achieve higher attendance rate?	For current 8th graders at Strivinghigher Middle School & comparison school attendance rates taken on first day of each quarter for last school year and this school year	Pull from computer database	Counselor's secretary	May	Plot a line graph of attendance over time to see if a break in the trend for Strivinghigher students, Murray's students by May 15
6. Do students show more engagement in class?	Evidence of engagement from randomly selected students at Strivinghigher Middle School and comparison school	Structured classroom observation Oct. and April	Yolanda & Stan	May 15	t-test comparing mean change scores for Strivinghigher students and comparison group, Yolanda/Stan by June
		Student survey Oct. and April	Teacher advisors	May 15	Correlation between student responses and teacher judgment on engagement
		Teacher survey Oct. and April			t-test comparing mean change scores for Strivinghigher students and comparison group, Yolanda/Stan by June
7. Do students choose more academic challenges?	Evidence collected from randomly selected students at Strivinghigher Middle School and comparison school showing inclination to choose more academic challenge	Student survey Oct. and April	Teacher advisors	May 15	Correlation between student responses and teacher judgment on selecting challenge
		Teacher survey Oct. and April	Murray	May 15	t-test comparing mean change scores for Strivinghigher students and comparison group, Yolanda/Stan by June

Evaluation Question	Evidence	Data Source	Responsible	Date	Analysis
8. Do students show a more positive attitude?	Evidence of attitude collected from randomly selected students at Strivinghigher Middle School and comparison school	Student survey Oct. and April	Teacher advisors	May 15	Correlation between student responses and teacher judgment on attitude
		Teacher survey Oct. and April	Murray	May 15	t-test comparing mean change scores for Strivinghigher students and comparison group, Yolanda/Stan by June
9. Do students show more willingness to take responsibility?	Evidence of willingness to take responsibility collected from randomly selected students at Strivinghigher Middle School and comparison school	Student survey Oct. and April	Teacher advisors	May 15	Correlation between student responses and teacher judgment
		Teacher survey Oct. and April	Murray	May 15	t-test comparing mean change scores for Strivinghigher students and comparison group, Yolanda/Stan by June
10. Do students show more perseverance?	Evidence of perseverance collected from randomly selected students at Strivinghigher Middle School and comparison school	Student survey Oct. and April	Teacher advisors	May 15	Correlation between student responses and teacher judgment on perseverance
		Teacher survey Oct. and April	Murray	May 15	t-test comparing mean change scores for Strivinghigher student and comparison group, Yolanda/Stan by June
11. Do students exhibit greater self-efficacy?	Evidence of self-efficacy collected from randomly selected students at Strivinghigher Middle School and comparison school	Student survey Oct. and April	Teacher advisors	May 15	Correlation between student responses and teacher judgment on attitude
		Teacher survey Oct. and April	Murray	May 15	t-test comparing mean change scores for Strivinghigher students and comparison group, Yolanda/Stan by June
		LeTendre/Lipka Self-Efficacy Scale Oct. and April			
12. Are students ready for rigors of high school?	Opinions of 9th and 10th graders who attended Strivinghigher Middle School	Student Survey	High school Vice-principal	March	Create frequency table Disaggregate by 9th and 10th grade, Murray's students by June
	H.S. teacher opinions	Teacher survey	High school Vice-principal	March	Create frequency table comparing student and teacher response, high school vice principal by June.

A Evaluation question	B Information needed?	C Using what method?	D Who will collect?	E By When?	F How Analyze
13. What's going smoothly? Not so smoothly?	Opinions of staff, students, parents	Student survey	Students on Murray's team	December	Create frequency tables
		Teacher survey			Disaggregate students by grade level
		Parent telephone interview (sample)			Compare responses of students, teachers, parents, and principal
		Interview with principal			Murray's students by February 1
14. Are we getting our money's worth?	Costs and benefits associated with block scheduling Cost per pupil at Strivinghigher Middle School and comparison school (making adjustments for size Gain scores in achievement for both schools	budget	MBA students at university	March	Aggregate costs both outright expenditures and intangibles (time, productivity, etc.) and compare Strivinghigher with comparison school, MBA students by April 15

Figure 3.9   Cross-Walk of Qualitative Data Collection Methods/Developed by Murray and Colleagues

Evaluation Questions	Reviewing		Observing		Asking									
					Written Questionnaire					Interview				
	Documents	Artifacts	Structured	Unstructured	Teachers	Non-cert.	Principal	Families	Students	Teachers	Non-cert.	Principal	Families	Students
6. more engagement			X		X				X					
7. more challenge					X				X					
8. positive attitude					X				X					
9. more responsibility					X				X					
10. more perseverance					X				X					
11. self-efficacy			X*		X				X					
12. H.S. rigors					X				X					
13. going well?					X			X	X			X		

*LeTendre/Lipka Self-Efficacy Scale

3.21—Resources

Print Resources

References recommended in earlier chapters have an * by them. The number of *'s indicates the number of previous recommendations.

Brainard, E. A. (1996). *A hands-on guide to school program evaluation.* Bloomington, IN: Phi Delta Kappa Educational Foundation.

> Gives concise, understandable explanations of various data collection methods such as surveys, rating scales, checklists, structured interviews, and focus groups. Includes helpful examples of each method.

Drew, C. J., Hardman, M. L. & Hart, A. W. (1996). *Designing and conducting research: Inquiry in education and social science.* Boston: Allyn and Bacon.

> Gives a complete discussion concerning the rights of human subjects and other ethical issues in chapter 3.

Ebel, R. L. (1979). *Essentials of educational measurement* (3rd Ed.) Englewood Cliffs, NJ: Prentice Hall.

> Contains a glossary of 125 terms used in educational measurement. A good source for an educator who encounters an unfamiliar term while working with standardized tests and testing.

**Fink, A. & Kosecoff, J. (1978). *An evaluation primer.* Thousand Oaks, CA: Sage Publications.

> A gem of a book despite the 1978 copyright date. In chapter 4 provides excellent examples showing how to collect data: using performance tests, rating and ranking scales, archive review, observations, interviews, questionnaires, and achievement tests.

Hubbard, R. S. & Power, B. M. (1993). *Art of classroom inquiry.* Portsmouth NH: Heinemann.

> Targeted at practicing teachers (Pre K–12) who wish to conduct research that will inform their work with children. Written in a collegial tone with many detailed samples of data collection and data analysis techniques. Examples come from the work of practicing teacher-researchers (listed in the appendices of the book). Focuses primarily on using qualitative research methods. Chapter 2 covers note taking while "kid watching," surveys, student work and classroom artifacts, sociograms (one of the best explanations and examples of how to do this and what it can tell you as a teacher), and the use of audio and video tape transcriptions. Chapter 3 includes a good discussion of how to find and refine a research question. Finally, chapter 4 ably illustrates how to take qualitative data gathered through observations and interviews and make sense out of them. Provides exact examples of moving from raw field notes to "cooked" notes and, finally, to conclusions.

Lester, Paula E. and Bishop, L. K. (1996). *Handbook of tests and measurement in education and the social sciences.* Lancaster PA: Technomic Publishing Co., Inc.

> Includes a review of over 80 instruments that educators can use to take stock and determine effectiveness. Categorizes measurement instruments

under 32 topics, ranging from alienation to self-efficacy. In some cases includes actual instruments.

National Center for Service Learning in Early Adolescence. (1994). *Student Evaluators: A guide to implementation.* New York City: City University of New York.

> HIGHLY RECOMMENDED. Asks that you, the middle school educator, make a "leap of faith" and empower "young people to conduct evaluations of the projects in which they are involved." (p. iii) Provides a step-by-step explanation of how to engage young adolescents in planning and conducting program evaluations.

Internet Resources

NOTE: You can easily access the Websites we recommend below by simply going to our Web page located at

http://www.pittstate.edu/edsc/ssls/letendre.html

From our Web page, a simple click of your mouse will take you straight to the selected Website. We regularly verify these sites and add others that we find worthy of our recommendation.

American Educational Research Association
http://aera.net/resource/resource.html
Connects to a database containing many of the papers presented at the annual meetings (1985 to 1993) of the American Educational Research Association. Some include excellent examples of program evaluations that may provide you with ideas on how you might conduct your own evaluation. Also includes a copy of *The Program Evaluation Standards* that set the benchmark for credible evaluations.

National Research and Development Center
http://www.ed.gov/offices/OERI/At-Risk/center1.html
Connects to the National Research and Development Center which then links to three other centers: (1) The Center for Research on the Education of Students Placed At Risk, (2) The Center for Research on Education, Diversity and Excellence, and (3) The National Research Center on the Gifted and Talented. Provides excellent examples of program evaluations that can spark your own planning.

Tools for Understanding
http://www.ups.edu/community/tofu
Maintained by the University of Puget Sound in Washington. Filled with resources and ideas for involving students in collecting, organizing, analyzing, and presenting data. Bills itself as a Resource Guide for Extending Mathematical Understanding in Secondary Schools. Under both the "Math Concepts" and "Integrated Lessons" sections includes complete lesson plans for teaching students how to identify and clarify problems; collect, organize, and analyze real-world data; and clearly communicate results either orally or in writing. Contains "think sheets," available for down-loading, that guide students through all stages of the problem-solving process from planning to presenting findings.

Trochim, William M. K.
http://trochim.human.cornell.edu/kb/
Connects to Professor Trochim's Website at Cornell University entitled *The Knowledge Base, An Online Research Methods Textbook.* An excellent resource and further

treatment of many of the topics we cover in this book. Includes interesting graphics and clear explanations that provide enough detail without overwhelming the reader. Provides excellent information under the section "Introduction to Research" on sampling procedures, measurement, and research/evaluation design.

CHAPTER 4

Doing Evaluations

Step 4—Gather Data

4.1—Introduction

At this point in the evaluation process, you have completed the crucial thinking required to focus your evaluation. You have posed the evaluation questions you want answered, established the criteria you will use to judge the program, and made a detailed plan of how you will get your questions answered. Now, comes the "doing" part, where you actually gather the data you need. Let's begin by quickly reviewing some concepts about data and data collection we covered previously in Chapter 3.

Data can consist of numbers or words. We call numbers *quantitative data* because we are looking at quantities—"How many of this?" and "How much of that?". We gather quantitative data by counting things, events, or people. We can also gather quantitative data by measuring various characteristics of things and people, such as the age of middle school teachers or the level of math problem solving skills of middle school students. With quantitative data, we can add, subtract, multiply, divide, find averages, and calculate ratios. (There will be more information on this in chapter 5 when we discuss ways to analyze data.

We classify word data as *qualitative data*. We collect qualitative data by reviewing documents, asking, or observing. Rather than simply counting things, events, or people, we record our data in the form of words. Some examples of qualitative data include:

- Student comments about how they perceive the quality of the school's learning atmosphere
- Teacher judgments as to how students presented their portfolios during conferences with parents
- Explanations given by students as to why they got involved in after-school clubs.

Although we can count the number of students who responded "YES" to a question on a survey, we cannot calculate averages on qualitative/word data. We can, however, report percentages. For example, we could report that 76% of the parents surveyed said that they "often" talk with their child about school matters during the weekend. In chapter 5, we will more thoroughly discuss ways to analyze qualitative data.

4.2—How to Gather Data

No matter what type of data you collect (numbers or words), you gather information using three basic methods:

- *Reviewing* documents or artifacts
- *Asking* people for facts or opinions
- *Observing* situations and behaviors

Reviewing documents might include examining correspondence, grant applications, student records, and even printouts of test scores. Reviewing artifacts might mean examining objects such as student art work, History Day displays, or bulletin boards.

Asking people for facts or opinions is another method you can use to collect data. When gathering information by asking, you can interview individuals, groups, or conduct a survey.

Finally, you can also gather data by observing situations or specific behaviors. Your observations can be structured or unstructured. Let's look first at an example of a structured observation. In two of her seventh grade classes, a middle school teacher taught the history of the American Civil War by using video clips from a laser disc interspersed with various group activities. In her other classes, she used only the group activities. Now, she wants to know if using the video clips made a difference in how well students remember information about the American Civil War. She gives all her classes a written test. This written test is really a structured observation of her students' knowledge of the Civil War.

Now, let's examine an example of a less structured observation. Rather than giving a test, the teacher simply noted the reactions and comments of her students in all her classes while they were learning about the American Civil War. She then could ascertain any patterns in the students' comments that might emerge.

4.3—Getting Access to Existing Data

In chapter 3, we stressed that you should keep your collection efforts simple. Keeping it simple means relying on existing data when you can, and collecting new data only when you need to do so. As a matter of course, schools collect all sorts of information which then gets tabulated and filed somewhere. Whenever possible, find it and use it rather than collecting new data. Furthermore, most middle schools or district offices have extensive databases of information about students and staff that contain information you will find helpful.

In gaining access to existing data, you should keep several things in mind. First, you should be very clear about what information you need. Most likely, you won't be allowed to rummage through the file cabinets or computer database. It simply wouldn't be practical and confidentiality concerns may exist. However, clerical workers can often easily retrieve the data for you if they know exactly what information you need. We suggest that you actually share your evaluation questions with the clerical workers and then *ask them* what would be the easiest way to gather the information you want.

For example, let's say you are taking stock of the expertise within your school's staff and want to know the number of staff development credits teachers at your school have earned over the past three years. This information probably exists in each teacher's personnel file. You visit with the secretary in the district's personnel office and he suggests that he can go into the computer database and easily pull up the school's entire roster of certified staff and then run a report that shows the total number of staff development credits earned by the school's staff in the past three years. Furthermore, he can supply you with a list of topics these credits represent. However, he emphasizes that he will not supply you with any names because that would violate privacy.

Second, you should prepare for the possibility that existing data will not come in the exact format you need. You may have to translate the data into a more usable form. For example, almost every school collects some type of standardized student achievement data, whether the test comes from the state department of education or a publisher. These test results often come back to the school in two types of reports: individual reports showing the performance of each individual student and a summary report indicating the average performance of all students in the seventh grade. But for your purposes, you want to look at the average performance of only those students who attended your school for less than six months before taking the test. This means you will have to select the scores of particular students and then calculate the average score for this group.

Third, you may need to seek permission before you can gain access to certain types of school data. For example, in our previous example where you wanted information about the number of staff development credits earned by your school's staff, it is highly unlikely that the personnel office secretary would release this data to you without first checking with his boss, even if the data included no names. Most often administrators will happily release a summary report, as long as it includes no names.

4.4—Make a Plan

Simplicity in data collection also applies to collecting new data. Common sense and practicality should always guide your efforts. Making a plan using the Evaluation Planning Matrix (Figure 3.1) and the Cross-Walk of Qualitative Data Collection Methods (Figure 3.5) and following that plan will keep you focused and efficient. These planning documents will help you see how you can work smarter by consolidating your efforts. For example, if several evaluation questions require many different bits of information contained in student cumulative records, create a data collection form and collect *all* these data at one time rather than going into the student records several different times.

4.5—K.I.S.S. Your Data Collection

K.I.S.S. stands for Keep It Simple, Sweetheart! K.I.S.S.ing your data collection also requires that you keep data collection activities easy for both those who provide the data and those who collect the data. Those who provide you with data can include parents who answer a survey, teachers who report the amount they have spent out of their own pockets for classroom supplies, or students who tally up the number of minutes of television they watch in a week. You want to clearly state what information you need in language that everyone can understand.

Furthermore, you want to make it easy for people to provide you with the data. You might need to create a form that people can easily complete. Figure 4-1 illustrates a simple data collection form students might fill out to report the number of minutes they watch television. In later chapters, we will provide additional examples of how to keep your data collection simple. Chapter 9, in particular, will show how you can design surveys that people can easily and accurately complete.

Making your data collection easy for those who actually collect the data means keeping in mind the following advice:

- Spread the burden of data collection among several people if possible. Don't feel that only you can collect the data. Enlist the aid of other staff members, parents, community members and even students. Indeed, we highly suggest that you involve students in collecting data. This provides them with a real-world experience and hones skills that they will use for the rest of their lives.

- Devise clear, efficient procedures and forms that people can easily use to collect data. Figure 4.2 shows an example of a protocol a clerical worker could use to pull information from student cumulative records about grades made during elementary school.

Getting Kids Involved!

Christine Smith's eight grade mathematics students at Charleston (MO) Middle School have a solid reputation as "statisticians." They are always using numbers to solve real-world problems. One year, the superintendent asked if they would help prepare the bid specifications to build outdoor basketball courts at the elementary school. The students first calculated the dimensions of the concrete pad and then determined the amount of cubic yards of concrete needed to build the courts. Once the superintendent saw the bid specs, he requested that the students also obtain bids for the concrete work and present their recommendations to him. The students did just that and now the superintendent is waiting for available funds before taking the students' recommendations to the School Board for approval. Soon the elementary students will have several outdoor basketball courts thanks to the work of Christine's students.

Another year, Christine's students served as the official "statisticians" for the Jaywalkers, a local walking club made up of Charleston teachers. Each member of the walking club pledged to walk six miles each week for six weeks. Each week the Jaywalkers turned their walking miles into Christine's students who then organized the data for each

Figure 4.1   Example of a Form Students Can Use To Report The Number of Minutes They Watch TV During a Week

Student's Name _____   Week of _____

Directions: Each block represents 15 minutes. Mark with X for each 15 minutes you watch TV.

TIME	MONDAY	TUESDAY	WEDNESDAY	THURSDAY	FRIDAY	SATURDAY	SUNDAY
6 AM							
7 AM							
8 AM							
9 AM							
10 AM							
11 AM							
12 noon							
1 PM							
2 PM							
3 PM							
4 PM							
5 PM							
6 PM							
7 PM							
8 PM							
9 PM							
10 PM							
11 PM							
12 midnight							

Comments:

Figure 4.2   Protocol for Gathering Data from Student Cumulative Records Concerning Elementary Grades

Student Code number _____

Number of elementary schools attended: 1 2 3 4 5 6 7 8 9 10 more than 10 (circle one)

Grades repeated: K 1 2 3 4 5 NONE (circle one)

Directions: Record letter grade assigned each marking period. If no grade found or assigned, please make comment.

	READING		COMMENTS	MATHEMATICS		COMMENTS
2nd grade	1st semester	2nd semester		1st semester	2nd semester	
3rd grade						
4th grade						
5th grade						

COMMENTS:

individual walker and the group. At the end of the six weeks, the students calculated the mean, median and mode for the Jaywalkers group. Then integrating writing with math, the students wrote individual congratulations letters to all club members, giving a summary of the individual member's walking statistics and those of the group as well.

4.6—Use Reliable Methods

Not only should you keep your data collection simple, you should also collect information in a reliable manner. This means you should use methods that are both systematic and impartial. Let's look first at how you can systematically collect your data. You want to be consistent in the procedures you follow to collect information that you get the same results each time. To get this consistency, we suggest that you first establish a written protocol (a set of directions) that you or whoever is collecting the data can follow. Second, we urge you to train your data collectors in following these protocols.

Perhaps a negative example can illustrate what we mean about systematic data collection. A middle school counselor wants to judge how well the conflict resolution training all sixth graders received during the first months of the school year is working. Her overall evaluation question is, *"Has the conflict resolution training caused the number of violent conflicts among students to diminish?"*.

She defines "violent conflicts" as those where students actually exchange blows. She examines the disciplinary referrals for the six months *before* the training and for six months *after* the training. As she begins to sort through the discipline referrals, she encounters several instances where one student simply shoved another student to the ground without the two students actually exchanging blows. Sometimes the counselor puts such a shoving incident into the "violent conflict" category and sometimes she puts it into the "non-violent conflict" pile.

Unfortunately, this type of data collection is haphazard and unreliable. The counselor needs to *clearly define* what she means by "violent conflicts" and then uniformly apply this definition to her sorting. Her definition and procedure should be so clear and consistent that she could hand the stack of discipline referrals to another person and that person would sort the referrals in the same piles as the counselor did.

Systematic data collection also requires that you carefully record your data. Sloppy handwriting or careless recording of information will only result in garbage data that you can't read and will lead to inaccuracies and unreliability.

When conducting a high-stakes evaluation where reliability and consistency are absolutely crucial, we suggest that you conduct a trial run of your data collection procedures before engaging in any real gathering of information. During this trial run, you can practice collecting the data and iron out any kinks in your procedures.

4.7—Strive for Impartiality

Reliability rests not only on systematic, consistent procedures, but also on impartiality. While collecting data you must guard against bias in:

- Your procedures
- The instruments you use to take measurements
- The method you use to select groups for study

Let's look first at an example of *bias arising from faulty procedures.* A middle school team began using journal writing during math class to help students consolidate their understanding of mathematical concepts. At the end of the first semester, the teachers collected their students' math journals and started analyzing the quality of the students' mathematical understanding. Each teacher analyzed a set of journals and then switched with a teammate, who then judged the set once again. The team members soon discovered that they judged the first five journals in each batch higher in quality than the last five. A bias spawned by fatigue had crept into their procedures. Furthermore, they found that they tended to judge the journals of the girls higher than those of the boys, because the girls generally had neater handwriting. Again bias raised its ugly head.

Bias that threatens reliability *can also spring from the instruments* that we use to take measurements. You want to use only tests that consistently measure a trait, knowledge or skill. If a school psychologist administers an IQ test to students in March and then again in October of the same year, you would expect the IQ scores to be similar (not necessarily the same) both times if the IQ test is indeed reliable.

Furthermore, the instruments/tests you use should be fair and non-discriminatory. For example, you might find that the test you used to measure your students' reading ability is biased against students who come from inner-city or rural homes. Many questions required that students draw on prior knowledge that only children living in the suburbs normally acquire. City and rural children generally do not have these experiences. Thus, this particular reading test systematically underestimates some students' reading ability.

If you plan to use any standardized test to collect data, first check its reliability by reading the section concerning reliability in the technical manual accompanying the test or by consulting *Buros' Mental Measurement Yearbook*. This yearbook includes a description and information on reliability for most standardized tests in publication. You can find the latest copy of *Buros'* in the reference section of any good college or university library. The Resources Section 4.14 at the end of this chapter includes additional sources (both print and Internet) you can consult about a test's reliability and validity.

Finally, bias can arise in *how you select groups or samples* from which you will gather data. Of course, in some cases, you will collect data from all members of a particular population. In these cases, you do not need to select a sample. However, at other times, you will want to select a sample.

4.8—Sampling Techniques

Should you decide to use a sample, you can easily minimize bias by using random sampling. The key is that you want to select a sample that looks similar to the entire group (also known as the population). Through random sampling, the laws of probability work in your favor to help ensure that the naturally occurring differences among people we see in the population also show up in our sample.

Evaluators use several methods to *randomly* select a sample from the entire population:

- Simple random sampling
- Stratified random sampling
- Cluster sampling
- Systematic sampling

In *simple random sampling,* all students have an equal chance of being selected. You can either draw names out of a hat, use a random number table, or employ a computer program that will randomly select students. Any college text on methods of research or statistics will include an explanation of how to use a random number table to select subjects. (See Section 4.14 Resources for suggested texts.) Microsoft's Excel™ includes a built-in function for generating random numbers and using these to randomly select subjects.

In *stratified random sampling,* we divide our population into relevant subgroups and then randomly select from those subgroups to form our sample. Evaluators use stratified random sampling when they don't want to leave everything up to Lady Luck. If an evaluator wants to match groups on a particular characteristic or wants to ensure that certain important subgroups get represented in the sample, she will use stratified random sampling.

Let's illustrate this procedure. The teachers at Uptodate Middle School want to evaluate the effectiveness of using laser disk images to augment their teaching of science concepts. They feel, however, that boys may react differently than girls. To control for the possible impact that gender might have, the teacher make sure the experimental and comparison groups include an equal number of boys and girls. They begin by dividing the population of all science students into two subgroups based on gender. (See Figure 4.3). They then randomly select 15 boys to be in the laser disk group and 15 boys to be in the non-laser disk group. They do the same for girls. They now have two groups of 30 students, each matched on gender.

Figure 4.3   Stratified Random Sampling

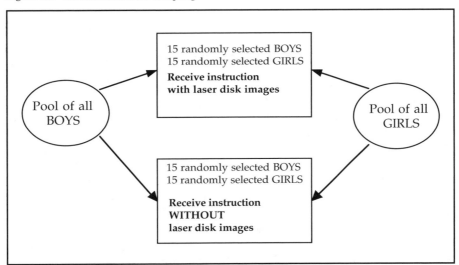

Another form of random selection is *random cluster sampling*. In this type of selection you randomly select whole clusters or groups from a population. For example, an evaluator may randomly select a whole neighborhood from a city and survey all the people living there. In schools, evaluators often randomly select intact classrooms and survey all the students in those classrooms. However, you need to keep in mind that you should use random cluster sampling only when all the classes in a group are essentially the same. You should not use random cluster sampling if classes differ substantially on relevant variables. For example, if you want to select a representative sample of language arts students and all your language arts classes are tracked by ability, then you should not use random cluster selection. However, if classes were created by randomly assigning students to classes, regardless of ability, then random cluster sampling would be appropriate. [Computer scheduling programs often randomly assign students to classes, thus creating classes that are essentially equivalent.]

Let's share an example of how one middle school used random cluster sampling to select a sample of parents to complete a survey about the school's climate. Knowing that if they sent out surveys to *all* parents only a certain type of parent would respond, the teachers in this school randomly selected seven teacher advisories and worked to get 100% of these students' parents to respond. Since the computer scheduling program randomly assigned students to teacher advisories, the teachers reasoned that this sample of seven classes would constitute a representative group of the school's parents. Using various incentives for students, teachers, and parents, the teachers did achieve a 98% response rate — much higher and more representative than they would have gotten if they had sent out surveys to all parents.

A fourth method of randomly selecting a sample involves using a procedure known as *systematic random sampling*. In this process, you take a list of names arranged alphabetically and select every nth name. For example, you might select every 10th name from a school roster and these students would participate in your study. CAUTION: This method may actually result in a *biased* sample. For example, taking every 10th name from an alphabetic list of students may result in certain ethnic groups being over, or under, represented since surnames often reflect ethnicity.

4.9—Avoid a Sample of Convenience

Thus far we've shared four sampling methods, all designed to select a representative sample from a population. Now we come to a method we strongly suggest you avoid—*convenience sampling*. The "person-on-the-street" interview survey is a perfect example of a convenience sample. You've seen folks conducting this type of sampling. They stand on the side walk and stop everyone who enters a store or building and ask some quick questions. Their data come from whomever happens to walk up and gives opinions. This type of sampling almost always results in biased data. For example, if an evaluator stands in front of Wal-Mart on a Saturday morning asking patrons their opinions about GettingBetter Middle School, she will get the viewpoint of only a certain segment of the community. Whereas, another evaluator who collects opinions from those who walk into the Neiman-Marcus store will most likely get a very different perspective. They both will get biased data simply because of who tends to patronize these two types of stores.

4.10—Some Final Pieces of Advice

Unfortunately, Murphy's Law ("If it can go wrong, it will.") often comes into play during the data collection stage. Despite your best laid plans generated during Step 3, things can go wrong or take an unexpected twist. We offer three suggestions to combat Murphy's Law:

1. Do a trial run of your data collection procedures so that you can iron out the kinks before you jump into the real thing. Also, this trial run can help you gauge just how long various tasks will take to complete.

2. Build into your timeline some mid-course checks on the progress of your data collection. If you encounter difficulties, you can make corrections and not lose time and data.

3. Strike a balance between collecting too much data and too little data. As you collect data, you may be tempted out of curiosity to collect more than you need. But your time and energy are precious. Use them wisely. Following a well thought out and parsimonious Evaluation Planning Matrix will help you avoid collecting extraneous data. However, you should also realize that collecting too little data is more of a problem than collecting too much data. Often, the opportunity for collecting usable data passes quickly and you simply cannot go back in time to get the information. Using the Evaluation Planning Matrix (Figure 3.1), along with the Cross-Walk of Qualita-

tive Data Collection Methods (Figure 3.5), will ensure that you collect just enough data for you to evaluate your program.

4. Finally, in chapter 3, we offered several pieces of advice on how to avoid bias during data collection. We won't repeat our suggestions here but encourage you to turn back to Section 3. 8 and review what we said. It would be a shame if you completed Steps 1, 2, and 3 with flying colors only to see your evaluation torpedoed by bias when you actually start collecting your data.

4.11—Chapter Highlights

Major Concepts

☞ Making a plan and following that plan will keep you focused and efficient.

☞ Bias can arise from faulty procedures, from the instruments you use to collect data, and from the method you use to select groups or samples.

☞ Evaluators use the following methods to randomly select a sample from the entire population:
  • Simple random sampling
  • Stratified random sampling
  • Cluster sampling
  • Systematic sampling

Advice

√ Rely on existing data when you can and collect new data only when you need to do so.

√ Keep several things in mind as you try to gain access to information:
  • Be very clear about what information you need.
  • Be prepared for the possibility that existing data will not come in the exact format that you need.
  • Seek permission before you can gain access.

√ Keep data collection activities easy for both those who provide the data and those who collect the data.

√ Make your data collection easy for those who actually collect the data.
  • Spread the burden of data collection among several people if possible.
  • Devise clear, efficient procedures and forms that people can easily use to collect data.

√ Use systematic and impartial methods to gather data.

√ Avoid a sample of convenience.

√ Do a trial run of your data collection procedures so that you can iron out the kinks before you jump into the real thing.

√ Build some mid-course checks on the progress of your data collection into your timeline.

√ Strike a balance between collecting too much data and too little data.

4.12—The Road Ahead

In this chapter we gave only a brief overview of Step 4: Gather Data. Later, in chapters 8, 9, and 10, we will provide more detailed examples of ways to efficiently and reliably collect data. In the next chapter, we tackle the task of analyzing data.

4.13—Murray Does Step 4

Figure 4.4   Evaluation Process Step 4

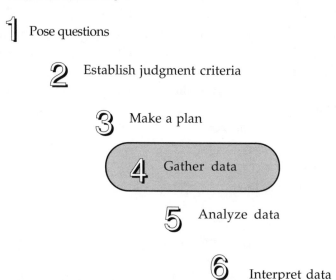

1 Pose questions

2 Establish judgment criteria

3 Make a plan

4 Gather data

5 Analyze data

6 Interpret data

All the powers-that-be have approved the plan Murray and his colleagues devised to evaluate the effectiveness of the school's block scheduling. At a recent meeting Yolanda and Stan passed out a GANNT Chart. (See Figure 4.5.)

"Hey, this is a great chart!" Murray commented. "You can really see what we have in front of us." Everyone seconded his opinion and also quickly agreed that Yolanda and Stan would take the lead in coordinating the data collection.

"We can collect some of the data," principal said. "But I see that our main job as a committee is to monitor the overall evaluation."

Over the next months, Yolanda and Stan met each month with the committee and gave them updates on how the data collection was going. Surprisingly, from September to February everything progressed like clock work. Yolanda convinced the middle school across town that uses a traditional schedule to act as a comparison group for the evalua-

Figure 4.5   Gantt Time Line for Block Scheduling Evaluation

TASK	Sept	Oct	Nov	Dec	Jan	Feb	March	April	May	June	July
Review state assessment scores			█								
Analyze state assessment scores									█	█	
Collect attendance data					█						
Analyze attendance data									█		
Conduct classroom observations		█						█			
Analyze classroom observation data		█							█		
Conduct middle school student survey (sample)									█		
Analyze middle school student survey data (sample)			█								
Conduct formative student survey											
Analyze formative student survey data					█						
Conduct middle school teacher survey		█									
Analyze middle school teacher survey data						█					
Administer Self-Efficacy Scale											
Analyze Self-Efficacy Scale data											
Conduct 9th and 10th grade student survey							█				
Analyze 9th and 10th grade student survey data							█				
Conduct high school teacher survey							█				
Analyze high school teacher survey data								█			
Conduct parent telephone interviews (sample)			█								
Analyze parent telephone interview data (sample)					█						
Conduct cost benefit analysis											
Write draft report										█	
Finalize report										█	
Prepare and present oral report to Board									█		
Prepare and present oral report to middle school faculty											
Prepare and present oral report to high school faculty											█

tion. Murray and the other two teachers on the School Improvement Committee enlisted the help of their students in designing a written survey to collect opinions from staff and students about what's working smoothly and not so smoothly with the block schedule. These students also crafted *and* conducted a telephone interview to solicit the opinions of parents.

Starting February 1, however, Murphy's Law starting kicking in. First, a computer glitch made it impossible to get attendance data for February 1, 1999. The clerk in the attendance office opted to use the data for February 15, 1999 instead.

Next, the teachers at the comparison school across town started balking about completing the post measurement surveys. They said it was a waste of time since they would get no benefit from participating. Stan finally convinced them that the pre-post information from their students' surveys would help them in their planning for the next school year.

By June 1, Yolanda and Stan were up to their eyeballs in data. They had reams of papers and stacks of computer disks loaded with Excel™ files. Luckily they had been able to stay up with the data entry. Plus, the students in Murray's classes had been really helpful in organizing some of the data.

Now, everyone was ready to make sense out of the data.

4.14—Resources

Print Resources

★ These references have been recommended in earlier chapters. The number of ★'s indicates the number of previous recommendations.

Harp, B. (1996). *The handbook of literacy assessment and evaluation.* Norwood, MA: Christopher-Gordon Publishers.

Can serve as a one-stop source of tools to gauge the literacy of students whether you're conducting a formative or summative program evaluation. Reviews 45 of the most popular literacy assessments in use today. Covers both teacher-made and commercially prepared tools for assessing student literacy.

Henderson, Marlene E., Morris, L. L.& Fitz-Gibbon, C. T. (1978). *How to measure attitudes.* Thousand Oaks, CA: Sage Publications.

Despite the 1978 copyright date, this book gives very practical advice that still stands today. Provides school-based examples on measuring attitudes by using word-of-mouth response (polls, interviews), written responses (questionnaires and attitude rating scales, logs, journals, diaries, and reports), and observation. Even covers sociometric procedures (measuring the type and depth of relationships among people in a group or class) and how to glean information by plowing through school records. Gives sound advice on selecting a measurement tool from existing tools, as well as step-by-step advice on developing your own questionnaires, attitude rating scales, interviews, written reports, observations, and sociometric instruments. Also includes a very readable chapter on validity and reliability of attitude instruments. Written for the intelligent, practitioner in a collegial tone. Gives what you need and no more, but does provide a list of references at the end of each chapter should you want to go more in-depth.

**Herman, J. L. & Winters, L. (1992). *Tracking your school's success: A guide to sensible evaluation.* Newbury Park, CA: Corwin Press.

HIGHLY RECOMMENDED. Well-written guide for educators interested in whole school improvement. Includes an excellent matrix showing the advantages and limitations of the common data collection methods: questionnaires, interviews, observations, performance tests, portfolios, archival information, and published achievement and attitude measures.

Hill, B. C. & Ruptic, C. A. (1994). *Practical aspects of authentic assessment: Putting the pieces together.* Norwood, MA: Christopher-Gordon Publishers.

Designed for elementary practitioners but middle school educators could easily adapt the over 140 assessment tools to their students. Very clear, understandable discussion of using a variety of methods for assessing the learning of students. Includes many forms for data collection. Excellent suggestions on observing students (growth in reading and writing). A How-to book on authentic assessment using student portfolio and teacher observations. Includes a list of annotated references for "Getting Comfortable" and "Fine-tuning" your knowledge base. Illustrates ways to collect data that go beyond the usual (but often inadequate) standardized criterion-referenced and norm-referenced tests that we so readily employ when we're trying to determine whether or not something worked.

*Hubbard, R. S. & Power, B. M. (1993). *Art of classroom inquiry.* Portsmouth, NH: Heinemann.

Targets practicing teachers (Pre K–12) who wish to conduct research that will inform their work with children. Written in collegial tone with many detailed samples of data collection and data analysis techniques. Examples come from the work of practicing teacher-researchers (listed in the appendices of the book). Focuses primarily on using qualitative research methods. Chapter 2 covers note taking while "kid watching," surveys, student work and classroom artifacts, sociograms (one of the best explanations and examples of how to do this and what it tells you as a teacher), and the use of audio and video tape transcriptions. Chapter 3 includes a good discussion of how to find and refine a research question.

Impara, J. C. & Plake, B. S. (Eds.) (1998). *The thirteenth mental measurements yearbook.* Lincoln, NE: Buros Institute of Mental Measurements.

Latest in the series of yearbooks on commercially available testing instruments. Don't buy this. Instead go to your local college or university library. It'll be in the reference section in book form or on a CD-ROM. Provides a description and critique of most commercially available tests. You can get much of the same information by visiting the Websites recommended in the Internet Resources section of this chapter.

Rea, L. M. & Parker, R. A. (1997). *Designing and conducting survey research: A comprehensive guide.* San Francisco: Jossey-Bass Inc., Publishers.

Provides solid advice on selecting a sample for survey research. Begins chapter 6 with a very understandable, coherent explanation of sampling theory designed for the research novice. Then moves on to describing a step-by-step procedure for determining the appropriate sample size. Rounds out with an explanation of all the acceptable methods for selecting a representative sample. Written for the research novice.

*Wiggins, Grant. (1998). *Educative assessment: designing assessments to inform and improve student performance.* San Francisco: Jossey-Bass Inc., Publishers.

Chapter 6 in this book provides a very clear discussion of performance testing, while chapter 7 focuses on constructing and using rubrics to judge the quality of a student's performance. Chapter 8, entitled Portfolio as Evidence, gives practical advice for creating, maintaining, and judging student portfolios.

Internet Resources

NOTE: You can easily access the Websites we recommend below by simply going to our Web page located at

http://www.pittstate.edu/edsc/ssls/letendre.html

From our Web page, a simple click of your mouse will take you straight to the selected Web site. We regularly verify these sites and add others that we find worthy of our recommendation.

Buros Institute of Mental Measurement
http://www.unl.edu/buros/
Takes you to the Buros Institute of Mental Measurement, the people who publish reviews of tests. Here you can search the database of test reviews and critiques to find information on a specific commercially available test or to learn about available instruments you can use to measure achievement, attitudes, skills, beliefs, and aptitudes.

Center for Equity and Excellence in Education (CEEE)
http://ericae.net/eac/
Using ERIC's Clearinghouse on Assessment and Evaluation Website as a gateway, connects to the Center for Equity and Excellence in Education (CEEE) located at George Washington University. Includes abstracts and descriptions of almost 200 tests commonly used with Limited English Proficient students.

Clearinghouse on Assessment and Evaluation
http://ericae.net/intass.htm
Connects to the home page of the Clearinghouse on Assessment and Evaluation sponsored by the Educational Resources Information Center (ERIC) funded by the U. S. Department of Education. A great jumping off site on a myriad of topics all related to assessment and program evaluation. Simply click on the category of your choice and immediately you see links to quality Internet resources on the topic. A sampling of categories includes action research, alternative assessment, fairness in testing, goals and standards, and program evaluation. Also includes links to various Listserves (discussion groups) all dealing with various aspects of assessment and program evaluation.

National Association of Test Directors
http://www.natd.org/
Connects to the Website sponsored by the National Association of Test Directors. Includes a copy of the Code of Fair Testing Practices in Education. Also provides excellent links to Websites all related to testing.

National Center for Research on Evaluation, Standards, and Student Testing (CRESST)
http://cresst96.cse.ucla.edu/index.htm
Takes you to the National Center for Research on Evaluation, Standards, and Student Testing (CRESST) which conducts research on important topics related to K-12 educational testing. Funded by the U. S. Department of Education. Allows you to search on keywords within the site's database which includes reports and newsletters on evaluation, standards, and student testing. You can even download sample performance assessments in social studies, mathematics, and science. Also contains an alternative assessments database which lists over 300 developers of new assessments, along with detailed information about the purpose, scoring, availability, and skills measured by each of the assessments. Would be of great interest to educators seeking ways other than standardized achievement tests to measure student learning.

Test Review Locator
http://ericae.net/testcol.htm
Connects to the Test Review Locator, a searchable database giving descriptions and reviews for various testing instruments. Sponsored by the federal government's Educational Resources Information Center (ERIC). Also allows you to search the 10,000 tests included in the Educational Testing Service (ETS) Test Collection. The Test Collection encompasses virtually all fields within education and the social sciences. Also includes a helpful document giving tips on selecting tests appropriate to your purpose.

CHAPTER 5

Doing Evaluations

Step 5—Analyze the Data

5.1—Introduction

At the end of Step 4 in the evaluation process, you'll have in hand a pile of data. In fact, you might have so much paper, that you may need a couple of file drawers to store it. Some of your data will probably be in the form of numbers, such as student scores on a reading test, the number of hours students volunteered at the local homeless shelter, or the number of graduate hours teachers have taken in the last year. Other data may consist of words, such as student opinions about the school's learning climate, teacher comments about the use of math journals, or parent reactions to the use of student portfolios to report their children's academic progress.

At this point you need to make sense of all this data. First, you need to organize all the data in some meaningful way. Next, you need to summarize and describe the data and, finally, in some instances, you need to perform statistical analyses to draw inferences from your data.

In this chapter, we tackle all three of these tasks:

- Organizing your data
- Summarizing and describing your data
- Analyzing your data

5.2—Organizing Your Data

Let's begin by looking at ways you can organize your quantitative data. Often the best way to organize such data is to put all your information in some sort of frequency table. Let's look at how one team of middle school teachers organized their number data into a frequency table.

The Zoo Team teachers at Standingtall Middle School want to spend this school year building a strong sense of self-efficacy* among their sixth graders. At the beginning of the school year, they ask their students and a comparable group

---

* Rather than believing that things simply happen by chance, people with a high sense of *self-efficacy* believe that through their own efforts or skills they can make a difference in their lives.

in another team within the school to complete the LeTendre/Lipka Efficacy Scale*, a 20 item test that measures a person's sense of efficacy and yields a score that ranges from 0 (very low sense of self-efficacy) to 20 (very high sense of self-efficacy). They want to examine these scores to see where their students now stand in terms of self-efficacy *before* implementing any of their special strategies.

The teachers begin by creating a frequency table of their students' scores to get some overall sense of the current level of their students' sense of self-efficacy. [They will eventually do the same for the comparison group, but right now they want to concentrate on their own students. They will use the pre-test information to help plan self-efficacy activities for the year.]

Task 1

They entered all 160 of their students' scores into a computer spreadsheet.[1] Figure 5.1 shows a page of this spreadsheet. At this point the teachers don't worry about the order of the scores. They simply make sure that the student identification numbers and the efficacy scores match.

Figure 5.1   Computer Spreadsheet

Column A Student ID#	Column B Sept. Score
0032	15
0453	10
0245	06

Task 2

They then sorted the data in Column B in descending order. You can consult the manual for the spreadsheet software you are using to find out how to do this. The purpose for sorting the data is to help tabulate how many students obtained each possible score.

Task 3

Using the listing generated in Task 2, the teachers then created a frequency table in another spreadsheet file. Figure 5.2 shows this frequency table with column B completed.

Task 4

At this point, the teachers inserted the needed formulas to calculate Columns C, D, and E.[2] Figure 5.3 shows the completed frequency table.

---

*Please note that no such test called the LeTendre/Lipka Efficacy Test exists. We have fabricated it only to illustrate the concepts of data analysis.

Figure 5.2   Frequency Table of September Self-Efficacy Scores

Column A	Column B	Column C	Column D	Column E
Possible Scores	Frequency (number of students who obtained this score)	Percentage of students who obtained this score	Cumulative Frequency	Cumulative Percentage
0	3			
1	5			
2	8			
3	0			
4	11			
5	15			
6	23			
7	1			
8	8			
9	3			
10	31			
11	15			
12	16			
13	0			
14	0			
15	3			
16	6			
17	9			
18	1			
19	2			
20	0			

Figure 5.3   Completed Frequency Table of September Self-Efficacy Scores

Column A	Column B	Column C	Column D	Column E
Possible Scores	Frequency (number of students who obtained this score)	Percentage of students who obtained this score	Cumulative Frequency	Cumulative Percentage
0	3	1.88%	3	1.88%
1	5	3.12%	8	5.00%
2	8	5.00%	16	10.00%
3	0	0.00%	16	10.00%
4	11	6.88%	27	16.88%
5	15	9.38%	42	26.25%
6	23	14.37%	65	40.62%
7	1	0.62%	66	41.25%
8	8	5.00%	74	46.25%
9	3	1.88%	77	48.12%
10	31	19.38%	18	67.50%
11	15	9.38%	123	76.88%
12	16	10.00%	139	86.87%
13	0	0.00%	139	86.87%
14	0	0.00%	139	86.87%
15	3	1.88%	142	88.75%
16	6	3.75%	148	92.50%
17	9	5.62%	157	98.12%
18	1	0.62%	158	98.75%
19	2	1.25%	160	100.00%
20	0	0.00%	160	100.00%

Now that the Zoo Team teachers have this frequency table showing their students' September self-efficacy scores, what can they do with it? What does it tell them? First, they can create a visual picture showing the distribution of their students' scores. Below is a bar graph showing the data from Columns A and B of the frequency table (Figure 5.4). Chapter 7—Sharing the Answers to Your Questions—will demonstrate more fully the value of graphs and tables to quickly summarize and communicate your data.

Figure 5.4   Bar Graph Showing Frequency Data on Self-Efficacy Scores

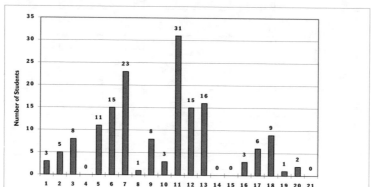

Using Column E of their frequency table in Figure 5.5, the Zoo Team teachers can also readily figure the percentile ranks of various students on the test of self-efficacy. Essentially, a percentile rank tells you what percentage of students scored at or below any particular score. Standardized achievement test scores often get reported as percentiles. "Danielle scored at the 95th percentile on the reading comprehension subtest." This means that she scored equal to, or better than, 95% of the students who took the test.

Looking at Column E in Figure 5.5, we can readily tell that a student who scored 5 (a low level of self-efficacy) scored equal to or higher than 26% of the students on the Zoo Team, while a student who scored 17 (a high level of self-efficacy) scored equal to or higher than 98% of the students. Overall, the table tells the Zoo Team teachers that over 67% of their students scored at or below 10, a score that represents only a moderate level of self-efficacy. The teachers vow to raise their students' sense of self-efficacy. The frequency table gives them some idea of just how far they need to go to attain their goal.

5.3—Tabulating Data By Hand

In our illustration thus far, the Zoo Team teachers used a computer spreadsheet to tabulate and create a frequency table. They could, of course, have done all this by hand. Below are three quick methods you can use to tally data by hand to fill Column B of your frequency table.

The Picket Fence Method

You're probably already familiar with this tally method. You simply draw lines with a slash each time you get to 5.

Doing Evaluations: Step 5—Analyze the Data 91

Figure 5.5 Illustrations of Percentile Ranks Using September Self-Efficacy Scores

Column A	Column B	Column C	Column D	Column E
Possible Scores	Frequency (number of students who obtained this score)	Percentage of students who obtained this score	Cumulative Frequency	Cumulative Percentage
0	3	1.88%	3	1.88%
1	5	3.12%	8	5.00%
2	8	5.00%	16	10.00%
3	0	0.00%	16	10.00%
4	11	6.88%	27	16.88%
5	**15**	**9.38%**	**42**	**26.25%**
6	23	14.37%	65	40.62%
7	1	0.62%	66	41.25%
8	8	5.00%	74	46.25%
9	3	1.88%	77	48.12%
10	**31**	**19.38%**	**18**	**67.50%**
11	15	9.38%	123	76.88%
12	16	10.00%	139	86.87%
13	0	0.00%	139	86.87%
14	0	0.00%	139	86.87%
15	3	1.88%	142	88.75%
16	6	3.75%	148	92.50%
17	**9**	**5.62%**	**157**	**98.12%**
18	1	0.62%	158	98.75%
19	2	1.25%	160	100.00%
20	0	0.00%	160	100.00%

Tukey's Box Method

John Tukey, who came up with many methods to graphically display data, invented a unique way to tally data by hand.

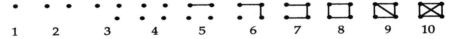

Stem and Leaf Plot

Tukey also invented another ingenuous method to tally data and then immediately turn your tallies into a graph. This method, however, only works with data where most scores have at least two digits.

Let's illustrate with a sample of 10 student scores.

60   62   53   59   66   41   43   48   101   64

You begin by first determining the "stem" for your group of scores. Generally, the "stem" includes all the numbers except the ones place. In this example, the "stems" would include:

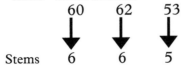

Now make a list of all possible "stems" in the group.

4
5
6
7
8
9
10

Notice that we included the full range of "stems" even though we have no numbers starting with 7, 8, and 9 in our sample.

Using graph paper, list your "stems" vertically in ascending order starting with the smallest number. The remaining digit (in the ones place) is the "leaf" for each number.

Thus, for the number 43,

4 is the "stem" and
3 is the "leaf."

You now put each "leaf" with its "stem," making sure that you keep everything in neat columns. This is where the graph paper comes in handy. In this example, you put one "leaf" in each graph box. Notice that for the number 60,

6 is the "stem" and
0 is the "leaf."

Below is the stem and leaf plot for our sample of 10 scores.

Figure 5.6   Stem and Leaf Plot

0				
1				
2				
3				
4	1	8	3	
5	3	9		
6	0	2	6	4
7				
8				
9				
10	1			

Now, this is where the ingenious part happens. If you simply rotate this plot 90° to the left, you have a graph showing the frequency distribution of the data.

Figure 5.7   Stem and Leaf Plot Transformed into a Graph

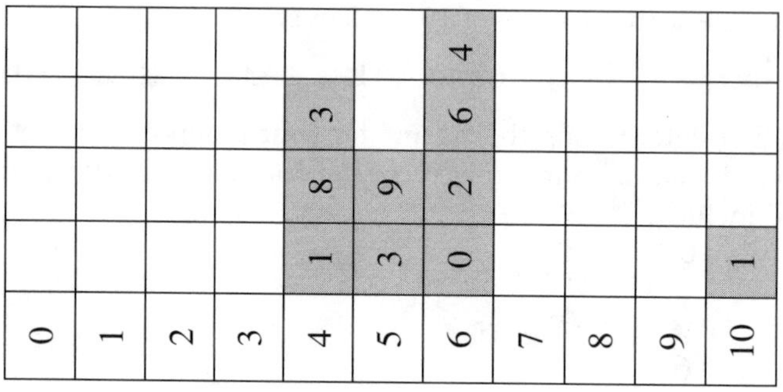

5.4—Organizing Word Data

We can also create frequency tables for word data. In Column A, rather than listing possible scores, you simply list the categories of possible responses. To illustrate how this is done, let's return to our Zoo Team teachers and their quest to build their students' sense of self-efficacy. At the beginning of the school year, the Zoo Team teachers not only gave all their students the LeTendre/Lipka Efficacy Test, they also asked them to complete a short questionnaire. One of the questions on the survey was:

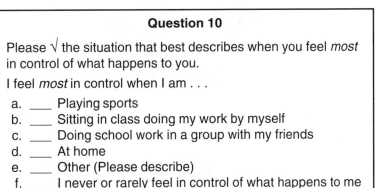

Question 10

Please √ the situation that best describes when you feel *most* in control of what happens to you.

I feel *most* in control when I am . . .

a. ___ Playing sports
b. ___ Sitting in class doing my work by myself
c. ___ Doing school work in a group with my friends
d. ___ At home
e. ___ Other (Please describe)
f. ___ I never or rarely feel in control of what happens to me

The Zoo Team teachers easily tallied the students' responses to each of the choices, a through f. They put this information in the usual frequency table format, but using Columns A, B, and C only. With discrete categories like we have in the above Question 10, cumulative frequencies and cumulative percentages aren't helpful. Unlike number/quantitative data, the Zoo Team teachers cannot talk about the percentile rank of student responses on Question 10. Percentile ranks simply don't make sense with data that come in categories.

Figure 5.8   Frequency Table for Student Answers to Question 10 on the Self-Efficacy Questionnaire Given in September

Column A	Column B	Column C
Possible Choices	Frequency (number of students who selected this choice)	Percentage of students who selected this choice
a. Sports	22	13.75%
b. Along in class	17	10.62%
c. With group in class	43	26.88%
d. At home	17	10.62%
e. Other	26	16.25%
f. No control	35	21.88%

As with number/quantitative data, the Zoo Team teachers can also create a visual picture showing the distribution of their students' responses. Figure 5.9

below shows a pie chart of the data from Columns A and B in the frequency table.

Figure 5.9   Pie Chart of Responses to Question 10 on Self-Efficacy Survey

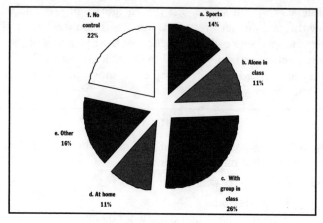

5.5—"Chunking" Word Data

In addition to creating the above frequency table showing the students' responses to Question 10 on the survey, the Zoo Team teachers took a closer look at the written responses given by the 26 students who marked "e. OTHER." Some students wrote simple phrases, while others wrote short paragraphs. The teachers first read through all 26 written responses noting emerging themes. From this first reading, they listed the following seven categories to use in sorting the responses:

- While playing music
- At church
- In my neighborhood
- At the mall
- While dancing
- With my friends
- At the "Y"

They then sorted through the open-ended responses and created the frequency table in Figure 5.10 summarizing how students who marked "e. OTHER" responded.

Figure 5.10 Frequency Table of Written Student Responses on Question 10 "e. OTHER"

Column A	Column B	Column C
Possible Categories	Frequency (number of students who responded this way)	Percentage of students who responded this way
Playing music	3	11.54%
At church	3	11.54%
In neighborhood	7	26.92%
At mall	4	15.38%
Dancing	1	3.85%
With my friends	7	26.92%
At the "Y"	1	3.85%

This "chunking" or clustering of open-ended responses into categories proves especially useful in summarizing any kind of word data, whether you gather the data through interviews or surveys. Indeed, "chunking" data is often the only way to make sense of qualitative/word data.

5.6—Summarizing Your Data

Thus far, we have shown you ways to organize your data, particularly by using computer spread sheets and frequency tables. In this section we will illustrate two major ways to summarize and describe your data by:

1. Reporting the "average" or central tendency of your data

2. Delineating the "spread" or variability (a.k.a. dispersion) of your data

5.7—Finding the Average

Often people want to describe data by calculating some sort of average or central tendency for their data. The family of "averages" includes three "siblings" and each has its unique advantages and disadvantages:

- The arithmetic mean

- The median

- The mode

5.8—The Arithmetic Mean

You already know about the *arithmetic mean* if you have ever calculated student grades by adding up a student's test scores and then dividing by the number of scores. Below (Figure 5.11) is a sample of 10 scores for a student with a possible 100 points on each test. The teacher wants to know the arithmetic mean (average) score for this group of test scores.

You can calculate an arithmetic mean on number data measured on a equal interval scale, such as a number line. However, it is not appropriate for word

Figure 5.11 Illustration of the Arithmetic Mean

	Test score	
Test #1	96	
Test #2	95	
Test #3	82	
Test #4	34	arithmetic mean = $\dfrac{\text{sum of all scores}}{\text{total number of scores}} = \dfrac{875}{10} = 87.5$
Test #5	94	
Test #6	97	
Test #7	91	
Test #8	89	
Test #9	99	
Test #10	98	
TOTAL	875	

data. It simply would make no sense to calculate the arithmetic mean to find the "average" response of students on Question 10 of the Zoo Team's questionnaire on self-efficacy where students indicated the situation when they feel most in control of what happens to them.

Besides the fact that calculating the arithmetic mean works only with number data, another major disadvantage exists when you use the arithmetic mean to describe the central tendency of a set of data that includes some scores very different from the majority. These so-called "outliers" can skew the arithmetic mean. Even just one extremely low score can pull down the arithmetic mean, giving you a somewhat distorted view of the data's central tendency or the "average" score. The same is true if one student scores much, much higher than the majority of scores. In this case, the one extremely high score can artificially shove the arithmetic mean upwards. Furthermore, the smaller the number of students in a group, the more impact outlying scores can have in distorting the "average" score.

Our scores for the 10 students in Figure 5.11 provide a perfect example of how just one outlier can skew the arithmetic mean. In our sample of 10 scores, all but one score fall in the 90's and 80's. Student #4's score of 34 is clearly an outlier. The arithmetic mean calculated with all 10 scores is 87.5, but if we don't include the "outlier" of 34, we get 93.44! As we can see, this one "outlier" pulled the overall arithmetic mean down by 5.95 points.

Despite its shortcomings regarding word data and outliers, the arithmetic mean enjoys wide popularity and acceptance. Indeed, when most people talk about the "average," they speak about the arithmetic mean. Furthermore, as you will see later in this chapter, the arithmetic mean is absolutely necessary in analyzing data using inferential statistics.

5.9—The Median

Another familiar type of "average" is the *median*, the midpoint that divides the distribution of scores in half, where 50% lie above the cutpoint and 50% below. Figuring the median for a set of data is quite easy. We'll demonstrate with our sample of 10 student scores. We begin by listing the 10 scores in ascending order. You then draw a line between the top 5 scores and the bottom 5 scores.

Figure 5.12 Illustration of Median with Even Number of Scores

Student A	34	
Student B	82	50% of the scores
Student C	89	
Student D	91	
Student E	94	
		94.5 the _median_ cut point
Student F	95	
Student G	96	
Student H	97	50% of the scores
Student I	98	
Student J	99	

But what happens if you have an odd number of scores? The procedure varies slightly. You still list the scores in ascending order. The median is the score in the middle, with an equal number of scores above and below. Figure 5.13 shows how this works with 9 scores.

Figure 5.13 Illustration of Median with Odd Number of Scores

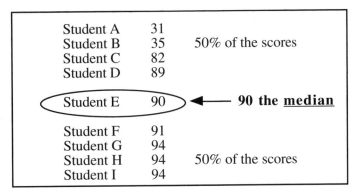

You can figure a median on many types of number data. However, like the arithmetic mean, the median is not appropriate for use with word data.

Despite this drawback, the advantages of using a median to describe the central tendency of a set of data are two-fold: First, the median is easy to figure.

Second, the median, unlike the arithmetic mean, is not overly sensitive to outliers. As we can see in Figure 5.12, Student #A's score of 34 did not artificially deflate our sense of what the average score was for this group of students. Thus, whenever you collect data where you have one or several outliers, you should consider reporting the median along with the arithmetic mean to describe the central tendency of your data.

5.10—The Mode

The final type of "average" is called the *mode* and is simply the number or category that has the greatest frequency in our frequency table. For example, 10 is the mode for the data shown in Figure 5.14. You should know, however, that a set of data may have NO mode or even have several. The set of data in Figure 5.12 on page 96 has no mode because no two students obtained the same score. But when we examine the data in Figure 5.15 we see that 7 students mentioned feeling most in control when they are in their neighborhoods and 7 others indicated that they felt most in control when they were with their friends. Thus, this set of data has two modes and we call this a bimodal distribution.

The mode as an "average" has two advantages: First, you can calculate a mode on both number and word data.

Second, you can easily and quickly figure the mode. Indeed, you simply have to "eyeball" your frequency table.

The major drawback of the mode is this: it is a rather crude measure of central tendency when you compare with its "siblings," the arithmetic mean and median. You simply can't go any further in calculations with the mode since no additional statistical techniques use the mode.

Figure 5.14 Illustration of Data Set with One Mode September Self-Efficacy Scores

Column A	Column B	Column C	Column D	Column E
Possible Scores	Frequency (number of students who obtained this score)	Percentage of students who obtained this score	Cumulative Frequency	Cumulative Percentage
0	3	1.88%	3	1.88%
1	5	3.12%	8	5.00%
2	8	5.00%	16	10.00%
3	0	0.00%	16	10.00%
4	11	6.88%	27	16.88%
5	15	9.38%	42	26.25%
6	23	14.37%	65	40.62%
7	1	0.62%	66	41.25%
8	8	5.00%	74	46.25%
9	3	1.88%	77	48.12%
MODE 10	31	19.38%	108	67.50%
11	15	9.38%	123	76.88%
12	16	10.00%	139	86.87%
13	0	0.00%	139	86.87%
14	0	0.00%	139	86.87%
15	3	1.88%	142	88.75%
16	6	3.75%	148	92.50%
17	9	5.62%	157	98.12%
18	1	0.62%	158	98.75%
19	2	1.25%	160	100.00%
20	0	0.00%	160	100.00%

Figure 5.15 Illustration of Data Set with 2 Modes (a.k.a. bimodal) Using Frequency Table of Written Student Response on "e. Other" of Question 10.

Column A	Column B	Column C
Possible Categories	Frequency (number of students who responded this way)	Percentage of students who responded this way
Playing music	3	11.54%
At church	3	11.54%
In neighborhood	**7 MODE**	**26.92%**
At mall	4	15.38%
Dancing	1	3.85%
With my friends	**7 MODE**	**26.92%**
At the "Y"	1	3.85%

5.11—Describing the "Spread" of Your Data

Describing only the central tendency (the "average") of your data gives a lop-sided picture. For a more complete description, you should also report how spread out the data are. Evaluators call this "spread" variability because it is a measure of the variation among the different pieces of data. Sometimes the "spread" provides a valuable perspective that you can't get from just looking at the average. For instance, in Figure 5.16 we show graphs illustrating the test results of two groups of students who recently took a science exam. Both groups have the same arithmetic mean (90), but clearly the spread or variability is very different between the two groups. In Group A, all the students cluster around the score of 90; in fact, all students made the same score of 90. This group shows no spread, no variability. In Group B, we have a very different picture, with the scores spread out across the whole spectrum with one student getting 0 items correct to 25 students obtaining the top score of 100. This group of student scores shows a great deal of variability.

Figure 5.16 Graphs Showing the Importance of Spread with Two Groups of Student Scores Having the Same Mean—90

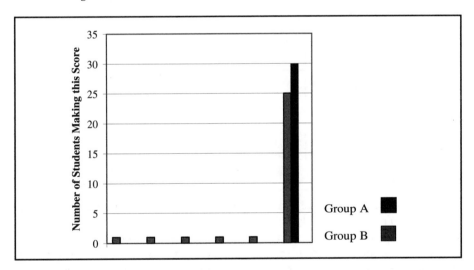

If you looked only at the measure of central tendency (the arithmetic mean) you might conclude that all the students in the two classes were indeed learning science materials equally well since, on the whole, each group scored well. But when you look at the spread, the variability within each group of scores, concerns immediately come to mind. By looking at Group A, you could conclude that these students are learning the science. Indeed, we believe that as teachers we should strive for the achievement "spread" in our classes to look more like this Group A, with everyone doing well.

As we examine the variability within the scores in Group B, major concerns about student learning arise. We must presume that some kids aren't getting it. Thus, we see that looking at both a data set's central tendency *and* spread gives us a truer picture of what's happening.

5.12—Reporting Spread: The Range

You can report the variability of a group of numbers in several ways. In this chapter we will focus on the three most frequently used measures of spread:

- The range
- The interquartile range
- The standard deviation

The *range* within a set of numbers is simply the distance between the highest score and the lowest score. Thus, in our sample of 10 student scores in Figure 5.17, the range is 65.

     99   minus   34   = 65 RANGE
    highest   lowest
     score   score

Figure 5.17 Illustration of Range

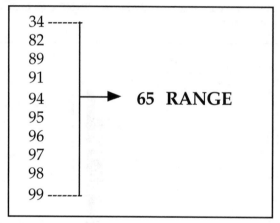

You can easily calculate a range for any data that come in the form of numbers. You can also legitimately report a range for word data if these data come in ordered categories such as "good, better, best" or "never, seldom, often." However, reporting the range for word data that comes in discrete categories such as "male/female" simply makes no sense. The same is true of data such as the student responses on Question 10 of the Self-Efficacy Survey shown in Figures 5.8 and 5.10. Really, the only way you can report the variability for such categorical data is simply to indicate the number of different categories that the data fall into.

5.13—Reporting Spread: The Interquartile Range

Another variety of range exists. You can report the interquartile range, which represents the spread of the middle 50% of the scores in a distribution. If you've chosen the median as your best measure of central tendency because of outliers in your distribution of scores, you should consider using the interquartile range as your measurement of spread. Both the median and the interquartile range are less sensitive to outliers. In fact, the interquartile range simply lops off the outliers at both ends.

Calculating the interquartile range is particularly easy, especially if you've constructed a frequency table that includes a cumulative percentage column like we have in Figure 5.18.

Before we can go further in our explanation of how to calculate the interquartile range, we need to introduce quartiles, the cutpoints that divide a distribution of scores in four equal parts, with 25% of the scores in each part. The cumulative percentage column in your frequency table can help you locate the cutpoints that divide each section.

For example, in Figure 5.18, the cutpoints between the 1st Quartile (the bottom 25%) and the 2nd Quartile is 1.5 (between 1 and 2), while the cutpoint between the 4th Quartile (the top 25%) and the 3rd Quartile is 3.5 (between 4 and 5). The interquartile range is 3.5 minus 1.5, or 2.

The interquartile range is simply the distance between these two cutpoints and represents the *middle* 50% of the scores. This way outliers don't have a distorting effect on the spread.

Figure 5.18 Illustration of Interquartile Range

Column A	Column B	Column C	Column D	Column E
Possible Scores	Frequency (number of students who obtained this scores)	Percentage of students who obtained this score	Cummulative Frequency	Cummulative Percentage
0	4	8.889%	4	8.89%
1	7	15.56%	11	24.44%
2	10	22.22%	21	46.67%
3	10	22.22%	31	68.89%
4	4	8.89%	35	77.78%
5	10	22.22%	45	100.00%

Interquartile Range = 2

5.14—Reporting the Spread: Standard Deviation

The range and interquartile range are a fairly crude measure of spread. A more precise measure of variability is the *standard deviation,* which tells you, on average, how far each of the scores deviates from the arithmetic mean of the data. The smaller the standard deviation, the less variability within a group of scores. Thus, a set of scores with a standard deviation of 7.09 would have more spread than a set of scores with a standard deviation of 2.02. As you will see later in this chapter, the standard deviation is absolutely crucial for doing various types of inferential statistics. Therefore, to answer some types of evaluation questions, you must calculate a standard deviation.

Any college statistics book (and we recommend some good ones in Section 5.28—Resources) can walk you through the calculations for standard deviation. But don't despair when you see the formulae for calculating the standard deviation. A computer spread sheet like Excel™ can easily do the calculations.

Getting Kids Involved!

When people in Charleston, Missouri, need data tabulated and analyzed, they turn to Christine Smith and her eighth grade students. Christine teaches mathematics at Charleston (MO) Middle School, a school of approximately 350 students located in rural southeastern Missouri. Over the years, her classes have tackled several real-world tasks involving mathematics. One of their specialties is tabulating, summarizing, and analyzing survey data. "People don't mind *giving* surveys," explained Christine, "they just don't want to do all the work that comes afterwards."

That's where Christine's students come in. For example, recently the school nurse contacted Christine and her students about a series of health services surveys she needed to send out to staff, parents, and students in the Charleston community as part of the school district's accreditation process. She explained that she would collect the data, but she needed help in tabulating, organizing, and analyzing all the data. Christine's students jumped at the task. Once they got the completed surveys, the students counted the responses to all the questions and constructed tables, complete with percentages, summarizing the data. From these tables, they then created circle graphs, visually depicting how people responded to each question. The nurse included all the students' work in the final report she submitted to the Missouri State Department of Elementary and Secondary Education.

5.15—Analyzing Your Data

Thus far, we have focused on organizing, summarizing, and describing data using descriptive statistics. Now we turn to analyzing data. In this stage, we can answer such questions as:

1. How confident can we be that our data from a small subgroup (a sample) actually represent the whole group (a population)?
2. Is there a significant difference between Group A, which got the special instruction, and Group B, which got only the usual instruction?
3. Does a relationship or correlation exist within the data?

To answer these questions, we turn to inferential statistics. This branch of statistics gets its name from the fact that we use information from a small subgroup (a sample) to make inferences about the whole group (the population). Let's say, we randomly select 75 students from the student population at Bestever Middle School and ask these students to complete a survey concerning the school's learning climate. Based on the responses of these 75 students, we then use statistics to *infer*, with some degree of accuracy, what the whole student population of 650 would have said about the school's learning climate if they all had completed the survey.

We want to emphasize up front that for the most part we perform inferential statistical analyses on data that come in the form of numbers. We've already hinted that much of inferential statistics requires that you first calculate an arithmetic mean and a standard deviation for your data and you can only do that with data measured on an equal interval scale. However, you can use certain statistical techniques to analyze and draw inferences using word data. Later in this chapter we will illustrate how you can use inferential statistics to analyze data that come in the form of categories.

5.16—How Confident Can We Be?

Let's begin our tour of inferential statistics by looking at the question:

> How confident can we be that our data from a small subgroup (a sample) actually represent the whole group (a population)?

Rarely, do evaluators (or researchers for that matter) have the luxury of collecting data from *all* subjects in a population. Often times, evaluators select a sample from the population and, by looking at this sample, draw inferences to describe the whole population. (See Figure 5.19) Whenever we use only a sample to try to describe a population, we always have some degree of error involved. We cannot describe the mean of a population with a 100% accuracy unless we collect data from *all* subjects. By selecting only a subgroup or sample, we always run the risk that, by chance, we chose a sample that is not fully representative of the total population.

Figure 5.19 Inferential Statistics

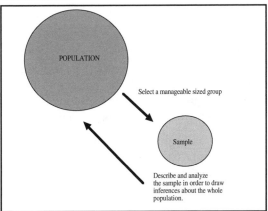

Perhaps an example will help illustrate the level of error that can occur when we try to describe a population by looking only at a sample. Let's say we want to gauge how the parents of the 650 students in our school feel about the learning climate of the school. About 35% of our students come from homes at or below the poverty level, 52% come from middle income homes, and the remaining 13% come from upper income families. During normal school hours, we conduct a telephone survey, going down an alphabetic list of students and calling every 10th parent. If no one answers, we go to the next name on the list. After contacting 65 parents, we organize and summarize our data. Unfortunately, we find that our sample includes 54 parents from upper income families. We suspect that more upper income parents are home during the day. Therefore our sample is skewed in favor of the upper income bracket. In this case, the data we collected might give us a very distorted view of what parents think about our school's learning climate since most opinions came from only one distinct group within the school community.

Using random sampling techniques, where every subject has an equal chance of being selected, can help to reduce the possibility of getting a skewed group like we did in the above example. But even with random sampling, there will always be some error, some loss of accuracy, as we try to describe a whole population by only looking at a sample.

5.17—Confidence Intervals

To compensate for sampling error, evaluators build a confidence interval around the sample's the arithmetic mean, saying that the true mean of the population falls, with some degree of accuracy somewhere within that interval. We see these confidence intervals whenever pollsters report the results of a national opinion poll. Figure 5.20 gives the results of a poll conducted in 1997 by Phi Delta Kappa asking a sample of 1,517 randomly selected U.S. parents of school-aged children their opinion about illegal drugs in schools. To generalize these results to the larger population of *all* parents of school-aged children in the United States, the researchers created a confidence interval of + or - 3 percentage points around each result. Thus, most likely the true percentage of parents *in the total population* who would answer "I prefer an educational approach" on the survey would fall somewhere between 49% and 55%.

Figure 5.20 1997 Phi Delta Kappa Poll Question on Drugs in Schools

---

Question: In your opinion, which is more effective for dealing with a drug problem in the public schools in your community—an educational approach, pointing out the consequences of drug use, or severe penalties for those violating the school drug policy?

I prefer an educational approach	52%
I prefer severe penalties	42%
I don't know	6%

Margin of error = ±3% points

From the 29th Annual Phi Delta Kappa/Gallup Poll Of the Public's Attitudes Toward the Public Schools published in the September 1997 issue of the *Kappan Journal* by L. C. Rose, A. M. Gallup, and S. M. Elam.

By convention, evaluators, researchers and pollsters set their confidence intervals at a 95% chance of being right. Most evaluators are willing to live with a 5% chance of being wrong. Sometimes, when the stakes are very high, evaluators will bump their chance of being right up to 99%, but they can never get to a 100% accuracy as long as they deal only with data from a sample rather than the total population.

Calculating a confidence interval by hand involves finding the mean and standard deviation for your sample, using these to derive what's known as the standard error of the mean, then consulting some statistical tables for a multiplier. Again, a good statistics text will hand-hold you through the calculations and Excel™ can do it in a flash.

Below we show what the 90%, 95% and 99% confidence intervals look like for a population when the sample mean is 150, the standard deviation is 5, and the sample size is 100. Notice the "band" around the sample mean gets larger as you increase your level of confidence. Essentially, we can say that we are "99% sure" that the population mean will fall within + or - 1.29 of the sample mean, or between 148.71 and 151.29.

	Confidence "Band"
90% confidence level = + or - .82	149.18 to 150.82
95% confidence level = + or - . 98	149.02 to 150.98
99% confidence level = + or - 1.29	148.71 to 151.29

5.18—Is There a Significant Difference?

In addition to using inferential statistics to describe a population by only looking at a sample from that population, we can use inferential statistics to answer a second type of question:

Is there a *significant* difference between Group A which got the special instruction, and Group B which got only the usual instruction?

Let's begin by looking at what we mean by *significant* difference. In a nutshell, a *significant* difference happens when we find it highly unlikely that the differences between the arithmetic means of two groups occurred by chance. By convention, researchers and evaluators establish their acceptable level of chance BEFORE they do the analysis and they typically set the level at 95%. In other words, they would be 95% sure that the difference between the mean score for Group A and the mean score for Group B did *not* occur by chance. Rather, we can infer that something other than chance, like our new instructional strategy, caused the difference.

As always, we can never be 100% sure that the difference did not happen by chance. Since we are looking only at samples rather than whole populations, we always must contend with some degree of error, that is, some possibility that the difference happened by chance and not because of our new instructional strategy worked.

For data that come in the form of numbers, we use a statistical *test of significance* to ascertain if a significant difference between sample means exists. Some common tests of significance include:

- z-test
- t-test
- F-test

In chapter 6 when we discuss Step 6: Interpreting the Results we will explain more about how these tests of significance work.

For data that come in the form of words, the usual statistical tests of significance such as the z-test, t-test, and F-test are not appropriate. Instead, you can use the Chi-Square Test for Goodness of Fit with categorical data and the Mann-Whitney U Test works well in analyzing rank-ordered categories. In Section 5.23—Resources we list several very readable statistics texts that provide in-depth explanations and illustrate how to calculate these tests. The Gravette and Wallnau (1996) book has some particularly helpful decision maps that can walk you to the appropriate test of significance to use.

5.19—Finding Relationships: The Descriptive Side of Correlation

To answer our final question, "*Does a relationship or correlation exists within the data?*", we begin with our analytical "feet" in the descriptive statistics arena. We simply want to describe if a two factors *co-relate*. For example, do men prefer wearing digital watches, while women prefer ones with hands? In other words, is there a relationship between gender and watch preference?

Another way to look at relationships, particularly with number data, is to see how two variables relate to one another. Does one variable go up as the other variable goes down? (↑↓) For example, do reading scores go up, as student suspensions go down? or, do both variables move in the same direction, as one variable goes up so does the other one. (↑↑) For example, do math scores go up as the number of community service hours performed by students goes up?

When we're dealing with number data, we describe correlations along two dimensions: direction and magnitude. In a direct (also known as a positive) relationship, both variables move in the same direction—as one goes up, the other goes up *or* as one goes down, the other goes down. (See Graph A in Figure 5.21.) In an inverse (also known as a negative) relationship, the variables move in opposite directions—as one goes up, the other goes down. (See Graph B in Figure 5.22.)

The magnitude of a correlation calculated on number data ranges from 0 to 1. A correlation of 0 means there is *no* correlation. A correlation magnitude of 1 signifies a perfect correlation, where as one factor moves up x number of points the other variable also moves the same number of points. Below we show the range of magnitudes for a correlation along with the words we generally use to describe these magnitudes.

Figure 5.21 Scatterplots of Direct/Positive and Inverse/Negative Relationships

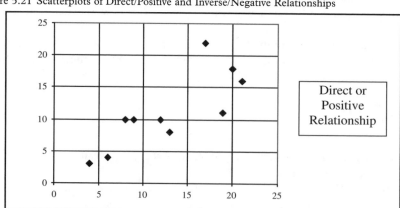

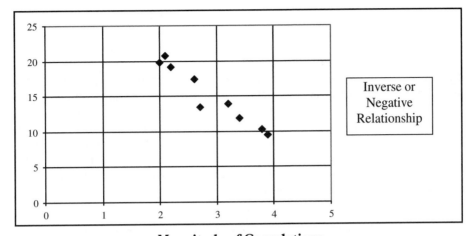

Magnitude of Correlations

0——.1——.2——.3——.4——.5——.6——.7——.8——.9——1
No   Weak   Moderate   Strong   Perfect

5.20—Determining if Correlations Exist

When it comes to number data, we have several options when we analyze data for relationships. First and foremost, we suggest that you create a scatterplot of your data. Figure 5.22 shows scatterplots for a number of relationships that vary both in direction and magnitude.

Figure 5.22 Scatterplots of Various Correlations

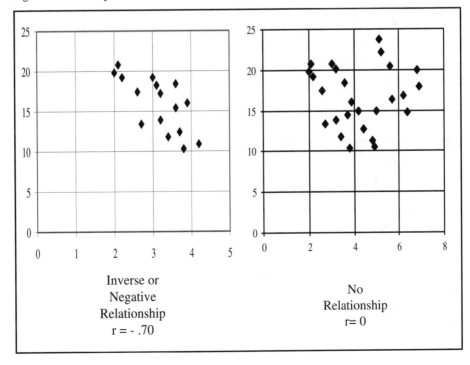

Figure 5.23 shows the scatter plot for data from a middle school that has been using a community service volunteer program for the past two years. The teachers at this school wanted to see if a relationship exists between the number of community service hours served by students and their scores in math achievement. In Figure 5.23, each ♦ represents the number of community service hours served by a student and the math achievement score for that same student.

As you can see, the scatterplot of the data for the 100 students slants upwards to the right indicating a direct/positive relationship and the ♦'s cluster fairly close around an imaginary line drawn through the scatterplot. Just from "eyeballing" the scatterplot, we can conclude that there exists a strong positive relationship between the number of community service hours served by students and their math achievement scores.

Figure 5.23 Scatterplot of Number of Community Service Hours Served by Students and Their Math Achievement Scores

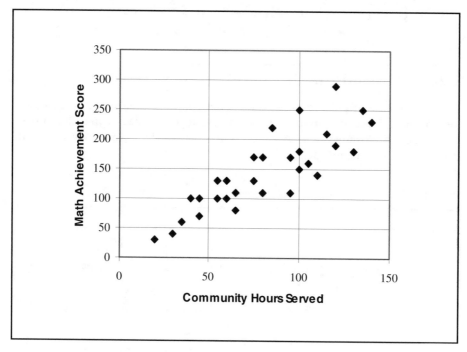

Although we can "eyeball" our data to get some sense of the direction and magnitude of a correlation, we can calculate more precisely the direction and magnitude of a correlation. The most popular procedure for doing this calculation involves computing what is known as the Pearson product-moment correlation coefficient, Pearson's r for short. Essentially, this procedure yields a number with a + or - sign, showing the direction of the correlation, and a number from 0 to 1, indicating the magnitude of the correlation. So, if the calculated Pearson's r for our data in Figure 5.23 yields the number **+ .8536,** we know that the correlation is "positive" in direction and "strong" in magnitude. Once again, a good college statistics text will help you do the hand calculation for Pearson's r and Excel™ can do it in nanoseconds.

Thus far, we've talked about finding correlations within number/quantitative data. What about word data? Can we determine if a relationship exists if our data come in words? The answer is yes. If you're dealing with categorical data, you can use the Chi-Square Test for Independence to determine if a relationship or correlation exists within the data. Later in chapter 6, Sections 6.8 and 6.10, we will give examples of how to use a Chi-Square Test for Independence. As always, any good statistics text will help you with the calculations.

5.21—Finding Relationships: The Inferential Side of Correlation

Thus far in our discussion of correlation, we have focused only on describing whether or not a relationship exists. However, if we want to answer the question:

> *Does the correlation we see in the sample represent a correlation that actually occurs in the population?*

we must turn to the inferential side of statistics. Essentially, we want to know the probability that the sample correlation reflects the population correlation.

We still calculate a correlation coefficient, but we go one step further and consult a set of probability tables (found in most statistics texts) to determine if our correlation is significant or not, answering the question *"What's the probability that this sample correlation reflects the reality of the population?"*. Again, a good college statistics book can step you through this procedure.

5.22—Correlation Does Not Mean Causation!

We want to alert you to a common misconception about correlations. Too often people erroneously believe that if two variables co-relate, one must *cause* the other. This is false! Just because you find a strong correlation between two factors, it does not mean one factor causes the other. It simply means that the two factors co-relate.

For example, if you created a scatterplot showing the relationship over a year's time between the amount of ice cream sold and the crime rate, you would find a strong positive correlation. Now, none of us would even entertain the notion that ice cream sales some how cause crime or vice versa. Something else is going on that's probably causing these two factors to co-relate. Most likely it has something to do with the weather. As the warm temperatures of spring and summer come, more people buy ice cream and more criminals are willing to brave the pleasant weather to ply their trade.

A strong correlation between two factors might get you to speculate that one factor does cause the other. But that's all you can do, just speculate. You'll have to conduct a carefully designed experiment to actually prove that one factor causes the other to go up or down.

5.23—Common Pitfalls in Data Analysis

Before we leave this chapter on data analysis, we want to alert you to three pitfalls that often trap people.

1. Too often people calculate and *report only one measure of central tendency*, thus giving a distorted view of the data. Such a practice is especially misleading when the data include outliers, scores that fall far below or above most of the other scores. We suggest that when you have number data, you get in the habit of calculating and reporting all three types of averages: the arithmetic mean, the median, and the mode. This way you present a well-rounded sense of central tendency.

2. Mark Twain once said, "There's lies, damned lies, and statistics." He must of have been talking about people who *simply state the average without indicating if that average is the arithmetic mean, the median, or the mode.* Indeed, the unscrupulous will select the "average" that best meets their need to persuade or simply to deceive others.

    For example, Anywhere Middle School just received its reading scores on the state assessment. The arithmetic mean for the 7th grade scores was 320, which placed the school just at the state average. However, the median test score was 240 and the mode was 230, well below the state average. A scan of the frequency table summarizing the individual scores revealed that 55 students got a perfect score on the test while 200 other students scored below the state average. These few "perfect score" outliers pulled up the school's mean. When it came time to publish the test results in the local newspaper, the school officials chose to report the "average" as 320, a score that raised no red flags with the public.

    However, when the district's Director of Special Programs submitted a grant proposal to get extra teachers to help with students at-risk for failure, she chose to report the school's reading average as 230, the mode. Again, we suggest that when you have number data, you report all three types of average along with some measure of variability/spread so that you convey a well-rounded view of your data.

3. Finally, beware of calculating arithmetic means or standard deviations on data that really are not measured on equal interval scales. Let's give an example of this pitfall. A parent questionnaire about family relationships asked the following question:

What is your current marital status?

1. Married
2. Engaged
3. Divorced
4. Widowed
5. Never married

The researchers entered the data into a computer spreadsheet putting in a "1" for married, "2" for engaged, and so forth. At the end, they added up all the numbers in the column and found that the arithmetic mean equaled 3.24. This simply does not make sense given the categories. Yes, they represented each category by a number in the spread sheet, but these numbers were simply codes, labels, and not real numbers. They could have easily entered "A" for married, "B" for engaged.

This seems awfully silly and you might never expect such foolishness to happen, but it does. Please don't let it happen to you. As you enter data into spread sheets for easy summarization, refrain from using numbers as labels. Use letters instead. This way you'll never be tempted to fall into this pit.

5.24—Issue Box

Likert Scales and Semantic Differentials

Although we just warned against treating word data as numbers that can be summed, subtracted, multiplied and divided, we want to call your attention to two accepted ways to turn word data into numbers. The first way is to use a Likert Scale (pronounced Lick´ert), a method invented by Renis Likert in 1932. Most likely you are probably very familiar with this scale. It consists of a series of forced choices with each response assigned a value. It is assumed that the distance between each choice is equal. Therefore, since this creates an equal interval scale, we can perform all the usual descriptive statistical analyses, including calculating an arithmetic mean and standard deviation.

Below is an example of a typical Likert Scale response to a question:

How often do you and your parents talk about your progress in school?

1. Never
2. Rarely
3. Sometimes
4. Most of the time
5. Always

When organizing this type of data, you simply key in the appropriate value (1, 2, 3, 4, 5) associated with the response and then find the arithmetic mean. If you obtained a mean of **2.3** for the responses to this question, you could conclude that most students speak with their parents about school work "rarely" to "sometimes."

A second accepted way of transforming word data into numbers is to use a semantic differential format for responses. A semantic differential consists of an equal interval scale with opposite words at each end. Each interval on the scale represents a number value with "1" (boring) being least favorable and "7" (exciting) being most favorable. Below is an example of a semantic differential response:

Circle the number that best reflects how you would rate the quality of instruction in your math class.

Boring — 1 — 2 — 3 — 4 — 5 — 6 — 7 —- exciting

As with the data from a Likert Scale, you simply key in the number value associated with the spot where the respondent marked the item and then find the arithmetic mean. If you obtained a mean of **6.56** for the responses to this question, you could conclude that most students find their math class tending towards "exciting."

5.25—Chapter Highlights

Major Concepts

☞ Analyzing your data involves three tasks:

- Organizing your data
- Summarizing and describing your data
- Analyzing your data

☞ "Chunking" data is often the only way to make sense of qualitative/word data.

☞ You can use the arithmetic mean, median and mode to describe the central tendency of a group of data.

☞ The most frequently used measures to report the variability or spread of a group of data include the range, the interquartile range, and the standard deviation.

☞ In analyzing data, you seek to answer questions such as these:

1.   How confident can we be that our data from a small subgroup (a sample) actually represent the whole group (a population)?

2.   Is there a significant difference between Group A, which got the special instruction, and Group B, which got only the usual instruction?

3.   Does a relationship or correlation exist within the data?

☞ A significant difference occurs when we find it highly unlikely that the differences between the arithmetic means of two groups happened by chance.

☞ Some common tests of significance for dealing with sample means include z-test, t-test, and F-test.

☞ Correlation has two faces: one side uses descriptive statistics to describe if a relationship exists within the data; the other side uses inferential statistics to determine the probability that the correlation we see in a sample actually reflects a correlation in the population.

☞ We describe correlations along two dimensions: direction and magnitude.

☞ Just because you find a strong correlation between two factors, it does not mean one factor causes the other. It simply means that the two factors co-relate.

☞ Two accepted ways to turn word data into numbers are the Likert Scale and semantic differential format.

Advice

√ Consider reporting the median if your data include outliers, scores far above or below the majority of scores.

√ Report both a measure of central tendency and a measure of spread to give people a more complete picture of your subject group.

√ Rather than reporting a single sample mean, build a confidence level around the sample mean to give people a sense of how likely it is that this number represents the population mean.

√ Don't assume that one factor causes the other if you find a strong correlation between the two factors.

√ Report all three types of averages: the arithmetic mean, the median, and the mode. This way you present a well-rounded sense of central tendency.

√ Specify exactly which type of average you're talking about. Use the terms mean, median, and mode rather than simply saying the average.

√ Beware of calculating arithmetic means or standard deviations on data that really are not measured on equal interval scales.

5.26—The Road Ahead

In this chapter we have focused on analyzing your data. Now, we move to Step 6: Interpreting the results of your analysis. Now the question becomes: What does it all mean?

5.27—Murray Does Step 5

Figure 5.24 Evaluation Process Step 5

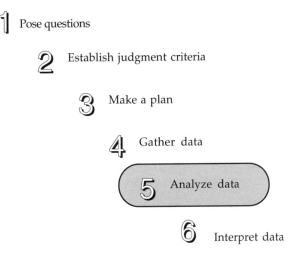

1 Pose questions

2 Establish judgment criteria

3 Make a plan

4 Gather data

5 Analyze data

6 Interpret data

Murray and his colleagues have worked hard. They have collected all the raw data. Furthermore, they are right on schedule. Now they need to organize all these data, put them into some understandable summary, and analyze them so they can move to Step 6, where they will interpret the data and finally answer the questions they posed in Step 1.

Over the past weeks, Murray's students have become graphing fools. They've learned a lot about making elegant graphs. They now know that the frequency *always* goes on the Y-axis. They plotted the data on attendance rates from both their school and the comparison school across town.

"I can't believe they get away with being absent so much," one student said in amazement as Murray's students examined the attendance data from the rival school across town.

They have also become very proficient at creating frequency tables and charts using Excel™. Back in December they examined the survey data collected from parents, teachers and students asking their opinions on how well the block schedule is working and how to improve it. They found that at first glance a lot of kids and adults were saying the same thing; they like it.

Finally, every student in Murray's team knows what it means to disaggregate data. "That's just a fancy term for pulling things apart," one student offered.

They created some very "neat looking" color charts showing how students in the various grade levels view the block schedule. They did the same thing when they compared the results on the surveys completed by the high school students and teachers.

While Murray's students have been busy organizing, describing, displaying, and analyzing the formative evaluation data, the doctoral students Yolanda and Stan have been working long hours analyzing all the achievement data, the pre-post survey data from students and teachers at Strivinghigher Middle School and the comparison school, and the classroom observation data.

Each day, Yolanda and Stan consult the GANTT chart they've created showing all the data analysis tasks they need to get done. So far things are going OK. Sometimes they feel overwhelmed, but Professor Everhelpful provided just the right amount of encouragement to get them going again.

Down in their office in the basement of the School of Education at the university, Yolanda and Stan have created a huge wall chart listing all the evaluation questions. (See Figure 5.25) As they complete each phase of the data analysis, they put a brief summary of the results by the appropriate evaluation questions. This way, when they move onto Step 6 to interpret their findings, they can use this chart to look for patterns.

Figure 5.25 A Portion of the Wall-Chart Showing Evaluation Results on Block Scheduling Conducted by Murray and his Colleagues

Evaluation Question	Judgment Criteria	Evidence Summaries	Conclusions	Judgment Criteria met?
1. Did students improve in reading comprehension?	1. Students on block schedule will master a higher percentage of items on state reading test.	• Line graph of scores since 3rd grade show rise starting in 7th grade. • t-test showed statistically significant difference between Strivinghigher students and comparison students.	1. Strivinghigher students outperformed comparison students in reading.	YES
2. Did students improve in math problem-solving?	2. Students on block schedule will master a higher percentage of items on state math problem-solving test.	• Line graph of scores since 3rd grade show rise starting in 7th grade. • t-test showed statistically significant difference between Strivinghigher students and comparison students.	2. Strivinghigher students outperformed comparison students in math problem-solving.	YES

5.28—Resources

Print Resources

★ These references have been recommended in earlier chapters. The number of ★'s indicates the number of previous recommendations.

Bernhardt, V. L. (1998). *Data analysis for comprehensive schoolwide improvement.* Larchmont NY: Eye on Education.

> HIGHLY RECOMMENDED. A dy-no-mite book!! Very practical. Written in easily understood language with a collegial tone. Thoroughly walks through how two schools (one elementary and one high school) used data to make decisions. Excellent illustrations. Gives suggestions on gathering, displaying, and analyzing data from the following dimensions: (a) demographics, (b) perceptions, (c) student learning, and (d) school processes. Illustrates 10 levels of analysis from "Snapshots of Measures" to "Interaction of all four measures, over time."

★★★Fink, A. & Kosecoff, J. (1978). *An evaluation primer.* Thousand Oaks, CA: Sage Publications.

> In 24 clearly-written pages, provides a conceptual understanding of both descriptive and inferential statistics. Does not focus on how to calculate various statistical tests, rather, helps the reader achieve a basic awareness of measures of central tendency and variability, correlation, regression, analysis of variance, analysis of co-variance, multivariate analysis of variance, and chi square.

Fink, A. and Kosecoff, J. (1998) *How to conduct surveys (2nd Ed.).* Thousand Oaks, CA: Sage Publications.

> Very user friendly and makes the assumption that the reader is an intelligent person who happens to be naive about conducting surveys. Covers the process from start to finish, from planning to designing to conducting to analyzing to presenting findings. Includes many real world examples. Gives

in chapter 6 an excellent overview of how to do various statistical analyses of survey data. Begins each chapter with a one-page overview. Can act as good reference on doing survey research and evaluation since you can easily turn to the section you want and get the information you need. For example, if you know how to plan, design, and conduct a survey but are fuzzy on how to analyze categorical data using inferential statistical procedures, you can turn to that section and readily get the guidance you need.

Fink, A. (1995). *How to analyze survey data.* Thousand Oaks, CA: Sage Publications.

Easy-to-use book with specific statistical tests compartmentalized so you can turn to the specific data analysis task you need. Ably covers summarizing data through graphing and descriptive statistics, examining the difference between two groups using the t-test and Sign test, and ascertaining relationships. Clearly illustrates the step-by-step calculation of the various statistical procedures, although some examples are very "mathy" with lots of symbols. Provides an excellent explanation of stanines.

Gravetter, F. J. & Wallnau, L. B. (1996). *Statistics for the behavioral sciences: A first course for students of psychology and education (4th ed.).* Minneapolis: West Publishing Company.

Everything you need to know about statistics and more. Excellent desk reference. Clear examples but sometimes goes too in-depth for the novice. Does give a step-by-step walk through of hand-calculating various descriptive and inferential procedures. Includes a *very useful* set of decision maps in Appendix A that can help you easily identify the appropriate statistical procedures you should use for a set of data.

Gronlund, N. E. (1981). *Measurement and evaluation for teaching (4th ed.).* New York: Macmillan.

Provides in Appendix A (pp. 537-554) one of the most readable treatments of basic statistics.

Holcomb, Z. C. (1997). *Fundamentals of descriptive statistics.* Los Angeles: Pyrczak Publishing.

Excellent discussion of the basics of using statistics to describe results. Assumes readers are intelligent but with no prior statistical training. Describes concepts in clear, non-mathematical terms, but also provides easily understandable step-by-step procedures for calculating measures of central tendency, measures of variability, standard scores, Pearson's r, and linear regression.

★★Hubbard, R. S. & Power, B. M. (1993). *Art of classroom inquiry.* Portsmouth, NH: Heinemann.

Targets practicing teachers (Pre K–12) who wish to conduct research that will inform their work with children. Written in collegial tone with many detailed samples of data collection and data analysis techniques. Chapter 4 ably illustrates how to take qualitative data gathered through observations and interviews and make sense of out of them. Provides exact examples of moving from raw field notes to "cooked" notes and, finally, to conclusions.

Jaeger, R. M. (1990). *Statistics: A spectator sport (2nd ed.)* Thousand Oaks, CA: Sage Publications.

One of the most readable of the many books on statistics that we've encountered. In the preface, the author states the following premise: "It is unnecessary to compute statistics in order to understand them," (p. ix) and proceeds to do just that in easy-to-understand language. Uses a conversational tone and explains the basics of both descriptive and inferential statistics. Augments every concept with real-world examples drawn from the field of education. After reading *Statistics: A Spectator Sport,* you'll come away with a clear understanding of when to use which statistical procedures and how to interpret them. You will, however, not learn how to *compute* statistics since this book contain *no* equations. But in this day of readily available computer software packages capable of easily performing statistical calculations, the absence of equations should not prove a hindrance.

Lindeman, R. H. & Merenda, P. F. (1979). *Educational measurement (2nd ed).* Dallas: Scott Foresman.

An oldie, but goodie. Despite the out-dated reliance on hand-held calculators, provides a cogent explanation of descriptive statistics (measures of central tendency and variability), correlation measures, and a *very* brief overview of inferential statistics. Also clearly describes the various measurement scales (nominal, ordinal, ratio, and interval) along with a brief overview of all the ways to measure academic achievement (teacher-made tests, norm-referenced tests, criterion referenced tests, performance tests, and observation). Also gives a thorough, but brief, explanation of the concepts of validity and reliability using many school-based, real-world examples.

Pyrczak, F. (1995). *Making sense of statistics: A conceptual overview.* Los Angeles: Pyrczak Publishing.

Lives up to publicity flyer's promise that this book "provides an overview without computations." Clearly explains in concise sections the basic concepts of both descriptive and inferential statistics. An easy to digest 118 pages of statistical knowledge. Gives you enough background to know when you can go it alone or when you should consult a statistician.

Pyrczak, F. (1997). *Success at statistics.* Los Angeles: Pyrczak Publishing.

A beefed-up version of Pyrczak's *Making sense of statistics: A conceptual overview.* Organized around a series of humorous riddles, covers both the concepts and computation of both descriptive and inferential statistics in a clear step-by-step fashion. Divided into 54, easily-digested sections. Also includes a basic math review.

*Rea, L. M. & Parker, R. A. (1997). *Designing and conducting survey research: A comprehensive guide.* San Francisco: Jossey-Bass Inc., Publishers.

In chapter 10, gives a clear, understandable discussion of various inferential statistical procedures (chi-square, Difference of Means Test, t-test, Difference of Proportions Test, Analysis of Variance). Keeps the math to a minimum, uses simple, easily understood examples.

Internet Resources

NOTE: You can easily access the Websites we recommend below by simply going to our Web page located at

http://www.pittstate.edu/edsc/ssls/letendre.html

From our Web page, a simple click of your mouse will take you straight to the selected Website. We regularly verify these sites and add others that we find worthy of our recommendation.

Glass, Gene
http://olam.ed.asu.edu/~glass/502/
Connects to Professor Glass' Website supporting his course "Introduction to Quantitative Methods" taught at the College of Education, Arizona State University. Provides clear explanations, with graphics, illustrating concepts dealing with data analysis. Periodically asks questions to check your understanding and then gives you answers. Includes hotlinks to other statistics resources for "another treatment" of the topics. Not heavy on the statistical/mathematical symbols. Concentrates on explaining the concepts, but does show how to calculate various descriptive and inferential statistics using a computer program.

Trochim, William M. K.
http://trochim.human.cornell.edu/kb/ANALYSIS.HTM
Connects to directly to the "data analysis" section of Professor Trochim's *The Knowledge Base, An Online Research Methods Textbook* at Cornell University. The best site we've found dealing with data analysis. Covers the concepts and procedures of organizing data, describing data, and using inferential statistics. Great graphics, clear explanations, with enough detail yet doesn't overwhelm the reader. Very user friendly.

End Notes

[1] You can use most computer spread sheets to create a useful frequency table. The spread sheet functions integrated into ClarisWorks™ and Microsoft Works™ work well. A more powerful and easier to use, stand-alone spreadsheet is Excel™. If you plan to simply summarize and describe your data, spreadsheets like ClarisWorks™ and MicrosoftWorks™ function well and can even create charts and graphs. However, if you plan to do more sophisticated statistical analyses of your data, we recommend that you use Excel™ since various statistical formulas are already embedded in the software program.

[2] You will need to consult the manual for the particular spreadsheet software you are using to get the correct format for specifying formulas. The following show the calculations for our example:

Column C: Percentage of students who obtained this particular score

$$\frac{\text{Number in Column A}}{\text{Total number of scores}} \times 100$$

If you want your spreadsheet to show the actual % sign in the column, most spreadsheets allow you to format the number as a percentage. If you do format the number as a %, you need to simply use the formula:

$$\frac{\text{Number in Column A}}{\text{Total number of scores}}$$

You don't need to multiply by 100 because the spread sheet automatically does this calculation when it puts your number into a percentage.

Figure 5.26 Calculating Column D: Cumulative Frequency

Column A Possible Scores	Column B Frequency (number of students who obtained this score)	Column C Percentage of students who obtained this score	Column D Cumulative Frequency	Column E Cumulative Percentage
0	3		3	
1	5	+ 3 =	8	
2	8	+ 8 =	16	
3	0	+ 16 =	16	

You should continue the calculations until your cumulative frequency equals the total number of scores in your group.

Figure 5.27 Calculating Column E: Cumulative Percentage

Column A Possible Scores	Column B Frequency (number of students who obtained this score)	Column C Percentage of students who obtained this score	Column D Cumulative Frequency	Column E Cumulative Percentage
0	3	1.88%		1.88%
1	5	3.12%	+ 1.88% =	5%
2	8	5%	+ 5% =	10%
3	0	0%	+ 10% =	10%
4	11	6.88%	+ 10% =	16.88%

(and so on until you include all your scores and the total percentage equals 100%)

19	2	1.25%		100%
20	0	0%		100%

CHAPTER 6

Doing Evaluations

Step 6—Interpret the Results of Your Analysis

6.1—Step 6: Interpret the Results of your Analysis: So What Does it Mean?

At this point in an evaluation, you have organized your data into frequency tables. You have also calculated numbers that summarize and describe your data in some fashion. Furthermore, you might have run some statistical tests to determine if differences or relationships actually exist. Now comes the fun part, the part you have been working so diligently towards—deciding what do all these data and analyses mean. Now, you can finally answer the questions you posed in Step 1.

No matter what type of questions you want answered, you follow a similar process in Step 6 to interpret the results of your analyses.

First, you review your analyses and *look for patterns*. Do most of the student opinions point to a positive learning environment within the school? When do most of the fights in the hall occur? Do students on the block schedule achieve as well as, or better than, those not on such a schedule?

Next, using these identified patterns, you then *draw conclusions*, conclusions that will withstand the scrutiny of supporters and critics alike. Finally, you apply the preestablished criteria you set in Step 2 and *make your judgments* about the program.

6.2—Looking for Patterns and Drawing Conclusions Through Pictures

One of the easiest way to ascertain patterns within data, whether your data come in the form of numbers or categories, is to create some sort of visual display. Often a picture can help you look beyond the "trees" and see the "forest."

For example, a group of middle school educators serving on an ad hoc committee on mobility used bar graphs to detect patterns in enrollment. These teachers became very worried about the high number of students who moved in and out of the school. Indeed, the district office calculated the school's mobility rate at 65%, meaning that 65% of the student body turned over during the previous school year. Only 35% of the students who began at the school in September were still at the school in May. Before they started crafting an action plan of what they could do to help these "move-ins," the educators wanted to see if any pattern existed in the enrollment. The attendance office produced the graphs in Figure 6.1 showing the number of new enrollees each month for the past three years.

Figure 6.1   Number of New Enrollees By Month for the Three Previous School Years

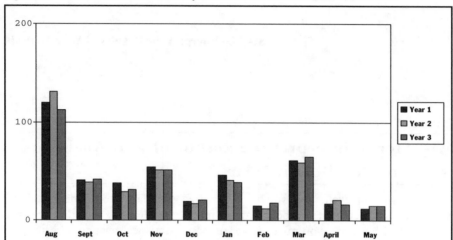

By looking at these graphs of new enrollees over the previous three school years, the teachers quickly saw patterns emerge. As expected, many new students enrolled at the beginning of the school year in August. However, regular dips and rises occurred during certain months. During November, January, and March, a substantial number of new students enrolled. Using this information, the teachers went on to design a special "newcomer" program for new students that focused particularly on providing services during August, November, January, and March.

6.3—Looking for Patterns and Drawing Conclusions Through Calculations

Various statistical calculations can also help you discern patterns and draw conclusions. In particular, statistics can help you determine if:

- A *significant* difference exists between the arithmetic means of two groups.
- A *significant* preference exists among the choices people make.
- A *significant* relationship (correlation) exists between two factors.

Does a Significant Difference Exist?

We often turn to statistical calculations when we want to determine if an innovative educational strategy actually works. To decide if a new program made a difference, evaluators frequently begin by selecting two groups of students. One group serves as an experimental group and gets the "treatment," while the other group serves as the comparison group and does not get the "treatment." (See Figure 6.2.) We then measure some relevant outcome, such as performance on a test, for both groups and calculate the arithmetic means for both the experimental and comparison groups. If we see a *significant* difference between the two means, we can then logically conclude that the "treatment" caused this difference.

Figure 6.2   Experimental Research Design

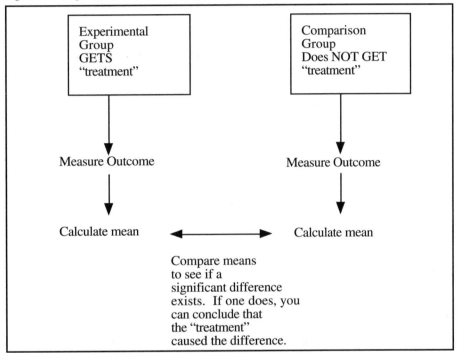

By *significant* difference, we mean that we are 95% sure that the difference we observe occurred not by chance, but because of some other factor, hopefully our new instructional strategy. Of course, we cannot be *absolutely* sure. Because we are looking at samples rather than whole populations, we always must contend with some degree of error. But for most evaluators, being right 95% of the time is good enough.

Evaluators commonly use two ways to ascertain if a significant difference exists between the arithmetic means of groups:

1. They calculate the group means, build confidence intervals around these means, and then plot these confidence intervals to see if the intervals of the two groups overlap.

2. They apply an appropriate statistical test of significance to their data.

6.4—Using Confidence Intervals to "Eyeball" Differences

Using confidence intervals built around the sample means of two groups, you can construct pictures that will illustrate whether or not a significant difference exists between the means. Figure 6.3 uses a plot to show the means and confidence intervals for Group A and Group B. The confidence intervals represent a 95% chance that the real sample mean falls within the range above and below the calculated sample mean. As you can see, the confidence intervals of the two groups in Figure 6.3 do not overlap. Thus, from just looking at the picture, we can conclude that possibly a significant difference exists between the mean scores of Group A and Group B. If the confidence intervals overlap as in Figure 6.4, then we can reasonably conclude that a significant difference does not exist.

Figure 6.3   Plots of Sample Means with Confidence Intervals Not Overlapping

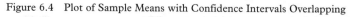

Figure 6.4   Plot of Sample Means with Confidence Intervals Overlapping

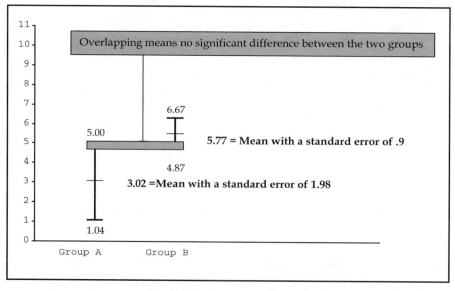

6.5—Using Tests of Significance

For a more precise method of ascertaining whether or not a significant difference exists, you can analyze your data using one of the many tests of significance. Gravetter and Wallnau (1996) provide a decision map in Appendix A of their book that can help you decide which one of the many tests of significance would be most appropriate for your data. Specifically, you can perform a test of significance:

- Between the mean of a sample and the known mean of a population (a rare situation)
- Between a sample mean and the expected mean of a population
- Between two samples means
- Among the means of three or more samples

No matter which of the various tests of significance you use, all the tests follow the same basic procedure known as hypothesis testing.

Figure 6.5   The Hypothesis Testing Process in Inferential Statistics

TASK 1 Write null and alternative hypotheses.
NULL Hypothesis:
    No significant difference exists between the two sample means.
ALTERNATIVE Hypothesis:
    There is a significant difference between the two sample means.

TASK 2 Set confidence level, the amount of error you're willing to endure. By convention 5% or 1%.

TASK 3 Using statistical tables, determine the critical value your CALCULATED test of significant must meet.

TASK 4 Calculate the appropriate test of significance.

TASK 5 Compare the calculated value with the critical value and decide whether to accept the NULL hypothesis or accept the ALTERNATIVE hypothesis.

Task 1

First, you write two hypotheses: a null hypothesis stating that *no difference* exists and an alternative hypothesis stating that a *difference does exist*. The null hypothesis acts as a "straw man" that you hope to knock down with your data. These two hypotheses act like a toggle switch. If you can knock down the null hypothesis with your data, you then can accept your alternative hypothesis and conclude that the innovative strategy worked. Of course, the opposite holds true as well. If you can't knock down the null hypothesis, you must conclude that a significant difference does not exist and your innovation did not work (at least not this time).

Task 2

Second, you need to decide how much error you are willing to endure. By convention, evaluators generally set the error at 5%, meaning that 5 times out of 100 they will be wrong. However, they might choose to live with a 10% chance of being wrong or, when the stakes are very high, lower it to a 1% chance of being wrong.

Task 3

Third, you should consult the appropriate statistical tables (found in any college statistics book) to determine the critical value your *calculated* statistical value must exceed for you to conclude that a significant (non-chance) difference indeed exists. [NOTE: Looking up the critical value in the appropriate statistical table is not as straightforward as you might think. You will need some basic statistical training in order to correctly use the various statistical tables.]

Task 4

Fourth, you can now collect your data and calculate the appropriate statistical value.

Task 5

Fifth, evaluate your hypotheses in light of your calculated statistic. You compare your *calculated* statistic to the critical value/standard you set in Step 3 and then decide one of two things:

1. If your *calculated* statistic *equals or exceeds* the standard from the statistical table, you can safely conclude that a significant difference does exist and you can reject the null hypothesis. When you reject the null hypothesis, our "switch" then toggles to the alternative hypothesis. You can then accept the alternative hypothesis and conclude that a difference *does* exist and your strategy *did* work.

2. If, however, your *calculated* statistic does *not* equal or exceed the standard, then you cannot knock down the null hypothesis. The "toggle switch" remains set at the null hypothesis. You then have to conclude that no significant difference exists and the difference you observed between the two means occurred simply by chance. This means that your innovative strategy most likely did not work. (Of course, Lady Luck might have been simply stacked against you this particular time. If you feel strongly that the strategy *does* make a difference, you can replicate the experiment and see if you get the same results again. Indeed, in clinical trials in medicine, researchers routinely do several replications to make sure that the patterns in the results hold true over several trials.)

6.6—The *t*-test at Work

Let's return to our Zoo Team teachers we met earlier in chapter 5 to demonstrate how this hypothesis testing procedure works.

As you will recall, the team decided to focus on improving the self-efficacy of their students. To evaluate their efforts, the teachers decided to collect data on their students and a comparable group of students within their school, the Power Team. Figure 6.6 shows their research design.

Figure 6.6   Zoo Team's Research Design

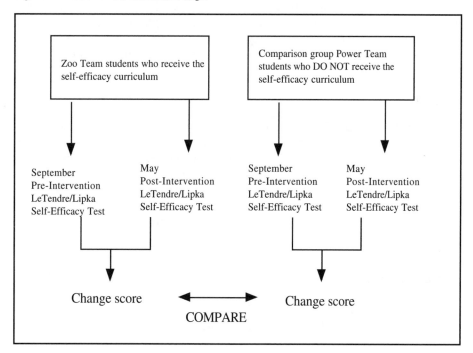

In September, they gave all 160 of their students the LeTendre/Lipka Test of Self-Efficacy and their colleagues on the Power Team gave the test to their 163 students. During the school year, the Zoo teachers implemented their self-efficacy curriculum while the Power Team teachers carried on as usual.

Now, at the end of the school year, the teachers want to see if their efforts at building self-efficacy have actually paid off. They begin following the hypothesis testing procedure we outlined above.

Task 1

They write their hypotheses.

Null Hypothesis:
> There will be no significant difference between the mean change scores for the Zoo Team students and the Power Team students.

Alternative Hypothesis:
> There will be a significant difference between the mean change scores for the Zoo Team students and the Power Team students.

The null hypothesis represents the "straw man" the teachers hope to knock down with their data.

Task 2

They decide they can live with a 5% chance of being wrong. So they set their confidence level at 95%.

Task 3

They consult the decision map in Gravetter and & Wallnau (1996) and find that for a non-matched comparison group pre-posttest design they should use a test of significance called a "t-test for independent means." Checking the critical values for t in a college statistics text, they determine that the critical value is + or - 1.98.

Task 4

The teachers then give LeTendre/Lipka Test of Self-Efficacy once again to the students in both groups. They now have 646 pieces of data, a pretest self-efficacy score and a posttest score on all Zoo Team and Power Team students. Using Excel™, they calculate the change score for each student by subtracting the September score from the May score. They then calculate the mean change score for both the Zoo Team and Power Team groups. Now, the teachers use Excel™ to calculate the t-value for their September-May data. They obtain $t = +2.48$.

Task 5

Now the teachers compare the critical value of t set in Task 3 (+ or –1.98) with the *calculated* t-value from Task 4 (+2.48). Because the *calculated* t-value is greater than the critical value, the teachers reject the null hypothesis and conclude that their efforts did make a difference. (See Figure 6.7.)

Figure 6.7   Comparing Calculated *t*-value with the Critical Regions

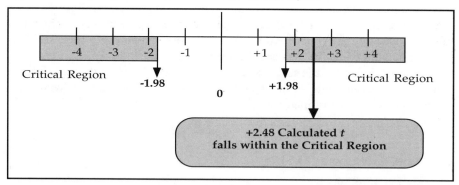

Since the Zoo Team teachers themselves are visual learners, they also calculated a 95% confidence interval around the means of the September test and the May test. They then graph these means with the confidence intervals, creating the plots you see below in Figure 6.8. As you can see in Figure 6.8, the confidence intervals *do not* overlap. Thus, we can see that a difference does exist and we can reasonably conclude that the Zoo Team's efforts to build their students' sense of self-efficacy paid off.

Figure 6.8   Confidence Interval Plot of Self-Efficacy Data for Zoo Team and Power Team Students

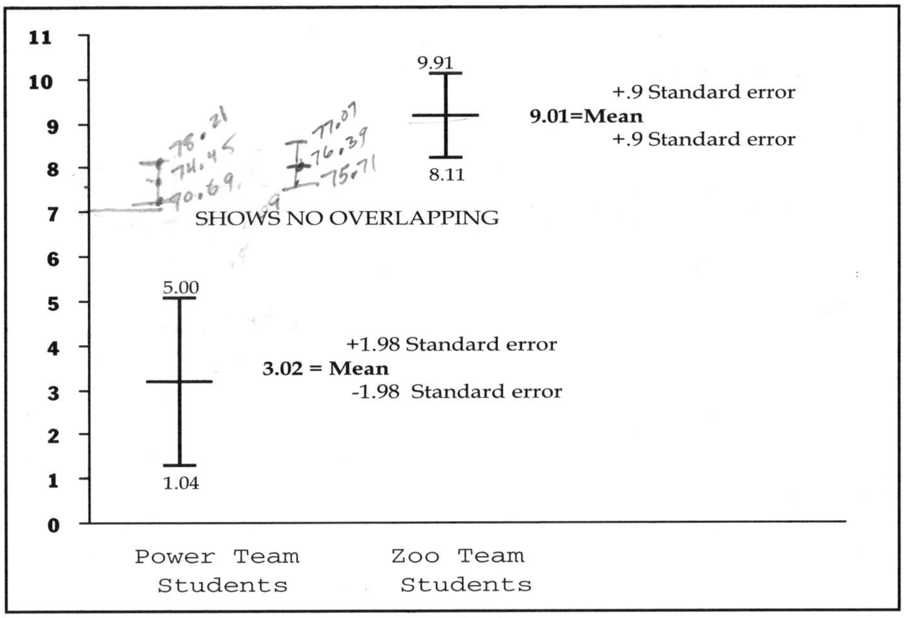

6.7—Statistically Significant vs. Educationally Significant

Given all this discussion about statistically significant differences, we need to sound a warning bell. Just because you find that an innovation performs statistically better than another strategy, it doesn't automatically mean you should continue using the innovative strategy. Popham (1975) reminds us that "Given enough subjects, even the most trivial difference in treatment effect may turn out to be *statistically* significant" (p. 239). We must remember that, as evaluators, we should be more interested in what is practically and educationally significant. We want to continue doing what's right for the kids. This means that we should base our judgments about a program on *many* pieces of information and not just one statistical test.

We need to also look at the benefits and costs of a program and consider the "rightness" of an innovation. Is it the *right* thing to do for students? For example, a program that pulls out academically able students and gives them a resource-rich and exciting curriculum, while all other students receive a dumbed-down, lifeless educational experience, will undoubtedly show significant gains for the academically able students. But is it morally right to deny the other students access to the "rich and exciting" experiences? Answers to questions like these go beyond a mere statistically significant difference.

6.8—Does a Significant Preference Exist?

The procedures we discussed in the previous section require that you have data that come in the form of numbers if you want to determine if a significant difference exists. But what about word data, data that come in the form of categories?

Can you ascertain whether or not a difference exists among categories? The answer is yes. But in the case of categorical data, we don't analyze for a significant difference. Rather, we calculate to see whether or not a significant *preference* exists among the various categories.

For example, a school asked 99 parents the following question in a telephone survey:

> What method would you most prefer we use to inform you
> about upcoming school events?
>
> ___ Send information home with my child weekly.
>
> ___ Mail information to my home.
>
> ___ Call me on the phone.

To determine if parents show a preference of one choice over the other, we use a statistical test known as a chi-square test-for-goodness-of-fit. Essentially, this statistical test discerns if a significant difference exists between what we *expected* to get and what we *actually* got.

Let's look at our parent survey questions. If no preference exists, we would expect that:

> 1/3, or 33, of the parents would select
>   Send information home with my child weekly.
>
> 1/3, or 33, parents would select
>   Mail information to my home.
>
> 1/3, or 33, parents would select
>   Call me on the phone.

As you can see from Figure 6.9, what we got and what we expected are two different things. By "eyeballing" the data it looks like parents do prefer the monthly calendar. But are the differences *significant* enough that we could say that parents really *do* prefer one choice over another? This is where the hypothesis testing process, combined with the chi-square test-for-goodness-of-fit, can help us decide if the differences are enough.

Figure 6.9   Frequency Table for Parent Question

Choice	Expected	Actual
Send home with child	33	33
Mail home	33	40
Phone call	33	26

Task 1

We begin by *writing two hypotheses:*

> No preference exists (null hypothesis).
>
> A preference does exist (alternative hypothesis).

Task 2

We *decide how much chance error* we're willing to risk. We set it at the 5% level.

Task 3

We *find the critical value our "calculated" chi-square statistic must exceed* for us to conclude that a significant, non-chance difference exists. Any statistics text will have a chi-square distribution table in the back. For the survey data in Figure 6.9, the critical value of chi-square is 5.991 (obtained from Chi-Square Table in a good statistics text).

Task 4

We *collect our data and calculate the chi-square statistic*. Unfortunately, most computer packages don't calculate the chi-square statistic. That's because it's so easy to do. Just lay out your data in a table and do some simple math. Again, a good statistics book will walk you through the calculations. The calculated chi-square value for the survey data in Figure 6.9 is 2.96.

Task 5

We *evaluate our hypotheses in light of your calculated chi-square statistic*. We compare our *calculated* chi-square statistic to the critical value/standard we set in Step 3 and then decide one of two things:

1. If the calculated chi-square statistic *equals or exceeds* the standard from the chi-square distribution table, we can safely conclude that a significant preference does exist and can reject the null hypothesis.

2. If, however, the calculated chi-square statistic does *not* equal or exceed the standard, then we cannot knock down the null hypothesis. The "toggle switch" remains set at the null hypothesis and we have to conclude that no significant preference exists

For the survey data in Figure 6.9, we find that the calculated chi-square value of 2.96 is less than the critical value of 5.991. Therefore, we must conclude that no significant preference exists. We retain our null hypothesis.

6.9—Does a Significant Relationship or Correlation Exist?

Thus far we have looked at how we can use statistical calculations to help discern whether a significant difference or preference exists. We can also use statistical tests to determine whether or not a significant relationship or correlation exists between two factors. The procedure for determining a significant relationship follows the now familiar Hypothesis Testing process with a few adaptations:

Task 1

You write a pair of hypotheses:
>   No relationship or correlation exists (null hypothesis).
>   A relationship or correlation does exist (alternative hypothesis).

Once again, these hypotheses operate as a toggle switch. If you reject the null hypothesis, you accept the alternative hypothesis, and vice versa.

Task 2

You decide how much error you are willing to endure. Will it be 1%, 5%, or 10%?

Task 3

You consult the appropriate statistical tables to determine the critical value your *calculated* statistical value must meet or exceed for you to conclude that a significant correlation does indeed exist.

Task 4

You collect your data and calculate the appropriate statistical value. With quantitative/number data you have several statistical techniques to use to determine if a relationship exists between two factors. Pearson's product-moment correlation coefficient is the most popular technique. For categorical/word data, you would most likely use the Chi-Square Test for Independence.

Task 5

You compare your *calculated* value/statistic to the critical value/standard you set in Step 3. If your calculated value equals or exceeds the standard, you can safely conclude a significant correlation does exist.

6.10—The Chi-Square Test for Independence at Work

Let's return to our Zoo Team one more time to illustrate how this procedure for ascertaining a significant relationship plays out in practice. As you recall, at the beginning of the school year, the teachers asked the Zoo Team's students to complete a short questionnaire that included the following question:

Question 10

Please √ the situation that best describes when you feel *most* in control of what happens to you.
I feel *most* in control when I am . . .
a. ___ Playing sports
b. ___ Sitting in class doing my work by myself
c. ___ Doing school work in a group with my friends
d. ___ At home
e. ___ Other (Please describe) _____
f. ___ I never or rarely feel in control of what happens to me.

As the Zoo Team teachers studied the students' responses, they wondered if boys tended to select certain situations when they felt more in control, while girls tended to select certain other situations. In other words, the teachers speculated that there might be a relationship between gender and the type of situation in which students felt most in control.

As always the teachers followed the Hypothesis Testing Process:

Task 1

They wrote two hypotheses.

Null : *There is no relationship between gender and the type of situation in which students feel most in control.*

Alternative: *This is a relationship between gender and the type of situation in which students feel most in control.*

Task 2

They set their confidence level at 5%.

Task 3

They consulted the decision map in Gravetter and Wallnau (1996) and found that they should employ a "Chi-Square Test for Independence" in analyzing the student responses. Checking the critical values for *chi square* in a college statistics text, they determine that the critical value is 11.07.

Task 4

The teachers sort the student responses to Question 10 on the survey by gender. They then calculate the chi square value for these data and obtain *chi square* = 13.87.

Task 5

They then compared the critical value of chi square in Task 3 (11.07) with the *calculated* chi square value from Task 4 (13.87). Because the *calculated* chi square value is greater than the critical value, the teachers reject the null hypothesis and conclude that a significant relationship/correlation does exist between gender and the type of situations where students feel most in control. It appears that boys felt more in control while playing sports or sitting in class doing their work alone, whereas girls felt more in control while doing classwork with their friends. This information helped guide the types of strategies the teachers chose to use with boys and girls during the school year to boost their sense of self-efficacy.

6.11—Qualitative Data: Looking for Patterns and Drawing Conclusions by Chunking

So far we have discussed how you can look for patterns in your data and draw conclusions by creating some sort of visual display of your data or by performing various statistical calculations. Now, we will examine a technique we call chunking to help you discover patterns and draw conclusions from qualitative/word data. Essentially chunking involves sorting words and phrases gleaned from surveys, interviews, documents, artifacts, and observations into bigger and bigger chunks so that you can see the big picture. The process works like a funnel to help you move from detail to generalizations, and from data to conclusions (see figure 6.10).

Figure 6.10   Data Funneling Down to Genealizations and Conclusions

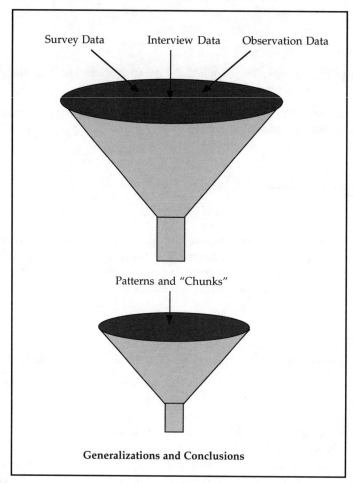

For example, as the Zoo Team teachers sifted through student responses on surveys, interviews and classroom observations, they wondered what characteristics tended to be present in situations where the students felt most in control. They began to satisfy this curiosity by examining all the various pieces of data where students spoke about the types of situations when they felt most in control.

From surveys, they found that students indicated that they felt most in control in the following types of situations:

- While playing sports
- While working with friends in class
- Sitting in class working by themselves
- At home

From interviews with 15 randomly selected students, they learned that these students felt most in control when:

- Hanging out with their friends

- Few adults were around
- Talking on the phone with their friends
- At the mall with their friends

From their observations in each others' classrooms, the teachers saw that students appeared most comfortable and in control in the following types of situations:

- When in a group of no more than three
- When in a group they chose to be in
- When doing an activity that involved physical movement
- When everyone was laughing together

Quickly the teachers saw that these 12 situations really represented five unique types of situations. They then chunked the 12 into the following five categories:

1. Situations involving activities desired by the individuals
2. Situations where individuals had some say about what they were doing
3. Situations where students *felt* they were free to make a choice
4. Situations involving fun
5. Situations where the individual was recognized as special

The teachers then asked themselves "What characteristics do these five situations have in common?" This question yielded the following four distinct characteristics that cut across all the situations where students felt most in control:

1. Choice of whom to be with
2. Physical movement
3. Lack of rigid constraints
4. Element of fun

As you can see, this process of chunking allowed various patterns to emerge. The teachers began with a massive amount of data gleaned from surveys, interviews, and observations. They then sorted these situations into five categories or chunks, and from these chunks identified characteristics that typify situations where students felt most in control. The Zoo Team teachers used this information to design learning situations within their classes that included these four characteristics.

6.12—A Warning: You *Can* Chunk too Much

Just as you can get hopelessly lost in a thousand bits of data, you can also pull back so far that you no longer see important patterns. For example, we humans on Earth are so close to the ground that we cannot actually see the interplay of land and oceans even though we know it's there. Only the astronauts circling in the shuttle can see these patterns of blue and green. But if these same astronauts traveled several light years away from our solar system, they would lose even this perspective. Earth would appear only as a small speck in even the most powerful of telescopes.

As an evaluator, you want to gather your data and wallow around in it, but you also want to be like the shuttle astronauts and pull back far enough to see the relevant patterns emerge. However, the trick is to chunk enough but not too much. You don't want to pull back so far that your conclusions become too general and meaningless.

Getting Kids Involved!

Ivy Diton currently serves as the assistant principal of Clarke Middle School in Westbury, New York. While she was in the classroom, she implemented a service learning curriculum within her Home and Career Skills course. At the end of the first year, Ivy and her students conducted an evaluation to determine the impact of the service learning component. Below, Ivy tells about the experience:

When a Home and Career Skills teacher retired, I was asked to teach two of her classes. Since I know little about "home" skills, I decided to focus on the career aspect of the program.

How do you teach middle school students about careers? I decided that the best way to do this would be to give them experiences where they can learn the skills necessary to become successful in the real world.

As part of the service learning curriculum, one class went to a nursing home and students were paired with senior citizens. The other class went to a day care center and became teacher assistants. Reflection in school focused on decision making and problem solving skills. Students were encouraged to think about how they may use newly learned skills, on the job and in their own lives.

Since this was the first time that service learning was used in the school's Home and Careers program, I was curious to learn how it was perceived by the students, parents, teachers, administrators, and community members. I proposed this question to my students and they, too, were also anxious to do the research, particularly since the students going to the nursing home thought that the students at the day care center were having a "better time."

Working with the National Center for Service Learning in Early Adolescence, [See Internet Resources for Chapter 9 for the Website of the National Service-Learning Clearinghouse which connects to a variety of resources.] my students were trained as student evaluators. They learned the language of research and evaluation, developed an evaluation design, created questionnaires, rehearsed interview questions, observed and questioned their "subjects," compiled their data, and then shared their work with the community at large.

The results were staggering. We learned that students would like to spend more time outside of school. We learned that students enjoyed the day care center more than the nursing home, but felt that the nursing home needed to have students visit. They recommended that students spend half a semester at a nursing home and half a semester at a day care center. (We followed through with this recommendation the following year.)

We learned that community perceptions of the school changed as students went out into the community to do their service. The recreation director of the nursing home commented that "The students were like a fountain of youth for our residents." We learned that parents are supportive and glad that their children have an opportunity to participate in the program. We learned that the day care staff relied on the students' visits each week.

We learned that the students were willing to continue their service on their own time. We learned that students felt that they learned more outside of school than inside of school and would be able to use these skills in whatever career they chose.

Information gleaned from this research encouraged the principal to change the course curriculum. We applied for a waiver from the New York State Education Department and implemented a new course entitled, "Careers and the Community."

6.13—Analyzing Qualitative Data: Triangulation and Conclusions

Drawing conclusions from word data requires that you be as meticulous as a police detective in moving from evidence (data) to conclusions. A conclusion drawn from just one piece of evidence lacks credibility, whereas an inference deduced from *several* pieces of evidence carries more weight. Just because parents say in a survey that they talk daily with their children about school, we cannot conclude that this is actually happening. We need further supporting evidence before we can legitimately seal our conclusion and state with conviction that, "The parents of Strivinghigher Middle School speak daily with their children about school." To get this supporting (or as the detectives say, corroborating) evidence, we might ask the students in a survey how often their parents speak to them about school. We might also interview randomly selected parents about their conversation habits with their children. You will recall from chapter 3, Section 3.6 (page 44), that we call this process of using multiple sources of data triangulation.

6.14—Cost Analyses

In our experience, teachers want to know, "Did it work?". But administrators, school boards, and even members of the general public also want to know, "Did we get our money's worth?". This is where cost analysis comes into play. A complete discussion of cost analysis goes beyond the scope of this book. Levin's *Cost-effectiveness: A Primer* (1983) provides one of the clearest discussions on this topic we've seen.

Briefly, cost analysis can take three forms:

1. **Cost Effectiveness analysis**

   In this type of cost analysis, the evaluator compares various innovations in terms of their costs and effects. Essentially, this analysis seeks to determine how much money it took to raise or lower some measure of an outcome. Perhaps the following example will make this clear:

   The EverExcellent Middle School served as the site for three different science programs meant to increase students' knowledge of science. As part of the evaluation, the students took the state assessment in science two times, once at the end of sixth grade and again at the end of seventh grade. The evaluator calculated the mean number of points gained by the students and the costs associated with implementing each of the three programs. These costs included the equipment, materials, teacher salaries, staff development, textbooks, consumable lab materials, special furniture, and remodeling of the science classrooms. Figure 6.11 shows the results of the cost-effectiveness analysis.

Figure 6.11   Example of Cost Effectiveness Analysis

Science Program	Cost per student	Average point gained (Effectiveness)	Cost/Effectiveness
Discovery 200	$1000	10	$100 per point gained
Snakes and Things	$1200	15	$ 80 per point gained
Everyday Science	$ 400	3	$133 per point gained

At first glance, before doing the cost effectiveness analysis, one might think that the Everyday Science program would be the way to go. Its per student cost looks very attractive. But when we calculate the cost associated with each point gained on the science assessment, the Snakes and Things program fares better. In this case, the Snakes and Things science program delivered the biggest bang for the buck.

2. **Cost Benefit analysis**

   In this variety of cost analysis, the evaluator compares innovations on the basis of both total program costs and total benefits. The evaluator calculates program costs in much the same way as when we do a cost effectiveness analysis. All costs associated with implementing the innovation are totaled up. Then the evaluator puts some kind of dollar amount on the benefits achieved by the program. This is where it gets tricky. All benefits must be translated into money even if we're talking about such intangibles as saving time, increasing productivity, expanding employment opportunities, and improving attitudes. Below, in Figure 6.12, is an example of a cost benefit analysis on three programs designed to improve school-community relations.

Figure 6.12   Example of Cost-Benefit Analysis

Strategy	Total Implementation Costs	Total Benefits	Cost/Benefits	Net Benefits
Reaching Out	$550,000	$450,000	1.22	-$100,000
School Partners	$400,000	$560,000	0.71	+$160,000
Back to School!	$150,000	$401,000	0.37	+$252,000

In Cost Benefit analysis, the "best" program is the one with the lowest cost/benefit ratio. For the three school-community programs, the Back to School! intervention appears to have the most desirable, cost/benefit ratio.

3. **Cost Utility analysis**

Evaluators use this form of cost analysis *before* implementation when decision-makers are trying to decide which innovation to adopt. The only available data come from implementors in other locales. Cost utility analysis requires the evaluator to compare potential innovations on the basis of both costs and utility. Costs associated with implementing a program are calculated in the usual manner, taking data from other sites. To determine the utility of a program, the evaluator first asks decision-makers to specify the desired outcomes or goals they hope to achieve by adopting and implementing one of the innovations.

Then, the evaluator asks decision-makers to make two judgments:

a. Estimate the probability that they will actually attain their goals should they adopt the program.

b. Rate the desirability of achieving each goal on a scale from 0 to 10, with 0 being "hardly desirable" to 10 being "extremely desirable".

The evaluator then calculates an expected utility index and a cost/utility ratio. Below, in Figure 6.13, is an example of a cost utility analysis as a hypothetical middle school contemplates which violence prevention program to adopt.

Given the data in Figure 6.13, it appears that the hypothetical Kid to Kid program would give the school the biggest payoff.

Figure 6.13   Example of Cost Utility Analysis

	P.R.E.V.E.N.T.	Kid to Kid
Probability of lowering the number of referrals for violence	0.8	0.5
Probability of lowering the number of suspensions due to violence	0.8	0.5
Utility of lowering the number of referrals for violence	9	9
Utility of lowering the number of suspensions due to violence	6	6
Expected utility	$(.8 \times 9) + (.8 \times 6) = 12$	$(.5 \times 9) + (.5 \times 6) = 7.5$
Cost per student	$24	$12
Cost/Utility ratio cost per point of utility	2	1.6

It's tempting to simply perform some sort of cost analysis and then mechanically make a decision by selecting the program with the "best" ratio. But Levin (1983) stresses that a cost analysis should not be the only piece of information that you examine. A cost analysis should stand as one among many pieces of information that decision-makers use to decide the worth of a program.

If you find yourself evaluating major, school-wide innovations, we suggest that you consider including some type of cost analysis as part of your evaluation plan. This is especially true when those who will make the decision about continuing a program are bottom-line, business-oriented people.

Unfortunately, we haven't seen a good how-to book on cost analysis for the novice evaluator. Even Levin's book (1983) doesn't get into the nitty gritty of calculating costs and benefits. We suggest, instead, that you seek experts to help you in doing a cost analysis. Professors and advanced graduate students in economics and business often have the necessary expertise. But Levin (1983) cautions that you "should not confuse expertise in accounting with expertise in C[ost] B[enefit] or C[ost] E[ffectiveness] analysis" (p. 142).

6.15—Building a Logical Chain of Evidence

Basing your conclusions on several pieces of credible evidence helps you to build a logical chain of evidence, especially when you're dealing with word data. We've found that using some sort of summary matrix helps us see the patterns emerge. Figure 6.14 shows just such a matrix, summarizing the evaluation findings for an after-school homework center. Later in section 6.20, we will show how Murray and his colleagues used this matrix to help them draw their conclusions.

Figure 6.14   A Portion of the Summary Matrix of the Homework Center Evaluation

Evaluation Question	Judgment Criteria	Evidence Summaries	Conclusions	Judgment Criteria Met?
1. Did home and school relations improve?	A higher percentage of students who use the homework center will indicate that their parents look favorably upon the school than those students who do not use the homework center. 98% of the school staff will indicate that they believe that home-school relations have improved since the start of the homework center. The average number of "Notes Home" per students will be higher since the start of the homework center.	• The student survey showed that 92% of the students who use the homework center indicated that their parents look favorably upon the school. • Only 74% of the students who DON'T use the homework center indicated that their parents look favorably upon the school. • 85% of the school staff indicated on the staff survey that they believe that home-school relations have improved. • The average number of "Notes Home" increased from 1.2 per student to 3.5 per student.	1. Although fewer staff members than hoped indicated that they believe that home-school relations have improved since the start of the homework center, the student survey data and "Notes Home" data show marked improvement.	YES

6.16—Moving from Conclusions to Judgments

Now, we come to the apex of our evaluation activities. We have our data, we have our conclusions, and now we use the criteria and standards we established in Step 2 of the evaluation process to make our judgments about the worth or value of the innovation. Again, a matrix like the one shown in Figures 6-12 can aid in helping you make your judgments. Sometimes, this judgment step is rather cut and dried; you simply march through each criterion and decide, based on your data analysis, if the program meets the standard.

For example, one of the Zoo Team teachers' criteria for judging the worth of their self-efficacy boosting program included the following:

> Zoo Team students will show a significant gain in their sense of self-efficacy over a comparison group of students who do not receive the self-efficacy curriculum.

After running a t-test on their data, the teachers find that a statistically significant difference does exist between the mean change scores of the two groups. Furthermore, the Zoo Team students showed greater gains. Thus, the Zoo Team teachers can indicate that this judgment criteria was met.

6.17—Dealing with Contradictory Evidence

However, applying the judgment criteria is not always so easy. Sometimes you encounter contradicting data. For example, 75% of the parents of Strivinghigher Middle School disclosed on a survey that they talk daily with their children about school. However, only 26% of the students indicated that they talk daily with their parents. Who should you believe, the parents or the students?

In reporting such contradictory information, you might report both pieces of information and let your readers decide who is more credible. Or, you might look for a third piece of evidence, collected from another source using another method, to serve as a tie breaker. You might also decide that students tend to be more honest in reporting the amount of communication, because parents might want to impress the teachers by saying they communicate daily with their children about school when they really don't. Or they simply don't remember how often they talk with their children about school. If they're like so many stressed-out parents today, they can barely remember what they did yesterday, much less last week! You might also decide that the students underestimated the amount of time they and their parents communicate about school because the students' perceptions are clouded by their overall feelings towards their parents.

So you see, dealing with contradictory information is not so easy. The key to sorting it all out is to ask yourself: What conclusions would a neutral third party find most credible? Then, go with those conclusions.

We also recommend that you consider using three other techniques when you find yourself with contradictory results. First, you might attach a minority report to your report. The minority report would include an alternative interpretation of the results. While the majority of your evaluation team might see the glass half full, the minority report might see the glass as half empty.

Second, you might follow one of the adversary-oriented evaluation approaches in planning and implementing your evaluation, particularly if you sense from the start that you will have much controversy (along with contradictory results) surrounding your evaluation. These adversarial approaches use a hearing format such as a jury trial, congressional hearing, or structured debate, where the evaluators thoroughly examine both sides of an issue, the pros and cons of a program. Worthen, Sanders, and Fitzpatrick (1997) do a good job in chapter 9 of their book *Program Evaluation: Alternative Approaches and Practical Guidelines* describing these various approaches.

Finally, you may simply want to list within your report both the strengths and weaknesses of the program, presenting a balanced perspective of the program.

6.18—From Judgments to Action

Once educators have conducted an evaluation of a program and made their judgments about its merit, rarely do they simply file this judgment away in some file cabinet. Most often, their judgments then guide their actions. Indeed, most evaluation reports end with a section entitled "Recommendations" that contains suggestions about the future of the program under investigation. These recommendations might include an outright statement to continue or discontinue the program. Or, the recommendations might offer ways to improve the existing program.

Earlier in this book, we indicated that most educators embark on an evaluation because they have questions that fall into one of three broad categories:

1. Questions that take stock or gauge the health of a program or school

2. Questions that determine effectiveness

3. Questions that seek solutions

If your evaluation seeks to take stock of your school or a program, then your judgments about the strengths and weaknesses of your school or program can help set the priorities for future action. If, however, your evaluation set out to determine if a strategy works or doesn't work, then your judgments will help you decide whether you continue, refine or discard the program. Finally, if you embarked on an evaluation to find a solution to a problem, your judgments about the core causes underlying the program can focus your brainstorming for solutions and eventually lead to an action plan.

6.19—Pitfalls in Interpretation

As you moved through the steps in planning and conducting your evaluation, you have carefully avoided the pitfalls of bias and inadequate procedures. Now, as you approach the final step of your evaluation, you again want to step around a final set of pitfalls that can too easily render all your hard work worthless. These pitfalls include:

*   Seeing what you want to see, rather than the facts. Too often educators will decide *beforehand* whether or not the program is a success and then bend their interpretation to conform with this preconceived judgment.

- Looking at the data only through a "microscope," thus failing to see the big picture. Good evaluators strive to use two sets of lenses, one set that allows them to see the minute details and one that requires them to pull back to see patterns and generalizations emerge.

- Performing only an "eyeball" test of significance and concluding that any change, even a one-point change, is significant. A 1-point decline or 1-point rise in the mean reading score of 7th grade students on a state assessment may *not* be statistically or even educationally significant. The difference may have simply occurred by *chance*. You really can't be sure, unless you run a statistical test of significance, and even then, there exists a margin or error.

6.20—Conducting Evaluations: Summary Advice

As we draw to the end of the six-step process for conducting program evaluations, we wish to summarize by reiterating the following advice—advice that will help *you* conduct professional evaluations that can withstand the scrutiny of supporters and critics alike:

1. Become more systematic and planful in doing evaluations. Use the Evaluation Planning Matrix even if you only take five minutes to sketch out an informal evaluation of a new teaching strategy.

2. Systematically define *beforehand* the criteria you will use to judge the worthiness of the program you are evaluating.

3. Consult a variety of stakeholders and then use a consensus building process to pose the questions and the judgment criteria that will guide your evaluation.

4. Be aware up-front of any potential threats to objectivity and take direct steps to minimize this bias.

5. Engage in both formative and summative evaluation whenever you embark on a new program/strategy.

6. Base your judgment concerning the worth of a program on many pieces of evidence.

6.21—Chapter Highlights

Major Concepts

☞ No matter what type of questions you want answered, you follow a similar process to interpret the results of your analyses:
- Look for patterns
- Draw conclusions
- Make your judgments

☞ It is possible for a program to statistically perform significantly better than another program, and yet not be either practically or educationally significant.

☞ Cost-effectiveness or cost-benefit analysis can help an evaluator determine whether or not we're getting our money's worth from an innovation.

☞ Cost Utility analysis can help decision-makers decide whether or not to adopt an innovation.

Advice

√ Look for patterns, through pictures and calculations.

√ Use chunking to help you see patterns and draw conclusions with qualitative data.

√ Use some sort of summary matrix to help you see patterns emerge.

√ Beware of these pitfalls:

1. Seeing what you want to see, rather than the facts.

2. Looking at the data only through a "microscope," thus failing to see the big picture.

3. Performing only an "eyeball" test of significance and concluding that any change is significant.

√ Build a cost-effectiveness or cost-benefit analysis into your evaluation plan if those who will decide the fate of your program are bottom-line, business types.

√ Use many different pieces of information as you decide whether or not a program is worth continuing.

6.22—The Road Ahead

Now that you've completed your evaluation, it's time to share the results. Our next chapter focuses on ways to you can share the results of your evaluation with a variety of audiences. It clearly would be a shame if you gather all your data, analyze it, draw your conclusions and then shelve it away in a file cabinet where it makes no impact on decisions or actions. Evaluations are meant to be shared and chapter 7 demonstrates some ways you can do this clearly and succinctly.

6.23—Murray Does Step 6

It's now June. The final evaluation report is due July 1. Murray, his colleagues and students, as well as Yolanda and Stan from the university, have collected the data, analyzed them, and now are ready to answer the question: *"What does it all mean?"*. Down in their office in the basement of the School of Education at the university, Yolanda and Stan have created a huge wall chart summarizing all the results from the data analyses. (See Figure 6.16.) They got the idea for this chart after seeing Murray and his students construct one to help them draw their conclusions concerning Evaluation Ques-

Figure 6.15   Step 6 of Evaluation Process

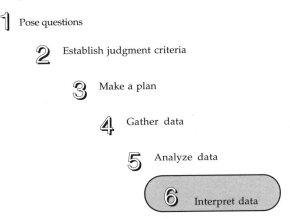

1   Pose questions

2   Establish judgment criteria

3   Make a plan

4   Gather data

5   Analyze data

6   Interpret data

tion 13, *"What's going smoothly? Not so smoothly with the block schedule?"*.

After mulling over the wall chart for several days, Yolanda and Stan jot down some tentative conclusions and then set up a time for the School Improvement Team to meet at their office so that they, too, can study the chart.

The Strivinghigher School Improvement Team reviews the wall chart while Yolanda and Stan share their tentative conclusions. Armed with this information, Murray and his colleagues now apply the judgment criteria they set in Step 2 to judge if block scheduling at the middle school is indeed worth continuing. After an hour's discussion, the committee comes to consensus: "Yes, it's worth continuing." They give Yolanda and Stan the go-ahead to write the evaluation report.

Figure 6.16   A Portion of Murray and Colleagues' Summary Matrix

Evaluation Question	Judgment Criteria	Evidence Summaries	Conclusion	Judgment Criteria Met?
1. Did students improve in reading comprehension?	1. Students on the block schedule will master a significantly higher number of items on the state criterion-referenced test in reading comprehension.	Line graph of mean percentage mastered by current 8th graders from May 1994 to May 2000 showed a slightly upward slope for Strivinghigher students when compared to a comparable group of 8th graders not on a block schedule. t-test comparing the mean change scores on the reading test from May 1999 to May 2000 showed a significant difference between the the Strivinghigher students and the comparison group.	Strivinghigher students showed significant gains in readings over comparison group.	YES

6.24—Resources

Print Resources

* These references have been recommended in earlier chapters. The number of *'s indicates the number of previous recommendations.

*Bernhardt, V. L. (1998). *Data analysis for comprehensive schoolwide improvement.* Larchmont, NY: Eye on Education.

> HIGHLY RECOMMENDED. Thoroughly walks through how two schools (one elementary and one high school) used data to make decisions. Gives suggestions on gathering, displaying, and analyzing the data. Excellent illustrations of using flow charting, affinity diagram, force field analysis, cause and effect analysis, and nominal group technique to make sense out of data.

*Gravetter, F. J. & Wallnau, L. B. (1996). *Statistics for the behavioral sciences: A first course for students of psychology and education (4th ed.)* Minneapolis: West Publishing Company.

> Everything you need to know about statistics and more. Excellent desk reference. Clear examples but sometimes goes too in-depth for the novice. Does give a step-by-step walk through of hand-calculating various descriptive and inferential procedures. Includes a *very useful* set of decision maps in Appendix A that can help you easily identify the appropriate statistical procedures you should use for a set of data.

Levin, H. M. (1983). *Cost-effectiveness: A primer.* Thousand Oaks, CA: Sage Publications.

> Gives a very readable explanation of the various methods of determining the cost-effectiveness of a program or strategy. Uses many examples drawn from education.

Internet Resources

NOTE: You can easily access the Websites we recommend below by simply going to our Web page located at

http://www.pittstate.edu/edsc/ssls/letendre.html

From our Web page, a simple click of your mouse will take you straight to the selected Website. We regularly verify these sites and add others that we find worthy of our recommendation.

Glass, Gene
http://olam.ed.asu.edu/~glass/502/
Connects to Professor Glass' Website supporting his course *Introduction to Quantitative Methods* taught at the College of Education, Arizona State University. Provides clear explanations with graphics illustrating concepts dealing with data analysis and interpretation. Periodically asks questions to check your understanding and then gives the answers. Includes hotlinks to other statistics resources for "another treatment" of the topics. Not heavy on the statistical/mathematical symbols. Concentrates on explaining the concepts, but does show how to calculate various descriptive and inferential statistics using a computer program.

Trochim, William M. K.
http://trochim.human.cornell.edu/kb/ANALYSIS.HTM
Connects to directly to the "data analysis" section of Professor Trochim's *The Knowledge Base, An Online Research Methods Textbook* at Cornell University. The best site we've found dealing with data analysis and interpretation. Covers the concepts and procedures of organizing data, describing data, and using inferential statistics. Great graphics, clear explanations, with enough detail yet doesn't overwhelm the reader. Very user friendly. Will soon have a section on drawing conclusions from your data.

CHAPTER 7

Sharing the Answers to Your Questions

7.1—Introduction

You've collected your data, done the analyses, interpreted your findings, and made your judgments. If you did all this simply to satisfy your own curiosity, then you can neatly file your evaluation away. However, we have found that frequently someone else wants to know the results. Even in the most informal of evaluations, a colleague down the hall will want to know what you've discovered. Remember, she's just as dedicated to improving her teaching as you are.

As with all other tasks in the evaluation process, sharing the results can range from a brief sketch to an elaborate report, complete with elegant graphs and tables. In this chapter, we will concentrate on producing the more elaborate report. You'll find that you can easily take much of what we say about constructing an elaborate report and scale it down to create a report customized to meet your specific needs.

The first step in sharing your findings is for *you* to thoroughly understand the results. You will not be able to clearly and succinctly communicate your evaluation findings to others unless you have spent time wallowing around in the data and know the results inside and out.

7.2—Tables and Pictures

We have found that two excellent ways to gain a thorough understanding of an evaluation's findings are:

1. Summarizing your findings into one or more tables

2. Experimenting with creating various pictures that display your findings

Later, you can use these same tables and pictures to clearly communicate your findings to your audiences.

In chapter 5 we talked about organizing your data into frequency tables whether you are dealing with numbers or words/categories (See Sections 5.2 and 5.4). These frequency tables not only organize your data, but can also display patterns that you can use to understand and, later, communicate your conclusions.

You can also use tables to summarize the various statistical analyses you conducted. Figure 7.1 gives the results of t-tests comparing the arithmetic mean scores of two student groups on a math achievement test: one group that received the new Hands-On Algebra program, and one group that received the usual algebra instruction. Although reading the table in Figure 7.1 requires a bit more background knowledge about statistics, it does communicate that a significant difference between the two groups was found.

Figure 7.1   Results of t-test Analysis on Mean Math Achievement Scores of Students Who Received Hands-On Algebra and Those Who Did Not

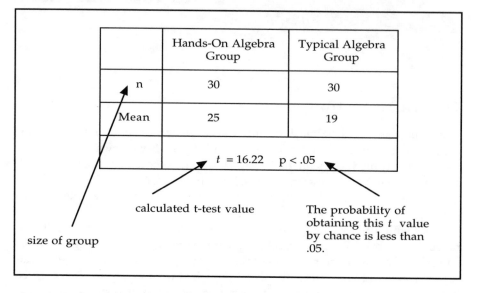

7.3—A Picture is Worth a 1000 Words

Pictures are another powerful way to summarize data and display patterns. Indeed, pictures can often be more powerful than tables in communicating information. Pictures can range from the simple to the elegant and come in two varieties: graphs and illustrations.

Some common graphs used to summarize data include:

- Bar Charts
- Line Charts
- Pie Charts
- Pictograms
- Scatter Plots
- Box and Whisker Plots

Below we illustrate each type of graph and give a brief explanation. Spreadsheet software such as Microsoft Works™, Claris Works™, and Microsoft Excel™ allow you to construct these various types of graphs and many more.

Bar Charts

A bar chart works well in graphing both numbers and categories. The frequency (your count) always goes on the Y-axis (the vertical axis), while your categories (for word data) or scores (for number data) always go on the X-axis (the horizontal axis). In Figure 7.2 we compare the mean math achievement scores attained by 6th, 7th and 8th graders. The use of different colored bars can further enhance your graphs.

Figure 7.2 Bar Chart Comparing Mean Math Scores for Grades 6, 7, and 8 at Strivinghigher Middle School May 1999

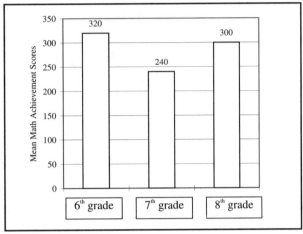

Line Charts

A line chart is one way to graph data across time to show trends. Essentially, you place dots to represent your data and then connect these dots. As with the bar chart, the frequency (your count) always goes on the Y-axis (the vertical axis), while your scores or, as in our example, years always go on the X-axis (the horizontal axis). Above we show the mean achievement scores for 6th grade students during 1996, 1997, 1998 and 1999.

Figure 7.3 Line Charts Showing Mean Math Scores for the 6th Graders Over Four Years at Strivinghigher Middle School

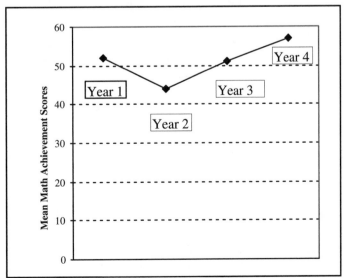

Pie Charts

Figure 7.4   Pie Chart Showing the Breakdown of Enrollment by Grade at Strivinghigher Middle School

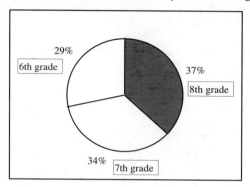

You're probably already very familiar with the pie chart. These graphs work well in displaying any data that come in percentages of a whole. For instance, Figure 7.4 shows the make up of a school's enrollment by grade level (using quantitative data). You could also use a pie chart to illustrate how students responded to a particular question on a survey. For example, in Figure 7.5 we show how many students responded "Yes," "No," "Don't Know," when asked if they found their experience volunteering at a homeless shelter to be valuable (using qualitative data). A tip to keep in mind: Refrain from using a pie chart if you have more than 10 "slivers" in the pie, or if you have one or more "slivers" that are equal to 5% or less. In both these cases, the pie chart simply gets too confusing and difficult to read.

Figure 7.5   Pie Chart Showing How Students Responded to the Question: Did You Find Volunteering at a Homeless Shelter Valuable?

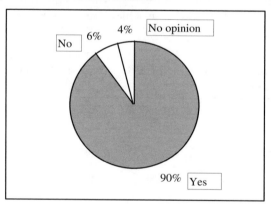

Pictograms

A pictogram is simply a snazzed up version of the bar chart. The newspaper *USA Today* often uses pictograms to report various polls. The only difference between a pictogram and a bar chart is that a pictogram uses some suitable picture (such as the stacked books in Figure 7.6) rather than plain bars to display the data. As with the bar chart, you can use a pictogram to illustrate both number and word data. As always, the frequency goes on the Y-axis, while your categories (for word data) or scores (for number data) go on the X-axis. In Figure 7.6, we compare the mean number of books read by students in the various grade levels.

Figure 7.6   Mean Number of Books Read by 6th, 7th, and 8th Graders per Student

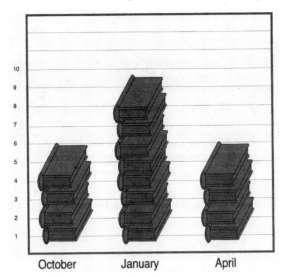

Scatter Plots

Scatterplots provide a visual display of the correlation between two variables measured on a number scale. In Figure 7.7, each dot represents the data for one student: that student's reading test score plotted with the number of books she read. As you might imagine, scatter plots work only with number data. You will have a number scale on both the X horizontal and Y vertical axes. Although reading a scatter plot requires some understanding of correlational statistics, you can usually estimate from such a scatter plot both the direction of a correlation (positive/direct or negative/inverse) and its magnitude. You can then verify your estimates by actually calculating a correlation coefficient such as Pearson's r. Indeed, if you suspect that two variables do co-relate, you should always construct a scatter plot, make your estimates, and *then* do the calculations.

Figure 7.7   Scatterplot Showing the Relationship Between Reading Score and the Number of Books Ready by 7th Graders

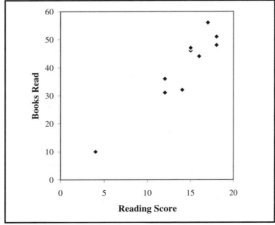

Box and Whisker Plots

Box and Whisker Plots graphically describe the spread among various groups. Sections 5. 11 through 5.13 give a complete explanation of what we mean by spread, or variability. The "box" represents the middle 50 percent of the distribution of scores (the interquartile range). The bottom of the box is the 25th percentile, while the top of the box is the cut point for the 75th percentile. The bottom "whisker" represents the minimum score obtained by someone in the group, while the top whisker indicates the maximum score obtained by someone in the group. The line through the middle of the box is the median, the midpoint for the distribution of scores. By comparing the distance between whiskers, or by examining the lengths of the boxes, you can readily tell whether or not the spread for two groups is similar or not. As you can see by examining the box and whisker plots in Figure 7.8, the scores in for the Power Team spread out more than those for the Zoo Team Student.

Figure 7.8   Box and Whisker Plot Showing the "Spread" of Power Team Group and Zoo Team Group

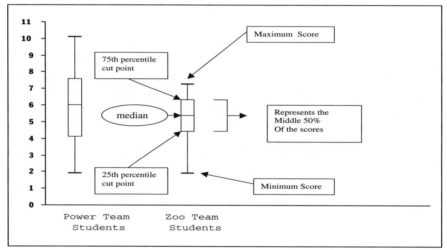

7.4—"Every Picture Tells a Story . . ."

Rod Stewart sings "every picture tells a story" and the same is true of illustrations. A good illustration can tell how something works. For example, the school board wants to know if Uptodate Middle School's Computer Awareness Class is actually expanding student knowledge about computers and information technology. As a way of explaining to the school board exactly what the Computer Awareness Class is, the teachers drew the diagram we see in Figure 7.9, showing the options available to students. Illustrations such as the one in Figure 7.9 can help you understand and eventually explain to others how something works. Indeed, we humans can often understand pictures much more rapidly and fully than written text. Furthermore, illustrations require those of us doing the explaining to boil down concepts and information to the essential parts, thus making our explanations clearer.

Figure 7.9   Illustration of the Various Options Open to Students Through the Computer Awareness Class at Uptodate Middle School

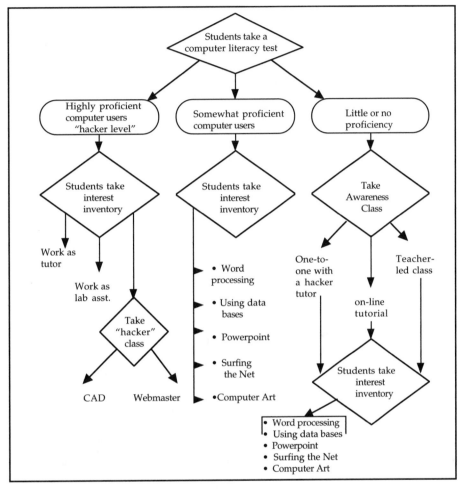

Illustrations can also provide a vivid method of visually displaying data without using tables or standard graphs. Joan's situation, introduced early in this book, provides a good example. Joan has just left four very angry 7th grade girls in the vice-principal's office, exclaiming "That's the second time today I've had to break up a shouting match between girls during passing period." She believes such verbal incidents are occurring much too frequently. Before Joan and her colleagues get down to brainstorming possible solutions, they want to take stock of just what's happening during the passing periods. Over the next week, Joan and her other team members plot on a map of the school *where* each of the 15 shouting matches and near fights occur. Figure 7.10 shows this map and as you can see, a pattern does seem to emerge. Although, such an illustration doesn't provide direct clues as to what's going on, it does indicate a starting point for investigation.

To summarize, before you can explain your evaluation results to others, you must first thoroughly come to understand your data. We've suggest that pictures in the form of graphs or illustrations provide an excellent technique for gaining

Figure 7.10 Map Showing Locations of Shouting Matches and "Near-Fights"

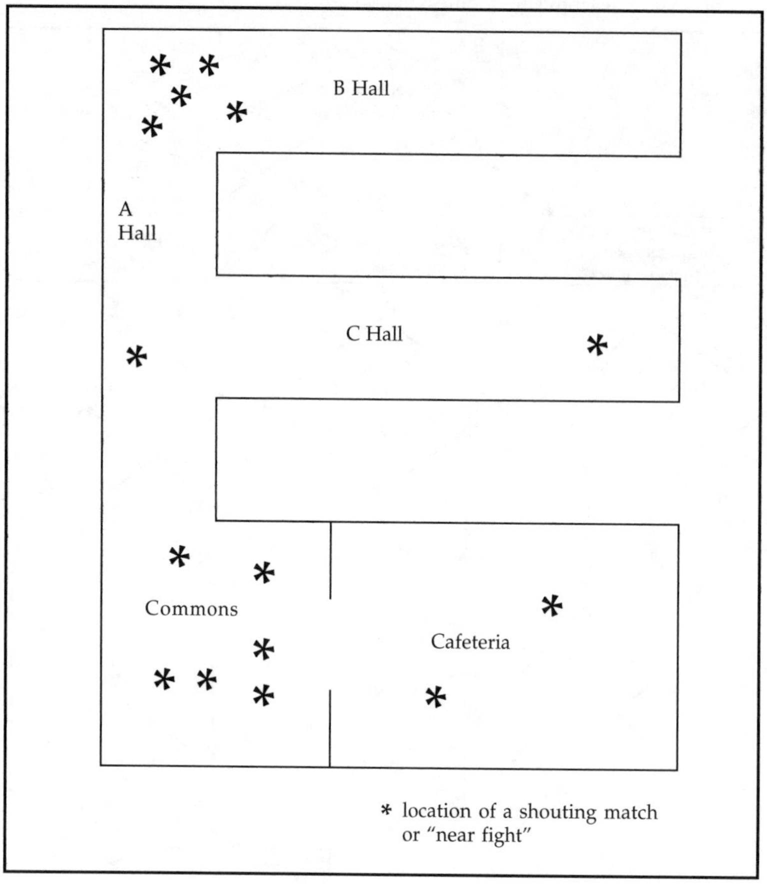

this understanding. Furthermore, you can use these same graphs and illustrations later to help communicate your findings to others.

7.5—Sharing your Findings

Now that you thoroughly understand your findings, it's time to share them with others. We suggest that you let the following three steps guide you:

First, determine what you want to accomplish by sharing your findings. A report, whether done orally or in writing, can serve one or several functions. The report can:

- Simply make people aware of your findings
- Urge people to make certain decisions and take particular actions
- Serve as a celebration of accomplishments
- Provide recommendations for fine tuning a strategy
- Supply the rationale for seeking additional support and resources

Second, decide who your audiences will be and what they will want to know. Rarely, will you have just one audience. Who will want to know about your findings? Those who have a major stake in the fate of the strategy under evaluation will of course constitute one of your audiences. The educators at your school, the students, their parents, the central office, the school board, and even the local media, are only a few of the possible audiences for your findings. In other cases, the interest in your evaluation findings might extend beyond the primary stakeholders in your school community. In some situations, you might find that educators across the district, the state, and even the nation might find the results of your evaluation worthwhile. You may find it most effective to have different presentations ready if you plan to present to very different audiences.

Once you have identified your audiences you need to answer the following questions for each audience. Your answers will guide the content of your report.

1. *What do the people in this audience want to know?*

   Here you should refer back to the ground work you did in Step 1 when you were posing the original questions to guide your evaluation. What did the various stakeholders say they wanted to learn from the evaluation?

2. *What prior knowledge do the people in the audience possess?*

   Make no assumptions. Find out what the audience already knows. Do the members know how the strategy actually works in the classroom? If not, your report will need to include a brief description of the strategy and how it was implemented. Do they understand research methods and data analysis techniques? If not, you will need to briefly provide some background.

3. *Will your audience be eager or reluctant to learn about your findings?*

   If your audience is eager to learn about your findings, then your job is easy. Simply explain your findings and offer your suggestions. However, if your audience is reluctant or downright uninterested in your findings, your job is much harder. You first need to get their attention. Showing them how the findings can help or affect them is a good tactic. Essentially you must *sell* the evaluation, writing in a tone of persuasion and, of course, clarity.

4. *Will your audience react in a hostile or sympathetic manner to your findings?*

   As you write your evaluation report, you should try to anticipate how your audience will react. Be honest with yourself. Don't assume that everyone will be overjoyed with your findings. Be prepared that some will be skeptical and some even outright hostile. Anticipate their questions and objections and be ready with answers. Better yet, you might even raise possible objections in your report and answer them preemptively.

The answers to the above four questions should help determine the tone of your report. Should you write it in a more *personal tone* using lots of "we found . . .", "we learned . . .", or should you stick with an *impersonal tone*? In our experience, we find that a more personal tone helps comprehension and builds a sense of ownership within your readers. [Indeed, we've tried to write this entire book using a personal tone.]

Your answers to the above four questions should also give you a clue about how much you will need to educate your audience. In particular, we find that most audiences need reminding about the following:

   • Multiple measures are better than one measure.

- Relying too heavily on scores from a one-shot achievement test to gauge your success can lead to erroneous conclusions. This would be akin to a physician using only your pulse rate to comprehensively and accurately measure your health. Pulse rate is a rather gross measure of physical health and mean scores on the state assessment are an equally gross measure of a school's health.

- Qualitative data such as people's opinions, perceptions, and judgments are just as real as quantitative data.

Furthermore, you will probably need to educate your audiences as to what outcomes they can reasonably expect from the strategy under evaluation. All too often, people, particularly school board members, want dramatic results fast. Such rapid success might simply be unrealistic and you should say so.

Thus far, you have determined what you want to accomplish by sharing your results, who your audiences are, and what they want to know. Now, you come to the final step in planning how you will share your findings. *Your final task is to ascertain how and when to share your findings.*

You can share your evaluation findings either orally or in a written report. In our experience, evaluators generally do both. Below we provide tips on how to create both an oral presentation and a written report.

However, before we discuss how to create a presentation or write a report about your evaluation findings, let's address the timing of your report, specifically who gets the report first. We suggest that you avoid hurt feelings and be politically savvy concerning the order in which you share your evaluation findings. Certain people legitimately should get the news first. Teachers, in particular, hate to be the last ones told about a program they have been implementing. If your evaluation results will be of interest to the local media, make sure that your primary stakeholders hear the results of the evaluation *first*, rather than reading about the results in the local newspaper.

Getting Kids Involved!

Earlier in chapter 3 we introduced you to the *Tools for Understanding* site maintained by The University of Puget Sound in Washington:

http://www.ups.edu/community/tofu.

This site provides a wealth of ideas (complete with lesson plans and student guides) on how you can involve your students in conducting program evaluations. We especially like how the lessons teach students to *clearly communicate* their results orally or in writing. These lessons mirror the real-world requirements that people in business face daily on their jobs. Lessons in both the "Math Concepts" and "Integrated Lessons" sections of the Website provide "think sheets" which guide students in preparing a memo, report or Powerpoint™ presentation that summarizes their findings and offers recommendations for action.

Tips on Sharing Your Evaluation Results in an Oral Presentation

As with the other tasks discussed in this book, you can make your oral presentation as formal as you want. Of course, presenting your results to the school board or an auditorium filled with patrons requires more preparation and polish than presenting your results to the five members of your teaching team. However, no matter the size of your audience, your oral presentation should rest on a foundation of careful analysis and interpretation of your data. Your thinking should be solid.

7.6—Making an Oral Presentation: Tip #1

Audiences tend to remember what they hear first and last. Therefore, we suggest that you use the Tell[3] Format in organizing your presentation:

- *Tell* them what you're going to say
- *Tell* them
- *Tell* them what you said

7.7—Making an Oral Presentation: Tip #2

K.I.S.S. (Keep It Simple, Sweetheart!) your presentation. Go for the important features of your findings rather than telling your audience everything you learned.

7.8—Making an Oral Presentation: Tip #3

Provide your audience with relevant numbers, but don't drown them in figures. Go for the most telling and relevant numbers. Too many numbers can fog the brains of your audience, stymie discussion, and even put people to sleep.

7.9—Making an Oral Presentation: Tip #4

Use visual aids to augment what you say. Most people are visual learners. They'll remember what they see much longer than what they hear. This is especially true when you share numbers. A clear, color-enhanced graph is worth a 1000 words. Also remember to K.I.S.S. your visuals as well. Use 18 point type or larger. Avoid making your graphs too busy, your lines too cluttered, or your type too small.

7.10—Making an Oral Presentation: Tip #5

Stay within your time limit. Audiences rarely forgive a speaker who goes too long. Practice your presentation so you can comfortably stay within your time limit without "speed" talking.

7.11—Making an Oral Presentation: Tip #6

Look at your audience. Make eye contact with individuals throughout the room, resting your gaze on a person for about five seconds and then move on, working your way randomly around the audience. Don't fall into the trap of finding one friendly face and talking only to that person. You'll soon lose the rest of the audience.

7.12—Making an Oral Presentation: Tip #7

Use illustrative stories and examples to explain your findings. People love stories that have a point, however, people hate stories that ramble on forever. So . . . practice your presentation to make sure that you can deliver your stories and examples succinctly, naturally and clearly.

7.13—Making an Oral Presentation: Tip #8

Create opportunities for your audience to participate during your presentation, even if you only ask for a show of hands.

This is how one speaker involved an entire auditorium of people when she shared the evaluation results of a successful district drop-out prevention program.

> She had the entire auditorium stand and said, "You represent all the students who enter our middle schools each year. Now, I want all of you who were born during the months of January, February, March, and April to sit down. You represent, the percentage of students (about 33%) who, before PROJECT SAVE began, dropped out of school." At this point, you could hear the audience gasp as they realized the enormity of the district's dropout rate. She continued saying, "Now, I want all of you who were born in January, February, and March to stand again. You represent the percentage of students PROJECT SAVE has kept in school since it began in 1994. Yes, we still have students dropping out, but now the percentage is 8% rather than 33%."

7.14—Making an Oral Presentation: Tip #9

As you give your presentation, anticipate the questions that your audience might want to ask and answer them within your talk. Also, provide time at the end of your presentation for audience members to ask you questions. When someone from the audience asks a question, always restate the person's question before you answer it. This gives you time to think about your response and makes sure that you understand what the person asked. This tactic also allows others in the audience to hear the question, since rarely in large groups can everyone clearly hear a question from the audience. Take your time in answering questions. You might even need to tell your audience: "I need to think on this one," then pause as you formulate your answer. Also, simply responding with "I don't know" is OK.

7.15—Making an Oral Presentation: Tip #10

Buy Malcolm Kushner's book *Successful Presentations for Dummies*™ for your school's professional library. While we don't particularly like the "dummies" implications, this book is crammed with excellent suggestions. The Additional Resources section at the end of this chapter gives the publisher's information for Kushner's book.

Getting Kids Involved!

Pat Campbell, Kathy Acerbo-Bachmann, and Karen Steinbruck with Campbell-Kibler Associates, Inc. spend their professional days conducting educational research and evaluations. In 1996, they received a contract to evaluate the services provided by Boston Children's Museum. As part of the overall evaluation plan, Pat Campbell and her associates included middle school students as part of their evaluation team. They placed notices at Little House, an alternative school in Groton, MA., seeking 13-year-olds to:

- Once a month from January to May, observe and interview students in the after-school program working on *Under The Rock* [a hands-on science program about insects]
- Meet with the rest of the evaluation team monthly to go over the findings and make plans for the following month, and
- Work on the final evaluation report.

The Campbell-Kibler evaluators selected five middle school students to join their team. The teen evaluators attended two, three-hour training and planning sessions where they helped pose the evaluation questions and create the data collection plan.

Starting in February, the teen evaluators met monthly to observe children as they participated in the *Under The Rock* program. They also interviewed staff and children, both those who took part in the *Under The Rock* project and those who did not. Each month they met with the Campbell-Kibler evaluation team for additional training and debriefing. They also crafted a monthly memo to the Children's Museum staff, summarizing their findings and offering suggestions for improving the *Under The Rock* program.

In May, the teen evaluators helped author the written evaluation report that went to the Children's Museum and the National Science Foundation. The teen evaluators also gave a presentation to the Little House Board of Directors.

"They took this seriously as a job," explained Ms. Acerbo-Bachmann, one of the Campbell-Kibler team, "It was incredibly real to them." Indeed, the teen evaluators even received a $200 honorarium (half paid in March and half in May) for their work.

Tips on Sharing Your Evaluation Results in a Written Report

Depending on your audiences and purposes, you can make your written report as elaborate as you want. If you plan to share your report widely, with audiences both inside and outside your school, you should consider writing a more formal report. If, however, you plan to share your findings with only your close colleagues (such as your teaching team) or to simply document your evaluation for your own purposes, then a less elaborate report will do the trick. However, we suggest that no matter how informal your evaluation, you should commit your findings to paper (or at least to a computer disk).

Below we offer some tips on writing a formal evaluation report. However, many of these tips can also apply to less elaborate reports.

7.16—Writing a Report: Tip #1

In its simplest form, your formal written evaluation report should include the following sections:

- *Executive summary*

  A one to two page summary of the entire report

- *Introduction*

  A couple paragraphs to set the context and provide your reader with a "road map" of your report

  Example of a road map:

  In this report we begin by describing the intervention itself and the students and teachers who took part in the program. We then list the evaluation questions that guided our study, along with the methods we used to answer these questions. In the next major section, we answer each evaluation question. Finally, we end the evaluation report with our conclusions and recommendations.

- *Description of the intervention or strategy under evaluation*

  Don't assume that everyone knows how your program works. Give a brief but clear explanation. You should also include a list of the outcomes the implementors hoped to accomplish.

- *Evaluation questions*

  A list of the questions that guided your evaluation

- *Methodology*

  A brief description of how you collected and analyzed the data. We suggest that you attach a more detailed Methodology Appendix that gives a complete description of how you collected and analyzed your data. The Methodology Appendix should also include a copy of any surveys, interview protocols, document review forms, or observation sheets you used to collect your data.

- *Results*

  An easy way to share your evaluation results is to answer each evaluation question separately. We suggest that you refrain from giving a blow-by-blow review of your results. Rather, your readers will appreciate summaries of your results, along with appropriate supporting graphs and tables. You can provide a full reporting of all your results (such as the tallies and percentages for every survey question you asked) in an appendix (which you can assume only the most interested people in your audience will read).

  Example

  Evaluation Question 3: Did student attitudes towards homeless people change as a result of their experience volunteering at the local homeless shelter?

  Both the survey and interview data showed that students saw homeless people in a more positive light after volunteering at the local homeless shelter. Table 3 below shows how students responded to various questions before and after volunteering.

- *Conclusions and recommendations*

  In this final section, you give your overall conclusions about the worth or effectiveness of the program you evaluated, along with any recommendations you might have about the fate of the program or how to improve the program. You should write this section carefully since in our experience most people simply turn to the "Conclusions and Recommendations" section and read only this part of the report. Therefore, this one section should say it all.

7.17—Writing a Report: Tip #2

As with the oral presentation, we suggest that you use the Tell[3] Format in organizing your written report.

- *Tell* them what you're going to say
- *Tell* them
- *Tell* them what you said

  Begin each major section with an advance organizer, a topic sentence that tells the reader what you will discuss. Then follow up with your discussion. At the end of the section, summarize the main points and include a transition sentence to cue the reader that you are now moving to a different topic. Keep repeating this formula until you get to the end.

7.18—Writing a Report: Tip #3

As we've said several times in this book, Keep It Simple, Sweetheart! In the Executive Summary, boil down your report to the absolute highlights. In the body of the report, you should elaborate a bit more, but opt for brevity and clarity. You can always include the details of how you gathered your data in a Methodology Appendix. You can even include the full results in the appendices.

7.19—Writing a Report: Tip #4

Write your report in an appropriate style. Match your style to your purpose. Use a *colorful style* when you want to persuade, sell or entertain. A colorful style creates word pictures; tells stories; uses vivid verbs, adjectives, and adverbs; and words to involve the reader.

Use a *personal style* when you want to create a sense of "we're in this together." A personal style also works well when you need to build cooperation. If you wish to write in a personal style, you should frequently use the pronouns "you" and "we," and all their variations. A smattering of "I's" also helps to create a personal style.

Use an *impersonal style* when you want to maintain objectivity or have a negative message. The impersonal style employs few pronouns and makes little attempt to draw the reader into the message. In this style, the writer steers clear of any emotionally-laden language and simply relates the facts—nothing but the facts.

In our experience, we find that readers relate best to a combination of the impersonal and colorful styles. Evaluation reports don't have to be dry, dense tomes. Rather, written reports should engage readers by balancing objectivity with illustrative examples.

7.20—Writing a Report: Tip #5

Write in *active* voice. When most of us have to write a report for others to read, we tend to fall into a dull, lifeless prose so often seen in college textbooks and research journals. Much of this lifelessness results from overusing all forms of the verb "to be." Whenever we use "is," "are," "was," "were," or "been," we have fallen into passive voice. Research shows that readers have a tough time comprehending passive voice. Active voice, where real subjects take real actions, fosters better understanding.

Let's demonstrate. Which of the following sentences do you find easier to comprehend?

A. It has been pointed out by several teachers that PROJECT SAVE was responsible for lowering the district's drop out rate.

B. Several teachers pointed out that PROJECT SAVE lowered the district's dropout rate.

We suspect that you find sentence B easier to understand. Not only does the writer of sentence B use active voice and fewer words, but the message comes across more clearly and forcefully than what we see in sentence A. Passive voice feels limp; plus it obscures meaning.

7.21—Writing a Report: Tip #6

Carefully edit your report before you share it with your audiences. We offer two editing processes to help you fine-tune your written report.

Reflective Editing

This type of editing works well when you have ample time to write your report. Not only do you have the luxury of time to think, organize, and compose, you also have ample time to edit. The best editing process involves reworking your document until you are satisfied *and* then letting it sit for a few hours. After this "wait time," you can come back again and edit one last time. The steps below work well when you can use *Reflective Editing.*

1. Box all subjects and verbs.
   - What words do the work?
   - Could I use more powerful words?
   - Do I use concrete subjects?
   - Do I use active verbs?
   - Do my subjects and verbs agree?
2. Put a △ around each "is" verb form.
   - Can I use active verbs instead?
3. Do I avoid needless, long warm-ups to my sentences?
4. Circle the prepositions.
   - Do I place the prepositional phrases as close as possible to the words they modify?
5. Spell check your document *or* check the spelling yourself by reading the document backwards, inspecting each word.
6. Read the document aloud.
   - Place commas wherever your voice pauses.
   - Listen for the flow of words.
   - Watch for missing words or words mistakenly repeated.

Editing on the Fly

Although most of us wish we lived in the "best of all possible worlds" and always had ample time to write and edit, rarely do we experience such luxuries. Often we barely have enough time to think, organize, and compose, much less time to edit. When you can't do Reflective Editing, try using the following shortened version.

1. Box all subjects and verbs.
   - Do I use concrete subjects?
   - Do I use active verbs?
   - Do my subjects and verbs agree?
2. Spell check your document *or* check the spelling yourself by reading the document backwards, inspecting each word.
3. Read the document aloud.
   - Place commas wherever your voice pauses.
   - Listen for the flow of words.
   - Watch for missing words or words mistakenly repeated.

7.22—Writing a Report: Tip #7

Give key stakeholders an opportunity to read and comment on the draft of your written report *before* you finalize it. Although, they will probably mark misspellings and poor grammar, have them read particularly for *errors* in facts and interpretation. You really don't want such errors in your final report.

Of course, when you give the draft report to stakeholders for their comments, you run the risk that they won't see the results in the same way as you do. What should you do if someone wants a change in the interpretation of the results and you don't agree? Most evaluators handle this situation in one of two ways. First, by mentioning in the body of the report that some people interpreted the results differently and explain this viewpoint. Second, by inviting the person to submit a minority report that you attach or incorporate into your report.

7.23—Maintaining an Archive of your Data and Findings

We've found that educators tend to fall into two categories: one group saves every scrap of paper, maintaining lesson plans from 10 years ago, while the other group rarely keeps anything except the essentials. When it comes to saving your raw data and the analyses, we suggest that you fall somewhere in between these two extremes. We recommend that you put all your raw data (such as interview notes, surveys, test score print-outs) into a box, along with your statistical calculations, and store the box in a safe, accessible place for at least three years. You may find that as you tackle problems in your school or work to refine programs that you will want to go back and refer to your original data. You might even want to look at the data with new lenses.

Of course, with the advent of computer disks, you could accurately enter all the data into a spreadsheet or data base and simply save the disk (with a backup in another safe location) and discard the raw data sheets.

You'll have to decide what works best for you. However, we want to emphasize that in our experience people *do* want to refer back to their original data, particularly it they want to gauge growth over several years.

7.24—Chapter Highlights

Major Concepts

☞ Two excellent ways to gain a thorough understanding of an evaluation's findings are:

   1. To summarize your findings into one or more tables

   2. To experiment with creating various pictures that display your findings

☞ Some common graphs used to summarize data include:

   • Bar charts

   • Line charts

   • Pie charts

   • Pictograms

- Scatter plots
- Box and whisker plots

Advice

√ Thoroughly understand the results of your evaluation before sharing them.

√ As you plan how you will share your findings:
  - Determine what you want to accomplish by sharing your findings.
  - Decide who your audiences will be and what they will want to know
  - Ascertain how and when you wish to share your findings

√ Tips for making an oral presentation about your findings:
  - Use the Tell³ Format in organizing your presentation
  - K.I.S.S. (Keep It Simple, Sweetheart!) your presentation
  - Provide your audience with relevant numbers, but don't drown them in figures
  - Use visual aids to augment what you say
  - Stay within your time limit
  - Look at your audience
  - Use illustrative stories and examples to explain your findings
  - Create opportunities for your audience to participate during your presentation
  - Anticipate the questions that your audience might want to ask and answer them within your talk
  - Buy Malcolm Kushner's book *Successful Presentations for Dummies*™ for your school's professional library

√ Include the following sections in your formal report:
  - Executive summary
  - Introduction
  - Description of the intervention or strategy under evaluation
  - Evaluation questions
  - Methodology
  - Results
  - Conclusions and recommendations

√ Tips for writing a report include:
  - Use the Tell³ Format in organizing your written report
  - Keep It Simple, Sweetheart!
  - Write your report in an appropriate style
  - Write in *active* voice
  - Carefully edit your report before you share it with your audiences
  - Give key stakeholders an opportunity to read and comment on the draft of your written report *before* you finalize it

7.25—The Road Ahead

At this point we've laid the foundation, albeit a quite substantial one. You now have under your belt the knowledge you need to conduct an evaluation and share the results, whether you do a full-blown formal evaluation or a quick, less formal one.

The last three chapters of this book will demonstrate how you, working either individually or with a team, can use this knowledge of evaluation to improve your teaching and your school. Chapter 8 will concentrate on answering questions that take stock, while chapter 9 will focus on getting answers to questions concerning effectiveness. Finally, chapter 10 will show how you can use evaluation techniques to answer questions that seek to find solutions.

Thanks for hanging in there with us! Now the fun begins!

7.26—Murray Shares the Results

It's June and Murray and his colleagues celebrate the end of a very productive school year. Even the kids agree it was a very good year. Some also want Murray to call them when the first draft of the evaluation report gets done. They want to read "The report those people from the University are writing." They especially want to know where their section on Evaluation Question 13 will go.

During the next two weeks, members of the School Improvement Committee review and give feedback to Yolanda and Stan about the final report. They even hold an open meeting with the faculty, sharing the draft of the executive report. Some teachers even ask to read the whole draft. Most of the feedback involves clarifications.

Murray also gives the draft report to the superintendent and high school principal for their feedback. Murray and the other members of the School Improvement Committee (especially the middle school principal) don't want any surprises.

Since they've been so involved in doing the formative evaluation piece of the project, about 20 of Murray's students get together over pizza at Travis' house one night to plow through the report. They beam with satisfaction as they realize that they *do* understand the report.

It's now June 21 and "B-Day" approaches. Yolanda and Stan will give a 30-minute presentation to the Board of Education on July 8, highlighting the evaluation results. They ask Murray if a handful of his students would like to help with the presentations. Murray is swamped with volunteers—about 10 kids. Murray suggests that they all spend the next week creating a PowerPoint™ presentation on Question 13 and then they can decide among themselves which three will actually do the board presentation.

The July 8th meeting of the Board of Education was unusually well-attended because the board planned to discuss the recommendations for redrawing attendance lines. Murray's students, Yolanda, and Stan were first on the agenda after the payment of bills. Murray beamed as his students gave their presentation and fielded questions from the board members with aplomb. Yolanda and Stan did well, but realized that the students were the "stars" of the evening.

The Board gave its stamp of approval for Strivinghigher Middle School to continue using the block schedule. One board member, struck by the excellent cost-benefit ratio for block schedule versus the traditional schedule, wondered why the other middle school and high school weren't considering a change to a block schedule.

Murray, his colleagues, and students left the board meeting elated. Their hard work had paid off. Now they had a welcomed vacation ahead. But there's more work ahead. Yolanda, Stan, and students will give another presentation to the parents and students of Strivinghigher Middle School at the open house scheduled in August, right before school starts. Plus they will give a short presentation to the faculty of the high school at an in-service day in October.

7.27—Resources

Print Resources

★ These references have been recommended in earlier chapters. The number of ★'s indicates the number of previous recommendations.

★★Bernhardt, V. L. (1998). *Data analysis for comprehensive schoolwide improvement.* Larchmont, NY: Eye on Education.

HIGHLY RECOMMENDED. Not only gives excellent suggestions on gathering, displaying, and analyzing the data, but also shows how you can communicate your results through charts. ("A good graph deserves a thousand words.") Also suggests numerous ways to disseminate the results of your evaluation through: local newspapers, public meetings, news conferences, newsletters, special events, school portfolios (includes to full school profile reports for two fictional schools, one elementary and one high school), websites, and summary reports. Also provides an example of a press release.

Career Track. (1996). *Writing High-Impact Memos and Letters.* Boulder, CO: CareerTrack Publications

Part of the *In a Pinch?* series. Provides big ideas in a booklet that fits into the palm of your hand. Published by CareerTrack Publications, Boulder, CO, 1-800-334-1018, **http://www.careertrack.com**

Fink, A. (1995). *How to report on surveys.* Thousand Oaks, CA: Sage Publications.

Volume 9 in *The Survey Kit* published by Sage Publications. You can purchase this 90-page compact volume separately as well. Covers the use of lists, pie charts, bar and line charts, and tables in written reports of survey data. Gives solid advice along with many examples of how to clearly and efficiently display your findings. Also gives tips on presenting your findings in an oral presentation. Provides the table of contents for both a technical and general report. A handy feature included in the book is a checklist to help make sure your report is comprehensive and accurate. Also includes an annotated bibliography of useful sources.

***Herman, J. L. & Winters, L. (1992). *Tracking your school's success: A guide to sensible evaluation.* Newbury Park, CA: Corwin Press.

HIGHLY RECOMMENDED. Focuses on whole school improvement by providing educators with the guidance and tools to answers the following questions:

• How are we doing?

• How can we improve?

• How can we share our successes

Includes in Chapter 3 a very useful set of guidelines for creating effective graphs and tables along with a helpful worksheet on how you can best communicate and act on the findings of your evaluation. Also provides a sample school report card (Report to Parents).

Kushner, M. (1996). *Successful Presentations for Dummies*™. Foster City, CA: IDG Books Worldwide, Inc.

A must for anyone who gives presentations. Funny, insightful and chocked full of tips on everything from preparing you presentation to dealing with "stage" fright.

Schmid, C. F. & Schmid, S. E. (1979). *Handbook of graphic presentation (2nd ed.).* New York: John Wiley & Sons.

Everything you wanted to know about making charts and more. Focuses on *all* the different ways to graphically present data and information: rectilinear coordinate charts (what we know as line graphs), bar and column charts, semi-logarithmic or ratio charts (representing rates of change over absolute changes), frequency graphs, pie charts, step charts, trilinear (pyramid) charts, scatter grams, growth curves, three-variable charts, fan charts, organizational charts, flow charts, ranking or rating charts, statistical maps, and pictorial charts. Readers will find chapters 1 and 2 quaint as they talk about drawing charts *by hand*. Remember this was before the personal computer and the easy-to-use charting software that comes bundled with most computers.

Torres, R. T., Preskill, H. S., & Piontek, M. E. (1996). *Evaluation strategies for communicating and reporting.* Thousand Oaks, CA: Sage Publications.

As its title promises, gives excellent practical advice for communicating and reporting the results of your evaluation. Particularly helpful on how to communicate negative findings. Covers the whole gamut of techniques for sharing your evaluation results with various audiences from how to write executive summaries to giving videotape presentations. Filled with numerous down-to-earth examples.

Wallgren, A., Wallgren, B., Persson, R., Jorner, U., & Haaland, J. (1996). *Graphing statistics and data: Creating better charts.* Thousand Oaks, CA: Sage Publications.

HIGHLY RECOMMENDED. For anyone who creates charts, graphs, or maps, this is a *must have* book. Should be in every middle school's library for students and teachers alike. Written by a group of Swedish statisticians (this explains the numerous examples that use Swedish data) for readers of all levels of sophistication. A well-written, well-illustrated, compact book. In 85 pages, the authors pack all you ever wanted to know about making elegant charts and graphs. Not only a useful overview, but a handy reference of particulars about making elegant charts and graphs. One excellent feature: Chapter 14 provides a check-list of questions that can help you plan and create elegant charts, graphs, and maps to display your data. Covers bar charts, charts that show frequencies (histograms, population pyramids, frequency polygons, stem and leaf charts, step function graphs and ogives, pie charts), charts that show development over time (time series charts, index charts, semilogaritmic charts, line charts), charts that show relationship (scatter plots, barometer charts), charts that show variation (box plots, Lorenz charts), charts that show flow, charts that show geographical variation (statistical maps, choropleth maps, square maps, isopleth maps, density maps, cartograms), and pictograms.

Internet Resources

NOTE: You can easily access the Websites we recommend below by simply going to our Web page located at

http://www.pittstate.edu/edsc/ssls/letendre.html

From our Web page, a simple click of your mouse will take you straight to the selected Website. We regularly verify these sites and add others that we find worthy of our recommendation.

National Institute for Computer-Assisted Reporting
http://www.nicar.org
Connects to the National Institute for Computer-Assisted Reporting based at the University of Missouri School of Journalism. Connects to a vast array of data bases useful to journalists. Includes links to various Websites maintained by newspapers. A handful of sites under the "On-Line CAR Projects" button include school report cards that newspapers have compiled and published.

Education Writers Association
http://www.ewa.org/other
Connects the Website for the Education Writers Association with links to Websites that include school report cards compiled and published by various newspapers across the United States. Provides some good examples of how to report data about your school.

CHAPTER 8

Taking-Stock Questions

Honest criticism is hard to take, particularly from a relative, a friend, an acquaintance, or a stranger.

—Franklin P. Jones

8.1—Introduction

Increasingly, we as middle-level educators must take stock of where we stand. *Just what are we doing right? What's working? What needs fine-tuning?* These efforts at taking stock might be prompted by our own need to know where we stand or as part of a requirement for accreditation. As individual teachers, we also take stock of what's happening in our own classrooms so we can use the information to improve our teaching.

Taking stock questions usually ask:

- Where are we NOW?
- What's going on NOW?
- How do we stack up against standards?
- How "healthy" is our school?
- How "healthy" are our classrooms?

The answers to these questions can be the beginning step in a school improvement process or simply serve as confirmation of a job well done. Depending on the purpose, your entire school community, a team, or yourself alone, as an individual educator, may be involved in taking stock of your school or classroom.

In this chapter, we will outline a taking stock process that you can scale up or down according to your needs. We will return to Beverly, a middle school educator, distraught by the local newspaper's allegation that her school is "shortchanging students." We will show how Beverly and her colleagues use the six-step evaluation process we explained in chapters 1 through 6 to gauge the health of their school and answer the newspaper's accusations. We will also show how you, as an individual teacher, can use taking stock questions to improve your own teaching.

8.2—Taking Stock of Your School

Let's begin with school-wide taking stock efforts. Whole school communities take stock of their current situations for a variety of reasons:

- As the first step in a school improvement process
- Because the state's school accreditation process requires that they do so
- As part of a voluntary accreditation process
- To satisfy their own need to confirm the "health" of their school
- In response to pressures to show results

Let's examine each of these situations more closely.

8.3—The First Step in School Improvement

Before a school can legitimately embark on improving itself, the school community members must take a good, hard look at all aspects of the school, discovering both the strengths and concerns of their school. This information can serve three purposes:

1. The school community can use the identified strengths as the foundation upon which to build solutions.

2. The school community can utilize the list of concerns that emerges from the taking stock process to set priorities for action.

3. The school community can employ the answers to their taking stock questions as a baseline measure against which they can subsequently gauge any progress they might make. Years later, teachers can look back at this baseline data and say, "This is where we were then. This is where we are now. Look how far we've come."

8.4—State Accreditation Requirements

All 50 states have some method for accrediting schools—judging whether a school or a whole school district meets a set of standards. Generally, schools that fail to meet accreditation standards suffer some sort of state sanctions. For example, depending on the particular state, the state department of education can close the school, withhold money, or actually assume control from the local authorities.

In most cases, the state department of education sets the standards used in accrediting schools, but in some states, the schools or districts themselves actually determine the standards, making sure they stay within parameters delineated by the state's department of education. Whether individual schools or the state sets the criteria and standards, these measures generally center around student achievement, safety, services offered, and fiscal responsibility.

Often, the state accreditation process specifies both the actual procedures schools must use to gather data and the instruments the schools must use. For instance, schools might have to distribute standardized surveys, conduct certain types of interviews, or present achievement data in a particular way.

As you can see, the taking stock process required for state accreditation might be quite prescriptive. Furthermore, it might take up to one full year to complete. For this reason, most states require schools or districts to go through an accreditation process only once every three to five years.

If you are not already familiar with your state's accreditation process, we suggest that you talk with your principal and find out about the process. Where is your school in the accreditation cycle? What kinds of data does the process require you to collect? Furthermore, we suggest that you get a copy of your school's last accreditation report and read it.

We believe that knowing about your school's accreditation efforts yields three benefits:

1. This knowledge places your own efforts as an individual educator into a context. You might see where you fit into the scheme of things and you also might better understand why you and your colleagues have to do things in a certain way.

2. You might find that you can use the data collected for the last accreditation cycle as a baseline in your own current taking stock activities.

3. You might want to use some of the data collection procedures or instruments used in the accreditation process rather than inventing your own.

8.5—Voluntary Accreditation

In addition to state-mandated accreditation, some schools opt to undergo a voluntary accreditation process. Many public and private middle schools in the Midwest seek accreditation from The North Central Accreditation Association of Colleges and Schools, while schools in other parts of the country look to five other regional institutions for voluntary accreditation. In section 8.55 under Internet Resources, we list the Websites for all six regional accreditation agencies. In the past, only high schools tended to pursue voluntary accreditation. Recently, however, more and more middle schools are also going through a voluntary accreditation process.

Similar to state accreditation processes, voluntary accreditation agencies often specify both the standards and procedures for taking stock of a school's health. Furthermore, the accreditation follows a set cycle.

As with state-mandated accreditation, you will find that a voluntary accreditation process yields valuable information that can serve as a baseline in answering your own taking stock questions. Furthermore, by examining the data collection procedures and instruments, you might get some ideas on how to collect useful data.

At the end of this chapter, in section 8.55, we provide the Internet Website addresses for various voluntary accreditation agencies you can visit for more information.

8.6—Confirm the School's "Health"

Sometimes, educators take stock simply to satisfy their own need to verify the "health" of their school or classrooms. As educators, we go to school every day and put in 110%. We believe that we are making a difference, but we want to know for sure. By taking stock in a formal way, we can confirm our feelings that we are indeed on the right track. This knowledge can often give us that extra boost we need to continue giving our 110%. We can and should celebrate the good things we are doing.

Furthermore, we believe schools don't toot their own horns enough. We know we're doing a good job, but we take for granted that the public also knows we're doing a good job. Unfortunately, too often that's simply not the case. Jamie Vollmer, an Iowa businessman, reminds educators that most members of our communities really view our schools through a rearview mirror. Their ideas about school date back to the time *they* graduated from high school. Our patrons remember schools as they were 20, 30, 40, and even 50 years ago, not as they are today. And, of course, schools are very different today. Unfortunately, many of the voting public judge this difference as worse rather than better.

We need to share the information we get from our taking stock efforts and let the public know what a good job we're doing. Indeed, by almost all indicators, American schools are now doing a better job of educating young people than at any other time in this century. We need to correct the misconceptions about the demise of public education. Otherwise, these misconceptions will come back and bite us in our budgets.

8.7—Pressure to Show Results

This brings us to the final reason why middle school educators might ask questions that take stock. Accountability is the watch word driving today's schools. Legislators, voters, and parents want results and by taking stock we can show our results.

Indeed, this is the very situation that Beverly and her colleagues face. They need to take stock of their school, particularly student achievement, if they are going to successfully answer the newspaper's allegation that the middle school is "shortchanging" students.

8.8—Taking Stock with the Six-Step Evaluation Process

Thus far we have examined the typical reasons why middle schools ask taking stock questions. Now, let's look at how you can get these taking stock questions answered, using the six-step evaluation process that we laid out in chapters 1 through 6:

1. Pose questions
2. Establish judgment criteria
3. Make a plan
4. Gather data
5. Analyze data
6. Interpret the results

We will walk through each of the six steps, showing how you can take stock of your whole school. We'll demonstrate how Beverly and her colleagues, faced with accusations in the local newspaper about "shortchanging" students, approach each step. At the end of the chapter, we will also give a brief example of how you, as an individual teacher, can take stock in your own classroom and use this information to improve your own teaching.

8.9—Taking Stock Step 1: Pose Questions

Figure 8.1   Graphic of Step 1

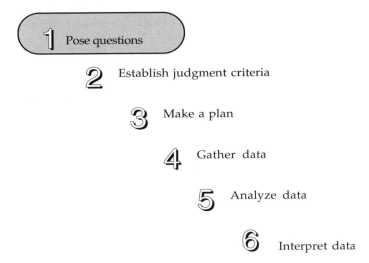

In taking stock, you want to get a good sense of what's happening *now* at your school or in your classroom. This picture of the "here and now" forms the foundation for improvement. Taking stock questions can flow from many specific sources.

1. Taking stock questions can come from mandated or voluntary accreditation procedures. Often these procedures delineate both the questions you must answer and the standards you must meet. For example, if a state accreditation standard for middle schools states: "The middle school will provide opportunities for all students to explore the fine arts," the taking stock questions you will generate will most likely include:

    • What fine arts courses do we offer to our students?
    • Do all students have access to these courses?
    • How many students actually take these courses?

    Furthermore, some accreditation processes actually provide you with a set of specific questions you *must* answer. These types of taking stock activities are fairly cut and dried.

2. Taking stock questions can emerge from your school's vision. For each component of the vision, ask:

    How close are we *now* to this piece of our vision?

Example

School's Vision	Taking Stock Question
Strivinghigher Middle School seeks to provide a safe environment,	How safe is the environment NOW?
empowering all students,	How empowered are students NOW?
to be self-confident,	How self-confident are students NOW?
ethical,	How ethical are students NOW?
responsible,	How responsible are students NOW?
creative problem-solvers,	How many students NOW are creative problem-solvers?
who will develop the skills to engage in life-long learning.	How many are NOW solidly on the road to developing skills for life-long learning?
these student will be actively involved in improving their community.	How many students are NOW actively involved in improving the community?

3. Taking stock questions can emanate from your school's goals. For each goal, ask:

   How close are we NOW to meeting this goal?

4. Taking stock questions can come from the standards set by various associations. Several associations have published standards that schools can use to judge themselves. We include a list of some of these in chapter 2. For example, the document *This We Believe* published by the National Middle School Association (1995) delineates the components of a middle school. Your taking stock questions can then ask:

   How close does our school align with each of these components?

5. Taking stock questions can come from asking stake holders what they want to know about the school. The list of stake holders includes:

   • Those who are directly affected by your school
     (students, teachers, administrators, support staff)

   • Those indirectly affected by your school
     (parents, patrons, community members, business people)

   • Those who will use the results of your taking stock efforts
     (the school board and many listed above)

   You can generate a vast array of useful taking stock questions by simply asking these folks:

   What should we find out about our school to help us create a complete picture of where we NOW stand?

8.10—Posing Meaningful Questions

No matter what method you use to pose questions to guide your taking stock questions, we suggest that you keep the following in mind:

> Pose meaningful questions that will yield information that *you* will find helpful.

Unfortunately, we sometimes get bogged down with asking (and answering) questions that simply don't get us anywhere. These questions waste our time and don't really give us a clear picture of the "here and now."

For example, one member of a team might suggest the following taking stock question:

> How many 2nd grade students within the district scored at grade level on the state-wide reading test in 1991, the year our current 7th grade students were in 2nd grade?

While this is an interesting question, we feel that it will probably yield little useful information about the current status of the school's 7th grade students. A more useful question might be:

> What percentage of our 7th graders answered the content reading comprehension questions correctly on last year's state-wide reading assessment?

The bottom line is this—ask questions that will yield information that *you* will find helpful in accomplishing your purposes.

8.11—General and Specific Questions

When you first start brainstorming questions to guide your taking stock efforts, you will often begin with general, overarching questions As you push forward, you will want to generate questions with greater specificity. For example, you might start with the general question:

> Where are we now?

Later, more specific subquestions, such as the following, will emerge:

- What strengths do our students, staff, families, and community possess?
- Where do our students stand on the various measures of learning?
- How many students take part in after-school clubs and sports?
- How many parents talk daily with their children about school?

As you can see, the general taking stock questions get you started, but the more specific taking stock questions really help you create a complete picture of the "here and now" of your school.

8.12—Beverly Does Step 1

Figure 8.2   Small Step 1 Graphic

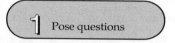

Beverly believes that the newspaper's accusations that her school is "shortchanging" students are untrue. She wants to gather information to counter the newspaper's report. Furthermore, she feels that it's high time the school let the community know just what a great job it's doing. As Beverly ponders how best to evaluate the school's health, she realizes that an internal audit may prove valuable to the staff in planning, but will hold little credence with critics, such as the local newspaper editor. Therefore, she feels that taking an *expertise-oriented approach* to evaluating her school will work best. In this approach, experts from outside the school visit the school, review documentation, observe the school in action, interview key stake holders, and then render a judgment using a set of published standards. Since the school is not scheduled to undergo a state accreditation review for another three years, Beverly begins looking for a suitable voluntary accreditation process. She learns that most schools in her area follow the process laid out by the BestEver Association of Voluntary Accreditation.

Beverly presents her idea about seeking voluntary accreditation first to her principal and then to the school's site council. Both the principal and the site council react positively. Beverly's principal tells her that just last month the State Department of Education agreed to give schools the option to use the BestEver Association's process or the state's procedure for accreditation purposes. In his eyes, conducting an BestEver review will give the school a leg up on the accreditation process.

Soon a committee of staff and parents forms and the group selects Beverly as chair. The committee's first order of business includes posing the questions to guide the school's evaluation.

Beverly's principal contacts the BestEver Association of Voluntary Accreditation and gets information about both the self-study the school must conduct and the school site visit that a team of experts will make.

Beverly's group begins by listing the questions the voluntary accreditation agency requires the school to answer. Then they consult the list of questions the state's own accreditation process specifies that schools answer as they take stock. Beverly knows that these questions reflect areas that the public deems important. The committee finds that the questions from the BestEver Association actually coincide with those from the state, so the members do not add any other questions to their list.

Beverly's school does have a vision statement and she and her colleagues formulate questions to ascertain how close their school is *now* to each component of the school's vision. For each component of the vision, they pose a general question—*How close are we NOW to this component?* Then they brainstorm a series of subquestions designed to further paint a portrait of their school's health.

Last year in compliance with state and district policy, Beverly's school set the following three goals:

1. The students will improve their ability to comprehend expository text.
2. The 6th grade students will improve their ability to solve multi-step, real-world mathematical problems.
3. The students will show respect towards themselves, others, and property.

As with the school's vision, the committee first poses the following general question, and then writes several subquestions.

How close are we now to meeting these goals?

Finally, Beverly learns that the news story containing the "shortchanging" allegations occurred because two weeks ago the state department of education released the school report card information for all schools in the state. To make sure that the evaluation specifically addresses the concerns raised in the news article, Beverly and her fellow committee members include questions about student achievement, absenteeism, and suspensions (all part of the school report card).

Now that Beverly and her committee have a list of 10 overarching questions and some 30 subquestions, they're ready for Step 2: Establish Judgment Criteria.

8.13—Taking Stock Step 2: Establish Judgment Criteria

Earlier in this book, in chapter 2, we made a strong case for establishing *up front* the criteria you will use to judge the success or failure of a program. Doing this not only makes explicit what you mean by success, but also helps define the kinds of data you will need to collect to make your judgments. In chapter 2, we suggested establishing your judgment criteria by:

• Polling those who have a stake in the results of the evaluation, asking them: What criteria and standards should we use to judge success or failure?

• Reviewing the purpose of the strategy (its vision and goals).

Figure 8.3   Step 2 Graphic

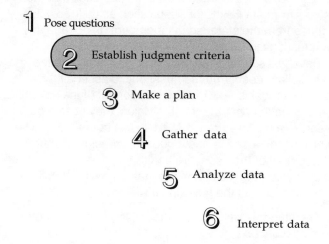

- Examining research literature to see what criteria and standards others have used to judge similar programs.

- Perusing checklists, standards, and guidelines published by various educational associations and agencies.

- Consulting with independent experts about what judgment criteria might be appropriate.

The key point to keep in mind is this: Establish your judgment criteria *before* you gather any data. This way you can avoid the whims of human subjectivity and also provide a focus for your data collection.

8.14—Beverly Does Step 2

Figure 8.4   Small Step 2 Graphic

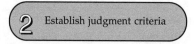

Rather than reinvent the wheel, Beverly and her colleagues begin establishing their judgment criteria by using as a foundation the list of standards set by the BestEver Association, the voluntary accreditation agency they have elected to follow.

However, Beverly and her colleagues also want to make sure they cover all their bases. Therefore, when they visited with various stake holders about questions to guide the evaluation of the school, they also asked for suggestions about suitable judgment criteria.

Furthermore, they turn to the school's vision statement and goals (as defined in the school's most recent improvement plan) and glean several other criteria to use in judging the current status of their school.

For example, the school's vision states:

Tiptop Middle School seeks to provide a safe environment empowering all students to be self-confident, ethical, responsible, creative problem-solvers, who will develop the skills to engage in lifelong learning.

From this vision statement, Beverly and her fellow committee members add the following judgment criteria to their list:

- Over 90% of the students will indicate that they feel physically safe at school.
- Over 90% of the students will indicate that they feel emotionally safe at school.
- Over 90% of the students will show that they are self-confident in their social and academic lives, ethical in their decision-making, responsible in their actions at school and in the community, and are creative problem solvers.
- Over 90% of the students will demonstrate that they are developing the skills they need for lifelong learning. Specifically, they are able to read for information, judge the credibility of information, organize new information in a meaningful way, and use print and electronic search techniques to find needed information.

The Taking Stock Committee further augments its judgment criteria by consulting with independent experts at the local university about what judgment criteria might be appropriate for judging the current status of their school.

Finally, Beverly and her colleagues review the components of the state's school report card which had prompted the news article in the first place. This report card shows how each school in the state stands on the following items:

- Scores on the state assessment in reading, math, writing, science and history
- Absentee rate
- Suspension rate
- Level of vandalism
- Number of students receiving remedial services
- Number of students taking advanced math and science classes
- The ratio between teachers and students
- The ratio between certified support staff and students

The committee knows that if they are to successfully counter the accusations cited in the newspaper article, they must make sure to include these report card items in their judgment criteria.

After taking all these steps to establish their judgment criteria, Beverly and her colleagues find to their surprise that most of the criteria and standards actually overlap. Therefore, they end up with a handful of criteria and standards representing the following seven major areas:

1. Student achievement
2. Curriculum offerings
3. Instructional strategies
4. School climate
5. Facilities and resources
6. Decision-making
7. Services for special student populations

At this point, Beverly and her group have their questions and the judgment criteria for determining the health of their school. They are now ready for Step 3: Make a Plan.

8.15—Step 3: Make a Plan

Figure 8.5   Step 3 Graphic

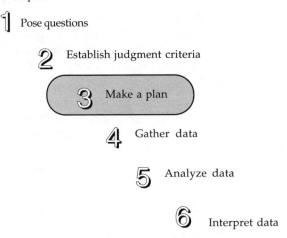

1 Pose questions

2 Establish judgment criteria

3 Make a plan

4 Gather data

5 Analyze data

6 Interpret data

In chapter 3 we provided a detailed look at this crucial third step: Make a Plan. This step requires that you establish a plan for getting your taking stock questions answered. You need to decide *who* will collect *what* data by *when* using *what methods*. You will also want to plan *how to analyze* the data you gather. Finally, you will want to very briefly outline the contents of your final *taking stock report* so that you can make sure that you collect all the data you will need to write the report.

We suggested in chapter 3 that you lay out your plan in a matrix (Figure 3.1). This same Evaluation Planning Matrix also works well when you plan how you will take stock of your school or your classroom. Of course, more formal taking stock efforts require a higher level of detail than the less formal efforts you, as an individual teacher, might undertake to ascertain the current status of your own classroom.

By completing the Taking Stock Planning Matrix such as the one we show in Figure 8.6, you can keep your data collection and analysis focused and efficient. Notice, this planning matrix looks exactly the same as the one we introduced in chapter 3, with one exception: We have changed the title to *Taking Stock Planning Matrix* to indicate the specific purpose of your evaluation efforts.

Figure 8.6   Taking Stock Planning Matrix

Column A Evaluation Question	Column B Information needed?	Column C Using what methods?	Column D By when?	Column E Who will collect?	Column F How analyze?
What kind of learning climate does our school NOW have?					

In column A, you simply list each of the taking stock questions you posed in Step 1. Then, using common sense mixed with your knowledge of good program evaluation techniques, build the rest of the matrix, planning how you will gather and analyze the information you need.

Completing Columns C through E of the Taking Stock Planning Matrix requires that you:

1. Attempt to corroborate your evidence
2. Find ways to collect data in a simple and reliable manner

Let's look at this need to corroborate your evidence first. At the end of your taking stock efforts, you and your colleagues will make a judgment of how well your school stacks up against the judgment criteria you established in Step 2. Rarely can you make credible, conclusive judgments using just one piece of evidence. Rather, you should base your judgments on *several* pieces of evidence that all point towards the same conclusion.

To make sure that you have several pieces of evidence upon which to draw your conclusions, we suggest that you use a second matrix known as a Cross-Walk of Qualitative Data Collection Methods, during your planning stage (Figure 8.7). For each taking stock question, you should try to collect data from a least two different sources using at least two different collection methods. Thus, you should have at least two "X's" in each row of the Cross-Walk matrix.

As you plan how to collect your data, you should keep two things in mind:

1. Keep it *simple*.
    *   Rely on existing data when you can. The principal's office and the district office already collect, summarize, and file much information about your school that you will find useful.

Figure 8.7   Taking Stock: Cross-walk of Qualitative Data Collection Methods

Evaluation Questions	Reviewing		Observing		Asking									
	Documents	Artifacts	Structured	Unstructured	Written Questionnaire					Interview				
					Teachers	Non-cert.	Principal	Families	Students	Teachers	Non-cert.	Principal	Families	Students

- When you do collect new data, stay focused by following the plan you laid out in the Taking Stock Planning Matrix (Figure 8.1). Periodically check to see if your timetable for collecting your data is indeed realistic. If not, make adjustments.

- Work efficiently by consolidating your efforts. For example, let's say that you have 15 questions you need to get answered by talking to the superintendent. Try to get all 15 answered in one visit rather than making numerous visits. The Taking Stock: Cross-Walk of Qualitative Data Collection Methods form in Figure 8.7 will help you see how to efficiently combine your efforts.

2. Keep it *reliable*. Remember that, unless you remain vigilant, bias can easily occur during your data collection and skew your results.

- Assume the role of a skeptic as you plan how to collect your data. Continually, ask yourself—*"Will this look credible in the eyes of our audience?"*

- Strive to collect data from multiple sources using different methods.

- Check with a neutral, third party as to whether or not your plans for collecting data appear objective and free of systematic bias.

In the final column of the Taking Stock Planning Matrix (Figure 8.6), you want to indicate how you will organize, describe, and analyze your data. In column F, you will specify *who* will analyze the data, *how* they will do the analysis, and by *when* you can expect them to complete their analysis. In chapter 5, we provided an extensive discussion of how your can accomplish these tasks.

8.16—Beverly Does Step 3

Figure 8.8   Small Step 3 Graphic

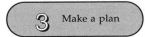

Because Beverly and her colleagues have opted to undergo a voluntary accreditation process, they use the procedures specified by the BestEver Association as a starting point in planning their taking stock efforts. However, to make sure that all tasks get covered, they also complete a Taking Stock Planning Matrix (Figure 8.9). Furthermore, as they complete the Matrix, they strive to keep their data collection simple and free of systematic bias. Since their time and energy are limited, they especially want to rely on already existing data as much as possible.

Since some of the evaluation questions rely on qualitative data (the opinions and perceptions of students, staff, and families), Beverly's team wants to make sure they gather information from multiple sources to triangulate their findings. (See Section 3.6 in chapter 3 for a refresher on triangulation.) To ensure that they collect corroborating evidence, the team creates a cross-walk of data collection methods.

Figure 8.9   A Portion of the Taking Stock Planning Matrix for Beverly's Middle School

Column A Evaluation Question	Column B Information needed?	Column C Using what methods?	Column D By when?	Column E Who will collect?	Column F How analyze?
What kind of learning climate does our school NOW have?	Student, staff opinions corroborating observations	Surveys designed by the BestEver Accreditation Association for students, teachers	January	Teacher Advisory, Vice principal	Scored by BestEver Association by February 1
		Interviews, observations by visiting BestEver expert team	March	Visiting team	Summary in report by visiting team by March 15

Finally, Beverly and her team sketch out the major sections they want to include in the final evaluation report they will present to the school board and the media. Of course, some parts of this report will follow the format specified by the BestEver Association for Voluntary Accreditation and some of it will even be written by the visiting team and not Beverly and her colleagues. Beverly's team decides on the following table of contents and makes sure that the evaluation plan includes strategies for collecting all the information they will need to write the final report:

- Executive summary
- Explanation of the voluntary accreditation process
- Evaluation questions
- Description of the middle school student population and school community
- Methodology
- Results
- Conclusions

Now, Beverly and her team are ready to implement their plan for taking stock.

8.17—Taking Stock Step 4: Gather Data

In Step 4, the Taking Stock Planning Matrix (Figure 8.6) serves as your blueprint for collecting data. As you will recall from chapter 4, evaluators collect information using three general methods:

1. Reviewing
2. Asking
3. Observing

Figure 8.10 Step 4 Graphic

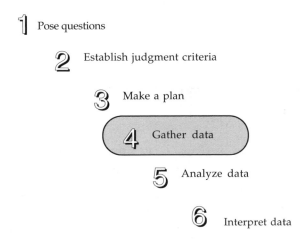

1   Pose questions

2   Establish judgment criteria

3   Make a plan

4   Gather data

5   Analyze data

6   Interpret data

In this chapter, we will focus primarily on *reviewing* school records, documents, standardized test results, and artifacts. In later chapters, we will highlight the other two general methods of data collection—asking and observing.

8.18—Reviewing School Records and Documents

Your school, like most institutions, abounds with records and documents that contain information you can use to answer your taking stock questions. Each day, as a matter of daily operation, clerks in the principal's office and teachers in their classrooms collect data. For example, school personnel create and maintain for each child a cumulative record that follows that child through the years. School clerks mark who is absent, who is tardy, who enrolls, and who withdraws. Cafeteria workers count how many breakfasts and lunches they serve. Furthermore, they know how many of these meals were free, reduced, or at full price. The school nurse records basic health information on students from their weight to the date of their last inoculations. Someone in the principal's office often keeps a running tally of disciplinary referrals. The principal and office staff maintain a set of ledgers showing all the financial transactions within the school's budget. Finally, in their classrooms, teachers record grades and other measures of student learning.

Often times, clerks regularly summarize information into reports that they then send to the district office or the state department of education. If the information you need to answer a taking stock question resides in such reports, then your job is easy. You simply need to ask for the right report and record the data.

Sometimes, however, asking for the right report can prove tricky. We suggest that whenever you have a set of taking stock questions you think can be answered by information collected through the school's office, you should approach the office staff and ask for their help. Show them your questions. In most instances they can quickly lay their hands on the appropriate reports. If the reports don't exist, they can provide you with valuable suggestions on how to collect the information you need.

In our experience, grant applications (especially those for federal money through Title I) can serve as valuable treasure troves of information. Most grant applications require an extensive needs assessment section. This means that someone has already toiled to pull together a myriad of facts showing the current status of your school and district. Often these grant applications include current information about:

- Student achievement on standardized tests
- Drop out rates
- Absentee rates
- Parent and community participation in school activities
- Socioeconomic status of the students and their families

You might also find that the persons who wrote the grant application have even more data that they did not include in the document. Thus, we strongly suggest that you visit personally with whomever wrote the grant application. Show them your taking stock questions. If they have the information you need, you're in luck. If they don't, they often can give you suggestions on how to get the information you need.

Of course, if we lived in the best of all possible worlds, all the data we need to answer our taking stock questions would already exist in some easily accessible report. But we don't live in the best of all possible worlds. Often times, you will find that the information you need lies *embedded* in a report. In such cases, you need to tease out the information that pertains specifically to your school. Unfortunately, this "teasing out" can take much effort. Under such circumstances, we have found that going back to the original data serves as the best starting point.

At other times, the information you need exists in bits and pieces scattered through various files and places. In these situations, you will need to plow through the files and paperwork to collect it yourself. When this happens, we suggest that you design a data collection sheet that you (or others) can easily use to record the information you need. Furthermore, we suggest that as you design your data collection sheet keep in mind how you will ultimately organize and analyze your data.

For example, let's say the staff of Beverly's middle school has generated the following taking stock question:

What are the top three reasons why students get referred to the principal's office for disciplinary action?

In most schools, teachers complete some sort of form whenever they refer a student to the principal's office for misbehavior. Figure 8.11 shows the disciplinary referral form that teachers use at Beverly's school.

The Taking Stock Committee members begin by designing a data collection sheet, keeping in mind that they eventually want tallies for both the reasons for referral and the types of disciplinary strategies teachers use within their classrooms. Figure 8.12 shows the data collection sheet they created.

Notice that the Data Collection Sheet (Figure 8.12) clearly lays out what data the committee wants. Yes, someone will have to sort through all the referrals, but this sheet makes tabulation and summarization a simple task. Furthermore, the committee can easily enter the totals into a computer spread sheet to calculate percentages and create graphs.

Figure 8.11 Disciplinary Referral Form Beverly's Middle School

| Student _____ Date: _____ Time:_____ |
| Referring teacher: _____ |
| Reason for referral: |
| What strategies did you (the teacher) use before referring the student? |
| Signed: _____ |

Figure 8.12 Data Collection Sheet for Disciplinary Referrals

Number of Referrals   from _____ to _____
                                (date)   (date)

   Total number of referrals _____

   Total number of students (unduplicated) referred _____

   Number of students referred more than 5 times _____

Reasons for Referral
                    Tally

Conflict with another student _____
Name calling, obscenity   _____
Defiance of authority   _____
Other:

Disciplinary Strategies Used by Teachers Prior to Referral

                    Tally

Conference with student   _____
Conference with parent   _____
Other:

Not only do the committee members need to design a data collection sheet, they also need to decide beforehand how to record ambiguous information. For instance, what sort of behaviors will go under the "Defiance of authority" category? Under what category would you place "Jill made explicit drawings of sexual intercourse and passed these around to her friends?"

Of course, the committee will probably not anticipate all the ambiguous data situations that may arise. Whoever sifts through the disciplinary referrals may have to make some judgments at the time. No matter who or when decisions get made about how to handle ambiguous data, data collectors should always strive for consistency in sorting.

For example, if a data collector decides to put Jill's explicit drawings under the "Use of Obscenity" category, then she should place all other similar behaviors under that same category. Furthermore, the data collectors should make notes about how they handled the various instances of ambiguous data. By documenting their decisions, they can readily explain to others how they handled the ambiguity.

8.19—Reviewing Achievement Test Results

Student achievement will always figure prominently in any taking stock effort. You can measure achievement through:

- Teacher judgment of progress
- Student judgment of progress
- Review of student portfolios
- Grades
- Standardized achievement tests
- Performance tests
- Teacher-made tests

We believe that all seven methods can provide you with valid measurements of student achievement. Each method has its own strengths and drawbacks. Because so many middle schools across the United States give standardized achievement tests, in this chapter we will focus on how you can review the results from these tests to gain new, and perhaps more meaningful, insights into student academic progress.

8.20—Standardized Achievement Tests

Generally standardized achievement tests attempt to measure a student's overall knowledge and skill mastery in a specific subject area. For example, the *Iowa Tests of Basic Skills*® assesses students in reading, understanding sources of information, language, social studies, science, and mathematics. Most often state departments of education and national publishing houses devise these tests, with students throughout the state or nation answering the same or similar test questions by bubbling in answers in a test booklet. (Recently, however, some standardized achievement tests have started requiring students to show their work or to construct written responses rather than simply bubble in answers.) Principals then bundle up these test booklets in a box and ship them to the testing company or scoring service, which then scores the tests and provides printouts showing the results for individual students, along with summaries for the whole school or district.

Standardized achievement tests come in two varieties: norm-referenced or criterion-referenced. Norm-referenced achievement tests, such as the *Iowa Tests of Basic Skills®,* the *California Achievement Test,* and the *Stanford Achievement Test,* compare your students' scores to the performance of students in a norming group. The norming group supposedly represents the variety of students found in the nation's schools. Thus, when the test results come back saying that Susan scored at the 56th percentile on the math problem solving subtest, this means that Susan scored equal to or better than 56 percent of the students in the norming group.

Criterion-referenced tests, on the other hand, compare an individual student's performance against a preset standard for mastery. For example, if the preset standard requires that students correctly answer 12 out of 15 questions on the math problem solving subtest for mastery and Susan correctly answers 13 items correctly, her test results would show that she mastered the math problem-solving skill. Many states now have criterion-referenced tests tied directly to the state's curriculum frameworks.

FYI

- Students in the United States spend 20 million school days taking standardized tests.
- Teachers and students spend 200–300 million school days preparing for standardized tests.
- Schools spend .7 to .9 billion dollars annually on purchasing, administering and scoring standardized tests.

—from Gage and Berliner, 1992

8.21—Using Standardized Test Data to Take Stock

Since most schools give some form of standardized tests by choice or mandate, the question now becomes—"How can standardized achievement tests help you take stock of your school?"

First, standardized achievement tests can help you *take stock of your curriculum,* detecting both the strengths and gaps in your curriculum. By analyzing how many students correctly answered each item on a standardized test battery, you can determine whether or not your curriculum includes various skills and knowledge. For example, the teachers at one school found that over 90% of their sixth graders missed all the items dealing with library skills. A review of the language arts curriculum revealed that the sixth grade curriculum contained no mention of library skills. By analyzing the standardized test data, these teachers found a hole in their curriculum which they quickly remedied.

Second, standardized tests can help you *take stock of your instruction.* By analyzing how students performed on various items, you can gauge the adequacy of your instructional strategies. For example, let's say you worked hard on teaching students how to read graphs, yet when you look at the test data you find most students missed all the items dealing with graphs. Hopefully, these data will cause you to carefully examine the effectiveness of your teaching strategies.

In another case, standardized test data can reveal when you haven't spent enough instructional time on a particular skill. For example, you find that only 10% of your students correctly answered all the test items dealing with proper punctuation. Upon reviewing how much class time you spent on developing various writing skills, you find that you really spent only a couple of hours during the year working on punctuation. Perhaps you may now want to increase your emphasis on cultivating punctuation skills.

Third, you can use standardized test data to *ascertain whether or not students show even growth* in their learning across subject areas. Do students score equally well in reading, math, written language, science, and social studies? Or do the data show weaknesses in some of these areas? Finding such discrepancies can help you focus on specific areas of concern within your curriculum and instructional practices.

Finally, standardized achievement tests provide an easy, although somewhat crude, *quantified measurement of student progress.* By comparing pretest and posttest scores, we can get some overall sense of students' growth in achievement.

8.22—Drawbacks of Standardized Achievement Tests

Analyzing standardized achievement test data can give you a very *general* picture of how well your students have learned the skills and knowledge assessed by the test. Notice we say "the skills and knowledge assessed by the test." One of the major drawbacks of any standardized test is that it may not align with *your* curriculum. It may not test what you have actually taught. Thus, your students may score poorly simply because they were not exposed to the particular knowledge assessed by the test.

Furthermore, please remember that standardized tests actually provide a very crude measure of student achievement. They judge a student's knowledge by looking at *only one* day's performance out of the whole year. This is akin to a physician judging your entire health based on your blood pressure during one visit to the doctor's office. Furthermore, that one measure of your blood pressure may or may not accurately reflect your normal blood pressure. Indeed, it's highly likely that it will be abnormally elevated because of "white coat syndrome," the anxiety many of us feel whenever we go to the doctor. Students may suffer a similar abnormal reading of their math skills on the day of the achievement test.

We also want to alert you to some additional negative consequences that often result when schools or districts rely too heavily on standardized achievement tests as a measurement of student progress and school health.

- The test may *become* your curriculum. If raising test scores becomes the ultimate goal, your curriculum may include only the skills and knowledge assessed by the standardized achievement test. We know of districts where teachers explicitly state: "If it's not on the test, I don't teach it. There's no time for anything else." Now, if the skills and knowledge assessed by the standardized achievement test represent those you deem worthy for students to learn, then you're home free. But if the skills and knowledge measured by the test embody only trivia, then you may want to question the wisdom of allowing such a test to drive your curriculum.

- Students may show a marked disinterest in doing academic work as they come to believe that external forces such as test scores control their fates. They may adopt the attitude of "why bother?" and even rebel when asked to take standardized achievement tests. We've seen bubble sheets carefully blacked in to spell a four-letter word beginning with "F."

- As students come to see the standardized tests as high stakes assessments, they may engage in various inappropriate test-taking strategies. Research conducted by Paris et. al (1991) demonstrated that, "Adolescents compared with elementary students were more likely to cheat, to become nervous, to have difficulty concentrating, to guess, and to look for answers that matched the questions without reading the passage" (p. 16).

- The inordinate emphasis on standardized achievement tests may also narrow the assessment strategies that you use as a regular part of your everyday instructional program. If the standardized achievement test asks students to respond to multiple-choice questions, this multiple-choice format, with its insistence on the *one* correct answer, may become the primary method teachers use to measure student academic progress. Other assessment methods, such as performance tasks, written assessments, and portfolios will drop by the way side.

- Teachers and even students may come to resent the amount of time they must spend on preparing and taking standardized achievement tests—time that they believe could be better spent on more interesting and compelling learning activities.

- Finally, the over-emphasis on standardized achievement test scores as *the* measure of a school's success can lead to the public (parents, patrons, voters, and policy makers) to base their judgment about a school's worth on just one set of numbers—that year's test scores. Indeed, in many communities the local newspaper publishes the test scores in a kind of school report card format that equates high test scores with school quality. Furthermore, in many suburbs and small cities across the United States real estate agents use these school report cards as a selling point in marketing houses.

8.23—Issue Box

Selecting Standardized Achievement Tests

Individual teachers rarely have a say as to whether or not a school or district will use a standardized achievement test to gauge its success. However, if you do get the opportunity to give input, we would like to offer some guidance in helping to determine which standardized test your students should take. Foremost, we suggest that you take a systematic approach to selecting a standardized test.

In, 1981, Jim Popham generated a series of guiding questions that Gage and Berliner (1992) later adapted. Answering these questions can increase your chances of selecting a standardized test that will prove helpful.

1. **What view of learning is enhanced by the test?**
   Does the test view learning as isolated bits and pieces, or as a complex act tied to some context? For example,

does the test include narrow questions like "What is a gibbous moon?"* or does the test require students to tackle richer conceptual questions such as "What causes the seasonal changes of weather?".

2. **Does the test provide an adequate description of the behaviors being measured by the test?**
   Does the test measure the behaviors (skills and knowledge) that you want to know about? Does it test the skills and knowledge you deem important for children to learn?

3. **Does the test include a sufficient number of items to adequately measure the your students' knowledge or ability?**
   Is it okay to make decisions about student achievement in long division with only one or two test items? How many items per behavior do you see as an adequate measure of your students' achievement?

4. **Does the test measure what you teach?**
   How closely does the content of the test match your curriculum?

5. **How reliable is the test?**
   Are the confidence bands capturing the score narrow enough for the kinds of decisions you must make as an educator? For example, is the test reliable enough to use in making high stakes decisions such as placement in pre-algebra and enrichment programs?

6. **Will you get the test results back in time to make decisions for next year?**

7. **Can you get the test results reported in the format you need them?**
   What reporting formats are available and at what cost? Will these data fit your needs? Can the data you receive be converted into standard scores for statistical analysis?

8. **Does the test provide feedback to students and parents?**
   Will you need to keep a psychometrician on speed dial or will the analysis include printouts that both parents and students can easily understand?

9. **Is the test appropriate for the age and developmental level of the students who will take the test?**
   Do testing instructions call for long sessions with few

---

*A gibbous moon represents that phase when the moon is more than half-full but less than full.

breaks or can you give the test in a way that fits the needs of middle school youngsters?

10. **Does the test include any obvious biases?**
Although no test is completely free of all bias, do most of the items appear relevant and connected to the lives of your students?

11. **Is the test easy to administer?**
Are you able to administer the test to large groups, small groups, or individuals? Are the directions for giving the test clear, or do you need speed dial again to get help from the resident psychometrician?

12. **Does the test promote a positive view of students?**
As you review the test directions to be read out loud to the students, do you get the impression that the test developers see all early adolescents as born evil? born good? or somewhere in between? Do the student directions contain numerous "DO NOT's" and other threatening legalese?

13. **Does the test have retest potential?**
Does the test come in equivalent forms, with appropriate fall and spring norms, that you can give as part of pretest/posttest evaluation design?

14. **Is the cost of the test acceptable?**
How much of the .9 billion dollars will come from your school district? A test that costs 50¢ per student to administer sounds like a deal until you realize it costs $6.50 per student to score!

8.24—Reviewing Artifacts

Thus far we've discussed reviewing records, documents and test results. Now we turn to reviewing artifacts. But let's first define artifact. An artifact is an object, created by a human, that has some permanence (at least until it gets stuffed into a back pack and breaks into a million pieces!). Some examples of artifacts you might find in schools include students' art work (both two and three dimensional), photographs, videotapes, dioramas, sewing projects, shop projects, Power Point™ presentations, and science fair displays. The list is almost endless.

8.25—Using a Protocol to Review

As with any other data collection method, we suggest that you review artifacts in a manner that is both *simple* and *minimizes bias*. Therefore, we suggest that you design a set procedure or protocol for reviewing artifacts. You may have to develop different protocols for reviewing different kinds of artifacts. For example, you may design one protocol for reviewing three-dimensional art projects, such as pottery and sculpture, and another protocol for reviewing multi-media projects.

You should decide *beforehand* what you want to look for and record. Below (see Figure 8.13) is an example of a protocol for reviewing multimedia projects. Notice that this protocol asks the reviewer to follow a set procedure for looking at the project as well as what elements to examine.

Figure 8.13 Example of a Protocol for Reviewing an Artifact Multi-media Project

Step 1:   Get a sense of the overall project

Purpose of the Project:

Types of media used:

Source of media used:

Length of project:

Step 2:   View the project once without taking notes.

Step 3:   View the project once again taking note of the following:

Devices used to attain flow:

Techniques used to visually display information:

Skills used in creating project:

8.26—Using Rubrics for Judging Quality

When reviewing artifacts, you may also want to judge the quality of that artifact rather than simply describing it. To judge the quality of an artifact, we suggest that you use some sort of a scoring guide. This scoring guide should list both the elements you examine and how you will judge the quality of each element. Today, many educators use various scoring rubrics that specify not only the elements and standards for performance, but also give samples of exemplary, satisfactory, and poor performances. You can, of course, devise your own scoring guide for reviewing various artifacts, but you can also turn to some of the resources we list at the end of the chapter in the section 8.55 Resources for already developed scoring guides and rubrics.

Figure 8.14 shows a rubric for judging the quality of a multi media project. Notice how it differs from the protocol for reviewing a multi-media project we show in Figure 8.13. The protocol in Figure 8.13 simply specifies the procedure for looking at the project and asks the reviewer to record facts and observations without making judgments about quality. Whereas, the rubric in Figure 8.14 requires that the reviewer take the next step and *judge the quality* of the project.

Figure 8.14 Example of a Rubric for judging the quality of a multi-media project

	Exemplary 4 Points	Excellent 3 Points	Satisfactory 2 Points	Needs improvement 1 Point	Unsatisfactory
Topic Coverage					
Preparation	Storyboard shows detailed planning and indicates thorough use of resources (more than 5)	Storyboard complete and organized. Shows planning and good use of resources (4-5)	Storyboard shows organization and adequate use of resources (2-3)	Incomplete. Inadequate use of resources. (1 or less)	No storyboard completed
Documentation	All sources are accurately and completely documented	All sources are documented with few errors	All sources are documented, but information is incomplete or in incorrect form.	Sources are not documented	No additional sources used
Content	Detailed development of topic is interesting, creative, and accurate	Development shows organization. Facts are interesting and accurate	Satisfactory development of topic, but may lack originality.	Indicates lack of organization. Few or no examples	No supporting facts or examples Indicates lack of organization
Multimedia Effects					
Type and Color	Creative use of type and color enhances content	Type style relates to topic, is readable. Color enhances content.	Minimal use of type and color.	Type and color overpower content. Type may be hard to read or obscured.	Type not formatted. No color formatting
Clip Art & Pictures	Enhances presentation. Pictures are clear, help explain topic.	Adds to presentation. Relates to topic.	Clip art emphasized over photos	No photos, Clip art does not relate to topic	Not used
Sounds/Music	Enhances mood of presentation	Adds to presentation.	No clear relation to topic.	Overpowers presentation.	Not used
Transitions, Builds, Timings	Effective use. Moves presentation smoothly. Used for emphasis of content	Effective use.	Occasionally slows presentation.	Slows presentation Used more for special effect	Not used

Developed by Barbara Queen, Multimedia Teacher at Webb City High School, Webb City, MO.

8.27—Beverly Does Step 4

Figure 8.15 Small Step 4 Graphic

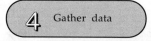

The voluntary accreditation process that Beverly's school has decided to pursue requires that the school conduct a self-study prior to a visit by a team of experts. It's November and the team will come in March. Beverly and her team of six simply can't do it all by themselves. They discuss their plight at a faculty meeting and soon almost every staff member, including many of the non-certified support staff, volunteer to help. Parents from the school's PTA also volunteer. Finally, Beverly approaches her students asking if they want to help collect, analyze, and interpret data. The students eagerly jump at the opportunity.

Using the Taking Stock Planning Matrix (Figure 8.9) they devised in Step 3, Beverly, the staff, students, and parents collect the data they need to answer their taking stock questions. Within a month, they have amassed a pile of data. Now, they need to make sense of all this information.

Getting Kids Involved!

In Fall, 1998, the staff, parents, and students at Showalter Middle School in Tukwila, Washington, a suburb of Seattle, kicked off their efforts to transform their school into an Accelerated School, where all students accelerate their learning. As the first step in this transformation, the Showalter school community formed committees to take stock of their school. These committees will conduct surveys, interview people, review documents, and observe their school all in an effort to get a complete picture of the "here and now." Students at Showalter will participate every step of the way. Not only will they fill out surveys giving information and opinions, they will also help design and conduct the surveys, tabulate the data, and write the final Taking Stock reports. Alex Glass, a 6th and 8th grade math teacher who is helping to spearhead the Accelerated School effort, plans to make these activities an integral part of his math classes. He's already introduced his students to the basics of descriptive statistics in preparation for the tasks ahead.

To further utilize their evaluation skills, Showalter Middle School students will also help teacher Robin Totten and her colleagues at three nearby elementary schools in their taking stock efforts. Periodically, the Showalter students will walk to the elementary schools to collect data. They will return to their classrooms where, as part of a class project, they will tabulate, organize, and analyze these data. Later, the students will present a Taking Stock report to the teachers at the three schools.

8.28—Taking Stock Step 5: Analyze Data

Figure 8.16 Step 5 Graphic

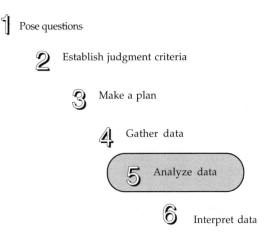

1 Pose questions

2 Establish judgment criteria

3 Make a plan

4 Gather data

5 Analyze data

6 Interpret data

To make sense out of your taking stock data, you must first organize it in some meaningful way. In chapter 5, we showed you how to create frequency tables and graphs to organize both number and word data. Next, you need to summarize your data by using descriptive statistics. We suggest that you report some measures of both central tendency (average) and variability (spread). Finally, in some cases, you will want to perform additional statistical analyses to draw inferences from your data. For example, if you want to know whether or not the drop in standardized achievement scores from one year to the next represents a statistically significant drop, you will need to compare the two means using a t-test.

In chapter 5 we provided an introduction of how to organize, summarize and analyze your data. In this chapter, we want to extend your understanding by discussing the various ways test companies describe student scores on standardized norm-referenced tests. Furthermore, we want to show how you can compare student scores on different standardized tests.

8.29—Reading Standardized Criterion-Referenced Test Printouts

As we suggested in section 8.21, you can use standardized test data to take stock of both your curriculum and instructional practices. By reviewing the results from a criterion-referenced test, you can ascertain what skills and knowledge your students have mastered. This information can help you pinpoint both strengths and gaps in your curriculum and instruction. For example, if you see that almost every student mastered the items involving multi-step math computations, then you could conclude that you're doing a find job of teaching that skill. However, if you find that few students correctly answered the items that required students to identify relevant and irrelevant information within a math problem, you may conclude after analyzing your curriculum that you simply don't explicitly teach this skill. Or it may be that you do teach the skill, but your instructional strategies simply didn't work.

All standardized criterion-referenced tests, whether developed by state departments of education or publishing companies, provide printouts showing the kind of skill analysis you need to take stock of your curriculum and instructional practices. Even most norm-referenced achievement tests also offer a scoring service that shows how individual students, as well as whole classes, scored on the various test items and subtests.

Even through the *Iowa Tests of Basic Skills*® is a norm-referenced achievement test, for a fee, Riverside Publishing will provide an individual or building-level, criterion-referenced skill analysis as part of the test results schools receive. In Figure 8.17 we show the Student Criterion-Referenced Skills Analysis for fifth-grader Alicia Wilson. Notice that the section marked ❶ shows the following:

- The number of items included on the Problems and Data Interpretation Subtest
- The number of items on this subtest attempted by the student
- The percentage of items on this subtest *this student* answered correctly
- The average percentage of items on this subtest that *her class* answered correctly
- The average percentage of items on this subtest that *students across the nation in the norming group* answered correctly

With careful analysis, printouts like the one in Figure 8.17 can help you diagnose areas of difficulty within your curriculum and instructional practices. You can also use the information to help you tailor learning activities to specifically meet the needs of individual students.

8.30—Reading Standardized Norm-Referenced Test Printouts

Publishers of standardized norm-referenced achievement tests offer printouts that report test results in various formats. Later in section 8.39 we list all the various formats one publisher offers. Other major test publishing companies provide similar services. Some printouts will report the various measures of central tendency: the arithmetic mean, median and mode. Other printouts will indicate the range of scores, showing the highest score and lowest score attained by students within the school.

We also want to share six other popular methods of reporting standardized norm-referenced achievement tests results:

- National percentile rankings
- Standard scores
- NCE's or Normal Curve Equivalents
- Grade equivalents
- Quartiles
- Stanines

Figure 8.17 Printout of Service 1:Student Criterion-Referenced Skills Analysis

We'll discuss each of these reporting methods by looking at various printouts available for the *Iowa Tests of Basic Skills*®.

8.31—National Percentile Rankings

Let's begin by looking once again at Figure 8.17, labeled Service 1: Student Criterion-Referenced Skills Analysis. This is a printout showing the results for a fictional fifth grader, Alicia Wilson. Find ❷ near the top next the label "National Percentile Rank."

To create the National Percentile Rank, the test developers begin by ranking the scores of all the students in the norming group. To establish *percentiles*, they divide the distribution of scores into 100 equal parts, with 1% of the students in each of the parts. They then calculate which scores are associated with which percentile. For example, the current norms for the "Vocabulary" subtest on the *Iowa Tests of Basic Skills*® show that Alicia's raw score falls at the 63rd percentile. This means Alicia scored equal to or better than 63% of the students in the norming group.

Using percentile rankings, we can examine a student's performance in comparison to various groups. For example, let's say the scoring services had provided not only the national percentile rank for Alicia which you see in Figure 8.17 ❷, but also had calculated percentile ranks using three additional comparison groups: her school, the district, and the state. Using these additional percentile rankings, we show in Figure 8.18 Alicia's reading performance compared to other students in her school, her district, and her state, along with her national percentile ranking. Notice, that although Alicia scored quite well when compared with other 5th graders across the nation, she only scored at the 45th percentile when compared with the other 5th graders attending her school. This means that Alicia attends a school where most the students scored very well on the reading test.

Why might we want to see the kind of comparisons shown in Figure 8.18? Such comparisons help us to reexamine our expectations for Alicia. If we only compare her performance with that of her fellow classmates, we might think that Alicia is performing *below* par in reading. However, in reality she is probably doing better than OK, especially when we look at her performance in comparison to other 5th graders in the state and nation.

8.32—Standard Scores

Now locate ❸ in Figure 8.17. A standard score represents a raw score that has been transformed onto a standard scale so that we can compare student performances across various tests. Essentially, standard scores allow us to compare apples to oranges by transforming all the fruit into grapes. By transforming the scores on various tests into standard scores, we can compare student achievement even when one student took the *California Achievement Test* and the other student took the *Iowa Tests of Basic Skills*®. Or we can compare achievement scores across time even when students took the *Stanford Achievement Test* during sixth grade and CTB McGraw-Hill's *TerraNova* during the seventh grade.

Most standard scores discussed in basic college statistics books use the mean and standard deviation of a norming population to create a scale that places the

Figure 8.18 Alicia's Percentile Rankings in TOTAL Reading for her School, District, State, and Nation

Alicia's Percentile Rank in relation to other 5th graders **at Washington School**	45%ile (requires additional calculations)
Alicia's Percentile Rank in relation to other 5th graders **in the district**	51%ile (requires additional calculations)
Alicia's Percentile Rank in relation to other 5th graders **in the state**	55%ile (requires additional calculations)
Alicia's Percentile Rank in relation to other 5th graders **across the nation**	60%tile (from Figure 8.17)

mean at the center and then measures "how many standard deviation units a person is from the mean and whether the person is above or below the mean" (Pyrczak, 1996, p. 81).

One common type of standard score is the z-score which uses the scale we see in Figure 8.19. Using this scale, if Adam scored at the population mean, he would have a standard z-score of 0, while Jennifer who scored one standard deviation above the mean for the population, would obtain a standard z-score of +1. Finally, if Wesley scored one standard deviation below the mean, his standard z-score would equal -1.

Figure 8.19 The z-score scale

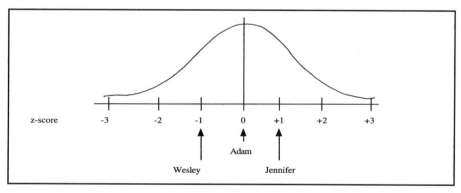

Although z-scores can prove especially helpful in comparing across tests, most publishers of standardized achievement tests don't report z-scores. Rather they have created their own versions of a standard score, ones that don't include negative scores. (Many people feel that reporting standard scores such as -1.2 only confuses and demeans people.)

Figure 8.20 shows the standard score scale created for students taking the *Iowa Tests of Basic Skills*® during the spring.

Figure 8.20 Iowa Test of Basic Skills® Standard Score Scale

Grade	K	1	2	3	4	5	6	7	8	9	10
Standard Score	130	150	168	185	200	214	227	239	250	260	268

Alicia Wilson's standard score of 223 (next to ❸) on the "Vocabulary" subtest means that her performance is just about like that of a typical 6th grade student in spring of the school year. Thus, Alicia performed well on the "Vocabulary" subtest.

8.33—NCE's or Normal Curve Equivalents

❹ on the Service 1 printout (Figure 8.17) marks the listing for Alicia's Normal Curve Equivalent (also known as NCE) scores. Test makers recently developed this version of a standard score primarily to meet the reporting needs of various federally-funded programs such as Title I. The Normal Curve Equivalent standard scale has a mean of 50 with a standard deviation of 21.06. (You can refresh your knowledge of means and standard deviations by reviewing sections 5.8 and 5.14.) Normal Curve Equivalent scores roughly equal percentile ranks, but not quite. Alicia's NCE score of 54 on the "Reference Materials" subtest means that she scored better than about 56% of the students who took the test.

8.34—Grade Equivalents

Now find ❺ on the Service 1 printout (Figure 8.17). The second listing for Alicia Wilson is her grade equivalent score—perhaps the most widely used and *misunderstood score.* Alicia took the ITBS during the seventh month of the 5th grade. Thus her 5.7 grade equivalent score for "Maps and Diagrams" has Alicia scoring at grade level. Alicia's score of a grade equivalent of 9.4 on the "Math Computation" subtest indicates that she scored as well as a typical 9th grader in the fifth month of the school year would score on *this* test—Grade 5, Level 11, Form K. We cannot say that Alicia is doing 9th grade work in math because there are many things that a 9th grader has learned that are not on this 5th grade test! Because people so often misunderstand grade equivalent scores, we suggest that you *not* use them to report tests results to students and their parents.

8.35—Quartiles

Now let's turn our attention to Figure 8.21 which shows a sample of the Evaluator's Summary Reports available for the *Iowa Tests of Basic Skills®*. Find the section marked ❻. This section reports the number of students in the school who score in each quartile of the national norming group. Like the national percentile rankings we discussed in section 8.33, test publishers create quartiles by first ranking all the students' scores and then dividing the distribution of scores into four equal parts, with 25% of the students in each quartile. Thus, the four quartiles include students who scored within the following percentile rankings:

Figure 8.21 Printout for Services 24a and 24b: Evaluator's Summary Reports

Iowa Tests of Basic Skills

Service 24a:
Building Evaluator's Summary

Building:	WASHINGTON	Grade:	5
Bldg Code:	99C001101	Form:	M
System:	PORT CHARLES	Test Date:	4/96
Norms:	SPRING 1995	Page:	12
Order No.:	901-A4000052-00-002		

	Reading: Vocabulary	Reading: Comprehension	Reading: Total	Language: Spelling	Language: Capitalization	Language: Punctuation	Language: Usage/Express	Language: Total	Mathematics: Concepts/Estim.	Mathematics: Probs/Data Interp.	Mathematics: Total *	Core Total *	Social Studies	Science	Sources of Info.: Maps & Diagrams	Sources of Info.: Ref. Mat'ls	Sources of Info.: Total	Composite *	Math Computation
Student Count	51	51	51	51	51	51	51	51	51	51	51	51	51	51	51	51	51	51	51
Grade Equivalent																			
Average	7.21	7.41	7.29	6.66	6.96	7.26	8.14	7.18	7.21	8.50	7.43	7.20	7.76	8.30	8.64	7.85	8.20	7.57	6.83
Standard Deviation	1.83	2.14	1.78	2.28	3.13	2.97	2.84	2.46	1.97	2.62	1.81	1.80	2.19	2.72	3.04	2.56	2.64	1.87	1.67
GE of Average SS	7.1	7.2	7.2	6.5	6.6	7.1	7.9	6.9	7.0	8.2	7.3	7.1	7.6	8.0	8.4	7.6	8.0	7.4	6.7
PR of Average SS:																			
National Student Norms	74	68	72	61	61	64	70	64	72	77	73	70	72	75	77	73	75	73	67
National School Norms	89	84	88	72	66	73	86	77	87	95	87	84	87	93	94	88	92	88	81
High GE	12.3	12.4	11.9	12.9	14.0	13.9	13.9	13.3	12.1	13.3	11.6	12.2	12.8	13.6	13.7	12.8	12.8	12.2	10.2
Low GE	4.0	1.4	3.9	3.3	3.1	3.0	1.8	3.7	3.0	3.5	4.3	4.5	4.2	3.4	2.8	3.6	3.5	4.4	3.9
90th Percentile	9.80	10.31	10.25	10.40	12.42	12.87	12.54	11.94	9.25	12.15	10.24	9.34	10.65	11.83	12.83	11.15	12.11	10.24	9.40
75th Percentile	8.13	8.86	8.36	7.38	8.62	8.64	9.81	8.28	8.33	10.04	8.39	8.31	9.21	10.81	11.86	9.80	10.28	8.58	7.82
50th Percentile - Median	7.18	7.36	6.89	6.30	5.89	6.20	7.32	6.63	6.83	8.28	7.50	7.00	7.57	7.70	8.48	7.32	8.00	7.34	6.61
25th Percentile	5.99	5.84	6.03	5.17	4.61	4.74	6.02	5.53	5.94	6.31	6.03	6.19	5.71	6.30	6.04	5.73	6.03	6.04	5.54
10th Percentile	5.01	5.36	5.41	4.26	3.71	4.35	4.91	4.29	5.36	5.55	5.21	4.82	5.16	5.08	4.96	4.89	4.76	5.06	4.71
Standard Score																			
Average	230.6	231.4	231.1	222.3	225.1	229.0	239.9	229.1	229.0	243.2	232.4	230.9	236.1	241.0	244.6	236.3	240.4	235.0	224.8
Standard Deviation	20.6	25.5	20.0	26.4	36.6	34.1	32.5	27.9	23.0	28.3	20.4	19.8	24.1	29.5	33.5	28.5	28.3	21.0	20.6
National Stanine																			
Average	6.3	6.0	6.2	5.4	5.3	5.5	6.2	5.7	6.1	6.7	6.3	6.1	6.2	6.3	6.5	6.3	6.5	6.4	5.9
Standard Deviation	1.6	1.5	1.5	1.7	1.6	1.5	1.5	1.5	1.7	1.7	1.6	1.4	1.4	1.7	1.7	1.7	1.6	1.5	1.6
Normal Curve Equivalent																			
Average	63.6	60.2	62.4	54.4	53.9	55.6	61.1	57.2	61.7	67.0	63.7	61.3	62.6	64.0	65.3	62.8	65.0	63.6	58.0
Standard Deviation	16.8	15.9	14.9	17.8	16.9	16.6	16.2	16.6	18.3	17.8	16.6	15.4	14.7	16.7	18.7	18.1	17.9	16.1	16.6
N in PR Group ❻																			
75-99	27	19	18	12	16	18	21	14	22	26	26	19	23	23	26	24	26	25	19
50-74	12	19	25	19	12	13	20	22	19	16	14	22	14	20	14	13	15	15	12
25-49	11	11	6	13	17	17	8	8	5	8	8	9	13	5	9	10	9	11	16
1-24	1	2	1	7	6	3	2	7	5	1	3	1	1	3	2	4	1		4
% in PR Group ❼ — National																			
75-99 — 25%	52.9	37.3	37.3	23.5	31.4	35.3	41.2	27.5	43.1	51.0	51.0	37.3	45.1	45.1	51.0	47.1	51.0	49.0	37.3
50-74 — 25%	23.5	37.3	49.0	37.3	23.5	25.5	39.2	43.1	37.3	31.4	27.5	43.1	27.5	39.2	27.5	25.5	29.4	29.4	23.5
25-49 — 25%	21.6	21.6	11.8	25.5	33.3	33.3	15.7	15.7	9.8	15.7	15.7	17.6	25.5	9.8	17.6	19.6	17.6	21.6	31.4
1-24 — 25%	2.0	3.9	2.0	13.7	11.8	5.9	3.9	13.7	9.8	2.0	5.9	2.0	2.0	5.9	3.9	7.8	2.0	[illegible]	7.8
N in Sta9 Group ❽																			
7, 8, 9	22	17	19	12	11	12	21	12	22	26	24	16	23	23	26	24	25	21	19
4, 5, 6	28	32	31	33	34	36	29	36	24	24	25	35	28	25	23	25	25	30	29
1, 2, 3	1	2	1	6	6	3	1	3	5	1	2	[illegible]		3	2	2	1	[illegible]	3
% in Sta9 Group ❾ — National																			
7, 8, 9 — 23%	43.1	33.3	37.3	23.5	21.6	23.5	41.2	23.5	43.1	51.0	47.1	31.4	45.1	45.1	51.0	47.1	49.0	41.2	37.3
4, 5, 6 — 54%	54.9	62.7	60.8	64.7	66.7	70.6	56.9	70.6	47.1	47.1	49.0	68.6	54.9	49.0	45.1	49.0	49.0	58.8	56.9
1, 2, 3 — 23%	2.0	3.9	2.0	11.8	11.8	5.9	2.0	5.9	9.8	2.0	3.9	[illegible]		5.9	3.9	3.9	2.0	[illegible]	5.9

*Includes Mathematics Computation

Top or 4th quartile	Includes students who scored at the	75%ile to 99%ile
3rd quartile	Includes students who scored at the	50%ile to 74%ile
2nd quartile	Includes students who scored at the	25%ile to 49%ile
Bottom or 1st quartile	Includes students who scored at the	1%ile to 24%ile

As you can see in the printout in Figure 8.21, of the 51 students at Washington School who took the test, 27 scored in the top quartile on the "Vocabulary" subtest, while only 1 student scored in the bottom quartile.

Just below these numbers in the section marked ❼ in Figure 8.21, the printout shows the percentage of students at Washington School who scored in the various quartiles. As you can see, 52.9% of the students scored in the top national quartile even though you would expect only 25% of the students to score that well. This means that the students at Washington School performed very well on the "Vocabulary" subtest.

8.36—Stanines

Like percentiles and quartiles, stanines also rely on ranking scores. This time, however, the test publishers divide the distribution of scores into nine parts. Indeed, stanine is short for "standard nine point scale." Stanine 1 captures the lowest 4% of the scores and Stanine 9 includes the top 4% of the scores. Starting at the bottom of the distribution, the percentages are as follows:

Stanine	Percent of Scores
9	4%
8	7%
7	12%
6	17%
5	20%
4	17%
3	12%
2	7%
1	4%

To explore stanines, find ❽ on the printout in Figure 8.21. On the "Vocabulary" subtest, 22 out of the 51 Washington School students scored in the top three stanines (Stanines 7, 8, and 9), while only 1 child scored in the bottom three stanines. Notice that the printout writes "Sta9" for stanine.

Now look at ❾ on the printout in Figure 8.21. This compares the percentage of Washington School students with the expected percentage for each group of stanines. While 23% of the national norming group scored in the top three stanines, a whopping 43.1% of the Washington students scored that high on the "Vocabulary" subtest. The percentages for the middle stanines are right at what we would expect, while the Washington percentage of students scoring in the bottom three stanines is way below what we would expect. This shows that Washington students, overall, score above national expectations on the "Vocabulary" subtest.

Not only can we make local, state, and national comparisons using stanines, we can also attach the following adjectives to each stanine and use these ratings to communicate with parents and other audiences. People often find such ratings more meaningful. Rather than saying "10% of the students scored at the ninth stanine," we could say, "10% of the students scored in the very outstanding category" and people would understand us instantly.

Stanine	Description
9	Very outstanding
8	Outstanding
7	Greatly/considerably above average
6	Slightly above average
5	Average
4	Slightly below average
3	Greatly/considerable below average
2	Poor
1	Very poor

8.37—Local Norms

Thus far, we have talked about test developers establishing percentiles, quartiles, and stanines by using the norming group. With some scoring services, you can ask for percentiles, quartiles, and stanines based on your students only. To establish what is known as *local norms*, the scoring service rank orders the scores of *your* students and then establishes the percentiles, quartiles, and stanines based on this ranking rather than the ranking of the norming group.

8.38—Gain Scores

Let's now look at a final sample printout: Service 11: Pre/Post Report available from Riverside Publishing, the publishers of the *Iowa Tests of Basic Skills*®. (See Figure 8.22.) This testing report includes information that you can use in the pre/posttest evaluation designs we introduced in chapter 6, section 6.6, and will discuss more fully in chapter 9. While we use the language of "change scores," the ITBS employs the term "gain scores." Both terms mean the same thing. Gain scores come in handy, particularly when we evaluate the effectiveness of a new strategy and want to see if a significant difference exists between the achievement of those students who got the innovation and those who didn't.

For example, let's say that the fifth grade teachers at Northeast Elementary have spent the year using an innovative reading program while the fifth grade teachers at Southwest Elementary across town continued to use the usual program. To ascertain the effectiveness of the innovative reading program, the Northeast Elementary teachers could perform a statistical test of significance comparing their school's mean gain score of + 11.1 on the Total Reading Test of the ITBS (marked ⑩ in Figure 8.22) with the mean gain score for the students at Southwest School. If they found a statistically significant difference, they could reasonably conclude that the innovation worked (assuming that all other factors were similar between the two groups of students).

Figure 8.22 Service 11: Pre/Post Report

Posttest		Pretest	
Test:	ITBS 5/94		ITBS
Test Date:	04/15/94		03/15/93
Normal Date:	SPRING 1992		SPRING 1992
Order No.:	000-A5100094-00-002		000-A5100093-00-002

Service 11: Pre/Post Match
List Report of Student Scores
Score Reported: Normal Curve Equivalent
Chapter 1 Reading

Building:	NORTHEAST ELEMENTARY	
Bldg Code:	PORT CHARLES	
System:	000-A5100094-00-002	Grade: 5
Order No.:		Page: 19

Student Name	Birth Date	G/Sex	Grade		READING VOCABULARY	READING ADV SKILLS/COMPREHENSION	READING TOTAL	LISTENING	SPELLING	CAPITALIZATION	PUNCTUATION	LANG ADV SKILLS USAGE/EXPRESS	LANG TOTAL	MATH CONCEPTS/ESTIM	MATH ADV SKILLS PROBS/DATA INTERP	MATH TOTAL	CORE TOTAL	SOCIAL STUDIES	SCIENCE	MAPS & DIAGRAMS	REF MATLS	SOURCES TOTAL	COMPOSITE	WORD ANALYSIS	MATH COMPUTATION
TRIMBLE TRAVIS ID=255433932 C1=R	3/83	F	5 11 POST		30	49	41		81	65	78	52	69	62	47	53	56	29	32	36	32	34	43		58
TRIMBLE TRAVIS ID=255433932 C1=	3/83	F	5 10 PRE		4	28	12		75	83	80	47	73	44	38	41	46	42	32	24	50	36	40		44
			GAIN		+26	+21	+29		+6	-18	-2	+5	-4	+18	+9	+12	+10	-13	0	+12	-18	-2	+3		+14
WILLIAMS TAMECA ID=253416538 C1=R	5/82	F	5 11 POST		10	36	21		46	70	47	39	52	38	44	41	38	29	39	24	43	32	35		39
WILLIAMS TAMECA ID=253416538 C1=	5/82	F	5 10 PRE		1	30	10		41	67	58	40	54	25	41	33	34	34	40	24	43	32	33		42
			GAIN		+9	+6	+11		+5	+3	-11	-1	-2	+13	+3	+8	+4	-5	-1	0	0	0	+2		-3
WILSON BOBBY ID=254439231 C1=R	1/83	M	5 11 POST		26	36	31		25	28	36	27	26	33	33	32	28	35	35	33	32	31	29		5
WILSON BOBBY ID=254439231 C1=	1/83	M	5 10 PRE		22	24	20		15	32	24	14	16	16	44	31	20	31	16	30	25	26	19		14
			GAIN		+4	+12	+11		+10	-4	+12	+13	+10	+17	-11	+1	+8	+4	+19	+3	+7	+5	+10		-9
WINTER DERRICK ID=037541746 C1=R	11/82	M	5 11 POST		26	38	32		31	22	16	7	13	28	33	30	23	32	29	43	37	40	27		37
WINTER DERRICK ID=037541746 C1=	11/82	M	5 10 PRE		25	30	27		26	32	20	9	17	9	24	15	17	27	23	24	29	25	18		23
			GAIN		+1	+8	+5		+5	-10	-4	-2	-4	+19	+9	+15	+6	+5	+6	+19	+8	+15	+9		+14
WONG BRIAN ID=259450537 C1=R	7/83	M	5 11 POST		37	32	32		27	31	36	15	23	33	30	31	27	20	23	24	25	23	22		41
WONG BRIAN ID=259450537 C1=	7/83	M	5 10 PRE		4	12	1		39	46	51	30	41	34	27	30	24	25	12	28	11	11	18		28
			GAIN		+33	+18	+31		-12	-15	-15	-15	-18	-1	+3	+1	+3	-5	+11	-4	+14	+14	+4		+13

Averages for Grade 5

		Reading			Listening	Spelling	Capital	Punct	Lang Adv	Lang Total	Concepts	Math Adv	Math Total	Core	Social	Science	Maps	Ref	Sources	Composite	Word Anal	Math Comp
Posttest only	N-Count Mean S.D.				⑩											29.0	32.0 2.0				14.0		40
Posttest and Pretest	N-Count Post Mean Pre Mean Gain Post S.D. Pre S.D. Gain S.D.	40 23.7 13.0 +10.7 1.6 9.7 1.9	40 30.3 22.1 +8.2 9.1 10.4 1.3	40 25.3 14.2 +11.1 10.5 9.6 .9		40.7 33.4 +7.3 18.7 17.4 1.3	35.3 34.8 +.5 20.1 20.8 2.8	36.4 35.6 +.8 19.2 19.2 .2	26.9 26.4 +.5 13.4 11.7 1.7	32.4 29.4 +3.0 16.1 17.6 1.5	27.9 21.6 +6.3 13.0 13.7 4.8	30.8 23.4 +7.4 7.1 11.5 3.2	27.9 20.7 +7.2 15.3 15.2 3.4	27.3 19.3 +8.0 13.1 13.0 3.0	27.8 23.9 +3.9 11.9 11.8 3.1	24.7 25.7 -1.0 13.1 10.1 3.0	31.0 23.5 +7.5 11.8 11.3 3.6	28.7 26.9 +1.8 15.0 15.0 1.2	28.9 23.1 +5.8 13.0 13.0 1.7	25.1 18.9 +6.2 12.3 12.5 1.7		29.8 23.6 +6.2 15.9 13.9 2.0
Pretest only	N-Count Mean S.D.	18.0 11.5	18.0	18.0		18.0	15.0	16.0	18.0	9.0	35.0	21.0	26.0	10.5 9.5	19.0	32.0	15.0	24.0 5.0	22.5 10.5	16.0 11.5		16.0

8.39—Issue Box

**Getting Data Reported from the
Test People in the Ways *You* Need It.**

Giving a standardized achievement test to your students costs a great deal of money and time. Therefore, you should get your money's worth. Unfortunately, many educators don't know how to get the data they need from the testing company. Often times, the scoring service will send back a summary printout that really doesn't meet your needs. Therefore, we suggest that before you spend the money and time to give a standardized achievement test you clearly delineate how you plan to use the results. Then talk with the testing company to negotiate getting the data reported in a way most useful to you.

For example, let's say your school wants to use the results from this year's and next year's *Iowa Tests of Basic Skills®* to take stock of the curriculum. You particularly want to identify the strengths and gaps in your curriculum by analyzing how well your students scored on specific items measuring skills in mathematics. This means that you need to know how many students answered each item correctly on the math subtest. You contact the company representative for Riverside Publishing (a Houghton Mifflin Company), which publishes the *Iowa Tests of Basic Skills®,* and find out that you can get that information by ordering Scoring Service 3 listed below.

Indeed, the *Iowa Tests of Basic Skills* (1996) offers the following scoring services:

  1* Student Criterion-Referenced Skills Analysis (Figure 8.17 shows a sample printout of this report.)
  2 Student Profile Narrative (Parent or Teacher copy)
  3 Building Criterion-Referenced Skills Analysis
  4 Superintendent's Report (Group Narrative, Test Graphs, Skill Graphs, and Questionnaire Data)
  6 Group Item Analysis
  7 Counselor's Report
  8 Press-on Labels
  9 List Report of Student Scores with Class, Building, and System Averages Report
10 Frequency Distribution
11 Pre/Post Report (Figure 8.22 shows a sample of this report.)
12 Individual and Group Performance Profiles
13 Class, Building and System Averages
14 Ranked Lists by Skills, Tests
16 Student Data on Disk with Student Data Management System Option

18 Coded Summaries and Graphs
21 Class/Building/System Diagnostic Report
22 Summary of Achievement by Ability
23 Class Item Response Record
24 Evaluator's Summary Reports (Figure 8.21 shows a sample of this printout.)
25 Bar Code Identification Service
29 Customized Skills Report
30 Comparative Norms Reports
33 Individual/Group Longitudinal Profile
34 National Performance Standards Report

* These numbers refer to the designations assigned by Riverside Publishing to the various scoring options.

Testing services will often honor out-of-the-ordinary requests for data if you let them know in advance. They will, of course, charge an extra fee. The bottom line is this: ask for what you need. Most often the testing companies will find a way to help you.

Note: If you work in a district with several schools, often someone at the district office makes the decision about the format the testing company will use in reporting scores. This person may be the testing coordinator, a curriculum director, or assistant superintendent. Visit with this person and request that the test results come back in a format most useful to your needs.

8.40—Analyzing Test Data

Once you have organized and summarized your taking stock data, you can begin analyzing your data. Continuing our focus on standardized achievement tests, in this section we will give examples showing various ways to analyze test results. We will discuss five specific techniques for analyzing test data:

- Comparing test scores over time to see whether or not trends emerge.
- Disaggregating test results based on various student characteristics.
- Ascertaining whether or not a relationship exists between two variables.
- Building confidence intervals around means.
- Determining whether or not a significant difference exists between two groups.

8.41—How Do Test Scores Compare Over Time?

Taking stock of your school often means looking for trends over time. A good way to spot trends is to plot data from at least three observations on a graph. (Two data points do not make a trend!) For example, Figure 8.23 shows the number of community service hours students performed over a three-month period, while Figure 8.24 shows the school enrollment count taken on September 1 for the past four years. Figure 8.25 shows how you can graph qualitative or word data over time.

Figure 8.23 Number of Community Service Hours Performed by Students Over a Three-month Period

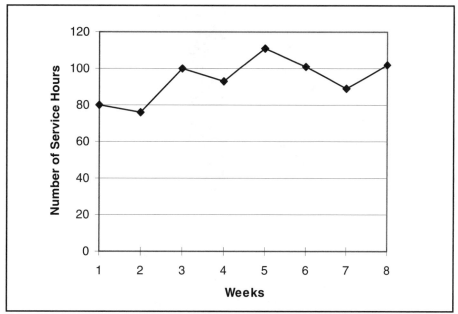

Figure 8.24 School Enrollment Counts on September 1 for the Past Four Years

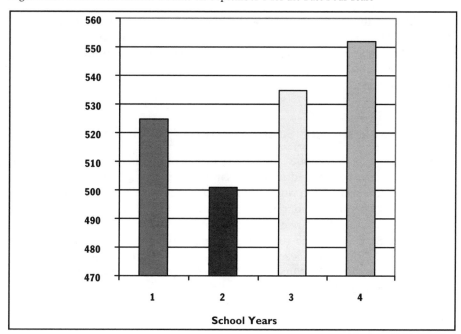

Figure 8.25 Number of Students Who Indicated That They Feel Emotionally Safe at School Comparing Data From Last Three Years

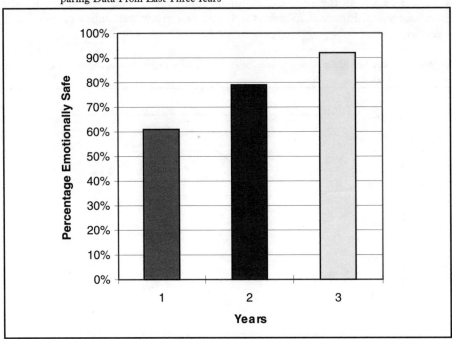

When comparing average achievement scores over time you can do it two ways:

1. Track the same group of students over time as they move from grade to grade.

2. Compare the achievement test data for students in the same grade over time.

When taking stock, we suggest that you do both so that you can obtain a richer portrait of student achievement in your school as measured on standardized test. You can do these comparisons of achievement across time whether you use a norm-referenced or a criterion-referenced test, although the procedures are slightly different for each type of test.

8.42—Tracking the Same Students Over Time

If you want to get a feel about the quality of teaching and learning within your school or district, you should track the same group of students over time. This method requires some extra work, but it allows you to see how well you're doing with students who stay in your school or district long enough for you and your colleagues to make a difference in their learning.

Figure 8.26 shows the reading achievement scores on the commercially available standardized achievement test (C-ASAT) for the same group of students at Beverly's school as they moved from 6th grade to 8th grade. As you can see, the graph line stays rather flat with a slight rise in the 8th grade year. This means that the students, on average, scored basically the same in relation to the norming group over the three years.

Despite the flatness of the line, this graph really indicates strength. Because the average reading achievement scores for all three years are slightly above the national norms, we would expect the scores to remain relatively the same over time. We should worry only if scores take a significant dip from one year to the next. Such a dip would not necessarily mean the teachers taught less or students learned less. Many things from a change in testing format to inadequate curriculum or even sheer chance can cause a dip in scores. Should your school experience a significant drop in test scores, we suggest that you (and your school board) resist the temptation of grabbing at the first solutions that come to mind. Instead, we strongly recommend that you turn immediately to chapter 10 in this book and use the Targeted Problem-Solving Process to discover the reasons for the significant drop in scores and find solutions that *really* address the problem.

Figure 8.26 Time Series of Same Group of Kids Over Three Years on Commercially Available Standardized Achievement Test (C-ASAT) on Reading Achievement

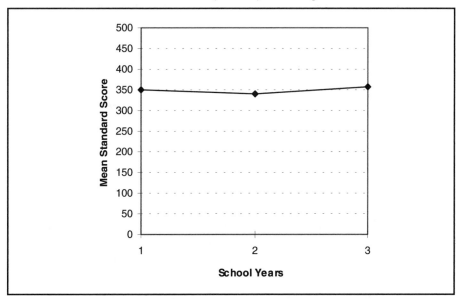

You're probably wondering how we can graph these achievement data over the three years when students take a different form of the ITBS each year. As you might guess, we can't simply graph the average raw score or even the percentage correct because the test the students took in 6th grade might have 30 possible right, while the test they took in the 8th grade might include 50 possible right.

To equalize everything, we graph *mean standard scores.* Using mean standard scores works well even when students took a totally different brand of norm-referenced test from one year to the next. For example, you can use standard scores to plot the achievement scores of student who took the *Stanford Achievement Test* during their 6th grade year and the *Iowa Tests of Basic Skills®* in their 7th grade year. To get the mean standard score, we must transform the raw scores into standard scores. Actually, the testing company will do this for you, or you can calculate standard scores by reading the Technical Manual that comes with the standardized norm referenced test. Standard scores rely on two measures from descriptive statistics: the arithmetic mean and the standard deviation for the norming group. The most common standard score reported by testing companies is the *Normal Curve Equivalent (NCE)*.

8.43—Comparing Achievement Test Data Within the Same Grade Over Time

A second way to track achievement data over time involves looking at the mean achievement scores for the same grade level over several years. If you're plotting mean test scores from the same test over time, you simply need to use the reported mean score, because you're comparing apples to apples. But what if you're comparing apples to oranges? What if the 6th graders took the *Stanford Achievement Test* one year and the next year took the *California Achievement Test*? Once again, standard scores come to the rescue. You simply transform the students' scores into standard scores and calculate the mean standard score. You then plot the mean standard score for each year.

As with most things in life, plotting student achievement at the same grade level over time has its advantages and disadvantages. The foremost advantage is that it's easy to do. Most testing companies report overall scores and you simply have to sift through the past years' printouts to make your graph. However, you must always contend with possibility that one group of 6th grade students differs significantly in ability and experiences from another group of 6th grade students.

8.44—What Does Disaggregating the Data Tell Us?

Rather than simply examining overall mean scores, you may want to also look at the achievement of particular groups of students. Sometimes disaggregating (separating out student scores according to various relevant student characteristics) can reveal new insights and give you an even richer picture of your school's achievement. You may want to disaggregate your standardized achievement data so you can answer questions such as:

- Do students who have attended our school all year perform differently than those who have attended for only 9 weeks or less?
- Do boys score differently than girls?
- How do the scores of students receiving special education services compare with those who don't receive such services?
- Do students with more than 10 absences in a semester score differently than those who have less than 4 absences a semester?
- Do students who qualify for free or reduced lunches score differently than those who don't qualify?'

   Caution: As you disaggregate data to examine how certain groups of students score on the test, please don't fall prey to faulty assumptions that expect that certain students, just because they are boys, come from low SES homes, or speak a primary language other than English, should perform in a particular way on a standardized test. The reason for disaggregating data is not to identify students and then hold differing achievement expectations for them, but rather to see if we are systematically under serving and failing to educate certain groups of students. If certain groups of students show under achievement, we can then find strategies to rectify the situation. We should not, however, simply accept statements like: "You really can't expect much from this group of kids. Their background simply gets in the way!"

You can disaggregate achievement data (and other data as well) in many ways. Figures 8.27, 8.28, and 8.29 illustrate several ways the teachers at Beverly's school disaggregated the achievement data to look at how various groups of students performed on the commercially available standardized achievement test (C-ASAT).

Figure 8.27 Standardized Achievement Scores Disaggregated by Number of Absences in a Semester

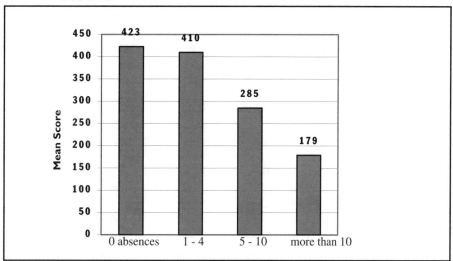

Figure 8.28 Standardized Achievement Scores Disaggregated by Gender

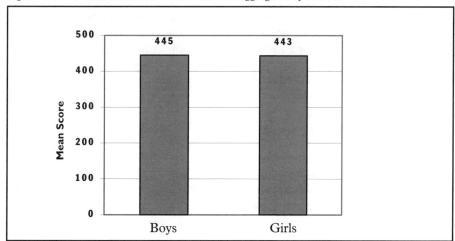

Figure 8.29 Standardized Achievement Scores Disaggregated by Socioeconomic Status (SES)

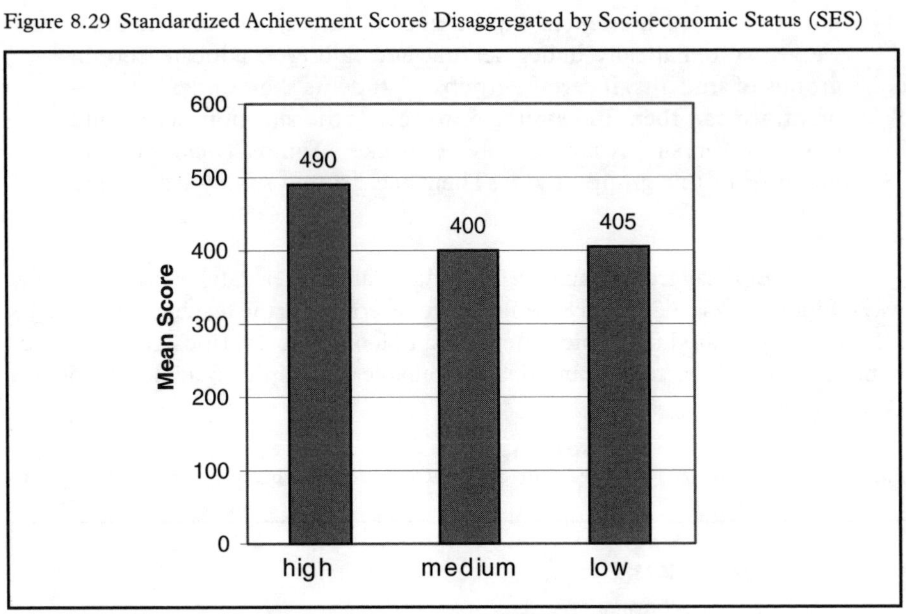

No matter how you decide to disaggregate the data, you should always try to do so in ways that seem relevant. For example, if your school has a high student mobility rate, then separating out scores by length of enrollment might make sense. At other times, disaggregating data may prove useless, particularly when the disaggregated group is so small that changes in just one student's achievement score radically alters the mean score for the entire group. For instance, if a school has only three students whose primary language is not English, tracking the mean score of these three students versus the mean score of the rest of the school may provide little useful information.

8.45—Tracking Criterion-Referenced Data Over Time

Not only can you track norm-referenced scores over time, you can also track criterion-referenced test results. As with norm-referenced tests, you can observe the same group of students as they move from grade to grade, or you can examine achievement at the same grade level across the years. However, instead of looking at the mean score or standard score, you plot the percentage of students meeting mastery. Figure 8.30 provides an example of how to plot levels of mastery as students moved from 4th to 8th grade.

8.46—Does a Relationship Exist?

Looking for relationships between two variables within your data is another way to find answers to your taking stock questions. As you will recall from chapter 5, you can examine both quantitative and qualitative data for relationships or correlations. Since we're focusing our attention in this chapter on standardized achievement data, we want to give you some examples of how you can look for correlations within test results.

Figure 8.30 Percentage of Current 8th Grade Students Attaining Mastery on the State Criterion-Referenced Reading Assessment Tracking Same Group of Students

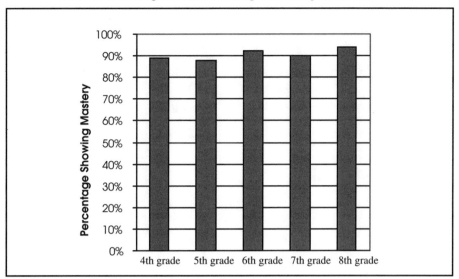

Let's begin, however, with a brief review about correlations within quantitative data. We describe how two variables co-relate along two dimensions: direction and magnitude. In a direct or positive correlation, both variables move in the same direction (↑↑ or ↓↓). For example, as reading scores go up so do math scores. In an inverse or negative relationship, the variables move in opposite directions (↑↓). For example, as student absences go up, test scores go down (See Figure 8.31).

The magnitude or strength of a correlation ranges from 0 to 1, with 0 meaning no correlation and 1 meaning a perfect correlation. So a -.90 correlation between absences and test scores, means that there exists within that group of scores a strong negative correlation between those two variables. Indeed, Figure 8.31 displays the scatterplot for this correlation.

Some possible relationships you might want to pursue include the correlation between:

- Various subject area subtests on the tests:

   Do math scores correlate with science scores?

- Scores on one achievement test with scores on another achievement test given to the same students:

   Do student scores on the reading subtest on the *Stanford Achievement Test* correlate with student scores on the *Gates-McGinity Standardized Test of Reading?*

- Standardized test scores and some other relevant variable:

   Do test scores correlate with absences?

This list could go on and on. We have only tried to prime the pump. Your needs, curiosity, available time, and energy level will dictate the possible correlations you investigate.

Figure 8.31 Scatterplot Showing a -.90 Correlation Between Absences and Math Test Scores

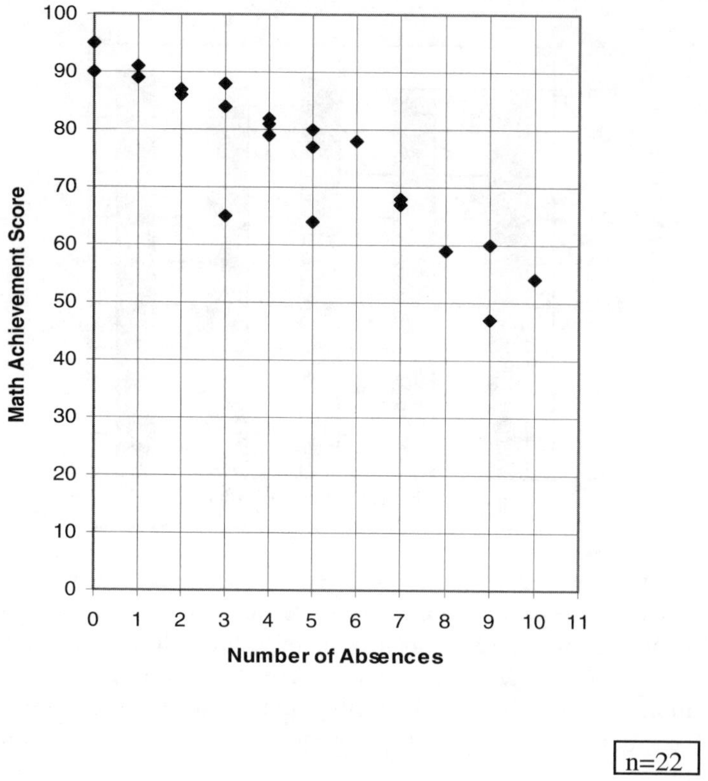

8.47—How Confident Can We Be?

If every hour on the hour throughout the day you took your blood pressure and recorded it, you would see fluctuations. One time you might get a 110 over 70, while another time you might get a 115 over 70. In fact, it is possible that each measurement will result in a different number. So what's your *true* blood pressure? Well, physicians have answered that question by designating a band of numbers rather than just one number as normal.

This same logic should apply to standardized test scores as well. Unfortunately, too often the media, the public, school board members, and even educators take the reported mean score for a group of students as an exact and true measure of student achievement. In reality, that one mean test score is only an *estimate* of the students' true test performance. If we gave similar (but not the same) achievement tests one week, two weeks, and three weeks apart, we would most likely get three different mean scores. Just like our blood pressure example, the true mean achievement score for your school lies within a band of numbers we call the confidence interval.

Let's say a reading specialist gives Shane, a 6th grader, an individual reading test. He scores 105 on the test. The mean score for the norming group is 100 with a standard error of the mean equal to 6.5. [The technical manual of any commercially available test should include the mean and standard error of the mean.] The reading specialist meets with Shane's parents and rather than simply telling them that Shane scored 105 (slightly above the mean), she decides to report the score with a confidence interval built around it. She wants the parents to understand that Shane's score of 105 is only an *estimate* and that his true reading score would fall with a band of numbers.

Statisticians have determined that the formula:

SCORE + and - [1.96 x the standard error of the mean]

will tell us, with a 95% confidence level, the range within which we could expect Shane's true reading score to fall. Applying the formula to Shane's score, we would expect, with a 95% confidence level, that Shane's true reading score would fall between 117.74 and 92.26.

$$105 + \text{ and } - [1.96 \times 6.5] = 105 + 12.74 = 117.74$$
$$105 - 12.74 = 92.26$$

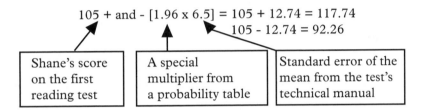

| Shane's score on the first reading test | A special multiplier from a probability table | Standard error of the mean from the test's technical manual |

You're probably thinking that this is a rather wide band (117.74 to 92.26). And, it is. But if we want to be reasonably sure about our prediction (right 95 times out of 100), Lady Luck requires that we use a wide band. If we want to be even surer with a *99%* confidence level, we would have a band that is even wider.

As you can see from looking at the example with Shane, a single test score is really only an *estimate*. Thus, we would suggest that you report mean test scores as a band of numbers rather than as a single number. Figure 8.32 shows a graph of the 6th grade math scores at Beverly's school tracked over the years using confidence intervals rather than single mean scores. This confidence interval readily communicates to audiences that test scores are not as exact as they might believe.

Generally, we create a 95% confidence interval around a mean score. A confidence interval of 95% means that we are 95% confident that the *true* mean achievement score for this group of students lies within that band. Section 5.17 in chapter 5 gives more information about confidence intervals. Some scoring services will even do these calculations for you if requested.

8.48—Does a Significant Difference Exist?

As you can see in Figure 8.32, the test scores for the 6th graders at Beverly's school experienced a drop from Year 3 to Year 4. Should alarm bells go off? Does this represent a downward spiral? Do these dips in mean achievement scores raise legitimate concerns or did these drops occur simply by chance? Statistics can help us answer these questions. We can use inferential statistics to ascertain whether or not a significant difference exists between the mean achievement score of one year and the mean score of another year.

Figure 8.32 Comparing Five Years of 6th Grade Math Standardized Achievement Scores Displayed Using Confidence Intervals

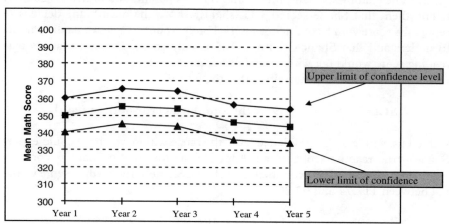

By "significant difference," we mean that the difference between the two means would have occurred by chance only 5% of the time.* Thus, if we find a statistically significant difference between the mean scores of Years 3 and 4, our alarm bells should sound. This drop probably represents a difference that didn't occur by chance and the faculty should try to figure out why the scores dropped.

Conversely, if we find that a statistically significant difference does *not* exist between the mean scores for 1997 and 1998, we can reasonably conclude that the dip occurred by chance. In this case, the faculty should take a stance of watchful waiting—no need to sound the alarm, but the faculty should monitor achievement to make sure that student *achievement* (not just test scores) is not making a slow, gradual decline.

Through the years, we have watched in dismay as central office administrators and school board members have placed increasing pressure on schools to raise test scores. Schools should definitely be held accountable for educating students. However, too often central office administrators and school board members only look at year-to-year fluctuations, differences that may have occurred by chance and *not* because teachers failed to do their jobs.

Let's give two examples. The Betterbegood Middle School charted the mean achievement scores for its 7th graders over a five-year period. As you can see in Figure 8.33, whoever did the graph elected to use only single points rather than confidence intervals. When the central office administrators saw this graph, they expressed dismay about the dip from Year 3 to Year 4 which leveled out in Year 5. They sounded the alarm bells and pressured the school's principal and teachers to raise the scores or else.

When the school's counselor redrew the graph using confidence levels rather than single scores (see Figure 8.34), it became apparent that the dip from Year 3 to Year 4 could have occurred by chance rather than due to a failure on the part of the teachers. Furthermore, inferential statistical analysis showed that no *significant* difference existed between the mean scores for Years 3 and 4. But the alarms set off by the central office had already damaged the school's reputation and morale.

---

*We can also do our calculations to reduce the level of chance to as low as 1%.

Figure 8.33 Comparison of 7th Grade Mean Reading Scores on the Commercially Available Standerdized Achievement Test (C-ASAT) Over a Five-year Period at Betterbegood Middle School Displayed Using Single Mean Scores

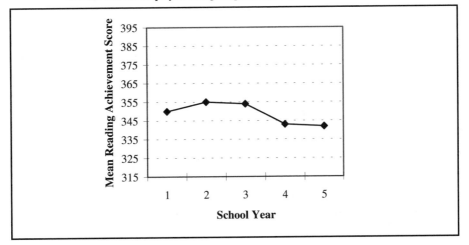

Figure 8.34 Comparison of 7th Grade Mean Reading Scores on the C-ASAT over a Five Year Period at Betterbegood Middle School Displayed Using Confidence Intervals

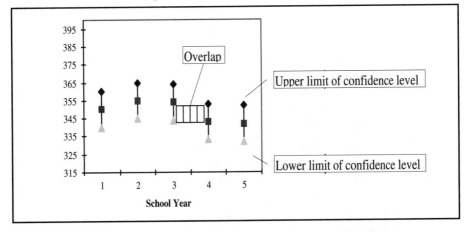

Another middle school in the same area also faced misplaced pressures. As part of the annual "state of the district" report, the superintendent included graphs showing student performance on the commercially-available standardized achievement tests (C-ASAT) over a three-year period. Figure 8.35 shows the graph for Pushedtothemax Middle School. As you can see, the students always scored above national norms. But the school board had set as one of its annual goals: "We will improve test scores in *all* schools." The school board members took one look at the flat line for Pushedtothemax Middle School and demanded improvement. Unfortunately, try as they might, the teachers at Pushedtothemax Middle School may not be able to raise the school's mean achievement test score. Their students already perform well on the test. Moving even a few points up will require an extraordinary effort that might better be spent *educating* students than improving test scores.

Figure 8.35 Comparison of 8th Grade Mean Reading Scores on the C-ASAT Over a Three Year Period at Pushedtothemax Middle School Displayed Using Single Scores

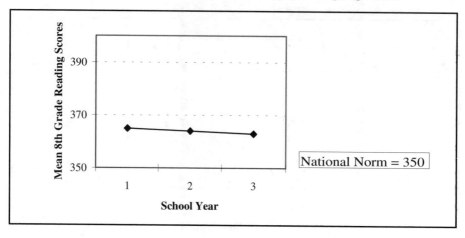

8.49—Beverly Does Step 5

Figure 8.36 Small Step 5 Graphic

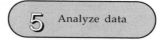

In Step 5, Beverly and her colleagues face three tasks:

- Organizing their data
- Summarizing and describing their data
- Analyzing their data

They begin by organizing all their taking stock data into frequency tables which they then enter into a spread sheet on Excel™. This way they can easily generate the various charts and graphs that will help them understand their findings. Furthermore, they plan to use Excel™ to do the inferential statistical analyses they might need.

Because the newspaper article that made the accusations about Beverly' school relied heavily on standardized achievement scores, Beverly and her colleagues make a graph of the school's results over the past four years on the criterion-referenced state assessment for 6th and 8th graders. They plot the "% mastered" for math, reading, writing, science, and social studies. Because the 7th graders don't take the state assessment, Beverly and her colleagues chart the mean scores on the norm-referenced *Iowa Tests of Basic Skills*® (ITBS) in math, reading, writing, science, social studies. For the 7th grade graph, they decide to chart a band of scores at the 95% confidence level, rather than single point mean scores.

The voluntary accreditation agency requires that the school present disaggregated achievement data as part of its self-study. Therefore, Beverly and her team disaggregate the scores for each grade level by:

- SES
- Gender
- Race and ethnicity
- Level of English language proficiency
- Level of absences

Additionally, they disaggregate the 7th and 8th scores for the past year by length of enrollment, putting students enrolled for less than one year in one group and the rest of the students in another group.

The accreditation self-study also requires that the school track the achievement of the same group of students over time. So, Beverly and her colleagues take the current 7th and 8th graders and trace their achievement back three years. This task presents some unique challenges since the elementary grades take the California Achievement and the 7th grade takes the ITBS®, but the team finds it can compare apples to oranges by using standard scores.

For the past year's ITBS® scores, the teachers create a table reporting the mean, median, and mode, as well as the range and standard deviation. They also constructed a plot comparing the school's scores with those of the norming group on the ITBS®. (See Figure 8.37). Just from "eyeballing", the school's scores don't seen to differ significantly from those of the norming group.

Figure 8.37 Grade Average Percent Correct Compared with National Average Percent Correct

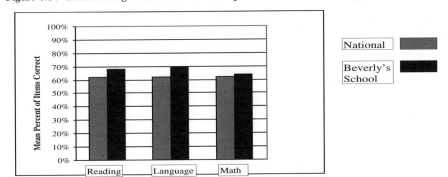

Beverly and her team also decide to showcase their success with those students who scored in the lowest quintiles in math and reading when they were in the 5th grade two years ago. So they create Figure 8.38 showing the number of students who moved from the bottom quintile in 5th grade to the upper quintiles in 7th grade.

Figure 8.38 Current Standing of Those 7th Grade Students Who Scored in the Bottom Quintile in Math Achievement During Their 5th Grade Year

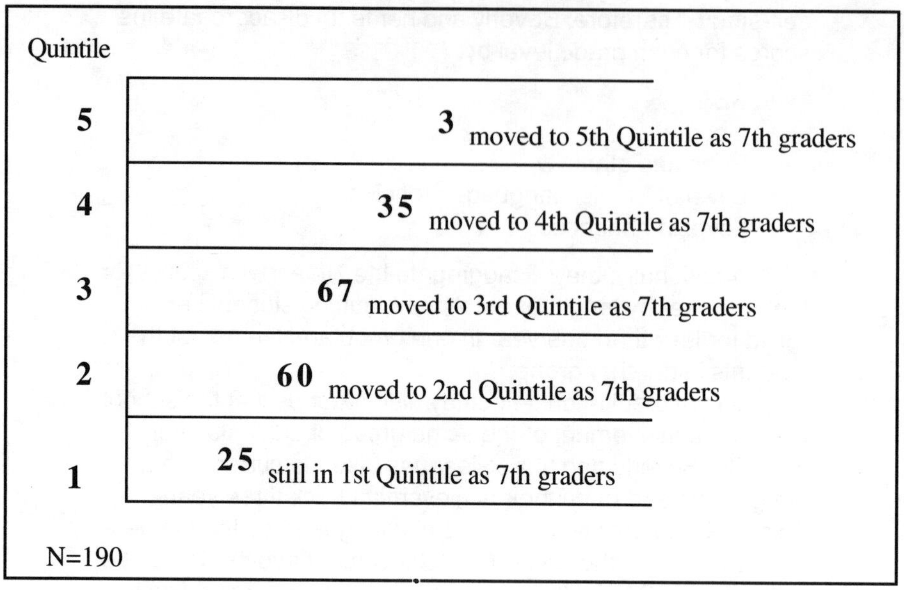

Quintile

5   **3** moved to 5th Quintile as 7th graders

4   **35** moved to 4th Quintile as 7th graders

3   **67** moved to 3rd Quintile as 7th graders

2   **60** moved to 2nd Quintile as 7th graders

1   **25** still in 1st Quintile as 7th graders

N=190

As part of the taking stock process, the team also created charts showing

- Number of suspensions over three years
- Number of different students suspended over the past three years
- Reasons for suspensions
- Number of absentees over three years charted by month
- Unduplicated count of absent students over three years
- Reasons for absences

8.50—Step 6: Interpret the Results

Figure 8.39 Step 6 Graphics

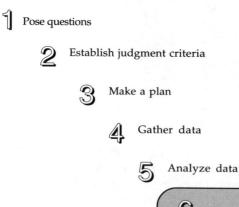

1 Pose questions

2 Establish judgment criteria

3 Make a plan

4 Gather data

5 Analyze data

6 Interpret data

Now, we come to the final step in our taking stock process. In this step, you must wallow around in your findings, looking for patterns. Chapter 6 offers guidance on how to use pictures, calculations and summaries to discover trends. Also in this step, you need to draw conclusions and finally render judgments about the health of your school.

Because of the nature of taking stock, sometimes you might simply describe the here and now, giving facts without judgment. For example, you might simply report the number of community service hours performed by your students without saying whether this is a good or bad thing. At other times, you must judge how well your school stacks up against the standards you set in Step 2. This is especially true if you have taken stock as part of a voluntary or mandated accreditation process.

In most cases, interpreting the results and rendering judgments are fairly straightforward tasks. However, we want to draw your attention to two particular difficulties you might encounter. First, you *may face contradictory evidence.* Suppose the mean reading achievement score on the 7th grade ITBS shows most students reading below grade level, while the mean reading score for these same students on the Gates-McGinity Reading Test shows them reading slightly above grade level. In such a case, we would encourage you to present both pieces of data and then collect a third or even a fourth piece of evidence to help you decide how to call it. Perhaps teacher judgment or a survey of the reading difficulty of books students have read for book reports might shed some light on the reading ability of students.

A second difficulty that you might encounter deals with *making painful judgments.* As you interpret your taking stock results and render judgments, you might have to reveal your school's "dirty laundry." Indeed, when faced with glaring gaps between where you are and where you want to be, you might be inclined to look at your results through rose-colored glasses, ignoring your school's failings. As you take stock, we strongly urge you to honestly delineate *both* your school's strengths *and* weaknesses. Indeed, you might want to refer to weaknesses as gaps or problems because such words connote eventual solutions rather than immutable characteristics.

In our experience, using multiple lenses during interpretation helps. For example, educators can easily generate a wall of problems by looking at their taking stock data, but they can just as easily create of wall of strengths if they put their minds to it. Putting on the "strengths" lens and then switching to the "gaps" lens yields a richer and more useful picture of your school.

8.51—Beverly Does Step 6

Figure 8.40 Small Step 6 Graphic

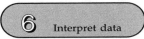

Beverly and the team of volunteers now scrutinize all their findings to the taking stock questions. They look for patterns and state their conclusions, always striving to have at least two credible pieces of evidence supporting each conclusion.

The Taking Stock Committee compiles their findings in a report and distributes the draft to all members of the staff and selected parents, community members, and students to review. The following week, committee members hold feedback sessions in the media center throughout Monday and Thursday so that they can get the reaction of staff members to the report. They also hold a before-school coffee and an evening chat session so parents and community members can give feedback.

In addition to the self-study report, the accreditation process also requires that the school staff create a document showing the staff's consensus about the school's standing on each of the accreditation standards. One afternoon at a faculty meeting after everyone has seen the draft report of the self-study, the teachers meet in groups of eight, discussing and eventually coming to consensus on each of the standards specified by the accreditation agency. Each group selects a representative who meets that afternoon with the representatives of all the other groups and the principal. This representative group then comes to consensus as to where their school stands on each of the standards.

Beverly, personally, finds this consensus process both exhilarating and painful. Exhilarating in that for the first time she sees all members of the staff taking ownership for the school. Furthermore, she hears her colleagues openly discussing issues that previously only stayed behind closed doors or on the teachers' parking lot. However, this openness prompts some pain. Beverly has to acknowledge the fact that her school does face serious problems and in some instances they are indeed "shortchanging" *some* students. "But not all the students," she quickly adds.

One month before the scheduled visit, The Taking Stock Committee sends the self-study report and consensus document to the site team visitors.

So far, we have described what Beverly and her team did as part of the required self-study prior to the visit by the team of experts. When they visit the school, the experts will also go through the same six steps, albeit in a more prescribed manner since the accrediting agency has already specified the taking stock questions, the judgment criteria, the data collection plan, and the data collection methods the team will use during their evaluation visit. At the end of the visit, the team of experts will analyze their data (Step 5) and render a judgment concerning the school's overall "health" (Step 6). The team then will share its judgment in an exit conference and follow-up with a formal written report.

After reading how Beverly and her colleagues responded to the newspaper's accusations that "Middle Schools Shortchanging Students," you're probably thinking that they overreacted, using a sledgehammer to swat a fly when a rolled up newspaper might have done the trick. Yes, Beverly and her colleagues could have responded with a scaled-back version of what we described above. For example, rather than undergoing a formal voluntary accreditation process that took much energy, time, and money (the school had to pay the expenses of the visiting team), Beverly and her colleagues could have simply kept everything local. They could have focused simply on questions raised by the school report card indicators published by the newspaper and not evaluated all aspects of the school as required by the voluntary accreditation process. If they had scaled back to just the questions raised by the school report card news article, data collection, analysis, and interpretation would all have been simplified.

We showed you a full-blown version of what Beverly and her colleagues could do in response to the newspaper article because, in our experience, people are more adept at scaling back than scaling up. Furthermore, the voluntary accreditation process circumvents one of the major criticisms that the newspaper and other critics might lodge against an in-house evaluation: That the evaluation was biased in favor of the school. Yes, Beverly and her colleagues could respond in a less elaborate way. But whatever evaluation they do must avoid systematic bias and withstand the scrutiny of critics and supporters alike.

Epilogue: Beverly's school received an "Exemplary" rating from the accreditation team. Furthermore, the faculty used the taking stock information to set new, more focused priorities for the coming school year. Finally, the school formed committees around each priority area. These committees followed the Targeted Problem-Solving Process described in chapter 10 to create action plans. As for the local newspaper, they ran a front page story highlighting the school's "Exemplary" rating.

8.52—Another Example: A Teacher Takes Stock of Her Classroom

Thus far in this chapter, we have focused on school-wide taking stock efforts. However, teachers can also take stock of their own classrooms as a first step in improving their teaching practice. The following is a drastically scaled back version showing how you, as an individual teacher, can take stock of your own classroom.

Let's say Ruth has been reading *In Search of Understanding: The Case for Constructivist Classrooms* written by Brooks and Brooks (1993). She's intrigued. She feels that she already does much of what the authors suggest, but also recognizes that she is not yet a fully constructivist teacher*. However, before she embarks on any wholesale changes in her classroom, she wants to see where she now stands. So she decides to take stock using the 6-Step evaluation process laid out in this book.

Step 1: Pose Questions

She turns to the pages listing the characteristics of a constructivist teacher and uses these characteristics to pose the questions that will guide her taking stock process.

Step 2: Establish Judgment Criteria

Again, she turns to the Brooks and Brooks (1993) book for guidance. Throughout the book, the authors describe criteria for judging whether or not a classroom is truly a constructivist classroom.

Step 3: Make a Plan

Using the Taking Stock Planning Matrix, Ruth spends about 15 minutes sketching out her plan for collecting and analyzing the data she will need to answer her taking stock questions. (See Figure 8.41.)

Figure 8.41 Handwritten Taking Stock Planning Matrix for Taking Stock of the Level of Constructivist Teaching Within an Individual Classroom

Column A Evaluation Question	Column B Information needed?	Column C Using what methods?	Column D By when?	Column E Who will collect?	Column F How analyze?
1. How much do I NOW encourage and accept student autonomy?	• Student opinions • Observations of lessons • Content of learning activities	Survey Video tape learning activities	March 15 March 22	Me Me	How: tallies Who: volunteer students By when: 3/22 How: tally # of times I encourage autonomy Who: Joan, partner teacher By when: 3/29

Step 4: Collect the Data

Ruth spends the next week gathering the data specified in her Taking Stock Planning Matrix. To her surprise, she finds that much of the data she needs already exists. She simply has to pull it together.

Step 5: Analyze the Data

First, Ruth organizes her data into frequency tables and then she runs some percentages using the spreadsheet function in Microsoft Works™. She's pleased she takes only about 15 minutes to enter the data and formulas into the spreadsheet and amazed that the computer takes only microseconds to do the calculations.

Step 6: Interpret the Results

Using the data she collected, Ruth now applies the judgment criteria she established in Step 2. She finds that indeed she does follow many of the practices of constructivist teachers, but she sees that she doesn't follow these practices daily. Rather, it's more a hit and miss proposition. Using this information, she now turns her thoughts to seeking a solution and flips to Chapter 10 of this book for guidance.

8.53—Chapter Summary

Major Concepts

☞ Taking stock of your classroom or school should not be an idle endeavor where you do it and then shelve it. Rather, you should take stock and then use it to:

- Guide improvement in your classroom or school
- Establish a baseline that will serve as a reference point for future evaluations of progress
- Provide a treasure trove of information that you can use in seeking solutions to your concerns

☞ In a school-wide effort, your taking stock questions can come from:

- Mandated or voluntary accreditation procedures
- Your school's vision
- Your school's goals
- The standards set by various associations
- Asking stake holders what they want to know about the school

☞ Grant applications (especially those for federal money through Title I) can serve as valuable sources of information.

☞ Standardized achievement tests come in two varieties: norm-referenced or criterion-referenced, both of which can help take stock of your school.

☞ Five specific techniques for analyzing test data include:

- Comparing test scores over time to see whether or not trends emerge
- Disaggregating test results based on various student characteristics
- Ascertaining whether or not a relationship exists between two variables
- Building confidence intervals around means
- Determining whether or not a significant difference exists between two groups

Advice

√ Use the six-step evaluation process that we laid out in chapters 1 through 6 to get your taking stock questions answered.

√ As you design your data collection sheet, keep in mind how you will ultimately organize and analyze your data.

√ Review artifacts in a manner that is both *simple* and *minimizes bias*.

√ As you disaggregate data to examine how certain groups of students score on the test, please don't fall prey to faulty assumptions that expect that certain students, just because they are boys, come from low SES homes, or speak a primary language other than English, should perform in a particular way on a standardized test.

8.54—The Road Ahead

This chapter has focused on a crucial first step in any school improvement process: taking stock of the "here and now." Whether you're striving to improve your classroom or the entire school, getting answers to your taking stock questions provides the foundation you need to move forward. In our next chapter, we will examine another set of questions integral to the improvement process: questions that determine effectiveness. Essentially, these questions ask, *"Did it work?"*.

8.55—Resources

Print Resources

★ These references have been recommended in earlier chapters. The number of ★'s indicates the number of previous recommendations.

★★★Bernhardt, V. L. (1998). *Data analysis for comprehensive schoolwide improvement*. Larchmont, NY: Eye on Education.

HIGHLY RECOMMENDED. Does an excellent job of showing you how to disaggregate (pull apart) data to examine how various subgroups perform. Uses examples from an elementary school and a high school to show how to disaggregate data by various factors such as ethnicity, grade level, and SES. Also discusses ways that educators can use disaggregated data to take stock and solve problems. Finally, Appendix C gives a rubric schools can use to gauge their commitment to continuous school improvement.

Bracey, G. W. (1998). *Put to the test: An educator's and consumer's guide to standardized testing*. Bloomington, IN: Phi Delta Kappa International.

HIGHLY RECOMMENDED. One of the best explanations of standardized tests we've seen. Gives an excellent overview of the purposes and uses of standardized test and then clearly explains how test makers construct norm-referenced and criterion-referenced tests. Also covers performance tests. Provides a jargon-free explanation of how to interpret tests, complete with sample printouts. Gives a brief but clear discussion of basic descriptive statistics in chapter 7. Parents, as well as educators, will appreciate this book.

Danielson, C. A. (1997). *Collection of performance tasks and rubrics: Middle school mathematics*. Larchmont, NY: Eye on Education.

Good for all middle school teachers, not just those who teach mathematics. Guides the middle school teacher in creating performance tasks in mathematics along with the rubrics for fairly evaluating student performance on those tasks. Gets into the nitty-gritty of designing a performance task to measure how well students have learned mathematical skills and tackles in clear fashion the complex task of developing and using rubrics to judge the quality of student performance on tasks. Also shows how to adapt existing performance tasks and rubrics to your needs. Includes 24 performance assessment tasks geared to middle school students.

Ebmeier, H. (1988). *Diagnostic assessment of school and principal effectiveness.* Topeka, KS: KanLEAD.

Commissioned by the United School Administrators of Kansas and developed at the University of Kansas. Normed using data from 23 schools from across Kansas, serving a largely white middle to lower class populations. Would work well in similar locales. Provides schools at all grades levels with machine-scoreable questionnaires that educators can use to take stock of their school's strengths and weaknesses. Focuses on estimating student growth in both academic and non-academic areas, gauging parent opinions about the school's effectiveness, and helping schools prepare for developing school improvement plans. Includes questionnaires for parents, students, supervisors, principals, and staff to complete. Costs of the instruments ranges from $250 to $450 depending on the school's size. Contact KanLEAD Educational Consortium Technical Assistance Center, 820 Quincy, Suite 200 Topeka, KS, 66612, or call 913-232-6566 for ordering information.

NOTE: Other administrator groups across the nation have also developed similar diagnostic materials for taking stock of a school's "health." Most are designed with the needs of a particular state in mind. Therefore, we suggest that you investigate what your state has to offer before ordering the Kansas material.

****Herman, J. L. & Winters, L. (1992). *Tracking your school's success: A guide to sensible evaluation.* Newbury Park, CA: Corwin Press.

HIGHLY RECOMMENDED. Written for practitioners (both teachers and administrators) interested in taking stock of their whole school as a first step towards improvement. Very readable and filled with examples. Focuses on providing educators with the guidance and tools to answer the following questions:

How are we doing?
How can we improve?
How can we share our successes?
Includes at the end of each chapter an annotated list of suggested readings.

*Hill, B. C. & Ruptic, C. A. (1994). *Practical aspects of authentic assessment: Putting the pieces together.* Norwood, MA: Christopher-Gordon Publishers.

Includes over 140 elementary school assessment tools that middle school educators could easily adapt to their students. Very clear, understandable discussion of using a variety of methods for assessing the learning of students. Includes many forms for data collection. Excellent suggestions on observing students (growth in reading and writing). A how-to book on authentic assessment using student portfolio and teacher observations. Illustrates ways to collect data that go beyond the usual (but often inadequate) standardized criterion-referenced and norm-referenced tests.

Hopfenberg, W., Levin, H., et al. (1993). *The accelerated schools resource guide*. San Francisco: Jossey-Bass Inc., Publishers.

Written to guide beginning Accelerated Schools in their efforts to transform their schools into learning communities where *all* students accelerate their learning. A first step in the process includes taking stock of the "here and now" of the school, identifying both strengths and challenges. Chapter 3 outlines the taking stock process that eventually helps the school community set its priorities. Even educators in non-Accelerated Schools can find guidance in this book on how to take the "pulse" of their schools.

*Leithwood, K. & Aitken, R. (1995). *Making schools smarter: A system for monitoring school and district progress*. Thousand Oaks, CA: Corwin Press.

Provides a comprehensive guide for taking stock of your school or district. Includes judgment criteria, as well as suggested indicators dealing with the following areas: mission, goals, organizational culture, strategic planning, management, leadership, instructional services, decision-making, policies, procedures, and school-community relations at both the district and school levels. Also provides sample surveys that you could use to collect the data you need to make your judgments.

National Middle School Association. (1995). *This we believe: Developmentally responsive middle level schools*. Columbus, OH: Author.

Excellent source for judgment criteria to determine how well your middle school embodies the philosophy and principles of middle level education.

*Schurr, S. L. (1992). *How to evaluate your middle school: A practitioner's guide for an informal program evaluation*. Columbus, OH: National Middle School Association.

A must for middle-level educators wanting to know if their programs fit the needs of their students. Provides over 25 survey and observation instruments based on the characteristics of exemplary middle schools that schools can use to take stock.

Internet Resources

NOTE: You can easily access the Websites we recommend below by simply going to our Web page located at

http://www.pittstate.edu/edsc/ssls/letendre.html

From our Web page, a simple click of your mouse will take you straight to the selected Website. We regularly verify these sites and add others that we find worthy of our recommendation.

Council of Chief State School Officers
http://www.ccsso.org/
Links to the Website maintained by the Council of Chief State School Officers. Serves as a gateway to Websites sponsored by state departments of education in all 50 states. By going to your state's Website, you can find the learning outcomes and accreditation standards your state expects schools to achieve. Great resource

for generating Taking Stock questions. Also, your state's Website may include basic data on all schools in the state (i.e. achievement scores) that you can use in your getting your Taking Stock questions answered.

Middle States Association of Schools and Colleges
http://www.css-msa.org/
Connects to the Website for the voluntary, non-governmental regional accrediting institution that accredits schools in DC, DE, MD, NJ, NY, and PA. Also accredits schools in the Caribbean, Europe, Africa and the Mideast. Provides information about other standards and the accreditation process, along with a roster of accredited schools.

National Education Association
http://www.nea.org/resource/keys.html
Connects to information provided through the National Education Association about the organization's KEYS Initiative. Using 11 keys to school quality gleaned from data collected from high-achieving schools across the United States, the KEYS Initiative helps a school staff take stock of their school and implement a "continual improvement strategy." KEYS includes both diagnostic instruments and a process for using information to improve the entire school environment.

National Study of School Evaluation
http://www.nsse.org/
Links to a gateway Website sponsored by the National Study of School Evaluation, a non-profit educational research and development organization sponsored by the six regional voluntary school accreditation institutions. Provides a map where you simply point to your region and then connect to the Website of the appropriate accrediting commission. You can also obtain information on the Opinion Inventory and Scoring Service offered at reasonable prices through the National Study of School Evaluation group.

New England Association of Schools and Colleges
http://www.neasc.org
Takes you to the Website for the commission that offers voluntary accreditation to schools within CT, MA, ME, NH, RI, and VT. Includes information about standards and the accreditation process itself, along with a roster of accredited schools.

North Central Association of Colleges and Schools
http://www.nca.asu.edu/
Links to the Commission on Schools that confers voluntary accreditation on schools in the Midwest: AR, AZ, CO, IL, IN, IA, KS, MI, MN, MO, NE, ND, NM, OH, OK, SD, WV, WI, and WY. Includes information on standards and procedures along with the latest announcements on member services and meetings. Also gives a roster of accredited schools.

Northwest Association of Schools and Colleges
http://www2.idbsu.edu/nasc/
Connects to the Website for the not-for-profit, non-governmental commission that accredits 1434 schools throughout the Northwest region of the United States (AK, ID, MT, NV, OR, UT, WA), as well as international schools in Bolivia, Canada, Czechoslovakia, Egypt, Jamaica, Macedonia, Poland, Republic of Panama,

Russia, and Western Samoa. Provides a listing of accredited schools and information about standards and the accreditation process. Also includes an electronic newsletter updated twice monthly.

Southern Association of Colleges and Schools
http://www.sacs.org/pub/Sa00003.htm
Takes you directly to the Commission on Elementary and Middle Schools site that offers voluntary accreditation for elementary and middles schools in AL, FL, GA, KY, LA, MS, NC, SC, TN, TX, and VA. Provides excellent information for educators and parents on the standards and process for accreditation, along with a roster of accredited schools.

Western Association of Schools and Colleges
http://www.wascweb.org/schools/schools.htm
Links to the Accrediting Commission for Schools which offers voluntary accreditation to middle schools in CA, HI, the Pacific, and East Asia. Provides complete information on the standards schools must meet for accreditation along with a full description of the process schools must undergo.

CHAPTER 9

Effectiveness Questions

Nothing that's good works by itself to please you.
You've got to make the goddamn thing happen.

—Thomas Edison

9.1—Introduction

Does it work?
Did we accomplish what we wanted to accomplish?
Is it worth continuing?

Questions such as these trip off the tongues of middle school educators every day. Always striving to better educate our students, we try new strategies and then want to know if our efforts have paid off. Unfortunately, however, we often use only our "gut feelings" to determine if our strategies worked. Such unsystematic evaluation can lead us to falsely conclude things "worked" when they really didn't. We then continue using faulty methods, wasting precious time, effort and money.

In this chapter we will share with you a more systematic way to determine the effectiveness of your interventions. We will show how the 6-Step Evaluation Process we introduced in chapters 1 through 6 can help you confidently answer the question, *"Did it work?"*.

9.2—A Reminder: The 6-Step Evaluation Process

To determine the effectiveness of your strategies, you should follow the 6-Step Evaluation Process we laid out in chapters 1 through 6:

Step 1: Pose questions

Step 2: Establish judgment criteria

Step 3: Make a plan

Step 4: Gather data

Step 5: Analyze data

Step 6: Interpret data

You can perform these steps as formally as you wish. For example, you can scale-up to conduct a year-long evaluation of a school-wide violence prevention program, or you can scale-down to determine if the new pre-reading strategy you're using in your own classroom actually worked. Furthermore, the 6-Step Evaluation process can help both individual teachers or groups of educators evaluate their efforts.

9.3—Determining Effectiveness Step 1: Pose questions

In Step 1, you pose the questions that will guide your investigation. To determine the effectiveness of a strategy, you can begin by asking:

- Did it work?
- Did it accomplish what we wanted to accomplish?
- Is it worth continuing?

Of course, you may want to pose additional questions that break down these overarching questions into more manageable subquestions.

Step 1 requires that you pose your evaluation questions *before* you begin the evaluation process. However, please realize that rarely can you anticipate all the pertinent questions you might want to answer. So, during the evaluation process, stay flexible and remain open to additional evaluation questions that might emerge. At the same time, however, guard against getting side-tracked by too many questions. Sometimes evaluators let their curiosity run rampant and fail to answer the really important questions because they spend too much time examining interesting, but not very useful questions.

9.4—Who Should Pose Questions

No matter how narrow or far-reaching your evaluation, we suggest that you seek input from a variety of people as you pose the questions that will guide your evaluation. Ask them, *"What information do we need to decide if our strategy worked or not?"*.

We urge that you seek input from the following sources:

- **Those who will use the results of your evaluation to make decisions**
  This might include you, as an individual teacher, your colleagues, the principal, the central office administrators, or even the school board. By asking these people for their input, you ensure that your evaluation efforts will generate the information that decision-makers will need to determine the effectiveness of the program and judge its worthiness.
- **Those directly or indirectly affected by the intervention**
  Teachers, students, parents, and community members may all have a stake in the outcome of your evaluation. These folks provide valuable perspectives and may generate important questions to guide your evaluation.
- **The intentions of the program's initiators**
  Those who initiated the idea for the intervention hoped that the program would accomplish certain outcomes. Sometimes you can find these inten-

tions spelled out formally in a proposal, while at other times, initiators have not made explicit what they hoped to accomplish. You should, however, get them to clearly define the outcomes they hoped to achieve and then use these outcomes to generate your evaluation questions.

9.5—Where to Look for Questions

In addition to seeking input from various decision-makers and stakeholders, we suggest that you *consult the educational literature* for ideas about questions to guide your evaluation. Someone out there has probably already implemented and hopefully evaluated a program similar to yours. By reviewing articles and evaluation reports concerning programs similar to yours, you might get some additional thoughts concerning questions to guide your evaluation. Examining the ERIC database or surfing the Internet can yield valuable ideas. At the end of this chapter in Section 9.56 Resources we list several Websites that you might find helpful.

Also you might want to *consult experts at your local university*. These people can provide a fresh perspective and possess expertise in evaluation that goes beyond the scope of this book.

9.6—Formative vs. Summative Evaluation

Earlier in the Introduction of this book, we differentiated between formative and summative evaluation. The distinction between these two types of evaluation centers around the *timing* of the evaluation. Seeking to help implementors "form" the program, formative evaluation occurs *during* implementation and often is ongoing throughout the implementation phase. Formative evaluation provides you with information that tells you if you're on the right track or if you need to make some mid-course adjustments. Such information can often mean the difference between a program that succeeds and one that fails. You really shouldn't wait until the end to discover that if only you had slightly tweaked your action plan, things would have gone smoother and more successfully.

During implementation, *formative evaluation asks* questions such as:

- Is it working?
- What's going right?
- What's going wrong?
- How can we make it better?

Summative evaluation, on the other hand, occurs *at the end* of the implementation process and provides a "summary" of your program, giving you information about the program's effectiveness, usefulness, and worth. *Summative evaluation asks* questions such as:

- Did it work?
- Did it accomplish what we wanted to accomplish?
- Did it make a difference?
- Is it worth continuing?

And sometimes

- Why did it work?
- Why didn't it work?

Whether you decide to conduct *both* formative and summative evaluations, or just a summative evaluation, you should use the same 6-Step Evaluation Process to guide your efforts. You need to pose questions, set judgment criteria, make a plan, gather data, analyze data, and interpret data.

9.7—Jaime Does Step 1

"Wow, things really got dusty over the summer," Jaime, an 8th grade teacher at Gettingeverbetter Middle School exclaimed to Suzanne and Rob, his colleagues on the Challenge Team. "Look, I can even write my name in the dust."

"That's because they've been renovating the basement," Suzanne explained. "Everything in the school is covered with a fine coat of dust."

"Well, let's don't mess with the dust just yet," Jaime said. "I want to talk with you about something I would like to do this school year."

"OK, let's go down to the Media Center," Rob suggested. "It's air-conditioned and besides I bet it's dust-free. I noticed that the maintenance staff in there yesterday cleaning."

The Challenge Team teachers troupe down to the Media Center, lugging curriculum guides, calendars, and plan books.

"So what's on your mind?" Suzanne asked.

"You know last year we started the year off with the Family and Community unit and it was great success," Jaime began. "The service learning component was especially successful."

"Yea, our 8th graders served over 2000 volunteer hours at the police department, juvenile court, daycare centers, nursing homes, the YMCA, the homeless shelter, the food bank, the Red Cross, and the local sheltered workshop for developmentally disabled adults," Rob proudly ticked off all the sites on his fingers. "The kids really got alot out of those experiences."

"So far we've been just telling people what wonderful things this service learning is doing for our kids.," Jaime continued. "Perhaps we should heed the saying on the poster that hangs in my room: 'Facts speak louder than opinions.' I think we should do some sort of evaluation of our service learning program."

"I agree," said Suzanne. "We need to conduct an evaluation that will show the facts."

The next day the Challenge Team teachers meet and quickly pose the following general questions to guide their evaluation.

- Does service learning work?
- Are we achieving what we set out to accomplish when we began the service learning component of our Family and Community unit?

Last night Jaime had gone to the local university library and checked out a book recommended by one of his professors, *Program evaluation: Alternative approaches and practical guidelines.* (2nd ed.). by Worthen, B. R., Sanders, J. R., & Fitzpatrick, J. L. (1997). He had turned to chapter 11 and scanned the section comparing the various approaches to evaluation and decided that the Objectives-Oriented approach fits their situation.

"In this approach, we take the objectives we set for the unit and then gather evidence to see if we met these objectives," Jaime explained.

The group pulled out the syllabus for the Family and Community unit, looked at the objectives they set for the service learning component and wrote the following additional evaluation questions:

- Do students improve their real-world, problem-solving skills?
- Do students show an increased sensitivity towards people who are different?
- Do students demonstrate a greater willingness to take responsibility for their actions?
- Do students demonstrate increased social competence in dealing with different people and situations within the school and outside the school?
- Do students show an increased sense of self-efficacy, that *they* can make a difference in their world?

"That's a good start," Rob commented. "I'm concerned, however, that some community members might say that the kids aren't learning the basics of reading, writing, math and science because we're spending too much time on volunteering. Shouldn't we add those to our evaluation questions as well?"

"Definitely," said Suzanne. And the team generates the following additional evaluation question:

- Does participation in service learning activities increase students' achievement in reading and math?

The team also decides to get input from their students. So two weeks later when they introduce the "Family and Community" unit and explain the service learning component, the teachers ask their students: "What information do we need to help us know whether or not service learning is working and if we should continue using it?" The students added two other evaluation questions to the list:

- Does participation in service learning activities improve attendance?
- Do student volunteers have a positive effect at the sites where they volunteer?

Jaime and the Challenge Team are now ready for Step 2 of the evaluation process where they will specify the criteria and standards they will use to judge whether or not they have met their objectives.

9.8—Determining Effectiveness Step 2: Establish Judgment Criteria

In Step 2, *before* you begin your evaluation, you need to explicitly answer the question:

On what basis will I judge the effectiveness of the program?

Answering this question requires that you *specify both the criteria and the standards* that you will use to judge whether or not your intervention worked. You must define *exactly* what you mean when you say "it worked."

You begin by itemizing the *criteria,* or components, you will examine to determine a program's effectiveness. For example, if we are evaluating the success or failure of thematic teaching, some of the criteria we might want to investigate might include:

1. Student achievement in expository writing
2. Student motivation to complete learning projects

Once you have delineated the criteria, you then must set the *standards,* or the specific levels of performance, you wish to attain. Criteria tell you what to look at, but standards tell you how to judge the quality of the performance.

Continuing with our thematic teaching example, below we show some standards we might use to judge the quality of the two criteria we set:

CRITERIA	STANDARD
1. Student achievement in expository writing	1. Over 50% of the students will improve their ability to write an essay.
2. Student motivation to complete learning projects	2. The students will indicate a greater willingness to complete learning projects than students who do not take part in the thematic unit. Over 80% of the students will successfully complete a major group learning project.

9.9—Who Should Set the Judgment Criteria

In setting the criteria and standards you'll use to judge the effectiveness of your program, we suggest that you cast your net wide just as you did in Step 1 when you delineated your evaluation questions. In section 2.5, we offer the following techniques to ensure that you gather a wealth of suggestions about the judgment criteria you establish to determine the effectiveness of your program:

- Seek judgment criteria *from stakeholders* by asking them:

    1. What evidence will prove to you that the program worked?

    2. What evidence would indicate to you that the program failed?

- Gather judgment criteria by *reviewing the purpose of the strategy.*   Every intervention, large or small, has a purpose whether that purpose is implied or formally laid out in writing. These expected outcomes can help establish the criteria and standards you will use to judge the project's effectiveness.

- Garner judgment criteria by *examining research literature.*   A quick review, on the Internet or in a library, of articles describing programs similar to yours will often yield several valuable ideas about criteria and standards you might use in evaluating your own program.

- Draw judgment criteria from *checklists, standards, guidelines.*   Educational associations, accreditation agencies and state departments of education often establish checklists, standards, and guidelines that can provide you with useful ideas on how to determine whether or not your program worked.

- Collect judgment criteria by *consulting with experts.*   Independent experts working at local colleges or universities, in your state department of education, or at an educational service center serving your area can also prove helpful in helping you establish judgment criteria.

9.10—Jaime Does Step 2

Jaime, Suzanne, and Rob, the Challenge Team teachers, have had a busy week. Today, they spent their entire planning time laying out the evaluation questions and establishing the criteria and standards they would use to judge whether or not the service learning program is accomplishing what they hope it will.

They pulled from input given by their students, the principal, and some parents. They also went on-line and gleaned some ideas about judgment criteria from other evaluations done on service learning projects at schools across the country. Figure 9.1 shows the judgment criteria they set.

Now, the Challenge Team teachers need to work on a plan for getting all these evaluation questions answered. They decided to see if their students would be interested in helping to plan and conduct parts of the evaluation. This project could be real-world learning at it's best!

Figure 9.1 Judgment Criteria for Service Learning Evaluation

Evaluation Question	Judgment Criteria
1. Do students improve their real-world problem-solving skills?	1. Challenge students will show a statistically greater ability to solve real-world problems than a comparable group of students who have not engaged in service learning activities.
2. Do students show an increased sensitivity towards people who are different?	2. Challenge students will show a statistically significant greater sensitivity towards others than a comparable group of students who have not engaged in service learning activities.
3. Do students demonstrate a greater willingness to take responsibility for their actions?	3. Challenge students will demonstrate a statistically significant greater sense of responsibility than a comparable group of students who have not engaged in service learning activities.
4. Do students demonstrate increased social competence in dealing with different people and situations within the school and outside the school?	4. Challenge students will demonstrate a statistically significant greater social competence than a comparable group of students who have not engaged in service learning activities.
5. Do students show an increased sense of self-efficacy, that they can make a difference in their world?	5. Challenge students will show a statistically significant greater sense of self-efficacy than a comparable group of students who have not engaged in service learning activities.
6. Does participation in service learning activities increase students' achievement in reading and math?	6. Challenge students will show a statistically significant gain in reading and math achievement over a comparable group of students who have not engaged in service learning activities.
7. Does participation in service learning activities improve attendance?	7. Challenge students will show a statistically significant higher attendance rate than a comparable group of students who have not engaged in service learning activities.
8. Do students make a positive impact at the sites where they volunteer?	8. 95% of the volunteer sites will indicate that the student volunteers have had a positive impact.

9.11—Determining Effectiveness Step 3: Make A Plan

No matter how big or small your evaluation, you should make a plan specifying how and when you will collect and analyze the information you need. In chapter 3 we suggested that you lay out your plan using an Evaluation Planning Matrix. (See Figure 9.2.) In chapter 3 we also discussed the various issues you should keep in mind as you develop your evaluation plan. In particular, we stressed:

- Keeping your data collection simple and reliable
- Reviewing the judgment criteria that you established in Step 2 to make sure your evaluation plan indicates collecting *all* the data you will need to determine the effectiveness of your program

• Sketching out the table of contents of your final evaluation report (if you plan to write one) to make sure your Planning Matrix includes plans for collecting *all* the information you'll need to write your report

Figure 9.2   Evaluation Planning Matrix

A Evaluation Question	B Information needed?	C Using what method?	D Who will collect?	E By when?	F How analyze?

9.12—Using a Research Design to Establish Causation

Answering the question, *"Did it work?"*, requires that we determine, what *caused* the changes we see. Of course, we hope the changes occurred because our new strategies worked. However, something else might have actually produced the changes we see. Using a classic experimental research design can help us determine if our intervention really *caused* the changes we see.

In classic experimental research designs, we create two different situations in which we hold all factors the same except one. The only difference between the two situations is that in one situation the subjects *receive* the intervention and in the other situation the subjects *don't receive* the intervention. We take measurements under both conditions and compare. Hopefully, our comparison will show that the subjects who received the intervention did better than those who didn't receive the intervention.

9.13—The "Big Picture" of Experimental Research Design

Experimental research designs come in two broad categories:

1. Comparison group designs
2. Single group designs

Figure 9.3   Classic Experimental Design

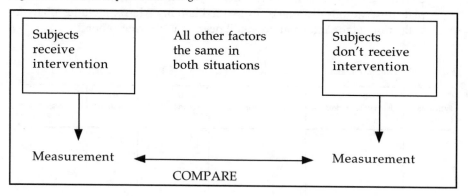

Furthermore, research designs vary along three dimensions:

1.   How subjects are selected for the various groups,

2.   When measurements are taken

3.   How many measurements are made

Figure 9.4 shows a breakdown of selected research designs. In the next few sections we will examine and critique each of these five selected designs. Please know that *many* variations on these basic designs exist. We highlight only a handful that we feel will prove most useful to you as an educator. Several of the books listed in section 9.56 Resources provide a more thorough listing and explanation of the various research designs.

9.14—Validity of Your Results

Before we get into the specifics of the selected research designs shown in Figure 9.4, we need to define some key terms. First, you need to know that the validity of your results rests on how much you can trust that your conclusions accurately depict the reality of the situation. Can you say without a reasonable doubt that the intervention *caused* the changes you observe?

To help ensure the validity of your results, you need to use a research design that identifies your intervention as the cause of the changes you observe and rules out all other possible explanations. In sections 9.16 through 9.22, we will discuss the factors that can contaminate or invalidate your results. We will also offer some suggestions that can help eliminate or minimize this contamination.

9.15—Variables

You also need to know that a variable is a trait, state, characteristic or dimension that varies from person to person or from situation to situation. Some examples of variables associated with middle school students might include:

•   Gender

•   Self-esteem

•   Reading ability

Figure 9.4   Classic Experimental Research Designs

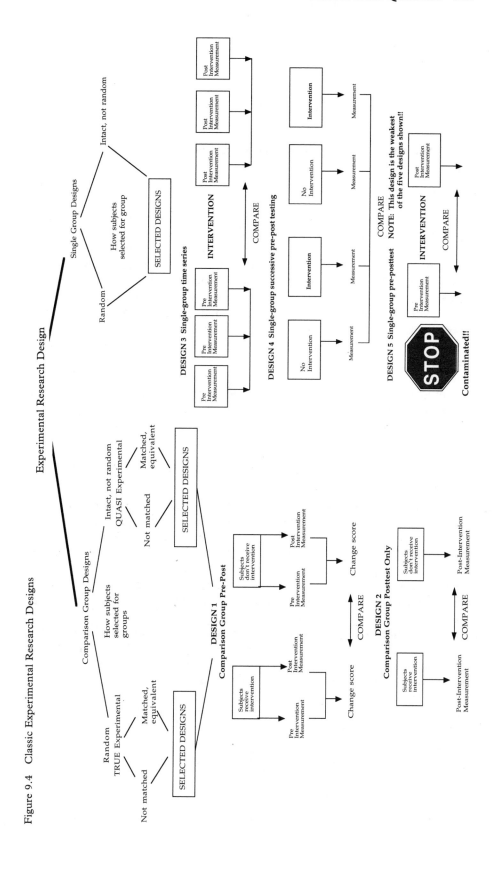

- Sense of efficacy
- Attitudes towards authority
- Learning style

Some situation variables might include:

- Class size
- The number of computers available to students
- Length of class period
- Instructional strategy used

Variables can also include those *things that we manipulate* as we set up an experiment. We call these variables *independent variables*. For example, if we want to see if using laser disk images helps students better understand science concepts, we would teach one group of students using the the laser disk images and another group using the same lesson but with no laser disk images. We would then measure the students' understanding of science concepts and compare the scores of the two groups. In this example, our independent variable, the variable we manipulate, is the use of laser disk images during the science lesson.

Another category of variables includes *dependent variables*, those outcomes we measure as part of the experiment. As Suter says in his *Primer of Educational Research* (1998), dependent variables "are the 'blank' in the expression ' . . . as measured by _____.'" In our example concerning the effectiveness of laser disk images, the dependent variable is the test we give students to gauge their scientific understanding.

9.16—Extraneous Variables

A final, and often troublesome, group of variables includes *extraneous variables*, those factors that might get so tangled up with our independent variable that we cannot tell whether our intervention or some other factor caused the changes we observed. Unless we carefully control for these extraneous variables in our research design, these outside factors can contaminate the results of our experiment, making it impossible for us to say with any certainty that our intervention worked. Indeed, these extraneous variables can threaten the validity of your evaluation.

Let's return to our example concerning the effectiveness of using laser disk images to teach science concepts. We teach one group of students using the the laser disk images and another group using the same lesson but with no laser disk images. We then measure the students' understanding of science concepts and compare the scores of the two groups. In this instance, the students who got the laser disk instruction did much better than the other group. We rejoice! The laser disk instruction worked!

But did it? Unfortunately, many other factors besides the use of laser disk images might account for one group doing better than the other group. Some rival explanations that stem from extraneous variables might include:

- The students in both groups learn better during a particular *time of day*. Students in both groups were predominately "morning" people who think and learn better from 8 a.m. to 11 a.m. The laser disk group received their instruction from 9 to 10 a.m., while the non-laser disk group got theirs from 2 to 3 p.m. right before the end of the school day, putting them at a disadvantage.

- The laser disk group students performed better on the science test because they are generally more *motivated to learn science* than the non-laser group students.
- The laser disk group learned more because the teacher had a more positive *rapport* with them than she did with the non-laser group students.
- From the outset, the students in the laser disk group had an advantage because they possessed a higher *level of prior knowledge* about science concepts than the students in the non-laser disk group.

Of course, we could generate many other plausible explanations for why the laser group students performed better than the non-laser group. We have selected these four rival hypotheses to illustrate how you can use research design to rule out these explanations.

9.17—Controlling Extraneous Variables

Fortunately, we can control many extraneous variables through careful design of our experiment. Let's return to our evaluation of the effectiveness of laser disk images in teaching science concepts. If we want to rule out the rival explanation that the laser disk group did better because they received their instruction from 9 to 10 a.m. while the non-laser disk group got theirs from 2 to 3 p.m., we simply need to present the lessons to the student groups at the same time of day. In this way, we eliminate "time of day" as an extraneous variable.

Three other design techniques can also help minimize or rule out rival explanations:

1. Random selection of subjects for each group
2. Matching the groups on relevant variables
3. Pretesting both groups to ascertain if any preexisting relevant differences exist between the two groups

Although the above three techniques can help control extraneous variables, few research designs are totally free of threats to conclusions. When we evaluate human behavior, we simply can't control *everything*. Our advice is this: Choose the design technique that controls for the extraneous variables that you think will be most problematic.

9.18—Using Random Selection to Control Extraneous Variables

Through the "luck of the draw," random selection helps to spread the normal variations among students across both groups. For example, all students vary in their motivation to learn science. Some are more motivated than others. To make sure that one group does not include a disproportionate number of highly moti-vated students, we can randomly select from a large pool of students who will be in the class that get laser disk instruction and 30 additional students who will not get laser disk instruction. (See Figure 9.5) The laws of probability work in our favor to help form comparable groups where both groups have some highly mo-tivated students, some less motivated students, and even some unmotivated stu-dents. [Other variable characteristics, such as rapport with the teacher, would also be evenly represented in each group as well.]

Figure 9.5   Random Selection

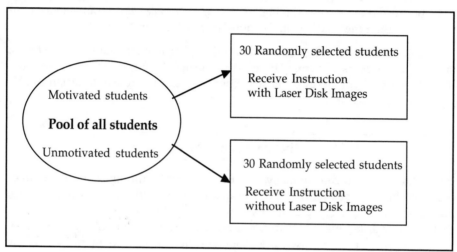

To get the laws of probability working in our favor, we must use certain procedures in selecting our student groups. In chapter 4, section 4.8, we intro-duced you to four common methods of randomly selecting a group:

1. Simple random sampling

2. Stratified random sampling

3. Cluster sampling

4. Systematic random sampling

9.19—Using Matching to Control Extraneous Variables

Another technique for controlling extraneous variables and thus ruling out rival explanations involves matching groups of subjects on relevant variables. Match-ing ensures that our groups *will* be comparable on important characteristics or variables.

Let's illustrate once again with our evaluation of laser disk science instruc-tion. If we think that gender might influence how students will respond to science instruction, we can control for this variable by making sure that both our groups include equal numbers of boys and girls. We can accomplish this matching by using a stratified random sampling procedure. (See Figure 9.6) We begin by dividing our population of all science students into two subgroups based on gender. We then randomly select 15 boys to be in our laser disk group and 15 boys to be in our non-laser disk group. We do the same for girls. We now have two groups of 30 students, each matched on gender.

In this case, we have continued to use random selection to make sure that we randomly distribute the natural differences that exist among students between the two groups. But, we don't want to leave gender to chance. Now, we can rule out gender differences as a rival explanation as to why the observed differences in science scores occurred.

Figure 9.6   Stratified Random Sampling

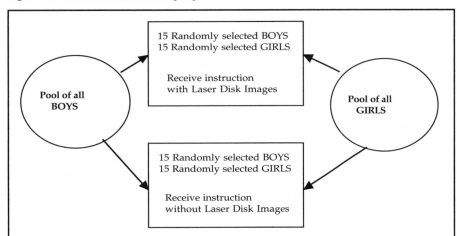

9.20—Matching Existing Groups

Matching on key variables becomes particularly important when we find ourselves in situations where random selection is impossible and we must use existing groups. This is often the case in schools. Indeed, we bet that as we've been talking about our example of evaluating laser disk instruction, you've been muttering to yourself that random selection in a real school is out of the question. And you're probably right. We would most likely have to use existing science classes rather than creating some special randomly selected classes for our study.

When random selection is not possible, we suggest that you choose two intact, existing groups that are as comparable as possible. You need to first decide which characteristics are relevant and then match your groups on these variables. Matching the groups on relevant variables can help rule out rival explanations caused by preexisting differences between the groups.

In our evaluation of laser disk instruction, we might want to identify two existing science classes that are *similar* in not only gender but also in size, reading ability level, ethnicity, race, and attendance. [Note: "Similar" does not mean exactly the same. Rarely will you be able to find two existing groups that match exactly on all relevant variables.] The key is to match the groups on any extraneous variables that might contribute to an increase in science understanding. You must hold everything else constant between the two groups so that you can logically conclude that the laser disk instruction *caused* the difference in performance.

Of course in the real world of schools it is almost impossible to hold *everything* constant. However, in designing your study, you should strive to keep as many factors the same between the two groups as humanly possible.

Figure 9.7 shows see how matching can help control some of the extraneous variables in our evaluation of laser disk instruction.

> Note: In some schools, early in the school year, intact classrooms may actually represent random samples of students. This is the case if the school doesn't track students by achievement and the school's computer scheduling program randomly assigned students to classes. Beware, however, because sometimes a scheduling program will begin by assigning students to specialized classes offered only once in a schedule (such as Concert Band) and then these students get tracked together. It may be that the students in Concert Band represent a group of students qualitatively different from the rest of the student body.

9.21—Using Pretesting to Control Extraneous Variables

Pretesting groups on relevant variables can also help control for extraneous variables. By pretesting groups, you can ascertain if the groups have any preexisting differences that might confound your results. If your pretesting shows that the groups are comparable from the outset, you can then rule out many rival explanations for your results. Often groups formed using random selection will show no substantial differences from the outset because the randomization usually spreads the differences equally between the groups.

If, however, your pretesting indicates that major differences *do* exist from the beginning, you may have to go back to square one and redesign your study to control for these differences.

Let's illustrate once again with our evaluation of laser disk instruction. Random selection of students has proved impossible, so we've decided to use two existing science classes for our study. We give a pretest of scientific knowledge to the students in both existing classes *before* we teach our special lessons. We find that students in Group A possess substantially more prior knowledge about science than students in Group B.

At this point, we have two options:

1. We can pretest other existing science classes and find a class that scores similarly to Group A and use that class as a comparison group rather than Group B.

OR

2. We can stay with Groups A and B, compare change scores (the difference between pretest scores and posttest scores), and simply acknowledge that we weren't able to completely rule out the possibility that differences in prior knowledge from the outset might have given Group A an advantage over Group B.

We would select option 1 if at all possible, but unfortunately in our experience, we have often had to settle for option 2 when conducting evaluations in real schools.

Caution: Before we move on, we want to alert you to problem with pretesting as a technique for controlling extraneous variable. Although pretesting can help control extraneous variables, it can also contaminate your results. The pretest might provide the students with just the right amount of practice so that they do better on the posttest no matter what type of instruction they get later. Or the pretest might signal that something's up and the students try harder than they normally would, thus scoring higher on the posttest whether or not they get the special laser disk instruction. Of course, it helps if both groups (the one that gets the special instruction and the one that doesn't) receive a pretest. Then the pretest would have similar impact on both groups.

Again, Figure 9.7 shows see how pretesting groups on relevant variables can help control for some of the extraneous variables in an evaluation of laser disk instruction.

Figure 9.7   Controlling Extraneous Variables

Extraneous Variable*	Possible Method for Controlling
1. The the level of prior knowledge the students have about science concepts	Random selection of students for the laser disk group, non-laser disk group OR Pretest/posttest design to compare change scores OR Match groups on some test of prior knowledge about science concepts
2. The time of day when the lessons are presented	Present the laser disk lesson and non-laser disk lesson to student groups at the same time of day [Easily done if students are on a block schedule. On Day A, the teacher presents lessons using laser disk images. On Day B, she presents lessons without laser disk images to another group of students.]
3. The rapport the teacher has with the students	Random selection of students for the laser disk group, non-laser disk group OR Match groups on some measure of rapport with the teacher
4. The motivation the students have to learn science.	Random selection of students for the laser disk group, non-laser disk group OR Match groups on some measure of motivation to learn science

*These are only four of the extraneous variables that immediately came to our minds. You could probably generate up to 10 more.

9.22— 🛑 STOP Warning!! Contaminated!! Single Group Pre-Posttest Design

Now that you have some basics about variables and design techniques under your belt, let's return to the experimental research designs displayed in Figure 9.4.

We begin with *the worst first: the single group pre-post measurement* * *design.* Design 5 is fraught with all sorts of contamination because it fails to control for many extraneous variables. Indeed, this design is so contaminated that some textbooks label it as "pre-experimental" (McMillian & Schumacher, 1997).

Unfortunately, many educators often rely on a single group pre-posttest design to generate "proof" that an intervention worked. However, with this design you cannot unequivocally conclude that the intervention *caused* the observed differences. There's just too much contamination by extraneous variables.

Let's illustrate. In chapter 5 we introduced you to the Zoo Team teachers who decided to spend the school year building a strong sense of self-efficacy among their sixth graders. To evaluate the effectiveness of their self-efficacy curriculum, they gave their students the LeTendre/Lipka Test of Self-Efficacy in early September and then again in April. Figure 9.8 shows their research design. (Note: After reading this book, the Zoo Team teachers added a comparison group and greatly strengthened their design.)

Figure 9.8   Zoo Team's Research Design

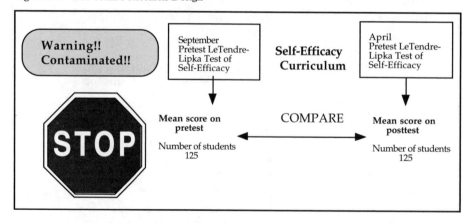

Let's say that Zoo Team teachers never had the benefit of this book and stayed with the research design shown in Figure 9.8. At the end of the year, they compared the pre- and posttest scores and found that the students scored significantly higher in self-efficacy in April. Is this cause to celebrate? Did their self-efficacy curriculum work? Can the Zoo Team teachers really attribute the increase in their students' self-efficacy to their special curriculum?

---

* We use the term "measurement" rather than "test" because measurement is more inclusive. Measurements can include indicators of skill, knowledge, behavior, attitude, or physical characteristics all gathered by asking, observing or reviewing documents and artifacts.

Let's take a moment and generate some rival explanations that might explain why the students' self-efficacy scores improved over the year and suggest some ways to control for these extraneous variables. Please remember we list *some* rival explanations not *all*. We're sure you could produce some of your own.

Rival Hypothesis #1:   The normal psychological growth of seventh graders from September to April caused the higher self-efficacy scores.

Without a comparison group of similar seventh graders who did not get the self-efficacy curriculum, the Zoo Team can not rule out *maturation* as a reason for the higher scores. Thus, by simply adding a comparison group and using Design 1 displayed in Figure 9.4, the Zoo Team could control for maturation.

Rival Hypothesis #2:   By taking the pretest in September, the students realized that their teachers were going to do something special about self-efficacy this year. So when they took the same test again in April, they knew how they *should* answer and scored higher.

By adding a comparison group and using Design 1 displayed in Figure 9.4, the Zoo Team could control for the *effect of pretesting*. The two groups would experience the same awareness about self-efficacy. If the Zoo Team students who received the special self-efficacy curriculum showed higher gains than the comparison group, the Zoo Team teachers could confidently say that their efforts made a difference in their students' sense of self-efficacy.

The Zoo Team teachers could also use Design 2 shown in Figure 9.4. This design also uses a comparison group but uses only a post-test measure, thus eliminating any effect the pretesting might have on performance. However, without a pretest, the Zoo Team may not be able to rule out Rival Hypothesis #1 concerning maturation effects.

Rival Hypothesis #3:   Unbeknownst to the Zoo Team teachers, 50 of their students also participated during the school year in the "I Am Somebody" program at the local YMCA. This program focused on improving the students' self-esteem. The higher self-efficacy scores in April may have resulted from the "I Am Somebody" program or in combination with the special self-efficacy curriculum.

The Zoo Team teachers can control for this *concurrent program interference* by simply removing the pre- and posttest scores of the 50 "I Am Somebody" students from the group and only looking at the scores of the remaining students. Or they could make sure that the comparison group of students who don't get the special self-efficacy curriculum also includes approximately 50 students who participated in the "I Am Somebody" program. Either way, the Zoo Team teachers could rule out the effects of this concurrent program.

Rival Hypothesis #4:   From September to April, 26 students left and 29 new ones enrolled. Those who left had a lower sense of self-efficacy than the newly enrolled students. Therefore, the 29 new students artificially boosted the average on the April posttest.

Of course, one way to control for the effects of the 29 new students is simply compare the pre- and posttest scores for the 99 remaining students who took both the pre- and posttest.

In summary, as you can see, Design 5 that compares the pre-post measures from only one group really has a tough time establishing, without a doubt, that the intervention caused the higher self-efficacy scores. Because of its inability to control for extraneous variables, we suggest that you rarely use this design, particularly if you want to prove effectiveness. Design 5 can help provide some broad sense of what works and what doesn't during the *early* stages of an intervention's development. But that's about all you can use it for.

9.23—The Best: Comparison Group Designs 1 and 2

If you wish to conclude that your intervention *caused* the positive outcomes you see, we suggest that you always use a research design that includes a comparison group. In Figure 9.4, both Design 1 and Design 2 use comparison groups.

We also suggest that you create your groups using random selection. In this way, you can use the laws of probability to make sure that various extraneous factors that might affect your outcomes get spread equally by chance throughout both groups. As we stressed in section 9.18, whether you use simple random selection or match your groups by using stratified random selection, randomization can help control many extraneous variables and allow you to rule out most rival hypotheses. Research designs that use random selection fall into the category of *true experimental* designs.

If, however, you find that you cannot use random selection and must rely on intact, existing groups, we suggest that you try to make your groups as comparable as possible by matching the groups on relevant variables. This procedure can help dispel several plausible hypotheses caused by extraneous variables. Experimental designs that use existing groups come under the category of *quasi-experimental* designs, which resemble true experimental designs in all ways except in how the groups are created.

Figure 9.9   Experimental Design 1: Comparison Group Pre-Post

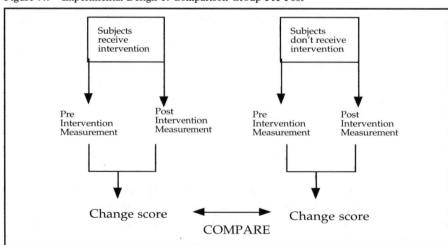

Design 1, shown in Figure 9.9, uses two groups: one receives the intervention and one does not. In Design 1, the evaluator collects a pre-intervention and post-intervention measurement on all subjects. The evaluator then compares the mean change score of the intervention group with the mean change score of the comparison group. As we mentioned in section 9.21 on using pretesting to control extraneous variables, pretesting subjects can possibly contaminate your results by providing subjects with practice on the outcomes measure or spurring them to try harder than they normally would. However, collecting pre-intervention measures does allow you to determine up front if preexisting differences exist between your two groups. This knowledge can help you explain away some rival hypotheses or signal that you might need to select another research design that will control for these preexisting differences.

Figure 9.10 Experimental Design 2: Comparison Group Posttest Only

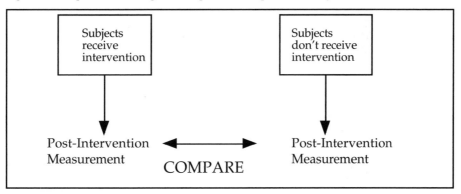

Design 2, shown in Figure 9.10, also uses two groups, but the evaluator collects only a post-intervention measure and compares the mean scores for the two groups. This design avoids the possible contaminating effects of pretesting but makes it difficult for you to ascertain if the groups have any preexisting relevant differences.

As with most things in life, there are trade-offs in using Design 1 over Design 2. You'll just have to determine what is more important to you: knowing about preexisting differences or avoiding the contaminating effects of pretesting.

9.24—Single-Group Design 3: Time Series

Figure 9.11 Experimental Design 3: Single-group Time Series

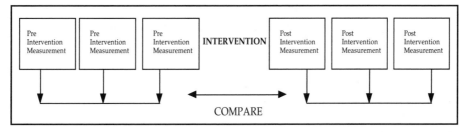

Sometimes as we conduct evaluations in the real world, we simply can't find a suitable comparison group. We must use only one group. Rather than settling for Design 5 with all its contamination, you might consider using a time-series scheme like the one we show in Design 3 in Figure 9.11.

Essentially, in a time-series design, you collect at least three measurements *before* the intervention to establish a baseline trend. You then collect at least three measurements *after* the intervention to see if your intervention breaks the pattern and results in better outcomes. [Note: Three measures rather than just two establishes the pattern.] The time-series design works best in situations where periodic testing is part of the routine. If all goes well and your intervention actually makes a difference, your data will show a break in the trend and look like this:

Figure 9.12 Display of Time Series Data

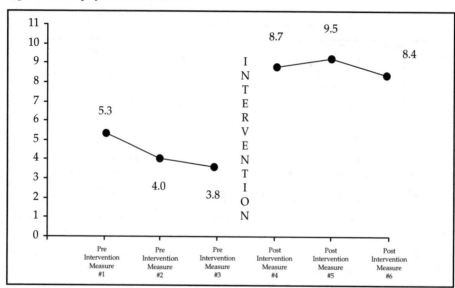

Although you may not be able to control for all extraneous variables, you can strengthen your design by doing the following:

- Randomly selecting your group and thus letting "Lady Luck" create a group that resembles the larger population
- Staying with the same measurement instrument over time
- Using data from only those subjects who take *all* the pre-intervention tests and *all* the post-intervention tests

The time series design has two distinct advantages:

1. It can show whether or not the effects of an intervention endure over time.
2. It controls for maturation since we can usually safely assume that natural growth would equally affect both the pre-intervention and post-intervention measures.

Despite its advantages, the time series design has four pitfalls:

1. Since you can legitimately examine only the performances of those subjects for whom you have ALL pre- and post-intervention measures, you *may end*

up with a remaining group that does not represent all the students. You can determine if major differences exist between those who remain and those who drop out by comparing what pre-intervention measures you do have. If you find that no major differences exist, then you can rule out that rival hypothesis. However, if you do find major differences, you may just have to acknowledge that you know that the intervention worked with only a certain type of student, not all students.

2. Taking so many measurements before and after the intervention might *trigger a practice effect or a "we'll try harder" attitude* among the students. Without a comparison group, you really can't rule out the possibility that the testing itself caused the change rather than the intervention.

3. Given that a time-series often has a long duration, you may run into *contamination from concurrent programs interference*, much like the Zoo Team teachers encountered with the "I Am Somebody" program interfering with their special self-efficacy curriculum. Without a comparison group or random selection, you really cannot rule out the possibility that the concurrent programs rather than your intervention *caused* the change.

4. Finally, when schools use a time-series design over several years to plot changes in student achievement scores, we find that too often they end up *using different achievement tests.* They end up comparing apples to oranges. For example, for the first two years before the intervention, the school has achievement data from the state's multiple-choice, criterion-referenced assessment. But then the testing "tide" turned and the state mandated the use of a performance-based, criterion-referenced assessment that is qualitatively different from the first test.

   What's a school to do? First, the staff can consult with the test designers and see if there is some way to appropriately standardize the student scores on both types of tests. Testing folks have done this with norm-referenced achievement tests by transforming student scores into Normal Curve Equivalents (NCE's). Or the staff can analyze the tests and find items that test similar knowledge and skills on both tests and use the results from these comparable items only. This second option may prove too time consuming and costly. So that brings us to a third option: Abandon the time series design and go with a more suitable plan.

9.25—Single-group Design 4: Successive Pre-Post Testing*

The final research design that we wish to highlight can also help establish causation by using only one group, created either by random selection or by using an existing intact group. Design 4 works particularly well in situations where you are evaluating an intervention that you can turn off or on.

For example, let's say you want to investigate the effectiveness of using study guides to improve your students' comprehension of the material in their social studies text. Figure 9.13 shows the research design for your evaluation. You begin by asking students to read their text without any special guidance. You then test

---

*In research circles, this design goes by the nomenclature ABAB design.

Figure 9.13 Design 4: Successive Pre-Posttesting

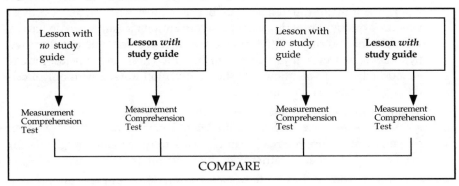

their comprehension of the material to set a baseline. Next, the students read the text, but this time they also use a study guide to help build their understanding. You again test their comprehension of the material. You repeat this same procedure for two more lessons, one without a study guide and one with a guide, always testing the students' comprehension. At the end, you compare the students' scores when they use a study guide to the the scores when they don't use a study guide. Hopefully, you'll see a pattern emerge like the one shown in Figure 9.14 that shows better scores when students use a study guide.

Design 4 can readily identify causality if our results look similar to those we see in Figure 9.14 where the students' performance without the intervention always drops back to the baseline level set by your first measurement. If, however, the students' performance remains high even when you withdraw the intervention, then you cannot conclude the intervention worked. You will have to look to factors other than the intervention as possible causes of the rise in student scores.

Figure 9.14 Results from Evaluation of Study Guide Use

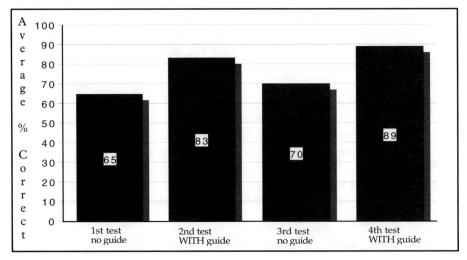

9.26—Jaime Does Step 3

"We want to do it!" the Challenge Team students reply when the teachers ask if they would like to help plan and conduct an evaluation of the service learning piece of the Family and Community unit that they been doing for the last two months. The teachers share the evaluation questions and discuss the various way evaluators collect data by reviewing documents and artifacts, asking, and observing. The teachers also share some of the basics concerning evaluation, such as validity and reliability.

They divide the students into 8 groups and each group tackles one of the evaluation questions. Jaime, Suzanne, and Rob act as consultants. The teachers show the students blank copies of an Evaluation Planning Matrix (Figure 3.1) and a Cross-Walk of Qualitative Data Collection Methods (Figure 3.5), explaining how to use these forms in planning the evaluation.

Jaime and his colleagues soon realize they need some extra help. They call the local university and find four graduate students willing to come into the class at various times during the week to help the student groups devise a plan for conducting the evaluation.

After two weeks of hard work, the Challenge Team teachers and students have completed a plan for getting all the evaluation questions answered. Figure 9.15 shows how one of the student teams (the Mighty B's) plans to answer Evaluation Question #3, "*Do students demonstrate a greater willingness to take responsibility for their actions?*".

At first, the students were simply going to give students, teachers, and parents a questionnaire *before* the service learning activities started and then again at the end of the school year. However, Jaime quickly reminded them that the service learning activities had already begun and they could not get the *before* data. Together they devised the following research design:

Soon several of the other student teams follow the design created by the Mighty B's.

Each of the 8 student teams has completed a draft Evaluation Planning Matrix, along with a Cross-Walk of Qualitative Data Collection to ensure that they are getting corroborating evidence. (They now know what "corroborating" means.)

The teachers give each team copies of all 8 plans with the assignment to "find ways that we can work together to collect the data." The students soon discover that that they really need to create only *one* student survey, *one* teacher survey, and *one* parent survey. They can put all their questions on the same one and send it out at the same time.

Figure 9.15 Evaluation Planning Matrix for Question #3

A Evaluation Question	B Information needed?	C Using what method?	D Who will collect?	E By when?	F How analyze?
Do students demonstrate a greater willingness to take responsibility for their actions?	A. Statements from students about willingness to take responsibility for their actions.	Survey completed by Challenge Team students and comparison group students	Betty, Bob, Belinda, and Blake (the Mighty B's	May 15	The Mighty B's %'s and summary for each question by May 22
	B. Judgment from teachers about whether or not their students demonstrate a greater willingness to take responsibility for their actions.	Survey completed by Challenge Team teachers and comparison group teachers (will get the Special teachers to do one as well)	Betty, Bob, Belinda, and Blake (the Mighty B's)	May 1	The Mighty B's %'s and summary for each question by May 22
	C. Judgment from parents about whether or not their children demonstrate a greater willingness to take responsibility for their actions.	Survey completed by parents of Challenge Team students and parents of comparison group students	Betty, Bob, Belinda, and Blake (the Mighty B's)	May 1	the Mighty B's %'s and summary for each question by May 22

The students create a giant time line across the back wall of the classroom, going from today (November 1) until May 30, the last day of school. Using sticky notes, they put each of the tasks they need to do on the time line. Soon they

Figure 9.16 Research Design for Service Learning Evaluation Question #3

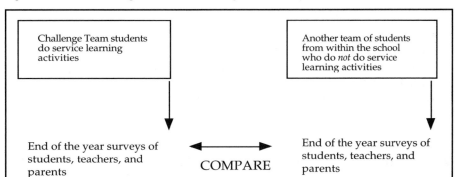

realize that they really don't need to start collecting data until mid-March. So the team decides to take a break from "evaluating," as the kids call it, and return to Step 4: Gather data after the winter holidays.

Meanwhile, Jaime contacts the teachers down the hall to see if they would be willing for their team of students to serve as a comparison group for the evaluation. The teachers consent.

9.27—Determining Effectiveness Step 4: Gather Data

Thus far in our endeavor to answer the question: *"Did it work?"* we have posed the questions that will guide evaluation, established our judgment criteria, and made a plan using the appropriate research design for collecting and analyzing our data. Now, we're ready to actually gather the data.

As you will recall, evaluators gather data by:

- Reviewing documents or artifacts
- Asking
- Observing

In this chapter we will focus on collecting data by asking people for information. We will give you tips on designing and conducting both surveys and interviews.

9.28—Featured Data Collection Method: Asking

Asking people for information or opinions through some sort of survey is probably one of the most frequently used data collection methods. You can gather information and opinions through surveys by:

- Interviewing individuals or groups
- Having people complete a written questionnaire

In the next sections we will deal with giving you advice on crafting a survey, selecting a sample, and actually conducting the survey. Whether you decide to use interviews or a written questionnaire, we suggest that you follow a six-task recipe for developing successful surveys:

Task 1:   Clearly define the information you want to find out through the survey.
Task 2:   Determine who will complete your survey.
Task 3:   Decide what method you will use to collect the survey information.
Task 4:   Prepare the survey materials.
Task 5:   Design your procedures for conducting the survey.
Task 6:   Pilot test your survey.

9.29—Developing Surveys Task 1:
Define What You Want to Find Out

As with any evaluation endeavor, you should always begin by clearly defining what information you need. The first task in survey development requires that you delineate as completely as possible what information you want to collect using your survey. This information generally falls into three categories:

1. *Demographic information* about the people completing the survey. Knowing such things as age, gender, and socioeconomic status about your subjects can help you describe the overall characteristics of your survey group.

2. *Factual information* about the subjects. Sometimes you want to know specifics about the subjects' background or behaviors. For example, if you're conducting a survey to ascertain the need for an after-school homework center, you may want to survey parents about their usual working hours. Or, you might want to ask students how often each week they have homework to complete.

3. *Opinions and attitudes* held by the subjects. Finally, many evaluators use surveys to systematically gather the opinions and beliefs of students and adults. Surveys, when done well, can effectively gauge public opinion.

As you define what information you want from the survey, you need to strike a balance between asking too little and too much. Generally, a survey is a one-shot data collection method. Rarely can you return to a survey respondent and ask for additional information. Thus, you need to make sure you do it right the first time.

Conversely, you should avoid asking so many questions that your respondents give up in disgust, leaving you with incomplete or garbage data. You can often pare the number of questions by asking only those questions that yield information you can't get elsewhere. For example, if you are distributing surveys only to fifth grade students, then you really don't need to waste space by asking students to indicate their grade level on the survey.

9.30—Developing Surveys Task 2:
Determine Who Will Complete Your Survey

Once you have delineated the information you want from the survey, you now need to define *who* you want to complete your survey. Of course, you can choose to survey the entire group or *population* of interest. For example, if you want to gather student opinions about the academic rigor of their classes, you could ask *all* the students in your school to complete a survey and, given the circumstances, you could easily get almost a 100% response rate. However, you may not want to tabulate that much data, so you might want to survey only a *representative sample* of students.

The key to getting a representative sample is to use some form of random selection. In section 4.8 we described four forms of of random selection that can help to minimize bias and ensure that naturally occurring differences among people get spread evenly throughout the sample:

- Simple random sampling
- Stratified random sampling
- Cluster sampling
- Systematic random sampling

Not only should you use random selection to choose your sample, you should also pay attention to the size of your sample. The number of respondents will determine just how confident you can be that your sample speaks for the larger population it represents. Remember, every time we use a sample rather than a whole population we have some margin of error when we generalize from the sample to the population. When we use sample data to indicate what people in the whole population might say, we need to build a confidence interval around our sample data.

Suppose we've conducted a survey among the parents of our school. We have approximately 1000 parents and from that population we randomly survey 600 parents and get 516 responses. Of those who responded, 75% said they feel that the teachers care about their children. But what would all 1000 parents have said if we had asked *all* of them? Using what our sample said, we can calculate a confidence interval and say, with some degree of accuracy (95%), that between 72% to 78% (margin of error = ±3% points) of all parents would have said the teachers care about their children.

As a rule, the larger your sample size, the smaller the margin of error. But a strange thing happens as your sample size edges beyond 1000 subjects. The margin of error really doesn't improve that much as you add subjects. Due to a quirk of probability, the margin of error for a sample size of 1000 is about the same when drawn from a population of 100,000, 1 million, or 100 million.

So what should your sample size be? Drawing from a very handy table on page 55 of Salant and Dillman (1994), you can use the following guidelines:

To achieve a margin of error of ±3 percentage points at a 95% confidence level use:

92 subjects	———>	when you draw from a total population of 100
203 subjects	———>	when you draw from a total population of 250
341 subjects	———>	when you draw from a total population of 500
441 subjects	———>	when you draw from a total population of 750
516 subjects	———>	when you draw from a total population of 1000
748 subjects	———>	when you draw from a total population of 2500
880 subjects	———>	when you draw from a total population of 5000

Of course, if you're willing to live with a larger margin of error (±10 percentage points) you can go with smaller sample sizes. Salant and Dillman (1994) give a complete table of recommended sample sizes on page 55 of their very readable book *How to Conduct your own Survey.* On page 79 of her book *Questionnaire Research: A Practical Guide,* Patten (1998) also provides another very usable table that gives recommended sample sizes

9.31—Developing Surveys Task 3: Decide What Method

Now that you have decided what information you want and who will complete your survey, you need to decide which survey method you want to use. Basically, you have five choices:

1. You can *directly administer* a written survey to a group.
    We often use this survey method whenever we ask our students to complete a survey during class time.
2. You can *mail the written survey* to your selected group.
    Sending a parent survey home with students falls within this category.
3. You can *drop off a written survey* and then return later to pick it up.
4. You can *telephone your sample* and conduct the survey.
5. Finally, you can conduct *face-to-face interviews* with your subjects.

Deciding which survey method would work best for your survey depends on several factors:

- How many respondents you wish to survey
- How quickly you need your information
- How much money you have to spend on conducting the survey
- How easy it will be to contact the people you wish to survey
- Whether or not you have the necessary staff to conduct the survey
- Whether or not you need to maintain anonymity
- What level of detail do you need when people answer your questions

The matrix shown in Figure 9.17 rates each of the five survey methods on these seven factors and lays out the advantages and disadvantages.

9.32—Developing Surveys Task 4: Prepare Survey Materials

Thus far in developing your survey, you have:

- Clearly defined the information you want to find out through the survey
- Determined who will complete your survey
- Decided what method you will use to collect the survey information

Now comes the crucial task of actually crafting the survey itself and preparing any other materials you need to successfully conduct the survey. We'll begin by looking at what it takes to design a written questionnaire. Then we'll move to the particulars of conducting interviews, both over the telephone and face-to-face.

Figure 9.17 Advantages and Disadvantages of Survey Methods

	A. Directly administer a written survey to a group	B. Mail the written survey to a selected group	C. Drop off written survey and then return later to pick it up	D. Telephone your sample	E. Conduct face-to-face interviews with a sample
1. Ease in reaching many respondents	◆◆◆	◆◆◆	◆◆	◆◆	◆
2. Quick turnaround	◆◆◆	◆◆	◆◆	◆◆◆	◆◆
3. Inexpensive	◆◆◆	◆◆	◆◆	◆◆	◆
4. Easy to contact people	◆◆◆	◆◆◆	◆◆	◆◆◆	◆◆
5. Few trained staff needed	◆◆	◆◆◆	◆◆	◆	◆
6. High level of anonymity	◆◆	◆◆◆	◆◆	◆	◆
7. High level of detail available	◆	◆	◆	◆◆◆	◆◆◆

◆ Good   ◆◆ Better   ◆◆◆◆ Best

	A. Directly administer a written survey to a group	B. Mail the written survey to a selected group	C. Drop off written survey and then return later to pick it up	D. Telephone your sample	E. Conduct face-to-face interviews with a sample
Advantages	• Allows for visual presentation of material • Respondents can get clarification on confusing questions • Provides think-time for respondents • Can clarify questions	• Allows for visual presentation of material • Provides think-time for respondents • Economical • Can easily automate the mailing process	• Often possible to get high response rates • Easy to follow-up on non-respondents • Provides think-time for respondents	• Can do at times convenient with respondent • Can probe for clarification and reasoning • Can conduct at a distance • Can control who in a household completes the survey	• Can do at times convenient with respondent • Can probe for clarification and reasoning • People more apt to participate
Disadvantages	• Can't probe for more detail • Need to consider length • Have to find a suitable time to administer • Respondents may get into a response rut answering all questions the same way • Difficult to follow-up with non-respondents	• Can't probe for more detail • Need to consider length • Respondents may get into a response rut answering all questions the same way • Difficult to follow up • Can't clarify questions • Respondents self-select for participation	• Sometimes logistical difficulties in getting staff to deliver and pick up questionnaires • Can't probe for more detail • Need to consider length • Respondents may get into a response rut answering all questions the same way	• Requires more, trained staff • Sometimes difficult to transcribe responses fast enough • People wary of unsolicited telephone calls	• Data may be skewed by interviewer characteristics • Requires more, trained staff • Sometimes difficult to transcribe responses fast enough
Comments	• Easy to use with student populations • Consent implied by completion and return of survey	• Good method to use when you have over 100 potential respondents to contact • Consent implied by completion and return of survey	• Good method to use when really need subjects to respond but difficult to arrange a face-to-face interview • Consent implied by completion and return of survey	• Need to obtain explicit informed consent	• Need to obtain explicit informed consent • Best used with small sample or when people won't respond using another method

9.33—Issue Box

Using Commercially Available Surveys

Rather than spend so much time and energy on designing their own written questionnaires, some educators decide to use an already-developed, standardized survey. A review of the educational research concerning programs similar to that you're evaluating may yield a suitable survey (free for the asking) that some evaluator or researcher has already developed. The ERIC Clearinghouse on Assessment and Evaluation on the Internet at http://ericae2.educ.cua.edu/ is a good source. Just click on *Test Locator* and then click again on *ETS/ERIC Test File*. You can then search by topic for the particular type of survey you need.

You may also find useful surveys by contacting your state department of education. Finally, some educational organizations and companies offer ready-to-use packages you can purchase to survey members of your school community. Often these package deals not only provide the survey materials, but also do the analyses as well.

Your decision to use already-developed standardized surveys should revolve around two questions:

- Does this survey fit your purpose and gather the information you need?
- Can you afford the cost of using a commercial survey?

Sometimes, just reviewing an already well-developed survey can give you guidance in developing your own. You can get ideas on how to successfully word and format questions. However, please do not simply lift questions from an existing copyrighted survey without prior permission of the authors.

At end of this chapter in section 9.56 Resources we list some sources where you can obtain already-developed surveys.

9.34—Designing Written Questionnaires

The steps in preparing a written questionnaire are the same whether you decide to directly administer your questionnaire, mail it out, or drop it off and pick it up later.

1. Carefully craft your questions.
2. Put the questions into a layout that not only invites people to respond but also allows for easy tabulation.
3. Prepare a cover letter that both explains the survey's purpose and persuades people to respond.

9.35—Crafting Questions for a Written Survey: Question Format

Typically, written survey questions fall into three broad categories:

1. Open-ended
2. Forced choice
3. Ranking

Each question format has its advantages and disadvantages. Deciding which format would work best for a particular question depends on several factors:

- The difficulty level in completing the survey
- The level of detail you need when people answer your questions
- How much time you can devote to tabulating responses
- What kinds of statistical analyses you wish to perform on the data

The matrix shown in Figure 9.18 gives examples of each of the various written survey question formats, along with a listing of the advantages and disadvantages of using each format. Hopefully, this matrix can help you decide which question format will work best for your survey.

9.36—Crafting Questions for a Written Survey: Advice

In section 9.56 Resources we list several books that contain excellent advice for devising written survey questions. We highlight ten suggestions we see as crucial.

1. Always KISS (Keep It Short and Simple) your questions. Few respondents will wade their way through long, convoluted questions.

2. Use clear, unambiguous language, avoiding vague words, technical terms, abbreviations, and jargon.

3. Include only *one* concept in a single item. Perhaps a negative example will demonstrate what we mean. Let's say 95% of the teachers in a middle school marked STRONGLY AGREE on the following item:

    Indicate the extent to which you agree or disagree with the following statement:

    1. Rigor and relevance are important components of a good middle school curriculum.
       ____   STRONGLY AGREE
       ____   MILDLY AGREE
       ____   UNDECIDED OR UNSURE
       ____   MILDLY DISAGREE
       ____   STRONGLY DISAGREE

Because the item includes both *rigor* and *relevance*, we can't say for certain that 95% of the teachers strongly agreed that both qualities are important components of a good middle school curriculum. Some teachers may have marked STRONGLY AGREE because they consider *relevance* highly important but really don't feel that strongly about *rigor*.

Figure 9.18 Advantages and Disadvantages of Various Question Formats

Format	Example	Advantages	Disadvantages	Comments

Closed, with ordered choices	A. My teachers make learning interesting.
	Strongly agree
	Agree
	Disagree
	Strongly disagree
		• Easy to tabulate
		• Lends itself to various statistical analyses that deal with ordered (ordinal) data
		• Demands little on the part of respondents
			• Requires careful crafting to make sure that the choices:
			  –flow in a logical order
			  –include all possible responses
			• May frustrate respondents who dislike constraints
				• Be sure that continuum follows an order that RESPONDENTS will find logical
				• Make sure to also include all possible choices in the continuum

Closed, with unordered choices	B. Which way would you prefer we share your child's academic progress with you? Mail the grade report to my home Hold a parent-teacher conference	• Easy to tabulate • Can perform a chi-square test for goodness-of-fit to ascertain if people prefer one choice over another • Demands little on the part of respondents	• Requires careful crafting to make sure that the choices include all possible responses • May frustrate respondents who dislike constraints • Can perform few statistical analyses other than calculating %'s or chi-square test for goodness-of-fit	• Best used when all possible choices fall within a reasonable number of categories
Partially closed	C. How would you prefer to be informed of upcoming events and programs at the school? Flyer sent home Weekly school newsletter Monthly calendar Phone reminder Other. Please specify	• Easy to tabulate • Allows for "free spirited" responses • Demands little on the part of respondents • Doesn't require as careful crafting as OTHER category acts as a catch all for unlisted choices	• OTHER category difficult to tabulate • People may shy away from OTHER category because they don't want to spend time writing • Can perform few statistical analyses other than calculating%'s or chi-square test for goodness-of-fit	• Best used when not sure of all possible responses people might make OR when the list of ALL responses is too long and only a few will fall in certain categories
Ranking	D. Please mark on the line the three most effective ways for you to learn. A Teacher lecture B Class discussion C Hands-on projects D Reading a textbook E Small group __ Most __ 2nd __ 3rd	• Lends itself to statistical procedures for analyzing ordinal data	• Very difficult for respondents to do, requiring much think-time	• Use sparingly
Open-ended	E. When you get angry, what do you usually do to calm down?	• Allows for richly detailed responses • Excellent when the evaluator doesn't know much about where people stand. (Later can use to create forced choice responses in the final version of the survey.) • Gives respondents opportunity to make comments. • Can use to find out "why" someone chose a particular response in a closed choice question • Can ask for precise information • Very demanding of respondents	• Very time consuming and often difficult to tabulate • May get "off-the-wall" and mean-spirited responses • Can do little statistical analysis other than calculating percentages • Use sparingly	• Leave adequate space for responses • Best used when the evaluator might have overlooked possible choices

4. Avoid using leading questions that suggest a preferred response. In particular, don't ask questions that make respondents disapprove of themselves.

    Again a negative example from a questionnaire sent to parents might best illustrate what we suggest.

    > Research shows that students whose parents talk to them daily about their school work make higher grades. How often do you talk with your child about the classes and activities at StrivingHigher Middle School?
    >
    >   _____ DAILY
    >   _____ SEVERAL TIMES A WEEK
    >   _____ ONCE OR TWICE A WEEK
    >   _____ RARELY

    Some slight revisions would make this question more appropriate.

    > How often do you talk with your child about school work?
    >
    >   _____ DAILY
    >   _____ SEVERAL TIMES A WEEK
    >   _____ ONCE OR TWICE A WEEK
    >   _____ RARELY

5. Request only information that respondents can reasonably provide. Don't ask respondents to recall minute details of their lives or give opinions on topics about which they know little to nothing.

6. Make the reading level of the items appropriate for the respondents. For parent surveys, you also may need to translate your survey into the parents' primary language.

7. If you use a forced-choice question format, make sure you include *all* possible choices a respondent might want to make.

8. Again, if you use a forced-choice question format where respondents must choose only one choice, make sure all choices are mutually exclusive.

    Once again a negative example from a student survey provides an illustration.

    > How many hours do you generally watch television on school nights?
    >
    > 1. I don't watch TV
    > 2. less than 30 minutes
    > 3. 30 minutes to 2 hours
    > 4. 1 to 3 hours
    > 5. more than 3 hours
    >
    > As you can see, responses (3) and (4) overlap and can cause confusion. And we suspect that most students would make an argument that responses (1) and (2) even overlap.

9. Keep your question format consistent. You might want to slightly vary your format to prevent boredom, but too much variation can confuse.

10. When gathering opinions about a certain topic, consider asking several different questions about the topic rather than just one question. This way you

don't have rely so heavily on just one response when you interpret your data.

9.37—Laying Out the Questionnaire

In designing an effective survey, you should not only consider how you write your questions, but you should also pay attention to the layout of the entire questionnaire. We offer the following advice:

1. Avoid a cluttered look by using ample white space.

2. Choose an easy-to-read font style and size.

3. Ask questions in an order that *respondents* will find logical.

4. Start with easier questions and then move to more difficult ones

5. Decide *where* to place demographic questions. Sometimes it makes more sense to put these types of informational questions up front and at other times they work better at the end of the questionnaire.

6. Don't start an item on one page and finish it on the next.

7. Consider ways you can make your questionnaire not only easy to complete but also easy to tabulate. This means that you might label your choices in some appropriate way.

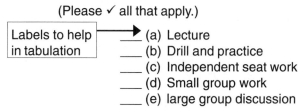

What teaching methods do you use *each day* in your class-room?

(Please ✓ all that apply.)

| Labels to help in tabulation | → | ___ (a) Lecture |

___ (a) Lecture
___ (b) Drill and practice
___ (c) Independent seat work
___ (d) Small group work
___ (e) large group discussion

9.38—Preparing a Cover Letter

If you plan to mail out your questionnaire, you also need to prepare a cover letter. A good cover letter will accomplish two things:

1. Explain the survey's purpose and

2. Persuade people to respond.

Through the years, survey researchers have found that the following helps convince people to respond to a written questionnaire:

a. People tend to respond when they perceive that the *cost of responding is low in comparison to the perceived reward.* If people feel that they are providing information that will help solve a problem or prompt an action they deem useful, they will take the time and effort to honestly respond to your survey. For example, teachers are willing to complete rather lengthy written surveys if they *know* that their voices will be heard in future planning that will help kids.

b. People are more willing to complete a questionnaire if the evaluator *in some way shows high, positive regard* for the respondent. Sincerely telling potential respondents that "their opinions count," can help persuade people to complete the questionnaire.

c. *Expressing appreciation* in advance to the respondent for completing the questionnaire also increases response rates.

d. Telling respondents that the evaluator is *consulting the respondent on an important issue* often persuades people to respond.

e. Response rate goes up if the evaluator *includes some incentive* that says, "Thanks for taking time to do the survey." We've seen schools get almost 100% response rate on parent surveys by having parents exchange a completed questionnaire for a lottery number tied to a drawing of prizes.

f. Telling respondents in your cover letter *how much time* it will take to complete the questionnaire also improves the response rate.

g. Finally, a cover letter *addressed to a specific person and signed* by the sender encourages people to respond. Such personal gestures tell the respondent, "You're special and we want to know what you think."

Dillman's *Mail and Telephone Surveys: The Total Design Method* (1979) listed in the 9.56 Resources section includes many more suggestions along with several examples of cover letters with proven track records in increasing response rate.

9.39—Crafting Questions for Telephone Interviews

Much of the advice we offered in section 9.36 about crafting *written* survey questions also holds when you devise questions for surveys conducted over the telephone. However, there is one big difference:

You must write for the "ear" and not the eyes of your respondents.

This means you must write the questions so that people can easily follow them by listening without the benefit of visuals. Particularly, you should avoid excessive wordiness and convoluted questions that lose your listener.

Other things to keep in mind as you craft telephone survey questions include:

a. Have a logical flow to the sequence of questions. You might consider starting with easy-to-answer questions and then moving to more difficult ones.

b. Consider employing the "funnel" questioning technique where you begin with open-ended questions that get your respondent talking and then go to confirming questions that the respondent can answer with a short answer, or a simple "yes" or "no."

c. Use a personal, more conversational tone in your writing. (Section 7.5 gives more details about writing in the personal style.)

d. Finally, build in probes. These are questions that allow you to clarify a respondent's answer or get more detail. Telephone interviews allow you to inquire more deeply and find out the "whys" behind a respondent's thinking.

9.40—Crafting Questions for Face-to-Face Interviews

Writing an interview protocol, the questions you'll use in conducting a face-to-face interview, should follow much of the same advice we gave in section 9.36 (crafting written survey questions) and section 9.39 (crafting questions for telephone interviews). However, you do have one advantage in a face-to-face interview that you don't have with other survey methods: You can *use visuals* to help clarify your questions. Some interviewers will actually give the respondent a copy of the questions to follow as they conduct the interview.

9.41—Developing Surveys Task 5: Design Your Procedures

Every task in designing a survey has two purposes:

1. To get reliable and valid information from respondents
2. To obtain a high response rate

Elsewhere in this chapter, we've discussed ways to ensure that the data you get from your survey are both reliable and valid. In this section, we want to focus on procedures that help increase the participation rate.

Let's start with *mail surveys*. The following are some suggestions that will help encourage potential respondents to participate in your survey:

a. Keep your survey reasonable in length. In our experience, parents and community members are willing to complete a one to two page survey. Teachers and other staff are generally willing to answer a longer survey, somewhere between four and six pages. Students, particularly if they answer the questionnaire during class time, can easily handle a questionnaire somewhere between two and four pages. Making your survey too long will tire respondents and you'll find that their answers become less valid and reliable.

b. Contact respondents prior to mailing to let them know a questionnaire is coming. If you have the luxury of time and money, you can do this by telephone or post card.

c. Include a self-addressed stamped envelope the respondent can use to return the questionnaire to you. No one likes to hunt around for a stamp just to return a questionnaire.

d. Make sure that the envelope and the cover letter don't look like junk mail. The envelope should be typed or handwritten for both the address and return address. Furthermore, you should address the envelope and cover letter to a specific person. "Dear Patron" rarely inspires people to respond to a questionnaire.

e. In your cover letter, specify a date for respondents to return their questionnaires. We suggest giving them about a week. If you allow more time, or don't put any deadline, you find your participation rate goes down.

f. Build in procedures to follow up those respondents who have not yet returned their completed surveys. To do this you can:

   1. Send a reminder letter that includes another copy of the questionnaire and a self-addressed stamped envelope. If respondents anonymously return the surveys, you have no way of tracking who has or has not re-

sponded. Therefore, you will need to send a reminder letter to *all* potential respondents. You may have to do as many as two follow-up mailings to get an acceptable participation rate. Be sure to ask those who have responded to discard the second and third copies and not complete another one.

2. If sending out reminder packets with another copy of the questionnaire is too expensive, simply send a reminder postcard.

3. Finally, some schools with automated calling equipment can call and remind parents to return questionnaires.

Through the years, we've worked with many schools that regularly survey parents. Often, these schools experience difficulty in getting an acceptable number of parents to return the completed questionnaires. However, below are some "tried and true" techniques successfully used by schools:

1. Find some sort of incentives for students and teachers to remind parents to return their questionnaires. One middle school offered a pizza party to all students whose parents returned completed questions, while the teachers whose classes had a high return rate received a lunch "on the town."

2. Send the survey in a packet with regular mailings from the school or other community organizations. One school mailed its parent questionnaire with first quarter grade cards.

3. Rather than mail or send home questionnaires, collect the survey data as part of a well-attended school event, such as an open-house or a music program.

Although *drop-off surveys* enjoy a fairly good history of high participation, some procedures that can increase participation rates include:

1. Setting an appointment for dropping off and picking up the questionnaire.

2. Having the same person both drop off and pick up the questionnaire. This way, the courier has an opportunity to build a personal relationship with the potential respondent. People tend to respond well to personal appeals for participation.

Direct administration of a survey is one of the easiest and fastest survey collection methods. The personal touch given by the person who hands out the survey and gives directions can really help increase participation. However, you may have to train those who will administer your survey so that confusion doesn't arise.

Telephone surveys require a bit more preparation than other survey methods if you want to ensure both the quality of your data and a high participation rate. Not only do you need to carefully prepare an interview protocol (including directions on how to select respondents), but you also have to train the people who conduct the interview. In this day and age, where the general public is wary of unsolicited phone calls, your interviewers must be skilled if you're going to get meaningful data from a telephone survey. Below are some suggestions to keep in mind:

1. Prepare an introduction that both explains the survey's purpose and persuades people to respond. The first few seconds of an unsolicited phone call

will determine whether or not the potential respondent decides to participate in your survey.

2. Use a scripted introduction but interviewers should read it in a conversational tone. We've all encountered stilted telephone solicitors that immediately turn us off.

3. Be ready to clarify. The beauty of an interview is that respondents can get misunderstandings clarified immediately. This makes for more valid and reliable data.

4. Have a logical flow to the sequence of questions.

5. Use procedures that allow the interview to flow at a comfortable pace *for the respondent*. This means you need to devise ways for your interviewer to quickly record the responses to the questions. Checklists of expected responses the interviewer can easily mark can help keep the pace moving quickly. For open-ended questions, allow space right on the interview protocol so that the interviewer can take notes. Finally, if you anticipate getting lengthy, unique responses during an interview consider asking respondents to allow you to audio record their interviews. You can easily record telephone conversations, *after gaining permission*, by using an inexpensive suction cup microphone that you can purchase at most audio/video stores.

The advice given about designing procedures for telephone interview also applies when conducting *face-to-face interviews*. However, there is one aspect of conducting face-to-face interviewing that warrants attention. You should be aware that certain characteristics of the interviewer may influence both a respondent's decision to participate and his or her responses to your questions. Physical appearance (gender, age, race, ethnicity, dress) can have an influence for good or bad, particularly when the interviewer is a stranger to the respondent. Within two minutes of meeting a stranger, we human beings generally form an iron-clad judgment of that stranger's character and this judgment influences our interactions with that stranger. Training interviewers in positive people skills and giving some thought as to whom potential respondents will most likely react favorably will help increase both the participation rate and quality of your survey data.

9.42—Developing Surveys Task 6: Pilot Test Your Survey

Whether you plan to use a written question or conduct interview, the final task in creating a survey involves performing a pilot test—you take it out for a "test drive" before you collect any actual data. During the pilot test, you need to examine three factors:

1. The individual questions themselves

2. The procedures you'll follow in conducting the survey

3. In the case of written surveys, the questionnaire layout

The following are seven questions to guide the "test drive" of your survey:

1. Is each question gathering the information you need?

2. Do respondents understand all the words?

3. Do respondents interpret each question in the same way?

4.   Does the overall questionnaire invite people to respond?

5.   Do you detect any systematic bias in the wording of the questions?

6.   Do you detect any systematic bias in the survey procedures?

7.   Do responses people give to each question make sense to you?

—(paraphrased from Salant and Dillman, 1994, p. 120–121)

Although several pretesting techniques exist, we suggest the following three because of their ease in use:

- Do a "think aloud" interview with a selected group of respondents, either while they complete the survey or immediately afterwards. Focus on finding out how they interpreted each question and why they answered the way they did. Often this will help you spot confusing questions and procedures.

- Instead of doing a face-to-face "think aloud" interview, you can simply include a series of follow-up questions at the end of a field test version of your survey. These debriefing questions ask respondents to indicate their reactions to various aspects of the questionnaire and explain how they interpreted the questions.

- A final method for pretesting a survey requires that you examine how often people leave a question blank or answer "don't know." Questions with a high number of blanks or "don't knows" often indicate trouble. Perhaps these questions confuse respondents, require too much effort to answer, or touch on sensitive issues.

> Author's note: As I was writing this section at my home computer, I received a telephone call from a market research group asking if I would answer several questions. The interviewer then proceeded in a very professional manner to explain that he was not selling anything and wanted to ask questions about our community. Feeling that I was providing important feedback, I answered all the questions concerning the local government, schools, business community, and media.
>
> Then the second half of the survey took a decidedly different turn. The interviewer now asked that I indicate whether or not I was familiar with a particular organization or product. He then asked me to make a series of judgments about the people who belong to these organizations or use these products. Essentially the questions wanted to know if I see these folks as healthy, neighborly people who spend their money wisely and are concerned with nature and the community? Everything was going well until we got to about the fifteenth product and the interviewer asked "How do you see people who drink Coca-Cola?" Then he moved on to "who drink Budweiser?" and finally "who drive a Mercedes car?" By this time, both the interviewer and I agreed that the "healthy-neighborly-thrifty-community-and-nature-minded" questions were ludicrous. Garbage data surely flowed at this point!

Lessons affirmed by this episode:

1. Beware of asking questions your respondents will find ridiculous and not worthy of a decent answer.

2. Avoid excessive repetition, so much that your respondents get silly or agitated.

Given the length and strangeness of the second half of this telephone survey, I wonder if these market researchers really did take their survey for a "test drive" before using it. I doubt it, since, in my opinion, the "engine" stalled midway through my interview.

—Brenda LeTendre, Co-author

9.43—The Ethics of Surveys

Aretha Franklin was correct! R-E-S-P-E-C-T is everything, especially when it comes to collecting survey data. Ethical standards require that you treat respondents with respect at all times. This respect comes in two forms—Respecting the rights of those who choose not to participate and ensuring confidentiality of those who do.

First, you must respect the rights of those who choose *not* to participate. You can persuade or remind people to participate, but you should never coerce someone into completing a survey. This right to refuse even applies to middle school students. Everyone, even a student, has the right to refuse participation. Furthermore, no one should suffer any negative consequences because of his or her refusal.

Second, you must ensure the confidentiality of respondents. Even when you, the evaluator, *know* an individual's name, you should never divulge individually identifiable responses without prior permission, particularly in reports. When you do collect names with survey information, remove any identifying information and assign a code number as soon as it's practical. Most often you'll have no difficulty ensuring confidentiality because respondents will complete the survey anonymously.

Sometimes in schools, students and adults will raise the issue of anonymity, particularly when dealing with a written survey. "They'll recognize my handwriting" respondents say. To get around this, you can either have the surveys tabulated by a trusted third party who is the only one to see the actual surveys OR you can design questions that require only check marks or circles, thus no handwritten answers. Some schools use bubble-in answer sheets that get "read" by a scanner.

9.44—Getting Students Involved

Students don't have to simply complete surveys. They can also design and conduct surveys. What better way to engage middle school students in real-world learning than empowering them "to conduct evaluations of the projects in which they are involved" (National Center for Service Learning in Early Adolescence, 1994, p. iii). Not only do students provide a needed service, but they also learn important research and writing skills and build a sense that *they* can make a difference in the world around them.

The coil-bound document *Student Evaluators: A Guide to Implementation* (1994) provides a road map for educators who wish to involve their students in designing and conducting surveys. The Guide also provides lessons on analyzing and reporting the results. Section 9.56 Resources has the information you'll need to obtain a copy of this valuable guide.

9.45—Jaime Does Step 4

The students return from the winter break hyper and eager to get started on "evaluating." The Challenge Team teachers remind the students that so far they have completed these tasks:

1. Posed the eight questions that will guide the evaluation of service learning
2. Established the judgment criteria they will use to determine if the service learning project accomplished its goals
3. Created a plan using an Evaluation Planning Matrix for getting answers to their eight evaluation questions

Now they are ready to actually collect data. Seven of the eight teams need to create surveys. The teams dealing with Evaluation Questions 2, 3, and 4 will work together to craft survey questions dealing with sensitivity towards others, willingness to take responsibility, and social competence. They will put these questions on three similar surveys, one that students will complete, one that teachers will do, and one that parents will fill out.

Jaime conducted a workshop on writing survey questions with all his classes. The students particularly got a kick out of the exercise he called "The Good, the Bad, and the Ugly" that asked students to identify and write examples of good, bad, and downright mean-spirited survey questions.

Jaime also showed them a question format invented by a man named Rennis Likert that allows them to write items that ask people to indicate how much they agree or disagree with a particular statement. The students immediately see that this format might work really well in gauging student, teacher, and parent attitudes and judgment about sensitivity, responsibility, community participation, and social competence.

The teams who will gather data for Evaluation Question 8, "*Has service learning made a positive impact at the sites where our students volunteer?*", are devising a special survey that they will mail out to the heads of the various agencies where students volunteer.

All teams working on surveys plan to conduct a pilot test of their instruments. The students express amazement at how difficult it is to write a *really* good survey question.

Two teams have been working with Rob to find suitable tests to measure real-world problem solving skills and self-efficacy. These teams want to use a commercially-produced test rather than creating one on their own. Rob tells them about a government site on the Internet, ERIC's Clearinghouse on Assessment and Evaluation, where they can search a list of commercial tests available for some idea of appropriate tests. He also reminds them that the school has very little money to spend on the evaluation so they should look for a cheap or free test.

The team tackling Evaluation Question 7, *"Does participation in service learning activities improve attendance?",* are pouring over attendance data that the principal's office supplied them.

One team has hit a major snag. This team is dealing with Evaluation Question 6 that asks if students increase their achievement in reading and math. The students want to use the scores from the state assessments they take each April. The problem is this: the test scores for April's test won't be back until after school's out.

Jaime suggests that these two teams carefully write a "recipe" for him to follow this summer to gather and analyze the data. The students get busy because they know Mr. Sanchez will want a very detailed recipe!

By May 15, the state assessments are over and all the student evaluation teams except the one dealing with achievement in reading and math, have collected their data. Now they are ready to make sense out of it. They have just two weeks.

9.46—Determining Effectiveness Step 5: Analyze Data

Let's refresh our memories about where we are in our six-step process for determining the effectiveness of an intervention. We've posed our evaluation questions, established our judgment criteria, made a plan, and collected our data. In Step 4: Gather Data, we digressed for a while to give a somewhat in-depth discussion about using surveys to collect data.

Now we come to Step 5 in our process for determining the effectiveness of a strategy. We're now ready to analyze our data.

Earlier in Chapter 5 we emphasized that analyzing your data involves three tasks:

1. Organizing your data
2. Summarizing your data
3. Analyzing your data

Sections 5.2 through 5.5 give many suggestions on how you can organize both quantitative (number) and qualitative (word) data, while sections 5.6 through 5.14 focus on the various ways you can describe the central tendency and variability of your data. You should take a few moments now and flip back to these sections just to refresh your memory. You'll find that many of the examples we used in chapter 5 deal with survey results.

Chapter 5 (sections 5.15–5.23) also gives an overview of the procedures you can use to answer the three major questions of inferential statistics:

1. Is there a *significant* difference between Group A which got the special instruction and Group B which got only the usual instruction?

2. Does a *significant* preference exist among the choices people make?

3. Does a *significant* relationship or correlation exist within the data?

In this chapter, we will focus on Question 1 since ascertaining if a significant difference exists lies at the heart of trying to determine the effectiveness of an intervention. Using Jaime's example we will show how a statistical procedure known as a *t*-test helped him and his colleagues decide if service learning activities worked and made a difference in their students' academic achievement.

9.47—Using a *t*-test to Answer the Question: *Did It Work?*

In chapter 6, we outlined how you can use statistical calculations to determine if an innovative educational strategy actually works. Generally, we use an experimental design (such as Designs 1 and 2 shown in Figure 9.4) and set up two groups. Keeping everything equal, one group gets the innovative program (the "treatment"), while the comparison group gets only the usual program. We collect outcome data on both groups (perhaps some sort of skill test) and calculate the mean score for each group. If we see a *significant* difference between the two groups, we can then logically conclude that the "treatment" caused this difference.

A *significant* difference is a difference that would rarely occur by chance. In fact, most evaluators will set their chance level at 5%. This means that the difference we observed between the two mean scores would occur by chance only 5 times out of a 100, should we repeat our experiment over and over with different samples.

One of the most common statistical procedures used to determine whether or not a *significant* difference exists between two mean scores is the t-test. Several varieties of the t-test formula exist:

- A single-sample t-test for comparing a sample mean with the expected (or hypothesized) mean of a population

- A related samples t-test for comparing the sample means of two matched groups or pre/post test means for one group

- An independent measures t-test for comparing the sample means of two independent (not matched) groups.

Any good statistics textbook (and we recommend some in section 5.28 Resources) can walk you through the calculations for a t-test statistic. Frankly, in this age of computers, you can readily find software that will do the calculations in a blink of an eye. Excel™ by Microsoft which comes bundled on many computers will easily handle the calculations for you.

But *you* have to do two things, tell the software package which t-test formula to use and then interpret the statistic.

First, you have to tell the software package which t-test formula to use. A good statistics book will help you decide whether to use a single-sample t-test, related samples t-test, or independent measures t-test. Page A61 in the Gravetter and Wallnau (1996) text *Statistics for the Behavioral Sciences (4th Edition)* that we recommend in Section 5.28 Resources contains a particularly helpful decision-tree that walks you straight to the appropriate t-test formula you should use.

Second, you have to interpret what the t statistic tells you. This is where the hypothesis testing process we covered in section 6.5 comes in handy. This process uses a combination of logic and statistics to help you decide if a significant difference exists between two means, thus helping you ascertain whether or not your innovative strategy worked.

Although we walked through a detailed example of how the Zoo Team teachers used the hypothesis testing process to show that their self-efficacy program worked in Section 6.6, let's refresh our memories about the hypothesis testing process.

Task 1

You write two hypotheses—a null hypothesis stating that NO DIFFERENCE exists and an alternative hypothesis stating that a DIFFERENCE DOES exist. If you can knock down the null hypothesis with your data, you then can accept your alternative hypothesis and conclude that the innovative strategy worked. Of course, the opposite holds true as well. If you can't knock down the null hypothesis, you must conclude that a significant difference does not exist and your innovation did not work.

Task 2

You decide how much chance error you're willing to risk. By convention, evaluators generally set the error level at 5%, meaning that 5 times out of 100 the results could happen by chance.

Task 3

You find the critical value your calculated t statistic must exceed for you to conclude that a significant, non-chance difference exists. You'll find this standard listed in a t distribution table provided in the back of any statistics text.

Task 4

You collect your data and calculate the t statistic using the appropriate formula (single-sample t-test, related samples t-test, or independent measures t-test).

Task 5

You evaluate your hypotheses in light of your calculated t statistic. You compare your *calculated* t statistic to the critical value/standard you set in Step 3 by looking in the t-distribution table of critical values and then decide one of two things:

- If your calculated t statistic *equals or exceeds* the standard from the t distribution table, you can safely conclude that a difference *does* exist and your strategy *did* work.

- If, however, your calculated t statistic does *not* equal or exceed the standard, then you cannot knock down the null hypothesis. This means that your innovative strategy most likely did not work.

9.48—Jaime Does Step 5

The student teams have worked hard. As the students finished a task listed on the giant timeline on the back wall of Jaime's classroom, they ceremoniously put a "DONE" sticker on the sticky note.

Suzanne showed them how to use Excel™ to enter the survey data, produce frequency tables, and create bar and pie charts displaying the data. Because so many of the survey questions used the Lickert format, the students also calculated arithmetic means and standard deviations on many of the survey items. (Boy, did the kids laugh at the term "standard deviation." They went around calling each other "standard deviates" for a week.)

Jaime worked after school with some very involved students showing them how to use Excel™ to run t-tests on their data comparing the survey responses of Challenge Team students with the responses of the comparison group. As Jaime explained the logic of a t-test, the students soon saw that it really relied on common sense. They just wished people would use a better name than t-test. It sounded so dull. They decided that the Dastardly Different Test sounded better.

The first week in May, the students created another giant wall chart on another wall in Jaime's classroom. This chart (See Figure 9.19) summarized of all the evidence they were compiling about each evaluation question. Once a team analyzed its data, they wrote a one page report summarizing their findings. They posted this report under the Evidence Summary column of the wall chart. They also posted their tentative conclusions.

9.49—Determining Effectiveness Step 6: Interpret Data

Now, we arrive at the final step in the evaluation process. We've got all our data, we've analyzed it, and now we're ready to make our judgments. At this point, we apply the judgment criteria we set in Step 2 of our process and decide two things:

1. Did our innovation work? Did we accomplish what we wanted?

2. Is our innovation worth continuing?

Throughout this chapter, we've spent considerable time discussing how we might judge whether or not an innovation worked. We've shown you how you can use both quantitative and qualitative data, particularly data collected through surveys to gather evidence that will either support or refute the effectiveness of a new strategy. But we really haven't spent much time talking about the question *"Is it worth continuing?"*.

In addition to asking *"Did it work?"*, decision-makers generally ask two other key questions, as they contemplate continuing a program:

Figure 9.19 A Portion of the Wall Chart Showing Evaluation Results on Service Learning Project
Conducted by Jamie and His Students

Evaluation Question	Judgment Criteria	Evidence Summaries	Conclusions	Judgment Criteria met?
1. Do students improve their real world problem-solving skills?	1. Challenge students will show a statistically greater ability to solve real-world problems than a comparable group of students who have not engaged in service learning activities			
2. Do students show an increased sensitivity towards people who are different?	2. Challenge students will show a statistically significant greater sensitivity towards others than a comparable group of students who have not engaged in service learning activities.			

1. Do the benefits outweigh the time and energy needed to continue the pro-
    gram?

2. Do the benefits surpass the money we would have to spend to continue the
    program?

To answer Questions 1 and 2 about benefits and costs we would need to use one of the varieties of cost analysis we introduced in section 6.14. And as we calculate costs, we should include not only actual expenditures of money, but also the human costs of implementing a program such as time, energy, and emotional stress, just to name a few.

We again want to stress that you should put many different pieces of information into the hopper as you decide whether or not a program is worth continuing. It is quite possible that innovation does not show a *statistically* significant difference in achievement scores but does show many other benefits, some of which we can assign a dollar amount and some of which we can't.

Furthermore, it's possible that an innovation would show a "poor" cost effectiveness ratio and yet be the right thing to do. For example, schools could certainly cut their cost per pupil if only they did away with individualized instruction tailored to the needs of students. But that wouldn't be right for the kids! Sometimes factors other than gains on achievement tests and thriftiness must come into play.

9.50—Jaime Does Step 6

It's May 27. It's almost time for the summer break. Surprisingly the Challenge students want to finish "The Evaluation." Today, during Jaime's class times, each student team mulls over the evidence it has accumulated concerning the evaluation question they tackled and make a judgment: "Was the judgment criteria met?" Each team also prepares a 2-minute oral summary of their findings. Tomorrow, the entire team of 165 students and three teachers will meet in the Commons Area in the morning to share their findings. The teachers plan to make 8½ x 11 copies of the giant wall chart summarizing everyone's judgments. The entire team will then look at all the conclusions and make an overall judgment about the worth of the service learning component of the Family and Community unit.

School's out! The students have cleared out their lockers and desks and visit quietly about yesterday's discussion of the service learning evaluation. The evaluation data showed mixed results and, of course, they still don't have the achievement data. The data indicated that Challenge Team students, when compared with the other students who did not engage in service learning activities, showed:

- Greater ability to solve real-world problems
- Greater sensitivity towards other people who are different
- Greater social competence
- Greater sense of self-efficacy

The students were also pleased to learn that 100% of the volunteer sites said that the students had made a positive impact.

However, they didn't find a significant difference between their attendance and that of the comparison group. They speculated that this was because their school had made such a "big deal" out of attendance this year and everyone was coming to school more regularly.

On the last day of the school year, Jaime, Suzanne, and Rob met after all the students had left and reflected about the year. It indeed had been a stressful one, but a good one just the same. The kids had really taken off with the evaluation of the service learning project! The Challenge Team teachers left school once again glad they were teachers!

9.51—Reporting Survey Results

In chapter 7 we gave much advice about successfully reporting the results of your evaluation. Here we want to highlight some suggestions that pertain specifically to reporting survey results.

As you report the results of surveys, *group the results conceptually*, reporting the results of similar questions together even if they didn't appear in that order in your survey. This way your reader can see patterns emerge.

To further help your reader see patterns, consider displaying your survey results in a graphic organizer like the one displayed in Figure 9.20. The evidence you show can come from responses on conceptually similar questions or from responses given by different groups to the same question. For example, one school asked the following question on surveys completed by students, teachers, and parents:

> In relation to the *appearance* of the building, what is your first feeling when you walk into Jefferson Middle School?
> (Please ✓ your answer.)
>
> ___ Very attractive and inviting
> ___ Pleasant
> ___ OK
> ___ Institutional and cold
> ___ No opinion

Figure 9.20 shows the patterns that appeared.

Figure 9.20 Survey Evidence Matrix

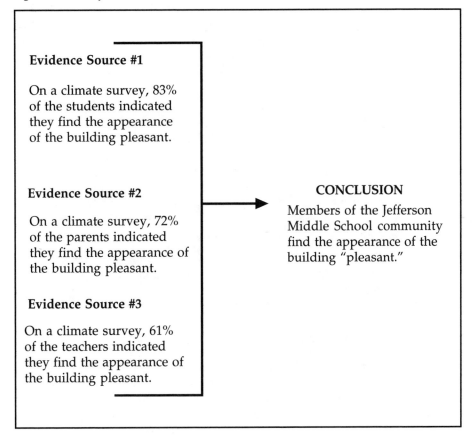

Evidence Source #1

On a climate survey, 83% of the students indicated they find the appearance of the building pleasant.

Evidence Source #2

On a climate survey, 72% of the parents indicated they find the appearance of the building pleasant.

Evidence Source #3

On a climate survey, 61% of the teachers indicated they find the appearance of the building pleasant.

CONCLUSION

Members of the Jefferson Middle School community find the appearance of the building "pleasant."

9.52—Issue Box

Handling "Mean-Spirited" Comments

Through the years, we helped gather survey data in many schools using anonymous written questionnaires and invariably a handful of respondents write some pretty nasty comments. Some students, parents, and teachers are often quick to vent on surveys about the incompetencies, real or imagined, of various staff members. Principals, because of their role as "bad guys" in disciplinary matters, often get many unkind remarks. It's going to happen, so we suggest that you decide up front how you will report these data. We see at least two choices:

1. Toss out these comments and don't report them. The trouble with this strategy is you report only a "rosy" picture. Highly critical comments may indicate a more pervasive problem that you need to address. However, these comments may just be the rantings of a very angry person in the heat of the moment. You'll have to be the judge.

2. Tally these comments in some appropriately labeled category, such as "highly dissatisfied" and report the number. This tactic gives a full picture of the situation, warts and all, but doesn't allow the venom to poison the evaluation. We suggest that you *never* report nasty comments verbatim or even with names left out. Someone will always figure out who Mr. X is, or at least they will speculate about his identity. Either way, hurts people's feelings and reputations.

The key is this—give a balanced report, but don't unnecessarily hurt people's feelings. No evaluation is served by mean-spirited remarks.

9.53—Another Example

Thus far, most of the examples in this chapter demonstrate groups of teachers tackling the question: *"Did it work?"* Now, we want to show how an individual teacher, Doug, used the six-step evaluation process to determine effectiveness of simulations in helping his students learn the complexities of American history.

For years, Doug has been searching for instructional techniques to bring American history alive for his students. This year, he has decided to use some of the "Activators"✱ materials published by Interact in El Cajon, California. He heard about them from Jillian, a fellow teacher, who used them to introduce her lessons. He looked at the catalog and decided to order the "Activators" dealing with the Great Depression and desegregation during the 1950's. The catalog described these activities as very short interactive simulations of key historical events.

When the materials arrive, Doug plans his lessons and an evaluation of the "Activators" materials using the 6-step evaluation process laid out in this book.

Step 1: Pose Questions

Doug begins by jotting down his main evaluation questions:

- Did using the 'Depression Soup Kitchen Activator' cause my students to learn and retain key concepts about the Great Depression?
- Did using the 'Montgomery Bus Boycott Activator' cause my students to learn and retain key concepts about the struggle to desegregate the South during the 1950's?

Step 2: Establish Judgment Criteria

Doug then writes down how he will judge whether or not his students have learned and retained key concepts about various aspects of American history. He decides on the following:

> A significantly greater number of students will achieve mastery on the end-of-unit tests for those units with include an "Activator" than those units with no "Activator."

Step 3: Make a Plan

Using the Evaluation Planning Matrix, Doug spends 5 minutes sketching out his plan for collecting and analyzing the data he will need to answer his evaluation questions. He decides to use an on/off/on/off design, something a book he's been reading calls a single-group successive pre-post design (See Figure 9.21.)

Figure 9.21 Doug's Research Design

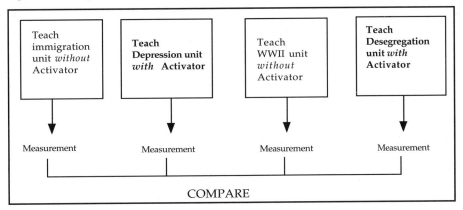

Step 4: Collect the Data

Over the semester, Doug teaches his lessons, gives the end-of-unit tests he's used in previous years, and then calculates the mean score for each test. He's having a hard time keeping his objectivity. The kids are really enjoying the "Activators," but the question still remains:

"Do they help students learn more?"

Step 5: Analyze the Data

After completing the Desegregation unit, Doug plots the mean scores for the four end-of-unit tests on a graph (Figure 9.19). He also consults with Jaime down the hall who tells him about using a statistical test called the t-test to determine if the differences he sees are statistically significant or not. One afternoon he and Jaime stay after school and run the calculations using Excel™.

Step 6: Interpret the Results

From just "eyeballing" the line graph, Doug speculates that the use of "Activators" did have a positive impact on student learning. The t-test calculations that he and Jaime did confirm that indeed a significant difference exists between the scores. Based on this data, he decides to use "Activators" more often. The Interact materials got him started, but he's sure he can think of some good "activators" on his own.

Figure 9.22 Doug's Line graph of the Mean Scores Made by Students on End-of-unit Tests

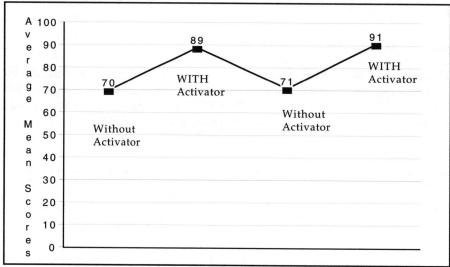

9.54—Chapter Highlights

Major Concepts

☞ To determine the effectiveness of your strategies, you should follow the 6-Step Evaluation Process we laid out in chapters 1 through 6:

Step 1: Pose questions
Step 2: Establish judgment criteria
Step 3: Make a plan
Step 4: Gather data
Step 5: Analyze data
Step 6: Interpret data

☞ Formative evaluation occurs *during* implementation.

☞ Summative evaluation occurs *at the end* of the implementation process and provides a "summary" of your program.

☞ Classic experimental research designs can help determine if your innovation worked or not.

☞ Extraneous variables are those factors that might get so tangled up with our independent variable that we cannot tell whether your intervention or some other factor caused the changes you observed.

☞ Three design techniques that can help minimize or rule out rival explanations include:

1. Random selection of subjects for each group

2. Matching the groups on relevant variables

3. Pretesting both groups to ascertain if any pre-existing relevant differences exist between the two groups

☞ A six-step recipe for developing successful surveys consists of the following tasks:

Task 1: Clearly define the information you want to find out through the survey.

Task 2: Determine who will complete your survey.

Task 3: Decide what method you will use to collect the survey information.

Task 4: Prepare the survey materials.

Task 5: Design your procedures for conducting the survey.

Task 6: Pilot test your survey.

☞ Typically, written survey questions fall into three broad categories:

• Open-ended

• Forced choice

• Ranking

☞ Statistical tests such as the t-test can help answer the question: "*Did it work?*".

Advice

√ Beware that pretesting to help control extraneous variables can contaminate your results by giving students practice or signaling them that something special is happening.

√ If possible, refrain from using a single group pre-post measurement experimental design. It's so contaminated by extraneous variables that you really can't legitimately use it to prove that some innovation works.

√ Always use a research design that includes a comparison group if you want to show that a strategy worked.

√ If you can't find a suitable comparison group, consider using a time-series design.

√ Keep the following in mind as you craft survey questions:

1. As always, KISS (Keep It Short and Simple) your questions.

2. Use clear, unambiguous language, avoiding vague words, technical terms, abbreviations, and jargon.

3. Include only *one* concept in a single item.

4. Avoid using leading questions that suggest a preferred response.

5. Request only information that respondents can reasonably provide.

6. Make the reading level of the items appropriate for the respondents.

7. If you use a forced-choice question format, make sure you include *all* possible choices a respondent might want to make.

8. If you use a forced-choice question format, make sure all choices are mutually exclusive.

9. Keep your question format consistent.

10. When gathering opinions about a certain topic, consider asking several different questions about the topic rather than just one question so you don't have to rely so heavily on just one response when you interpret your data.

√ When you devise questions for surveys conducted over the telephone, write for the "ear" and not the eyes of your respondents.

√ Take your survey for a "test drive" before you use it.

√ Respect your respondents' right to privacy and right to refuse to participate.

9.55—The Road Ahead

In this chapter, we've shown how you can use the six-step evaluation process to determine the effectiveness of an innovation. In chapter 10 we move to the last of our three types of evaluation questions—Those that seek solutions.

9.56—Resources

Print Resources

****Bernhardt, V. L. (1998). *Data analysis for comprehensive schoolwide improvement.* Larchmont, NY: Eye on Education.

   HIGHLY RECOMMENDED. Includes an excellent Appendix A on questionnaire design, along with examples of student, teacher and parent questionnaires geared to both elementary and secondary that educators can use to take stock of their school.

Bugher, W. (Author) & Duckett. W. (Ed.) (1992). *PACE: polling attitude of community on education manual revised edition.* Bloomington, IN: Phi Delta Kappa.

   If you want to conduct surveys like the pros (Gallup Organization) here's the guide for you. Consists of a comprehensive step-by-step manual (loose leaf three ring binder) on how to build a questionnaire and conduct a community survey. Includes all the questions and summaries of findings from the Annual Gallup Poll of the Public's Attitudes Toward the Public Schools of the U.S. commissioned by Phi Delta Kappa from 1969 to 1988. This pool of questions can prompt and guide the writing of your own questionnaire. Includes a 79-page guide on sampling written for the novice. Covers random sampling, systematic sampling, stratified sampling, cluster sampling, sampling by using telephone numbers, verifying the representativeness of the sample, handling the "not-at-homes," and sample size. Gives explicit directions on conducting telephone interviews. Includes a 20-page chapter on tabulating, dealing with sampling error, calculating confidence intervals, and using weighted subgroups. Provides sample questionnaires. You can contact Phi Delta Kappa by calling (800) 766–1156.

Committee on Privacy and Confidentiality. (1998). *Surveys and privacy.* Alexandria, VA: American Statistical Association.

Excellent discussion concerning the issue of a survey respondent's right to privacy. Written for the general public. You can download this document from the American Statistical Association's web site at **http://www.amstat.org/**. From the home page, click on the "Sections" option and then select the section on Survey Research Methods. From here you can select the document "Surveys and Privacy," produced by the ASA Committee on Privacy and Confidentiality.

Cox, J. (1996). *Your opinion, please! How to build the best questionnaires in the field of education.* Thousand Oaks, CA: Corwin Press.

Although only 103 pages, packed with solid advice about crafting questionnaires. Walks the reader through a seven-stage process that begins with establishing the guiding questions and moves all the way to marketing the questionnaire. Includes several sample questionnaires, instructions to respondents, and questionnaire formats. Walks through the full seven-stage process using two school-based situations. Has a very helpful checklist for finding flaws in questionnaires.

Dillman, D. A. (1979). *Mail and telephone surveys: The total design method.* New York: John Wiley and Sons.

THE book on doing mail and telephone surveys. Excellent reference, complete and very readable even for the novice. Virtually guarantees a high response rate if you follow the total design method. We've used Dillman's advice for years and it *does* work.

*Fink, A. and Kosecoff, J. (1998) *How to conduct surveys (2nd Ed.).* Thousand Oaks, CA: Sage Publications.

Very user friendly and makes the assumption that the reader is an intelligent person who happens to be naive about conducting surveys. Covers the process from start to finish, from planning and designing to analyzing and presenting findings. Includes many real world examples. Chapter 6 gives an excellent overview of how to do various statistical analyses of survey data. Begins each chapter with a one-page overview. Can act as a quick reference on doing survey research and evaluation since you can easily turn to the section you want and get the information you need.

Fowler, Floyd J. Jr. (1995). *Improving survey questions: design and evaluation.* Thousand Oaks, CA: Sage Publications.

A thorough treatment of the task of designing survey questions. Written in very understandable language with several examples. Novices as well as experts will find this book helpful. Focuses solely on the crafting of survey questions. Does not address design of the overall questionnaire, analyzing data, or implementing the questionnaire. Includes two very helpful appendices. One gives a ten-page overview of the various types of survey questions (format and purpose) and the other provides suggestions on how to measure age, gender, marital status, employment status, SES, religious preference or affiliation, race and ethnic background.

Morgan, D. L. & Krueger, R. A. (eds.) (1998). *The focus group kit*. Thousand Oaks, CA: Sage Publications.

Volume 1: Morgan, D. L. (1998). *The focus group guidebook*. Thousand Oaks, CA: Sage Publications.

Volume 2: Morgan, D. L. (1997). *Planning focus groups*. Thousand Oaks, CA: Sage Publications.

Volume 3: Krueger, R. A. (1997). *Developing questions for focus groups*. Thousand Oaks, CA: Sage Publications.

Volume 4: Krueger, R. A. (1997). *Moderating focus groups*. Thousand Oaks, CA: Sage Publications.

Volume 5: Krueger, R. A. & King, J. A. (1997). *Involving community members in focus groups*. Thousand Oaks, CA: Sage Publications.

Volume 6: Krueger, R. A. (1997). *Analyzing and reporting focus group results*. Thousand Oaks, CA: Sage Publications.

Available in a six-volume set (808 pages) but you can purchase each volume separately. Provides the basics, and slightly beyond, about using group interviews (a.k.a. focus groups) to gather data. Both novice and expert evaluators will find the kit helpful as a dependable reference, explaining each phase of focus group research. Written in understandable language with numerous examples.

Patten, M. L. (1998). *Questionnaire research: A practical guide*. Los Angeles: Pyrczak Publishing.

HIGHLY RECOMMENDED. Packed with sound, realistic advice on writing questionnaire items, pretesting your survey, selecting a sample, analyzing your data, and reporting your results. Written in easy-to-understand language designed for the intelligent novice with many examples. Can readily function as a quick reference on doing surveys.

**Rea, L. M. & Parker, R. A. (1997). *Designing and conducting survey research: A comprehensive guide*. San Francisco: Jossey-Bass Inc., Publishers.

A complete guide to developing, administering, analyzing and presenting the findings from surveys. Does a good job of presenting the pros and cons of mail surveys, telephone surveys, in-person interviews, and even focus groups. Shows sample time lines for doing the various tasks involved in survey research along with sample budgets. Although all the examples and illustrative cases are not school-oriented, provides clear and very understandable demonstrations. Gives a very understandable, coherent explanation of sampling theory for the novice with a step-by-step process for determining sample size. Also explains all the acceptable methods for selecting a representative sample. In chapter 10, gives a clear understandable discussion of the various inferential statistical procedures you can use to analyze survey data (chi-square, Difference of Means Test, t-test, Difference of Proportions Test, Analysis of Variance). Keeps the math to a minimum and uses simple, easily understood examples. Includes an excellent glossary.

Salant, P. & Dillman, D. A. (1994). *How to conduct your own survey*. New York: John Wiley & Sons.

HIGHLY RECOMMENDED. If you can purchase only one or two books on survey research for your school's professional library, we suggest that you get this one. Draws on Dillman's earlier book on mail and telephone surveys, but expanded to include face-to-face surveys as well. Lays out ten steps for success in conducting a survey and then spends one chapter illustrating each of the steps. Gives solid advice throughout augmented by both exemplary and poor examples. Chapter 6 on writing good questions is excellent.

*Schmuck, R. A. (1997). *Practical action research for change*. Arlington Heights, IL: IRI Skylight Training and Publishing, Inc.

Chapter 5 focuses on what the author labels "Proactive Action Research" where an educator seeks to find out whether or not a new strategy worked. Gives a step-by-step explanation of the action research process along with two case studies showing how two individual teachers used the process to improve their classroom climate and move from being the director of learning to the facilitator of learning. Would serve as an excellent companion to chapter 9 in our book *Getting Answers to Your Questions*.

Section on Survey Research Methods. (1993). *What is a survey?* Alexandria, VA: American Statistical Association.

A series of nine very short (12 pages) pamphlets distributed free of charge by the American Statistical Association (ASA). Written for the general public. For copies, write to the ASA at 1429 Duke Street, Alexandria VA 22314-3402 or visit the Section's website at **http://www.amstat.org/.** From the home page click on the "Sections" option and then select the section on Survey Research Methods. This will get you to the ASA Series "What is a Survey?" From here, you can actually download some of the information contained in the following pamphlets:
What is a survey?
How to plan a survey
How to collect survey data
Judging the quality of a survey
How to conduct pretesting
What are focus groups? (in preparation)
More about mail surveys (in preparation)
What is a margin of error? (in preparation)
What about surveys in the media? (in preparation)

The Survey Kit, Various Authors, Sage Publications (1995).

Volume 1: Fink, A. (1995). *The survey handbook*. Thousand Oaks, CA: Sage Publications.

Volume 2: Fink, A. (1995). *How to ask survey questions*. Thousand Oaks, CA: Sage Publications.

Volume 3: Bourque, L. B. & Fielder, E. P. (1995). *How to conduct self-administered and mail surveys.* Thousand Oaks, CA: Sage Publications.

Volume 4: Frey, J. H. & Oishi, S. M. (1995). *How to conduct interviews by telephone and in person.* Thousand Oaks, CA: Sage Publications.

Volume 5: Fink, A. (1995). *How to design surveys.* Thousand Oaks, CA: Sage Publications.

Volume 6: Fink, A. (1995). *How to sample in surveys.* Thousand Oaks, CA: Sage Publications.

Volume 7: Litwin, M. S. (1995). *How to measure survey reliability and validity.* Thousand Oaks, CA: Sage Publications.

Volume 8: Fink, A. (1995). *How to analyze survey data.* Thousand Oaks, CA: Sage Publications.

Volume 9: Fink, A. (1995). *How to report on surveys.* Thousand Oaks, CA: Sage Publications.

Available in a nine-volume set (over 1000 pages), but you can purchase each volume separately. The entire kit functions as a dependable reference, explaining each phase of survey research in clear, understandable language. Includes numerous examples. Both novice and expert evaluators will find the kit helpful.

Internet Resources

NOTE: You can easily access the Webssites we recommend below by simply going to our Web page located at

http://www.pittstate.edu/edsc/ssls/letendre.html

From our Web page, a simple click of your mouse will take you straight to the selected Website. We regularly verify these sites and add others that we find worthy of our recommendation.

American Statistical Association (ASA)
http://www.amstat.org/
Includes a series of nine very short (12 pages) pamphlets on conducting surveys that you can download. From the home page click on the "Sections" option and then select the section on Survey Research Methods. This will get you to the ASA Series "What is a Survey?" From here, you can download some of the information contained in the following pamphlets:

What is a survey?
How to plan a survey
How to collect survey data
Judging the quality of a survey
How to conduct pretesting
What are focus groups? (in preparation)
More about mail surveys (in preparation)
What is a margin of error? (in preparation)
What about surveys in the media? (in preparation)

Close Up Foundation
http://www.closeup.org/pubs.htm
Connects to the Website maintained by the Close Up Foundation located in Alexandria, VA. Publishes the materials designed to get students involved in collecting and analyzing data to solve community problems. Especially good is the Active Citizenship Today Field Guide [Middle School edition], which guides students in identifying problems, conducting research, and writing persuasively about community problems. Also publishes the Active Citizenship Today Handbook for Teachers and the Service Learning Teacher Training Manual.

National Opinion Research Center
http://www.norc.uchicago.edu
Connects to the National Opinion Research Center at the University of Chicago. Includes much practical, very understandable advice on conducting surveys. Also includes further print and Web resources. Under the "Links" button, connects to an extensive list of quality-rated Web resources dealing with survey research.

National Service-Learning Clearinghouse
http://www.nicsl.coled.umn.edu/
Connects to the National Service-Learning Clearinghouse which collects and disseminates information about the service-learning field. Includes a searchable database. Provides excellent resources, some with hot links to other Web sites, which you can access by clicking on one of the following questions:

Question 1: What do I need to know about the important issues involved in evaluating my service-learning program?

Question 2: Do you have a model of evaluation I can look at?

Question 3: Do you have an instrument I can use?

Question 4: If you can't send me the answer (an instrument or completed design), where can I go for help?

Question 5: Are there studies that "prove" (usually quantitative studies) service- learning is effective?

Question 6: What programs are out there for evaluation?

Question 7: Who has done evaluation/assessment of service-learning and how can I contact them?

CHAPTER 10

Solution-Seeking Questions

For every complex problem, there's a simple solution and it's wrong!

—H. L. Mencken

10.1—Introduction

Every day as middle school educators, we face problems as we work to do our best for kids. Some problems we face permeate the entire school, while others affect only our own classrooms. And every day we must solve these problems. One reason we ask questions and seek answers is because we want, indeed, we need solutions.

In this chapter, we will outline a process we call Targeted Problem-Solving, showing how you can pose and answer questions that seek solutions. We will demonstrate how Joan and her colleagues at a middle school plagued by shouting matches in the hallways used Targeted Problem-Solving to remedy student misbehavior. We will also show how Joan's team followed the six-step evaluation process we explained in chapters 1 through 6, not only to gather the information they need to solve the behavior problem, but also to judge the effectiveness of their solution. Finally, we will give an example of how an individual teacher used solution-seeking questions and Targeted Problem-Solving to solve a difficulty she faced in her own classroom.

10.2—Targeted Problem-Solving

Adapted from the Inquiry Process used by Accelerated Schools (Hopfenberg et al, 1993), Targeted Problem-Solving utilizes six clear-cut questions you can use to solve problems, both simple and complex. Individual teachers, grappling with problems in their own classrooms, as well as groups of educators, facing school-wide concerns, can use Targeted Problem-Solving. The key to the process is to correctly define the problem from the outset, so that the solutions you implement *really* do hit the *target* and solve the problem.

The six solution-seeking questions of Targeted Problem-Solving follow a sequence leading you towards successful solutions:

1. In general, what is the problem?

2. What are we striving for?

3. How close are we *now*?

4. What are the core causes of the problem?

5. How can we address these core causes?

6. Did our solution work?

Figure 10.1   Targeted Problem-Solving Graphic

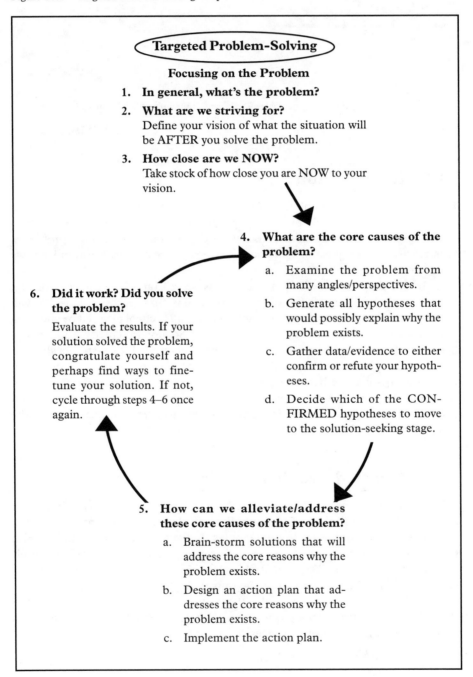

Author's Note   Since its inception in 1986, I've had the privilege of working with the Accelerated Schools Project founded by Henry M. Levin at Stanford University. I've seen school communities across the nation use the philosophy and process of Accelerated Schools to accelerate the learning of *all* their students. One of the most powerful processes within an Accelerated School is the Inquiry Process, a structured problem-solving procedure that helps teachers and administrators find solutions to the challenges they face. The Inquiry Process uses a procedure which begins with clearly defining the core reasons *why* a problem exists.

Unfortunately, many faculties get bogged down in the Inquiry Process because they fail to sufficiently focus and narrow their problem-solving efforts *before* they begin defining why a problem exists. They simply bite off more than they can chew. My work with teachers and principals in Accelerated Schools over the years has led me to make slight modifications to the original Inquiry Process and create what I call Targeted Problem-Solving.

Specifically, Targeted Problem-Solving (Figure 10.1) requires that problem-solvers explicitly focus and narrow their problem *before* they move into the next stages of the problem-solving process. This focusing results in making the original problem more manageable and thus more amenable to a successful solution.

Targeted Problem-Solving combines some of the stages in the original Inquiry Process. We've combined these steps in order to keep Targeted Problem-Solving simple and easily remembered.

—*Brenda LeTendre*, Co-author

10.3—Solution-Seeking Question 1: In General, What is the Problem?

Figure 10.2   Targeted Problem-Solving Graphic Solution-Seeking Question 1

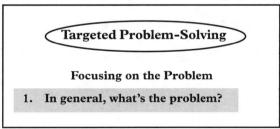

At this beginning stage of Targeted Problem-Solving, you need only state the problem in very *general* terms. In later stages, you will define more specifically the problem and its root causes. Below are some examples of *general* problem statements:

- The morale of adults and students in our school is low.
- Students can't successfully solve math problems.

- Teachers are so busy disciplining students they don't have time to teach.

- Students complain that school is boring.

- Parents aren't as involved in the education of their children as we want them to be.

- Students can't comprehend the texts used in science and social studies.

10.4—Joan Answers Question 1 of the Targeted Problem-Solving Process

Joan, a middle school math teacher, sits in a meeting of the school's Student Responsibility Committee. Members include Joan, three other teachers, four students (two 6th graders and two 7th graders), two parents, and the vice-principal, Ms. Collins. The group meets regularly every two weeks to deal with student behavior that hinders learning.

Today, Joan speaks up, "I think we have a problem that's escalating. Just yesterday I had to break up two shouting matches during the passing periods. And several other teachers had to do the same thing this week. I understand, Ms. Collins, you've already had eight students down in your office this week for the same thing and it's only Wednesday! I think we need to do something."

As Joan finished her statement, heads nodded around the table. Ms. Collins, the vice-principal and facilitator for today's meeting, suggested that the group use Targeted Problem-Solving to find a solution. "Joan, in general, what would you say the problem is?" Ms. Collins queries.

"In my opinion, *the problem is we simply have too many shouting matches during passing periods*," Joan replies. "I'm afraid that if we don't do something, these shouting matches will escalate into full-blown fist fights and someone's going to get hurt."

This general statement of the problem—too many shouting matches during passing periods—is enough to get the Targeted Problem-Solving process going. The group is now ready to pose and answer the next solution-seeking question.

10.5—Solution-Seeking Question 2: What are We Striving For?

Labeling situations as problems requires that you have an ideal situation already in mind. When you compare "what is" to "what should be," you see a glaring gap and call this a problem. Unfortunately, too often the ideal situation we have in mind is implicit, unspoken, and even quite fuzzy. By answering Solution-Seeking Question 2, you make explicit and clear what your ideal situation will look like.

Figure 10.3   Targeted Problem-Solving Graphic Solution-Seeking Question 2

<⟨ **Targeted Problem-Solving** ⟩>

Focusing on the Problem

1. **In general, what's the problem?**

2. **What are we striving for?**
    Define your vision of what the situation will
    be AFTER you solve the problem.

Later, you will take stock of just how close you are *now* to this vision. This comparison will help you identify where you need to start in solving your problem.

Your portrait of the ideal situation should refrain from describing *how* you will solve the problem. Rather, you should focus on painting a culminating portrait that not only specifies the behaviors that students and/or adults will engage in, but also describes the situation once the problem is solved.

For example, let's say the general problem you're addressing is this:

The students in your school can't successfully solve math problems.

You don't want to answer the question *"What are we striving for?"* by saying:

 We are striving for a new set of math texts that students can read more easily.

This answer is really a description of a *solution*. A more appropriate description of *"What are we striving for?"* is this:

We want our students to be able to successfully solve word problems, distinguish relevant from irrelevant information in problems, determine the appropriate order of operations, accurately complete the calculations, and clearly explain how they arrived at their answers.

Notice that this vision does not give any hint as to *how* you will solve the problem, but it does clearly define what you're striving for. This clear definition of what you want serves as the foundation for the third question in the Targeted Problem-Solving process: *"How close are we NOW?"*

10.6—Joan Answers Question 2 of the Targeted Problem-Solving Process

The members of the Student Responsibility Committee agree with Joan's general statement of the problem:

We have too many shouting matches during passing periods.

Now, Ms. Collins asks the group, "What are we striving for? What will things look like when the problem no longer exists?"

"Well, that's easy," pipes up Danielle, one of the 7th graders. "We won't have any shouting matches in the hallways."

"Right," Ms. Collins agrees as she charts Danielle's comment on the easel pad. "Any other behaviors we want to specify?"

"Students will greet one another in a friendly manner during the passing time between classes," says Ms. Jones, a parent.

"Students will refrain from using offensive name-calling, either in jest or earnest," offers Mr. Sanchez, a social studies teacher.

Everyone chimes in and Ms. Collins can barely write fast enough. In five minutes, the group has agreed that they are striving for the following behaviors:

- No shouting matches in the hallways
- Students will greet one another in a friendly manner
- Students will refrain from using offensive name-calling
- If a shouting match starts, it will quickly dissipate

The Student Responsibility Committee has stated the problem in general terms and specified the behaviors they hope to see once the problem is solved. Now, the committee needs to take stock of how close they are now to their vision.

10.7—Solution-Seeking Question 3: How Close are We Now?

Figure 10.4   Targeted Problem-Solving Graphic Solution-Seeking Question 3

> **Targeted Problem-Solving**
>
> **Focusing on the Problem**
> 1. **In general, what's the problem?**
> 2. **What are we striving for?**
>   Define your vision of what the situation will be AFTER you solve the problem.
> 3. **How close are we NOW?**
>   Take stock of how close you are NOW to your vision.

The next stage in Targeted Problem-Solving asks that you take stock of the current situation by answering the question: *"How close are you now to your vision?"*. This stage has three purposes:

a. To gather baseline data so that you will have a reference point when you later ask: "Did our solution work?".

b. To identify what's going *wrong* to help you distinguish symptoms from root causes
c. To recognize what's going *right* so you will know the strengths you can build upon when you design your solution

Taking stock in Targeted Problem-Solving follows a scaled-down version of the taking stock procedures we discussed in chapter 8 and uses the six-step evaluation process we laid out in chapters 1 through 6.

10.8—Joan Answers Question 3 of the Targeted Problem-Solving Process

The Student Responsibility Committee now needs to take stock of the current situation. Ms. Collins asks the group, "Just how close are we to this vision we wrote?" The committee uses the last 30 minutes of its regular meeting completing the first three steps of the evaluation process used in taking stock.

First, they pose their evaluation questions. They go straight to their vision for guidance:

VISION   No shouting matches.

Questions that take stock of how close we are NOW:

- How many shouting matches in the hallways occur daily? weekly?
- At what time of day do these shouting matches occur most frequently?
- Who perpetrates these shouting matches? The same people or different people?
- Who are the targets of these shouting matches? The same people or different people?
- What sets these shouting matches off?
- What do people say during these shouting matches?

VISION   Students will greet each other in a friendly manner in the hallways.

Questions that take stock of how close we are NOW:

- How many students greet one another in a friendly manner in the hallways?
- What do they say to one another?
- How many students greet each other in an unfriendly manner?
- What do they say?
- How many students greet no one as they pass to their next class?

VISION   Students will refrain from using offensive name-calling.

Questions that take stock of how close we are NOW:

- How many students engage in offensive name-calling in the hallways during passing periods?
- How much of this offensive name-calling appears to be in jest?
- Who tends to engage in offensive name-calling?
- What students do NOT engage in offensive name-calling in the hallways?

VISION   If a shouting match starts, it will quickly dissipate.

Questions that take stock of how close we are NOW:

- What happens when a shouting match occurs?
- How do the students who are directly involved respond?
- How do bystanders respond?
- How do adults respond?
- How long do these matches last before they stop?
- Who tends to stop these matches?

Second, they establish their judgment criteria.   Once again they turn to their mini-vision for guidance. They set the following standards for judging how close they are to their vision:

- No shouting matches in the hallways.
- Students will greet one another in a friendly manner.
- Students will refrain from using offensive name-calling.
- If a shouting match starts, it will quickly dissipate.

Third, they make a plan.   Quickly, they sketch out a data collection plan using the Taking Stock Planning Matrix. (See Figure 10-5.) Since they want to get moving on solving the problem, they decide to meet again next Monday afternoon.

Figure 10.5   Taking Stock Planning Matrix for Taking Stock of Shouting Match Problem

Column A Taking Stock Question	Column B Information needed?	Column C Using what methods?	Column D By when?	Column E Who will collect?	Column F How analyze?
Who perpetrates the shouting matches?	Names, What they say, how often	Observe Interview	Oct 20	Joan	Oct 20 Joan patterns

During the next two days (Thursday and Friday), members of the Student Responsibility Committee scurry to *collect the data* they need to take stock of the current situation. While the students on the committee informally observe behaviors during the passing periods, Ms. Collins and Joan station themselves in the halls. One passing period they stand at the intersection of A Hall and B Hall, and the next passing period they observe in the Commons. They try to be as inconspicuous as possible, since they don't want their presence to alter what usually happens. As she observes, Ms. Collins focuses on recording what goes right during the passing period. She notices friendly behaviors and helpful mediation attempts made by both students and adults whenever conflicts arise. Joan, on the other hand, records all that goes wrong. She even scripts one shouting match from start to finish as Mr. Stevens, the language arts teacher, hauls two boys down to the office.

After the committee members have done their observations, conducted their surveys, interviewed various members of the school community and reviewed the disciplinary referrals for the last three weeks, they quickly *organize, summarize and analyze their data.*

For example, Ms. Collins reviewed the disciplinary referrals over the past three weeks and plotted the location of each shouting match on a map of the school. Joan did the same thing for the past week and charted the times during the day when the shouting matches occurred. (See Figure 10.6.) Danielle, the 7th grader on the Student Responsibility Committee, created a matrix summarizing what students and teachers said when she interviewed them about shouting matches and what causes them. Ms. Jones, a parent member of the committee, summarized the survey results in a frequency table.

At Monday afternoon's meeting, the committee members presented their findings. Then the committee *interpreted their results* by comparing the taking stock information against their vision for friendly hallways. The committee sorted their interpretations into two categories:

Strengths	Gaps
Once a shouting match starts, it's over quickly	Some student bystanders egg on those involved
Adults act quickly to keep a fight from starting once they see a shouting match	More girls than boys engage in shouting matches
Student bystanders try to mediate when a shouting match starts	The same 15 students appear to engage in most of the shouting matches

Strengths	Gaps
Some students will run for an adult if the match appears to be escalating to a physical fight	Most shouting matches occur over the lunch hours and during the last passing period of the day
Shouting matches rarely occur before 11:00 a.m.	
Shouting matches rarely occur in front of the gym, in the cafeteria, at the main entrance.	Most shouting matches occur at the intersection of A & B Halls and in the Commons area.
90% of the students have not engaged in a shouting match during the last three weeks.	
Few shouting matches actually escalate to physical fights	

Figure 10.6   Hallway Map Showing Time and Location of Shouting Matches

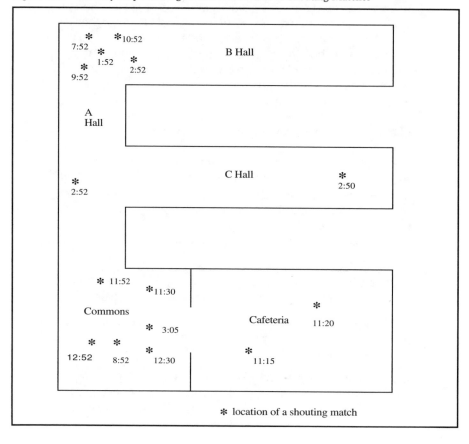

10.9—Doing Observations

As you see, the Student Responsibility Committee in our example relied heavily on observing to collect data. Before we move to the next question in Targeted Problem-Solving, we wish to offer some suggestions about doing observations. In earlier chapters when we examined the other data collection methods of reviewing and asking, we suggested that you keep your data collection simple and reliable. We offer the same advice for *observing*.

10.10—Keeping Observations Simple

Some ways to keep your observations simple include:

Use a simple form for recording what you see and hear during observations.

We suggest that you design an observation form keeping two things in mind:

1. Make it easy for you (or others) to use as you record data
2. Consider how you will ultimately organize and analyze your observation data

   You should try to anticipate what you might see during your observations and then include these things as checklists or options that the observer can simply check or circle. If you know that the events you'll observe have some sort of sequence (a beginning, middle, and end), then lay out the data collection form with this sequence in mind. Finally, if you know you want to count certain behaviors or events, include these on your form.

Focus on only a few important behaviors rather than trying to record everything.

You'll find that during observations, events unfold so rapidly that you rarely have enough time to record everything. Therefore, you need to decide beforehand which behaviors or events you *really* want to record. This way you'll assure that you get what you want.

When observing complex events, consider audio or video taping the events.

Audio or video taping allows you to view the event over and over so that you can accurately record the observation data. We, however, don't advocate using hidden cameras or audio recorders. Rather we suggest that if you plan to video or audio tape events, first acclimate students to the camera or audio recorder. The mere presence of a video camera can easily alter a situation and distort your data. If you want to observe classroom interactions, you can simply set up the camera in an out-of-the-way corner for several class sessions. Soon, the students will forget about the camera and you'll get a true picture of what normally happens in the classroom.

   Although videotaping can prove extremely helpful in collecting observational data, you need to understand its limitations. Specifically, the camera only records what is within the camera's line of sight. Furthermore, the sound track can be garbled or even overshadowed by ambient noise. Specialized equipment can amplify both the audio and visual tracks of a videotape, but most educators don't have access to such equipment.

10.11—Keeping Observations Reliable

While keeping your observations simple, you must also keep it reliable and minimize bias. Some ways to keep your data collection reliable during observations include:

Record the facts and only the facts.

Refrain from making assumptions about people's inner feelings. Rather than saying "She looked bored," state, "She looked out the window during the lesson, doodled on her paper, passed notes to her neighbor, didn't respond when the teacher asked her a question, put her head down on her desk."

Consider videotaping, audiotaping or photographing events.

This freezes the events in time and allows you to view them over and over so that you can check your accuracy in recording the observational data. Furthermore, you can double check the accuracy of your data collection by having other people view the same tapes or photographs, record their observations, and then compare their data with yours. This method is a particularly good way to check on what is called inter-rater reliability, the level of agreement between two or more observers about the same event.

Use multiple observers to record data about the same event.

Not only will multiple observers viewing the same event provide a check on inter-rater reliability, having additional eyes can extend the amount of data you collect. For example, both Joan and Ms. Collins observed during the passing periods. One person really couldn't adequately observe all that would happen during each passing period. So they decided to divide the job to make it more manageable and reliable: one looked for things that went right and one looked for things that went wrong during each passing period.

Use a protocol for both observing and recording data.

A protocol delineates the procedures for both observing and recording data. By designating exactly how to observe and how to record data, you help ensure that you'll systematically collect your data. Of course, you want to design these procedures so that you minimize bias. You'll also want to keep it easy to use.

Decide beforehand how you will record ambiguous behaviors.

Try to anticipate before observing how you will record ambiguous data. Which category will you place it under? Of course, you probably won't foresee all ambiguous situations. As you record, you'll have to decide on the spur of the moment how to handle the vagueness. Use your common sense and then move on. However, make sure that each time you encounter a similar situation, record it in the same way. Consistency helps keep your data collection reliable.

Train observers in viewing and recording events.

Trained observers increase the reliability and accuracy in data collection. Make sure that you and other observers understand the protocol for both observing and recording data. Before doing the real thing, observers-to-be should practice and debrief, noting ambiguities and difficulties.

Use observers who others would judge as impartial.

The one thing that can definitely skew your data collection is to use obviously biased observers, who see things one way and only one way. Of course, we humans cannot be completely objective, but when it comes to data collection we should strive for as much objectivity as possible. This means that sometimes you might want to use someone other than yourself to observe and collect data, particularly if you have a stake in the outcome of your own evaluation. Skeptics will quickly point out the bias that you bring to your evaluation. Therefore, if you plan to present your findings to a skeptical audience, we suggest that you consider using neutral people as observers.

Getting Kids Involved!

Steinbeck Middle School in San Jose, California, became an accelerated school in 1994. Since the beginning, students have played an integral part in transforming their school into a place where all students accelerate their learning. The school community forged a vision, took stock, and created committees called cadres to address each of its priorities. These cadres serve as "think tanks," examining the challenge areas and suggesting possible solutions. Below is an essay one of the students wrote describing her experience as an active member of a cadre:

I'm in 8th grade. My cadre is Communication/Involvement. My cadre is trying to make parents more involved at home with the students and with the students at school. We made a survey where we call the parents and ask them questions about how they can help their students succeed and how to get parents more involved at school. Some of the questions that were asked were if they needed a translator or if transportation was keeping them from being involved. So mostly it's questions about how to get parents involved.

Some of the surveys are in Vietnamese, Spanish and English. Since there were no adults on my cadre who speak Vietnamese, Michael and I helped translate the Vietnamese surveys to English. One of the teachers also helped translate the surveys from Spanish to English. After we translated the surveys, we took the surveys and tallied all the ones that said "yes" or "no". One of the other teachers wrote all the comments down and wrote an essay. We used the inquiry process to find out why there is low parent involvement.

(Thanks to Marilyn Zitzer, Resource Teacher and Accelerated Schools Coach at Steinbeck, for sharing this example.)

10.12—Solution-Seeking Question 4:
What Are the Core Causes of the Problem?

Let's focus once again on our problem-solving process. Thus far in the search for solutions using the Targeted Problem-Solving process, we have:

Figure 10.7   Targeted Problem-Solving Graphic Solution-Seeking Question 4

Focusing on the Problem

1. **In general, what's the problem?**

2. **What are we striving for?**
   Define your vision of what the situation will be *after* you solve the problem.

3. **How close are we NOW?**
   Take stock of how close you are NOW to your vision.

4. **What are the core causes of the problem?**

   a. Examine the problem from many angles/perspectives

   b. Generate all hypotheses that would possibly explain why the problem exists.

   c. Gather data/evidence to either confirm or refute your hypotheses.

   d. Decide which of the CONFIRMED hypotheses to move to the solution-seeking stage.

1. Stated the problem in very general terms

2. Described what we are eventually striving for

3. Taken stock of how close we now are to our ideal situation

Now, we come to an absolutely crucial stage in Targeted Problem-Solving—defining the core causes of the problem. Unfortunately, most people, including educators, often skip over this step. They simply leap at the first solution that occurs to them, even if that solution will not even come close to addressing the problem. Our culture is so bent towards action that when we see a problem we just act, often wasting time, money and energy on non-solutions that miss the target.

Answering the question: *"What are the core causes of the problem?"* requires completing four substeps:

4a. Examine the problem from many angles and perspectives to get multiple viewpoints about the root causes of the problem.

4b. Generate all possible hypotheses that might explain why the problem exists.

4c. Gather evidence to either confirm or refute your hypotheses.

4d. Decide which of the *confirmed* hypotheses to move to the solution-seeking stage.

Let's examine each substep in more detail.

10.13—Substep 4a: Examine the Problem from Many Angles

We humans are prone to see things one way, our way, closing our minds to other possibilities. Indeed, when it comes to problem-solving, we tend to "think" with our gut feelings rather than our brains. We settle on the first cause that occurs to us, saying "I know what's causing the problem. It's plain as day!", and then immediately shut our minds to other possibilities. Unfortunately, these gut feelings often center on symptoms rather than root causes.

To ensure that you consider all possible reasons why a problem exists, we suggest that you go to a wide range of people and ask the same question:

"What do you think is causing the problem?"

You should also consult the educational literature, examining what experts and researchers say might be the root causes of your problem. Finally, you should review documents, make observations, and examine your taking stock information, all the while asking, *What's causing the problem?*.

10.14—Substep 4b: Generate All Possible Hypotheses that Might Explain Why the Problem Exists

Hypotheses are educated guesses and complete the sentence: "*I believe the problem exists because...*" At this point in Targeted Problem-Solving, you want to draw on your work in substep 4a and state your hypotheses about the root causes of the problem you're addressing. You should exhaust the possibilities, brainstorming hypotheses until no one can think of any others. Remember the rules of brainstorming require that you simply list ideas and refrain from any judgment or culling at this point. That will come later.

Often times, groups find that some guiding questions can help get the brainstorming process going:

- Is there anything about our *curriculum* that might be causing the problem?
- Is there anything about our *instructional strategies* that might be causing the problem?
- Is there anything about how *we organize for learning* that might be causing the problem?
- Is there anything about our *procedures* that might be causing the problem?
- Is there anything about our *policies* that might be causing the problem?

Once you've generated as many hypotheses as you can, you need to first cull out duplicates and then sort the remaining into categories, trying to put similar hypotheses together.

As you go through the hypotheses, you might have to dig a bit deeper, generating additional hypotheses. For example, let's say the general problem we're addressing is:

"Students often fail to complete their homework."

Someone on the team offers this hypothesis:

"Students fail to complete their homework because their parents don't supervise their children's work at home."

We need to dig deeper with this hypothesis asking, *"Why don't parents supervise their children's work at home?"*. This question then yields further hypotheses:

- Because parents feel their children are older and therefore should be responsible for doing their homework without the parents hounding them.
- Because the parents aren't aware that their children have homework.
- Because the parents aren't at home in the evening.

As you can see, we can produce even more hypotheses as we dig deeper. If you're tackling a rather complex problem, you might generate as many as 20 to 40 hypotheses.

10.15—Substep 4c: Gather Evidence to Either Confirm or Refute Your Hypotheses

Again, we reach another crucial piece of Targeted Problem-Solving. When solving problems, people tend to implicitly generate hypotheses as to why a problem exists. Unfortunately, they usually generate only *one* hypothesis. Furthermore, they simply assume that this one hypothesis holds water and they never even bother gathering any real evidence. Instead, they think with their "guts" rather than with their brains.

Targeted Problem-Solving, however, requires that you actually gather data and specify evidence to either confirm or refute each of the hypotheses you generate. During this step, the key question you ask yourself is:

"What evidence, that others will deem *objective and credible,* do I have to either support or refute this hypothesis?"

Let's define evidence. In a court of law, evidence consists of "the data, in the form of testimony of witnesses, documents or other objects (such as a photograph, a revolver, etc.) identified by witnesses, offered to the court or jury in proof of the facts in issue." (The American College Dictionary) The same definition (minus the revolver) holds for Targeted Problem-Solving. Notice the key words in the preceding definition: "data" and "proof of the facts." There's no room for gut feelings. Targeted Problem-Solving requires that you look at the *facts* and draw reasonable conclusions from those facts.

In some cases, you might already have solid evidence. Often the taking stock information you gathered in answering Question 3: *"How close are we NOW?",* can provide evidence. However, in other instances you might have to gather new data using the methods we described in chapters 3 and 4.

Let's illustrate this substep of gathering data to confirm or refute hypotheses by returning to the problem: "Students often fail to complete their homework." Figure 10.8 below shows just three of the many hypotheses a team of middle school teachers generated concerning this problem. What *objective* and *credible* evidence could they use to either support or refute these hypotheses?

Figure 10.8   Hypotheses and Possible Sources of Evidence

	Hypothesis	Possible Sources of Evidence
1.	Students often fail to do their homework because parents feel their children are older and therefore should be responsible for doing their homework without the parents hounding them.	Parent survey, student survey Parent interviews, student interviews
2.	Students often fail to do their homework because the parents are not aware that the children have homework.	Parent survey, student survey Parent interviews, student interviews
3.	Students often fail to do their homework because the parents aren't at home in the evening.	Parent survey, student survey Parent interviews, student interviews
4.	Students haven't yet sufficiently developed a sense that they must take responsibility for their actions.	Parent survey, student survey Parent interviews, student interviews Observation of students

Of course, you need to check out *all* your hypotheses, not just your favorite ones that you feel might hold water. Happily, often times you'll find that one piece of evidence can serve to either support or refute several hypotheses. Thus, your work is easier than you might suspect.

10.16—Substep 4d. Decide Which of the CONFIRMED Hypotheses to Move to the Solution-Seeking Stage

Once the evidence is in, you then judge which hypotheses hold water and which don't. Generally, you will find that the evidence confirms *several* hypotheses. Complex problems always have complex causes and, often, even simple problems do too.

At this point in your problem-solving, we suggest that you use some sort of graphic organizer to summarize your findings about root causes. We recommend using one of the following:

- Force-field analysis
- Flow chart
- Fish bone analysis
- Is/is not T-chart

10.17—Force-field Analysis

This graphic organizer summarizes the forces that work for and against you in a problem situation. The line down the middle represents the problem you're addressing.

Arrows pushing from the left ——> indicate forces contributing to the problem. *Confirmed* hypotheses go on the left side. Arrows pushing from the right <—— represent forces that work to eliminate or minimize the problem. Strengths working for you go on the right side. Figure 10.9 shows the force-field analysis a team of middle school educators constructed to summarize their findings concerning the problem that students often fail to complete their homework.

Figure 10.9   Illustration of Force-field Analysis of the Homework Problem

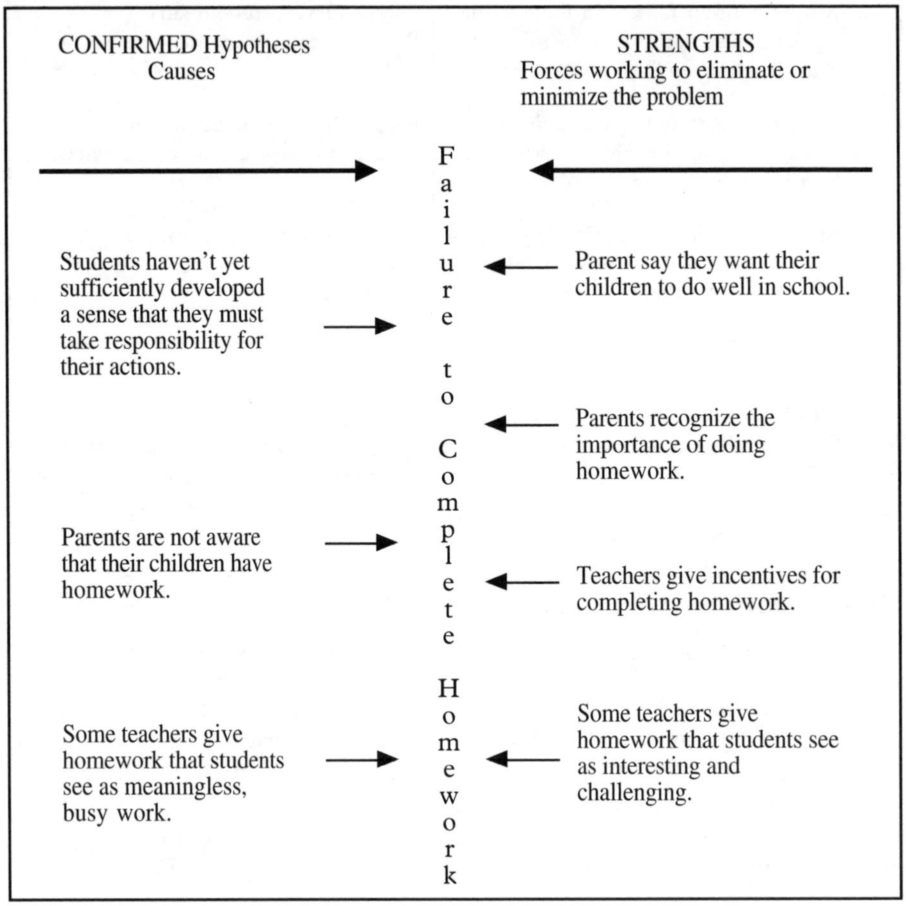

10.18—Flow Chart

Earlier we saw this technique used as a way to gain different perspectives about a problem and its causes. Here, we use a flow chart to summarize the results from the hypothesis testing. A flow chart can graphically display how an event or task unfolds from start to finish, showing all the decision points in the process and mapping out each of the pathways stemming from these different decisions. The teachers grappling with the homework problem constructed the flow chart shown in Figure 10.10 using the information they collected during the hypothesis testing stage. Notice they have highlighted the places in the process where difficulties start and causes begin to unfold.

Figure 10.10 Illustration of Flow Chart for the Homework Problem

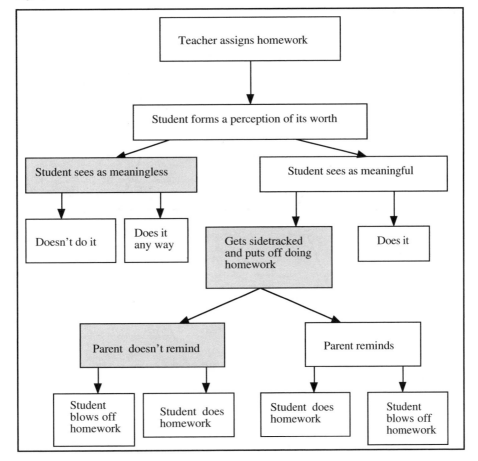

10.19—Fishbone Analysis

Also known as a cause-and-effect diagram, a fishbone analysis displays both the confirmed causes and the ultimate effect or problem you're trying to solve. Figure 10.11 shows the confirmed reasons for the homework problem laid out in a fish-bone diagram. Notice that we cluster the confirmed causes into related categories. Also note that unlike the force-field analysis, the direction of the lines do *not* differentiate strengths from causes. Indeed, you list *only* causes in a fishbone diagram.

10.20—Is/Is Not T-chart

This chart summarizes two categories: What *is* causing the problem and what *is not* causing the problem. Those hypotheses confirmed through evidence as root causes go under the IS column, while the refuted hypotheses go under the IS NOT column. Problem-solvers also list strengths under the IS NOT column. Figure 10.12 illustrates how the committee of teachers dealing with the homework problem summarized the results of their hypothesis testing. Later in this

Figure 10.11 Illustration of Fish-bone Analysis of the Homework Problem

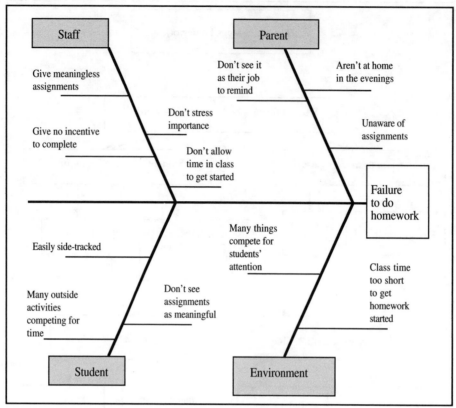

Figure 10.12 Illustration of Is/Is Not T-Chart of the Homework Problem

IS the Problem	IS NOT the Problem
Students haven't yet sufficiently developed a sense that they must take responsibility for their actions.	Parents say they want their children to do well in school.
Parents are not aware that their children have homework.	Parents recognize the importance of doing homework.
Some teachers give homework that sutdents see as meaningless, busy work.	Teachers give incentives for completing homework.
Most parents are not home in the evening to supervise homework.	Some teachers give homework that students see as interesting and challenging.

chapter, we will show how Joan and her colleagues used an Is/Is Not/Chart to summarize their observations of student behavior in the hallways.

10.21—Deciding Which Confirmed Hypotheses to Move to the Solution-Seeking Stage

Once you have summarized your hypothesis testing results, you need to decide which of the several confirmed hypotheses you wish to move to the solution-seeking stage. Of course, you can simultaneously try to address all the root causes, but this is often too difficult. So, we suggest that you prioritize your confirmed hypotheses using the following questions and then move only the top priority ones to the solution-seeking stage.

Are some of the confirmed hypotheses simply outside your sphere of influence? If *you* can't do anything about them, assign these hypotheses a low priority.

For example, let's say one of your confirmed hypotheses concerning the problem that children fail to complete their homework states:

> Parents aren't home in the evening to supervise homework.

You find out that a large percentage of parents in your community work the night shift at the local factory. You simply aren't going to be able to change the work shift assignments for parents, so this confirmed hypothesis goes to bottom of the list.

Is there a root cause that acts like the first domino in a chain reaction? If the solutions to a confirmed hypothesis sets off a chain reaction solving several other causes, you should give this confirmed hypothesis a high priority.

For example, the teachers dealing with the homework problem found their evidence supported the following hypothesis:

> Students haven't yet sufficiently developed a sense that t*hey* must take responsibility for their actions.

The teachers decided that if they could only build this sense of responsibility in students then they could solve the homework problem, as well as a slew of other problems within the school. Therefore, the team of teachers decided definitely to move this confirmed hypothesis to the solution-seeking stage.

10.22—Joan Answers Question 4 of the Targeted Problem-Solving Process

So far, the Student Responsibility Committee has stated the problem in general terms:

We simply have too many shouting matches during passing periods.

They also came to consensus about what they are striving for:
- No shouting matches in the hallways
- Students will greet one another in a friendly manner
- Students will refrain from using offensive name-calling
- If a shouting match starts, it will quickly dissipate

And they have taken stock of how close they *now* are to their ideal situation. Next, the committee moves to answer the question: *"What are the core causes of the problem?"*.

Substep 4a

Trying to identify the root causes for all the shouting matches in the hallways, Joan and her colleagues begin by *examining the problem from many angles and perspectives.*

They go to a handful of teachers, the principal, students who have seen a shouting match erupt, and students who actually engaged in a shouting match. They ask all these people the same question: *"What do you think is causing the problem?"*.

During her conferences with students sent to her office for taking part in shouting matches, Ms. Collins, the vice-principal, asks them to draw a flow chart of what happened. She also asks teachers and students who observed shouting matches to construct flow charts showing what happened from their viewpoints.

Joan and her fellow committee members consult the educational literature, examining what experts and researchers say about adolescent behavior. They also review documents, make observations, and examine their taking stock information, all the while asking *"What's causing the problem?"*.

After looking at the problem from many angles, the Student Responsibility Committee meets on Wednesday during its regular meeting time. The agenda includes the following tasks:
1. Generate all possible hypotheses that might explain why the problem exists.
   a. Cull out duplicates.
   b. Cluster hypotheses into related categories.
2. Decide how we will gather evidence to confirm or refute our hypotheses.
3. Set next meeting time.

Substep 4b

Joan facilitates today's meeting. After reviewing the agenda, she asks the group to *brainstorm hypotheses* by completing the following statement:

"We believe the problem of too many shouting matches exists because . . ."

The hypotheses flow fast and furious. Ms. Jones, the parent representative, charts the hypotheses and can barely keep up. The group follows the rules for brainstorming and refrains from judging any of the hypotheses. Soon they have 15 hypotheses.

As Joan scans the list of hypotheses, she notices that most put the blame on the students:

We believe the problem of too many shouting matches exists because:

- Students are angry at the world and the people in it.
- Students have little self-control when frustrated.
- Students want to build their reputations as being "tough."
- Students believe they can get away with it.
- Students have girlfriend/boyfriend troubles.
- Students want to intimidate weaker kids.
- Students need to save face when confronted by another student.
- Students are bored and want to spice up their life with a little conflict.
- "Fun" name-calling gets out of hand.
- Students follow the lead of the TV situation comedies they watch where nasty name-calling and shouting matches are par for the course.
- Students are mad at a teacher and take it out on a fellow student.
- Students forgot to take their Ritalin.
- Students are mad at their parents and carry their foul mood to school.
- Students see members of their families interact with each other using name-calling and shouting matches.
- Society says its OK to call names and have shouting matches.

Joan then challenges the committee to generate hypotheses that look at reasons besides those centered on the students and their deficiencies. She asks:

- Is there anything about our *curriculum* that might be causing the problem?
- Is there anything about our *instruction strategies* that might be causing the problem?
- Is there anything about how *we organize for learning* that might be causing the problem?
- Is there anything about our *procedures* that might be causing the problem?
- Is there anything about our *policies* that might be causing the problem?

These questions cause the group to view the shouting matches problem through different lenses and they generate additional hypotheses:

We believe the problem of too many shouting matches exists because:

- Few adults monitor the halls during passing periods.
- Adults often look the other way when student voices begin to raise in the excitement that signals the beginning of a shouting match.
- Students view the school's climate as oppressive.
- Teachers tend to ignore the emotional stressors of students.
- Nowhere in our curriculum do we teach conflict resolution skills.
- We encourage competition (some of which is "unhealthy") in all aspects of the school, in the classrooms and on the athletic fields.

They cull out duplicates and then sort the remaining into groups, trying to put similar hypotheses together. They also toss out one hypothesis they see as "off the wall", students forgot to take their Ritalin.

The committee ends up with nine major hypotheses to test.

We believe the problem of too many shouting matches exists because:

1. Students are angry at the world and the people in it.
   - Students view the school's climate as oppressive.
   - Students have girlfriend/boy friend troubles.
   - Students are mad a teacher and take it out on a fellow student.
   - Students are mad at their parents and carry their foul mood to school.
2. Students have little self-control when frustrated.
   - Nowhere in our curriculum do we teach conflict resolution skills.
   - "Fun" name-calling gets out of hand.
3. Students want to build their reputations as being "tough."
   - Students want to intimidate weaker kids.
   - Students need to save face when confronted by another student.
4. Few adults monitor the halls during passing periods.
5. Adults often look the other way when student voices begin to raise in the excitement that signals the beginning of a shouting match.
   - Students believe they can get away with it.
6. Teachers tend to ignore the emotional stressors of students.
7. We encourage competition (some of which is unhealthy) in all aspects of the school, in the classrooms and on the athletic fields.
8. Students are bored and want to spice up their life with a little conflict.

9. Students are surrounded by poor role models.
- Students see TV situation comedies where nasty name-calling and shouting matches are par for the course.
- Students see members of their families interact with each other using name-calling and shouting matches.
- Society says its OK to call names and have shouting matches.

Substep 4c

The committee members then take about 20 minutes to sketch out a plan on how they will *gather evidence to either confirm or refute their nine hypotheses.*

Before they adjourn, the group sets another meeting time in two weeks. They agree that they will have all the evidence collected and the data summarized by the next meeting. They plan to the use the next meeting to:

1. Identify the core reasons why the shouting match problem exists.
2. Decide which of the confirmed hypotheses to move to the solution-seeking stage.

Two weeks pass as committee members collect and summarize the data needed to confirm or refute the hypotheses they generated to explain why the shouting matches keep occurring in the hallways.

This time Mr. Sanchez, one of the teachers on the Student Responsibility Committee, facilitates the meeting. "Today, we want to share the information we collected and identify what we see as the core reasons why we have so many shouting matches occurring in our hallways." Members take turns sharing their data. As they share, Ms. Collins, the recorder for the day's meeting, creates the following Is/Is Not T-Chart (Figure 10.13) summarizing their findings.

Substep 4d

"Now, of our five confirmed hypotheses, which should we move to the solution-seeking stage?" Mr. Sanchez asks. The group examines each of the confirmed hypotheses, asking:

- Are some of the confirmed hypotheses simply outside your sphere of influence?
- Is there a root cause that acts like the first domino in chain reaction?

Based on their discussion, the committee prioritizes the confirmed hypotheses and decides to move the top two to the solution-seeking stage.

Figure 10.13 Is/Is Not T-Chart for Shouting Match Problem

IS the Problem	IS NOT the Problem
Students are angry at the world and the people in it.	Few adults monitor the halls during passing periods. Reality: Most teachers monitor the halls.
Students have little self-control when frustrated.	Adults often look the other way when student voices begin to raise in excitement that signals the beginning of a shouting match. Reality: Adults always pay attention if within earshot.
Students want to build their reputation as being "tough."	
We encourage competition (some of which is unhealthy) in all aspects of school.	Teachers tend to ignore the emotional stresses of students. Reality: Students say that teachers do care about their emotional stressors.
Students are surrounded by poor role models.	Students are bored and want to spice up their life with a little conflict. Reality: Students may be bored but not enough to use conflict to spice up their lives.

We believe the problem of too many shouting matches exists because:

Priority 1:   Students have little self-control when frustrated. They lack the skills to positively resolve conflict.
The committee members felt that the school could do something to alleviate this difficulty. They also believe that if students could positively resolve conflict and deal with frustration, many other problems around the school would disappear.

Priority 2:   We encourage competition (some of which is unhealthy) in all aspects of the school, in the classrooms and on the athletic fields.
Again, the committee members felt that not only could they, as educators, do something about this core reason but they also believe that if they lessened unhealthy competition in the school other problems within the school would dissipate.

Priority 3:   Students want to build their reputations as being "tough."
The committee members felt that by addressing Priority Reasons 1 and 2 they would minimize this cause as well.

Priority 4:   Students are angry at the world and the people in it.
Committee members see anger as a fact of life for both students and adults. They hope that by helping students develop skills for positively resolving conflict and dealing with

frustration, some of the students' anger will dissipate. However, the committee members also recognize that they may need to address this Priority Cause more directly later.

Priority 5:   Students are surrounded by poor role models. Committee members feel that they can do little about the way both society and TV condone name-calling and shouting matches as acceptable behavior. Committee members also feel somewhat powerless about changing how students' families interact with each other. However, they do agree to return to this priority later to see if any viable solutions exist.

Now, that the Student Responsibility Committee members have determined the root causes of the shouting match problem and decided which of the confirmed hypotheses to move to the solution-seeking stage, they are ready to brainstorm solutions and draw up an action plan for solving the situation.

Getting Kids Involved!

Earlier in this chapter, we introduced you to Steinbeck Middle School in San Jose California, an accelerated school since 1994. As part of the accelerated schools process, the school community formed committees called cadres around each of the school's major challenge areas. These cadres include staff, students and patrons and serve as "think tanks" examining the challenge areas and suggesting possible solutions.

One of the challenges assigned to the Program and Curriculum Cadre included whether or not the school should continue its Sustained Silent Reading program. During the cadre's meeting several staff members voiced their opinion that the students didn't use the time well and suggested dropping the program. A community member serving on the cadre asked, "Do we know what the kids think about it?" Quickly the students on the cadre offered to gather data to see what students actually thought about the Sustained Silent Reading time. They spent the next week talking with students during the lunch period. Using hand-held tape recorders, they recorded student answers to the following questions: "Should we keep Sustained Silent Reading or not? Why do you feel that way?".

The student evaluators then transcribed the interview data and reported back to the cadre that students overwhelmingly wanted to keep Sustained Silent Reading. Furthermore, the students stated that they felt that the program was helping them to read better. Based on the data compiled by the student evaluators, the Program and Curriculum Cadre recommended that the school continue with its Sustained Silent Reading program.

(Thanks to Marilyn Zitzer, Resource Teacher and Accelerated Schools Coach at Steinbeck, for sharing this example.)

10.23—Solution-Seeking Question 5: How Can We Address These Core Causes?

Figure 10.14 Targeted Problem-Solving Solution-seeking Question 5

Now, that you know the root causes of the problem, you are ready to find solutions. First, you need to *brainstorm possible solutions*. We suggest you begin by looking within your school for solutions. Is there a teacher in your school who appears to have solved a problem similar to the one you now face? Perhaps you can adapt her solution to meet your needs. Adapting a solution from within your own school helps increase your chances of success. Such a solution has shown that it works well within the unique context of *your* school.

After looking within your own school, next search outside your school for possible solutions. What have other schools done to solve similar problems? What do researchers say? A surf on the Internet, particularly through the ERIC database will most likely yield several possible solutions.

After brainstorming solutions, now comes the time to pick the best ideas and *design an action plan that addresses the root causes of the problem*. We suggest that in your action plan you specify *who* will *do what* by *when*. Plus, you should delineate how you will evaluate the effectiveness of your solution. We offer the form shown in Figure 10.15 as a guide in preparing your action plan. Notice that this form also requires that you specify your confirmed hypotheses along with the supporting evidence. This helps remind you to stay on target and write an action plan that specifically addresses the confirmed causes.

Figure 10.15 Blank Action Plan Form

Date: _____		Committee: _____	
Confirmed Hypothesis:			
Evidence confirming hypothesis:			
What do we need to do?	**When?**	**Who will do it?**	**How will be evaluated?**

As you design your action plan, please keep the following advice in mind:

- Use your common sense.
- Keep it do-able.
- Go with activities that will give you the biggest bang for your buck and energy.

10.24—Do You Pilot Test or Not?

Now, you're ready to *implement your action plan*. You can, of course, make wholesale changes. However, you might want to simply pilot test your solution before going school-wide. As you decide whether you should implement a full-blown plan or simply pilot test, weigh the following:

How much time, money and effort will the plan require for success?

If your action plan will take a great deal of time, money, and effort to implement, you should consider conducting a small-scale pilot test before making such a huge commitment of resources.

How high are the costs of failure?

If the consequences of failing are great, you should think about simply pilot testing your solution before scaling-up to a full-blown action plan. Doing a pilot can provide you with invaluable lessons that can help you fine-tune your solution. Also you should contemplate doing a pilot test if your action plan might result in irrevocable negative outcomes. Don't plunge into a solution if you feel you can't undo your mistakes.

How pressing is the problem?

Hopefully you won't always find yourself in a crisis situation that requires a solution *immediately*. Rarely, do quick fixes get beyond a "band-aid" solution that simply addresses the symptoms rather than the core reasons why a problem exists. If you have the luxury of time, do a pilot test. However, if you find yourself pressed for a solution now, by all means implement your action plan. But *do not skip* any of the Targeted Problem steps! Especially be sure you hypothesize why the problem exists *and* gather data that will either confirm or refute your hypotheses. Brainstorm solutions and create an action plan for only those hypotheses that your data confirm. Even when you're up to your neck in alligators, take time (albeit only a little) and define the problem. Otherwise, your quick fix will be no fix!

Do you have enough buy-in from the members of the school community to successfully implement your action plan?

Some action plans require that key members of the school community buy into your solution plan. If you don't yet have enough willingness from the key players, you should consider conducting a pilot test. Many teachers, administrators, students, and even parents will take a wait-and-see attitude if your action plans requires major changes on their part. A successful pilot test can go a long way towards convincing these folks that they should become part of the solution.

10.25—Joan Answers Question 5 of the Targeted Problem-Solving Process

> The Student Responsibility Committee has determined the following root causes underlying the shouting match problem:
> - Students have little self-control when frustrated. They lack the skills to positively resolve conflict.

- We encourage competition (some of which is unhealthy) in all aspects of the school, in the classrooms and on the athletic fields.
- Students want to build their reputations as being "tough."
- Students are angry at the world and the people in it.
- Students are surrounded by poor role models.

They also prioritized and decided to move the following two confirmed hypotheses to the next solution-seeking stage:

- Students have little self-control when frustrated. They lack the skills to positively resolve conflict.
- We encourage competition (some of which is unhealthy) in all aspects of the school, in the classrooms and on the athletic fields.

The committee members begin by brainstorming solutions to address the students' lack of conflict resolution skills. They decide to tackle the unhealthy competition reason later. First, they *look within their school for solutions*. A month ago, Ms. Kay in the Special Education Department taught her students conflict mediation skills. In the last three weeks, none of her 30 students has been involved in a shouting match, whereas two months ago Ms. Collins recalled seeing these same students daily in her office because of confrontations during passing periods. The committee puts Ms. Kay's conflict mediation program on the list of possible solutions and Ms. Collins volunteers to find out more about Ms. Kay's program by next Wednesday's meeting.

"Does any one else know of other programs in our school that help students deal positively with frustration and anger?" Joan asks the group. Mark and Julius, two sixth graders on the committee, raise their hands. "In our health class the other day, Mr. Stone talked about ways we can calm down when we get angry," explains Mark. "Julius and I could talk with Mr. Stone and get some more information."

"I'll check with the counselor and visit with the teachers to see if they are doing anything special on conflict resolution in their classes," volunteers Mr. Sanchez, the social studies teacher.

Next the committee draws up a plan to *search outside the school for possible solutions*. One member says she'll check with other middle schools in the surrounding districts. Ms. Jones, a parent, volunteers to surf the Internet for possible solutions. Joan offers to check out the university library to see what research has to say about helping youngsters resolve conflicts and deal with frustrations. Everyone agrees to report back at next Wednesday's meeting.

The committee members spend the following week looking both inside and outside the school for possible solutions. On Wednesday, November 5, the committee convenes and the members quickly share what they learned. They spend the next 45 minutes designing an action plan that addresses the students' lack of conflict resolution skills. Figure 10.16 shows the action plan the committee devised.

Since Ms. Kay's class served as a kind of pilot for the conflict mediation program, the committee opts to recommend a school-wide implementation of the Resolving Conflict Program. The committee members decide to evaluate the effectiveness of the action plan at the December 10 meeting. They also decide to tackle the second priority cause—We encourage competition, some of it unhealthy, in all aspects of the school—at the next meeting.

10.26—Solution-Seeking Question 6: Did our Solution Work?

You've implemented your plan, now you need to ask the tough question: *Did it work?* Chapter 9 provided detailed suggestions on how you can determine the effectiveness of your solution. Unfortunately, many problem-solvers never get to this step in Targeted Problem-Solving. They believe they have "solved" the problem simply because they implemented the plan. "How could it *not* work?" they say. "We carefully designed our solutions and even more carefully implemented it." But simply *doing something* doesn't always guarantee success.

No matter the scope of your intervention, whether it affects the entire school or just a few students, you should *always evaluate* the effectiveness of the program or strategy. As chapter 9 showed, an evaluation can consist of a year-long endeavor of gathering, analyzing, and interpreting evaluation data or a much less involved effort by one teacher collecting outcome data on her own students. You should keep the following key points in mind:

- Decide *before* you implement your solution, what kind of evidence will convince you (and others) that your solution succeeded or failed.
- Make a plan on how you will collect this evidence.
- Collect the evidence.
- Then *use* the evidence to judge success or failure.

If your evaluation of the solution's effectiveness shows your solution worked and successfully alleviated the problem, then congratulate yourself. If, however, you find that your solution fell short, you need to cycle through Steps 4 and 5, once again asking:

- What are the core causes of the problem?
- How can we address these core causes?

In some cases, you will simply have to fine-tune your solution. In other cases, you will have to start from scratch.

Figure 10.16 Action Plan to Address Shouting Match Problem

Date: _____ November 5 _____   Committee: _____ Student Responsibility _____

Confirmed Hypothesis: Students engage in too many shouting matches in the hallways because they don't have the skills to positively resolve conflict and deal with frustration.

Evidence confirming hypothesis: Student survey indicated that only about 35% felt they could successfully resolve a conflict. Interviews with students involved in shouting matches showed that only 1 in 10 could successfully resolve a conflict. Teacher observations showed that only about 30% of the students could successfully resolve a conflict without shouting or fighting. Interviews with counselor and principals indicated that only about 1 in 9 students could successfully resolve a conflict.

What do we need to do?	When?	Who will do it?	How will be evaluated?
1. Train all Teacher Advisory staff in conflict mediation.	November 17, 3:15–5:00	Ms. Kay and counselors	A. Chart the number of shouting matches that occur each day starting with September 15 until the end of the semester.
2. Start Peer Mediation Program.	November 18–21, during Teacher Advisory Period	Ms. Kay, her students and counselors	B. Survey students before beginning Peer Mediation Program and again at the end of the semester
3. Peer mediators and Teacher Advisors teach conflict mediation curriculum to students during Advisory Period.	November 24–27, during Teacher Advisory Period	Peer Mediators and Teacher Advisory staff	C. Survey teachers before beginning Peer Mediation Program and again at the end of the semester.

Figure 10.17 Targeted Problem-Solving Solution-seeking Question 6

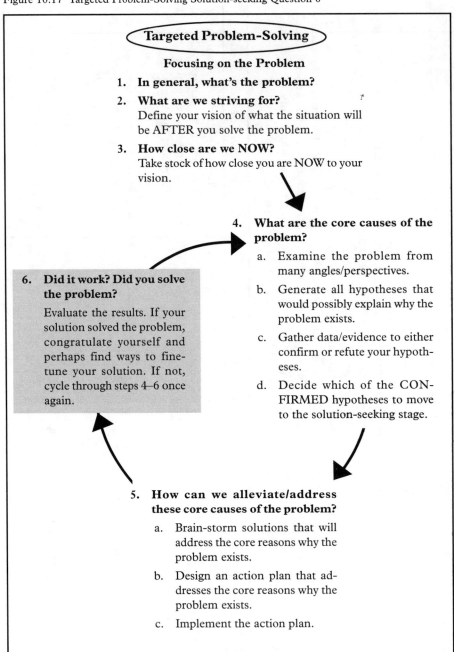

10.27—Joan and the Committee Members Do a Mid-Course Evaluation

It's been five weeks since the Student Responsibility Committee drew up an action plan to address the confirmed hypothesis:

Figure 10.18 Targeted Problem-Solving Cycling Through Again

Targeted Problem-Solving

Focusing on the Problem

1. **In general, what's the problem?**

2. **What are we striving for?**
   Define your vision of what the situation will be AFTER you solve the problem.

3. **How close are we NOW?**
   Take stock of how close you are NOW to your vision.

YES. Congratulations! Perhaps fine-tune your solution.

NO. Need to reexamine the problem, recycling through steps 4–6.

4. **What are the core causes of the problem?**

   a. Examine the problem from many angles/perspectives.

   b. Generate all hypotheses that would possibly explain why the problem exists.

   c. Gather data/evidence to either confirm or refute your hypotheses.

   d. Decide which of the CONFIRMED hypotheses to move to the solution-seeking stage.

6. **Did it work? Did you solve the problem?**

   Evaluate the results. If your solution solved the problem, congratulate yourself and perhaps find ways to fine-tune your solution. If not, cycle through steps 4–6 once again.

5. **How can we alleviate/address these core causes of the problem?**

   a. Brain-storm solutions that will address the core reasons why the problem exists.

   b. Design an action plan that addresses the core reasons why the problem exists.

   c. Implement the action plan.

Shouting matches are occurring too frequently in the hallways because students don't know how to positively resolve conflicts and deal with frustration.

Right after creating the action plan, Joan and her fellow members of the committee presented the plan to the principal, the School Advisory Council and the faculty as a whole. Everyone approved the plan and by November 12, the school community had begun implementing the action plan.

At the December 10 regular meeting of the Student Responsibility Committee, members reviewed how things were going thus far. Joan reported that all pieces of the plan were in place and going well after some initial fine-tuning. It seems that both the Teacher Advisory staff and Peer Mediators wanted on-going training. So now Ms. Kay and the counselors meet with the groups weekly for a 30-minute refresher session.

Ms. Collins, the vice-principal, informed the committee that discipline referrals for shouting matches in the hallways were down substantially in the past two weeks, but cautioned that "we might still be in the honeymoon period." She suggested that they continue to monitor referrals until the end of the semester in mid-January.

The students on the committee said that "things felt calmer and better" in classes and particularly during passing periods. Mr. Sanchez (the social studies teachers) and Ms. Jones (the parent) had conducted weekly observations in the hallways and lunchroom. They reported seeing no shouting matches during passing periods, but several conflicts during the lunch periods occurred each time they observed.

The committee set the January 21 meeting as the time when they would formally evaluate the Peer Mediation Program.

10.28—Joan Answers Question 6 of the Targeted Problem-Solving Process

It's January 21 and the Student Responsibility Committee members come to the meeting armed with facts and figures gathered to answer the question:

Did the Peer Mediation Program work?

The committee begins by reviewing the chart showing the number of hallway shouting matches that have occurred from September 15 to January 20. Ms. Collins also shares similar charts for the shouting matches that have happened in the lunchroom and elsewhere in the school.

Mr. Sanchez and Ms. Jones distribute a summary of their weekly observations in the hallways and lunchroom.

Danielle shares a frequency table showing how students responded to a survey on conflict and frustration before and after the implementation of the Peer Mediation Program. With the help of the counselors, her 7th grade teammates designed the survey, collected the data, and tabulated the numbers.

Joan shares a similar frequency table displaying the results of the teacher survey asking about students' skills in positively handling conflict and frustration.

"It's working!" exclaims Joan. All the data point to progress. Shouting matches have indeed substantially diminished, particularly in the hallways, and students do seem to be successfully using their conflict mediation skills in a variety of situations. However, the committee notes that shouting matches still tend to erupt too frequently in the lunchroom. They resolve to tackle this problem at next week's meeting. They also decide to continue charting disciplinary referrals for the remainder of the school year and reevaluate the Peer Mediation Program in June.

10.29—A Chronological Summary of the Committee's Work

Joan and the other members of the Student Responsibility Committee spent just under two months putting together a plan to address the core reasons as to why the shouting matches were occurring. Figure 10.19 shows a chronology of their work.

Probably two of your first thoughts as you review this chronology are:

1. "That's just too much time. Things would be in chaos by the time November rolled around!"
2. "It takes too much work and we teachers are working overtime as it is!"

Let's address the first issue—Targeted Problem-Solving process taking too much time. We want to stress that during the two months that the Student Responsibility Committee spent devising a solution, the staff of Joan's school did *not* just stand around and let the shouting matches occur and escalate. They did take action. They continued to monitor the halls; and they put extra adults in the Commons area and the intersection of A and B Halls during passing times; and they talked during Teacher Advisory with the students about being more courteous to one another at all times.

But the faculty knew these strategies only addressed the surface problem. That's why they encouraged the Student

Figure 10.19   Summary of Committee's Work showing all 6 Steps in Targeted Problem-Solving

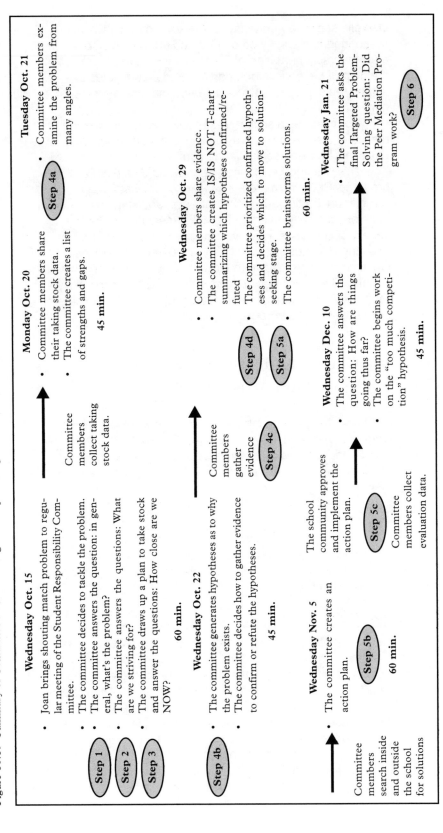

Wednesday Oct. 15

- Joan brings shouting match problem to regular meeting of the Student Responsibility Committee.
- The committee decides to tackle the problem.
- The committee answers the question: in general, what's the problem?
- The committee answers the questions: What are we striving for?
- The committee draws up a plan to take stock and answer the questions: How close are we NOW?

60 min.

Step 1
Step 2
Step 3

Monday Oct. 20

- Committee members share their taking stock data.
- The committee creates a list of strengths and gaps.

45 min.

Committee members collect taking stock data.

Step 4a

Tuesday Oct. 21

- Committee members examine the problem from many angles.

Wednesday Oct. 22

- The committee generates hypotheses as to why the problem exists.
- The committee decides how to gather evidence to confirm or refute the hypotheses.

45 min.

Step 4b

Committee members gather evidence

Step 4c

Wednesday Oct. 29

- Committee members share evidence.
- The committee creates IS/IS NOT T-chart summarizing which hypotheses confirmed/refuted
- The committee prioritized confirmed hypotheses and decides which to move to solution-seeking stage.
- The committee brainstorms solutions.

60 min.

Step 4d
Step 5a

Wednesday Nov. 5

- The committee creates an action plan.

Step 5b

60 min.

Committee members search inside and outside the school for solutions

The school community approves and implement the action plan.

Step 5c

Committee members collect evaluation data.

Wednesday Dec. 10

- The committee answers the question: How are things going thus far?
- The committee begins work on the "too much competition" hypothesis.

45 min.

Wednesday Jan. 21

- The committee asks the final Targeted Problem-Solving question: Did the Peer Mediation Program work?

Step 6

Responsibility Committee to spend the time and effort to devise a solution that would *really* address the underlying causes of the problem.

As you apply Targeted Problem-Solving to the problems you face, as a middle-level educator, you, too, may have to take some quick action to contain the situation, but please follow the lead of Joan's school and don't stop there. Go on to spend the time and effort to formulate a solution that will really be on target.

Now let's turn to the "It takes too much work" issue. Yes, teachers already work hard. However, in our experience as educators, much of that time is spent "containing" the situation. How much better it would be if we could get in place some *preventive* measures so that the situations in our classrooms and schools don't get to the point that we have "to contain" them? That's what Targeted Problem-Solving is all about—finding solutions that address the core causes of a problem and thus, devising strategies to address these causes. Targeted Problem-Solving helps us to "work smarter."

10.30—Another Example: A Teacher Makes a Difference

As you can see, Targeted Problem-Solving with its six solution-seeking questions can help guide a school community towards a solution addressing a school-wide problem. But what happens if you, as an individual teacher, face a problem in your own classroom and want to do something about it on your own? Does Targeted Problem-Solving help in such individual cases? The answer is a resounding YES! Targeted Problem-Solving works well with simple and complex problems, whether they exist school-wide or only in an individual classroom.

Let's illustrate with a problem that Janice, a middle school social studies teacher, faces. She's concerned because many of her students don't seem to understand the text she's using. Other teachers in her school may face a similar problem, but she feels that she needs to do something, even if it's on her own. She plans to raise the issue at the next grade level meeting, but she can't wait until then. She needs to act now before her students get even more lost and discouraged.

Saturday, September 15

Janice gathers up a pen and pad of paper and turns to the one-page graphic showing the Targeted Problem-Solving process (Figure 10.1). She's ready to begin. After such a trying week, she just couldn't think clearly Friday afternoon. But a good night's sleep has refreshed her and renewed her commitment to solve the problem.

She begins with Solution-Seeking Question 1:

Step 1   In general, what's the problem?

Too many students don't seem to comprehend our social studies text.

Next she jots down her answer to Solution-Seeking Question 2:

Step 2   What are we striving for?

After reading a chapter in our social studies text, students will be able to correctly answer comprehension questions whose answers:

- Are not explicitly stated in one place within the selection
- Require students to draw upon prior knowledge
- Demand that students apply knowledge to a novel situation.

Janice now comes to Solution-Seeking Question 3:

Step 3   How close are we NOW?

She takes about 15 minutes and creates a matrix summarizing her finding to Question 3. (See Figure 10.20.)

Figure 10.20 Matrix of Janice's Findings

Vision Component	Current State of Affairs in My Classroom
After reading a chapter in our social studies text, students will be able to correctly answer comprehension questions whose answers: • Are not explicitly stated in one place within the selection	Only 20% of the students correctly answered such questions on the last chapter review section.
• Require students to draw upon prior knowledge	On the last two chapter reviews, ony 15% of the sutdents showed evidence of drawing on their prior knowledge of history. On last week's chapter test,
• Demand that students apply knowledge to a novel situation	only 10% of the students could apply the knowledge to a novel situation.

Thus far, Janice has stated the problem in general terms, specified her vision, and taken stock of how close she is now to her vision. Now, she's ready for the crucial Question 4:

Step 4   What are the core causes of the problem?

She begins by listing all the "lenses" she might use to examine the problem.

My viewpoint
Students' viewpoint
What other teachers say

What test scores might reveal
Is there something about the way I'm teaching?
Is there something about the curriculum I'm teaching?
Is there something about the atmosphere in my classroom?

Putting on each new set of "lenses," she *generates possible hypotheses* as to why students don't understand the social studies text. After a few minutes she has 15 hypotheses.

My students don't understand our social studies text because . . .

1. My students don't try hard enough.
2. The students just don't want to read anything. They would rather just listen to me lecture than read it on their own.
3. The book is written at a 9th grade reading level.
4. The book is poorly organized.
5. Students find the book boring.
6. Students find the social studies content far removed from their own daily lives.
7. Students aren't motivated to learn; they would rather socialize than learn social studies.
8. Most of my students are reading below grade level.
9. Many of my students simply don't have the background experiences to help them understand the vocabulary in our text book.
10. I rely too much on the textbook to do the teaching job.
11. I don't provide enough guidance to help the students successfully handle the book.
12. These students have had six years of answering low-level comprehension questions where the answer is explicitly stated in the reading selection. Now for the first time they are faced with comprehension questions that require them to draw on prior knowledge and go beyond the text.
13. American History doesn't relate to the realities of my students' lives.
14. Our curriculum stresses "people and dates" over concepts and application.
15. The stress of competition in my classroom is so great that students are so afraid to make a mistake that they really don't try.

Janice then spends the next five minutes *culling out the duplicates and sorting her hypotheses into categories.* She finally ends up with the following list of seven hypotheses that she needs to test:

My students don't understand our social studies text because . . .

1. Students aren't motivated to learn.
    *   They would rather socialize than learn social studies.
    *   My students don't try hard enough.
2. The book is not "student friendly".
    *   Most of my students are reading below grade level.
    *   The students just don't want to read anything. They would rather just listen to me lecture than read it on their own.

- The book is written at a 9th grade reading level.
- The book is poorly organized.
- Many of my students simply don't have the background experiences to help them understand the vocabulary in our text book.

3. American History doesn't relate to the realities of my students' lives.
   - Students find the book boring.
   - Students find the social studies content far removed from their own daily lives.
   - Our curriculum stresses "people and dates" over concepts and application.
4. I rely too much on the textbook to do the teaching job.
5. I don't provide enough guidance to help the students successfully handle the book.
6. These students have had six years of answering low level comprehension questions where the answer is explicitly stated in the reading selection; now for the first time they are faced with comprehension questions that require them to draw on prior knowledge and go beyond the text.
7. The stress of competition in my classroom is so great that students are so afraid to make a mistake that they really don't try.

> Note: After reading Janice's list you might say, "Well, I don't see why she put that hypothesis with that one. I would have done it differently." Yes, it's quite possible that you would sort Janice's hypotheses into entirely different groups. There's really *no one right* way to sort. The key is this: Sort the hypotheses into groups that make sense to you. And Janice has done just that!

Janice has only 45 minutes before she has to take her sons to soccer practice so she quickly jots down a plan on how she will test each of her hypotheses. Next week at school, she'll *gather the evidence and either confirm or refute her hypotheses.*

Thursday, September 20

Janice sits in the media center, the school's only air-conditioned room. Indian summer's hit with a vengeance and she needs a cool spot to review the evidence she's collected. After about 30 minutes she's constructed a Force-Field Analysis Chart summarizing the results of her hypothesis testing.

Janice realized that all four confirmed hypotheses appear related and decides to move all four to the solution-seeking stage. At Friday's team meeting she'll pick the brains of her fellow team members for solutions. Friday night she wants to spend some time surfing the Net for ideas and Saturday afternoon after the boys' soccer games, she plans to drive to the university library to see what research has to say. Sunday, she'll put together her action plan and start making some changes Monday.

Sunday, September 23

Step 5   How can I alleviate/address these core causes of the problem?

Janice's excitement increases as she *sketches out her action plan.* Her search for solutions that address the core reasons why her students don't understand the

Figure 10.21 Force Field Analysis Chart Summarizing Hypothesis Testing

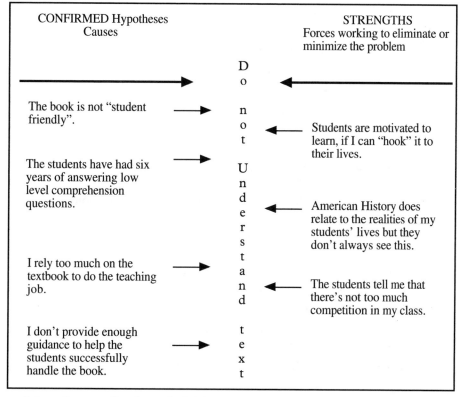

social studies text has been fruitful. She can barely wait until tomorrow so she can *try out her new strategies*. She decides to give herself a month before she formally evaluates her changes. Of course, she'll informally evaluate things as she goes along. She knows that she'll have to do some fine-tuning. She hasn't been this energized in a long time. She now feels she *can* make a difference.

Sunday, October 21

Janice and her students have had a good month. Her students seem to understand more and Janice feels she's making progress. Today, she pours over the evaluation data she collected over the past month as she implemented her action plan. Now, she must answer that tough final question of the Targeted Problem-Solving Process:

Step 6 *Did it work?*

All her data indicate she's on the right track. She just needs to keep fine-tuning her strategies. The year's off to a good start!

10.31—Chapter Summary

Chapter 10 has focused on using research and evaluation methods to seek solutions to problems. Furthermore, in this chapter we introduced Targeted Problem-solving which employs the following six solution-seeking questions to guide you towards successful solutions:

1. In general, what is the problem?
2. What are we striving for?
3. How close are we *now*?
4. What are the core causes of the problem?
5. How can we address these core causes?
6. Did our solution work?

Other key points from this chapter include the following Major Concepts

Major Concepts

☞ Answering Solution-Seeking Question 2: "*How close are we now to our vision?*" fulfills three purposes:

   1. To gather baseline data so that you will have a reference point when you later ask: "Did our solution work?".
   2. To identify what's going *wrong* to help you distinguish symptoms from root causes.
   3. To recognize what's going *right* so you will know the strengths you can build upon when you design your solution.

☞ Defining the core causes of a problem requires completing four substeps:

   1. Examine the problem from many angles and perspectives to get multiple viewpoints on the root causes of the problem.
   2. Generate all possible hypotheses that might explain why the problem exists.
   3. Gather evidence to either confirm or refute your hypotheses.
   4. Decide which of the CONFIRMED hypotheses to move to the solution-seeking stage.

☞ Some graphic organizers that can help you to summarize your findings about root causes to your problem include:

   • Force-field analysis
   • Flow chart
   • Fish bone analysis
   • Is/is not T-chart.

☞ Once you have determined the root causes of your problem, prioritize your confirmed hypotheses.

☞ Answering Solution-Seeking Question 5: "How can we alleviate/address these core causes of the problem?" requires that you:

   a. Brainstorm possible solutions
   b. Design an action plan that addresses the root causes of the problem
   c. Implement your action plan

Advice

√ As you answer Solution-Seeking Question 1: "What are we striving for?", refrain from describing *how* you will solve the problem. Rather, focus on painting a portrait that specifies the behaviors that will happen and will *not* happen once the problem is solved.

√ Strive to keep your observations simple and reliable.

√ Don't leap at the first solution that pops into your head. Whenever you try to solve a problem always ask: "What are the core causes of the problem?" *before* brainstorming solutions.

√ As you design your action plan:

- Use your common sense.

- Keep it do-able.

- Go with activities that will give you the biggest bang for your buck and energy.

√ Don't assume you have "solved" the problem simply because you have implemented some action plan. Check it out and and make sure your *data* tell you that it worked.

10.32—Resources

Print Resources

* These references have been recommended in earlier chapters. The number of *'s indicates the number of previous recommendations.

*****Bernhardt, V. L. (1998). *Data analysis for comprehensive schoolwide improvement.* Larchmont, NY: Eye on Education.

HIGHLY RECOMMENDED. In addition to providing comprehensive guidance to educators on how to gather, display, and analyze the data, also includes a rich description of how an elementary school and high school followed a problem-solving cycle (similar to the Targeted Problem-Solving Process described in this book) to meet complex, school-wide problems in their schools.

**Hill, B. C. & Ruptic, C. A. (1994). *Practical aspects of authentic assessment: Putting the pieces together.* Norwood, MA: Christopher-Gordon Publishers.

Provides numerous methods of observing students to assess their learning. Although written for elementary teachers, middle school educators could easily adapt the over 140 assessment tools to the middle-level grades. Includes many forms for data collection. A how-to book on authentic assessment using student portfolios and teacher observations.

*Hopfenberg, W., Levin, H., et al. (1993). *The accelerated schools resource guide.* San Francisco: Jossey-Bass Inc., Publishers.

Written to guide beginning Accelerated Schools in their efforts to transform their schools into learning communities where *all* students accelerate their learning. Fully describes, with rich examples from real schools, the Inquiry Process, a problem-solving process members of the Accelerated Schools use to find solutions to the challenges they face. The Targeted Problem-Solving Process described in Chapter 10 represents an adaptation of the Accelerated School's Inquiry Process. Even educators in non-Accelerated Schools can profit from reading how teams of teachers, administrators, parents and students work together to solve school-wide problems.

National Center for the Accelerated Schools, Stanford University. (1991). *The inquiry Process. Accelerated schools*, Volume 1 Number 3, Summer 1991.

An excellent, very brief explanation of the Inquiry Process in 8 pages. Also includes an example of how one school used the process to address the lack of family involvement in their students' educational lives. Available for downloading by accessing the Accelerated Schools Web page at **http://www.stanford.edu/group/ASP**.

**Schmuck, R. A. (1997). *Practical action research for change.* Arlington Heights, IL: IRI Skylight Training and Publishing, Inc.

Chapter 6 focuses on "Responsive Action Research" where an educator gathers data to help solve a problem. Gives a step-by-step explanation of the the action research process along with two case studies showing how two individual teachers used the process to solve the problem of unresponsive students and poor relationships among students of different racial groups. Would serve as an excellent companion to the Targeted Problem-Solving process covered in Chapter 10 of *Getting Answers to Your Questions*.

Internet Resources

Note: You can easily access the Websites we recommend below by simply going to our Web page located at

http://www.pittstate.edu/edsc/ssls/letendre.html

From our Web page, a simple click of your mouse will take you straight to the selected Website. We regularly verify these sites and add others that we find worthy of our recommendation.

Accelerated Schools National Center
http://www.stanford.edu/group/ASP
Includes a full-text version of all the Accelerated Schools Newsletters, published three times a year. Volume 1 Number 3 includes a succinct explanation of the Inquiry Process used by Accelerated Schools to find solutions to the challenges they face. Volume 5 Number 1 provides advice on maintaining the integrity of the Inquiry Process.

Center for Applied Research and Educational Improvement
http://carei.coled.umn.edu/
Connects to an excellent site sponsored by the Center for Applied Research and Educational Improvement. Includes a research and resources section organized around various innovative practices. A good guide when you get to the brainstorming stage in Targeted Problem-Solving.

Education Commission of the States
http://www.ecs.org/ecs/ecsweb.nsf
Links to the Website maintained by the Education Commission of the States. Includes a comprehensive catalog of school reform models, which you can download and may prove valuable when you get to Step 5 in Targeted Problem-Solving where you brainstorm solutions.

National Research and Development Center
http://www.ed.gov/offices/OERI/At-Risk/center1.html
Connects to The National Research and Development Center which then links
to three other centers: (1) The Center for Research on the Education of Students
Placed At Risk at Johns Hopkins University and Howard University, (2) The
Center for Research on Education, Diversity and Excellence, and (3) The National Research Center on the Gifted and Talented, located at the University of
Connecticut at Storrs. All three sites include an annotated bibliography on selected/relevant topics with links to relevant Websites. Can serve as an excellent
source of possible solutions once you get to Step 5 of Targeted Problem-Solving
where you brainstorm solutions that will address the core reasons why the problem exists.

National Staff Development Council
http://www.nsdc.org/
Connects to the Website maintained by the National Staff Development Council.
The "Library" button on the site's home page takes you to on-line text versions
of articles published in the organization's journal. Some articles deal with consensus decision-making, continuous improvement, and data driven decision making. Filled with down-to-earth advice.

Epilogue

As we come to a close, we want to leave you with three pieces of advice:

1. **Become more systematic in how you get answers to your questions.**

   Make a plan, even if it's just a quick checklist jotted down on the back of an envelope. Then follow that plan and let your data, rather than only your gut instinct, do the talking, helping you to decide what's best for the kids. It's time to work smarter. We're already working as hard as we can.

2. **Find partners to help you ask and answer your questions.**

   Surely you can find at least one "soul-mate" some where in your school who will be willing to embark on a more systematic process of asking and answering questions about educational practice. And we know of one group that will definitely jump at the chance to ask and answer questions—your middle-level students.

3. **Analyze the challenges you face by using Targeted Problem-Solving rather than simply leaping at the first solution that comes to mind.**
   This way you'll avoid wasted time, energy, and money. Plus you'll have a better chance of actually solving your problem.

   We're always interested in hearing about your experiences in asking and answering questions. So, please share them. Also we would appreciate any comments or suggestions you might have about this book. You can contact us at:

   > 303 Hughes Hall
   > School of Education
   > Pittsburg State University
   > Pittsburg, KS 66762
   > **http://www.pittstate.edu/edsc/ssls/letendre.html**

In closing, we offer a reflection we believe sums up what drives us all, especially when we find ourselves isolated and alone in our endeavors:

> I am only one, but I *am* one.
> I cannot do everything,
>   but I *can* do something.
> I *will* do what I can do.

> from *The Upper Room Daily Devotional Guide*

QA Bibliography

Barnhart, C. L. (Ed.). (1963). *The American college dictionary.* New York: Random House.

Brooks, J. G. & Brooks, M. G. (1993). *In Search of Understanding: The Case for Constructivist Classrooms.* Alexandria, VA: Association for Supervision and Curriculum Development.

Dillman, D. A. (1979). *Mail and telephone surveys: The total design method.* New York: John Wiley.

Drew, C. J., Hardman, M. L., & Hart, A. W. (1996). *Designing and Conducing Research: Inquiry in Education and Social Science.* Boston: Allyn and Bacon.

Gage, N. L. & Berliner, D. C. (1992). *Educational psychology (5th Ed.)* Boston: Houghton-Mifflin.

Hopfenberg, W., Levin, H. M., Chase, C., Christensen, G., Moore, M., Soler, P., Brunner, I., Keller, B., & Rodriguez, G. (1993). *The accelerated schools resource guide.* San Francisco: Jossey-Bass.

Levin, H. M. (1983). *Cost-effectiveness: A primer.* Thousand Oaks, CA: Sage.

McMillian, J. H. & Schumacher, S. (1997). *Research in education: A conceptual introduction (4th ed.)* New York: Longman.

National Middle School Association. (1995). *This we believe: Developmentally responsive middle level schools.* Columbus, OH: Author.

Paris, S. G., Lawton, T. A., Turner, J. C. & Roth, J. L. (1991). "A developmental perspective on standardized achievement testing." *Educational Researcher, 20* (5), 12-20.

Patten, M. L. (1998). *Questionnaire research: A practical guide.* Los Angeles: Pyrczak.

Popham, W. J. (1975) *Educational Evaluation.* New York: Prentice-Hall.

Popham, W. J. (1981). *Modern educational measurement.* Englewood Cliffs, NJ: Prentice-Hall.

Pyrczak, F. (1996). *Success at Statistics.* Los Angeles, CA: Pyrczak Publishing.

Salant, P. & Dillman, D. A. (1994). *How to conduct your own survey.* New York: John Wiley.

Suter, W. N. (1998). *Primer of Educational Research.* Needham Heights, MA: Allyn and Bacon.

Webb, E. J., Campbell, D. T., Schwartz, R. D. and Sechrest, L. (1965). *Unobtrusive measures.* Chicago: University of Chicago Press.

Worthen, B. R., Sanders, J. R., & Fitzpatrick, J. L. (1997). *Program evaluation: Alternative approaches and practical guidelines.* (2nd ed.). White Plains, NY: Longman.

Q A   **Appendix**

Accelerated Schools

An accelerated school is a school where ALL students *accelerate* their learning. Building on the ideas of Dr. Henry M. Levin and his colleagues at Stanford University, educators in an accelerated school seek to create a learning environment that nurtures all students, helping them to grow intellectually and socially. An accelerated school differs from conventional schools along the following dimensions:

- In an accelerated school, **all students are treated as gifted.** All students possess talents and strengths and the teachers in an accelerated school build on these talents and strengths to help students learn faster and better. Students learn not only facts, but they also learn how to use facts to think and solve problems.

- In an accelerated school, all members of the school community—teachers, administrators, students and families—**keep three principles at the forefront of all school activities:** (1) Unity of purpose (2) Decision-making coupled with responsibility, and (3) Building on strengths. Members of the accelerated school community strive to maintain a **unity of purpose** in all that they do. They make sure that all activities help further the school's vision for it's students. Furthermore, teachers, principals, and parents **make important decisions** about the school's curriculum, instructional practices and organization for learning and decision-making. Members of the school community **assume a real sense of responsibility** for making these decisions happen. Finally, members of the Accelerated School community alter their perceptions of themselves and their students. Rather than focusing on the deficits, they **build on the strengths** of their students, their colleagues, and their community as they change their school.

- In an accelerated school, teachers and administrators **examine the total school environment.** They believe that successful school reform must encompass ch!anges in the school's context, curriculum, and instruction. Each of these sides of the "triangle" must be changed. For example, if a school's science instruction is changed to include observation and experimentation, such a change will be successful only if the school's context for learning and curriculum support such instructional activities. Without changes in each side of the "triangle," efforts at reform will fail.

- In an accelerated school, **teachers, principals, and parents work together** to create an instructional program that draws on the unique strengths of their students and meets the needs of their students. They draw on their own expertise, common sense and research-proven strategies to find ways of addressing all three legs of the "triangle," the school's context for learning, its curriculum, and its instructional practices. Using a three-level approach to decision-making and problem-solving, members of the school community create their own unique Accelerated School.

- In an accelerated school, teachers and administrators promote **enriched learning opportunities for all students** rather than tracking, **avoid labeling** students, and find ways to change the school schedule to **allow staff to collaborate, reflect and problem-solve** on a routine basis.

- In an accelerated school, teachers make content **relevant** to students, encourage students to **make connections** across subject areas, and offer students opportunities to practice skills by **doing real-world tasks**. All students are expected to meet a common set of objectives. Teachers **stress broad-based skills** that apply to many learning situations rather than focus solely on discrete skills that have narrow application. Teachers in an accelerated school **emphasize critical thinking** over learning specific facts and **draw on current, real world situations** and personal experiences of students as a basis for study. Accelerated curriculum looks beyond textbooks to literature, source documents, magazines, reference books, and current and community events. Finally, the curriculum is **rich with opportunities for students to use language** for thinking and communicating.

- In an accelerated school, students **learn by doing**. They engage in learning activities that are real, meaningful and interesting rather than artificially contrived. Rote learning and drill are replaced by **discovery learning**. Rather than completing worksheets on money, students actually organize and run a class "store," learning how to run a business. Teachers use strategies that **build on the unique assets of youngsters**. Accelerated instruction focuses on the strengths of the students and finds their "giftedness." Additionally, accelerated teaching techniques **rely heavily on student-centered activities, emphasizing student responsibility for learning**.

- In an accelerated school, **parents play an important part** in nurturing their children's education. At home, parents affirm the goals and expectations of the school, monitor homework and encourage their children to do their best. At school, parents help out in classrooms and participate in making decisions for the school by serving on task forces and the school's steering committee.

- Finally, in an accelerated school, teachers, administrators and parents **follow a systematic process** to transform their school into an environment that accelerates the learning of all students. Members of the school community forge a common vision, take stock of the current situation, set priorities, and form task forces that use a problem-solving process known as Inquiry to find solutions to the challenges facing the school.

You can obtain more information by contacting:
Accelerated Schools Project
109 CERAS
Stanford University
Stanford, CA 94305-3084

Or, visit their Web site at: **http://www.stanford.edu/group/ASP**

Activators

Interact Learning Through Involvement publishes numerous simulations for use by students from primary grades to high school. Some of the simulations require several hours of class time. However, the Activators featured in our example in Chapter 9 take from 20 minutes to two class periods. These Activators give students a brief taste of a specific historical event through a direct experience. Prices for the classroom materials are quite reasonable. For a full listing of the Activators available contact the publisher at:

Interact
1825 Gillespie Way, #101
El Cajon, CA 92020-1095
Phone: 1 (800) 359-0961

Or, visit their Web site at: **http://www.interact-simulations.com**

Bay Area Writing Project

The Bay Area Writing Project is "a collaborative program of the University of California at Berkeley and [the San Francisco] Bay Area schools, dedicated to improving writing and the teaching of writing at all grade levels and in all disciplines" (from the Project's Website). The Project has expanded outside the San Francisco area and now supports a National Writing Project, residing at 160 colleges and universities across the United States.

The Website also includes a helpful on-line newsletter. You can reach the Bay Area Writing Project Website at: **http://www-gse.berkeley.edu/outreach/bawp/bawp2.html**

Constructivist Teaching

Constructivist teachers use teaching practices that rest on a theory of learning that says that people learn best when they *construct* their own knowledge. Brooks and Brooks in their book *In Search of Understanding: The Case for Constructivist Classrooms* (1993) provide a clear overview of the constructivist theory of learning and offer solid guidance to educators who wish to follow constructivist teaching practices. Brooks and Brooks (1993) lay out 12 benchmarks of constructivist teaching:

1. Constructivist teachers encourage and accept student autonomy and initiative.

2. Constructivist teachers use raw data and primary sources, along with manipulative, interactive, and physical materials.

3. When framing tasks, constructivist teachers use cognitive terminology such as "classify," "analyze," "predict," and "create."

4. Constructivist teachers allow student responses to drive lessons, shift instructional strategies, and alter content.

5. Constructivist teachers inquire about students' understandings of concepts before sharing their own understandings of these concepts.

6. Constructivist teachers encourage students to engage in dialogue, both with the teacher and with one another.

7. Constructivist teachers encourage student inquiry by asking thoughtful, open-ended questions and encouraging students to ask questions of each other.

8. Constructivist teachers seek elaboration of students' initial responses.

9. Constructivist teachers engage students in experiences that might engender contradictions to their initial hypotheses and then encourage discussion.

10. Cnstructivist teachers allow wait time after posing questions.

11. Constructivist teachers provide time for students to construct relationships and create metaphors.

12. Constructivist teachers nurture students' natural curiosity through frequent use of the learning cycle model (pp. 121–130).

For more information, please read:

Brooks, J. G. & Brooks, M. G. (1993). *In Search of Understanding: The Case for Constructivist Classrooms*. Alexandria, VA: Association for Supervision and Curriculum Development.

D.E.A.R

D.E.A.R. stands for Drop Everything And Read. During D.E.A.R. time, *everyone* within a school, students and adults alike, reads silently for a specified period of time. Some schools have D.E.A.R. time daily, while others opt to use it a couple of times a week. Generally, D.E.A.R. time lasts from 15 to 30 minutes. Most often students and adults may read any materials they wish (within the bounds of propriety), however, some schools focus on certain genres or topics. Below are the Websites of various schools that use D.E.A.R. This technique also goes by the term U.S.S.R. or Uninterrupted Sustained Silent Reading.

The Website of Saskatchewan Education in Canada gives an excellent overview of the D.E.A.R. strategy, along with very useful suggestions on how to successful implement a D.E.A.R. program. You can reach this Web site at:

http://www.sasked.gov.sk.ca/docs/ela/ela_ssr.html

A couple of Websites that can give you other ideas on implementation include: Acme Elementary School in Acme, Washington, site at:

http://www.mtbaker.wednet.edu/schools/acme/read.htm

Chatham Middle School site at:
http://chatham.k12.nc.us/ChatMid/daily.html

Hands-On Equations: Making Algebra Child's Play!

This is one of the frequent staff development workshops offered by Phi Delta Kappa, the national education fraternity. You're probably familiar with their monthly publication *The Kappan*. Conducted by presenters from Borenson & Associates, the workshop shows teachers how to "use the visual and kinesthetic HANDS-ON EQUATIONS patented teaching methodology for successfully presenting essential algebraic concepts to students in grades 3 to adult." (Phi Delta Kappa's Website.)

You can get more information by contacting:

Borenson and Associates
P.O. Box 3328
Allentown, PA 18106
Phone: (800) 993-6284
Website: **http://www.borenson.com**

Center for Professional Development and Services
P.O. Box 789
Bloomington, IN 47402-0789
Toll Free: (800) 766-1156 or (888) 792-2904, extension 2500
e-mail: cpds@pdkintl.org

Math Journals

In many middle school classrooms around the country, teachers are integrating mathematics and writing by incorporating *math journals* into their math lessons. By asking students to reflect and write on their problem-solving experiences, students can both consolidate and extend their mathematical understanding. Furthermore, by providing students with a variety of writing prompts, teachers can help students connect math with the real world. Two ERIC Digests (both available in fulltext versions on-line) give a list of resources that will provide you with information and suggestions on using math journals in your classroom:

Reed, M. K. (1995). *Making mathematical connections in middle school. ERIC Digest.* Columbus, OH: ERIC Clearinghouse for Science, Mathematics, and Environmental Education. (ERIC Document Reproduction Service No. ED 380 309)

Available on-line at:
http://www.ed.gov/databases/ERIC_Digests/ed380309.html

Peyton, J. K. (April 1993). *Dialogue journals: Interactive writing to develop language and literacy. ERIC Digest.* Washington, DC: ERIC Clearinghouse on Languages and Linguistics. (ERIC Document Reproduction Service No. D 354 789)

Available on-line at:
http://www.ed.gov/databases/ERIC_Digests/ed354789.html

Multiple Intelligences

Howard Gardner, a Harvard psychologist, suggests that we view human intelligence as a multi-faceted capacity to learn and interact with our environment and other humans. His ideas have challenged the narrow definition of intelligence held by researchers and educators alike. He suggests that humans possess at least eight types of intelligence:

- Verbal/linguistic
- Logical/mathematical
- Spatial
- Bodily-kinesthetic
- Musical
- Interpersonal
- Intrapersonal
- Naturalist

Furthermore, he posits that each person possesses all the various types of intelligences to some degree and everyone can further develop each of the intelligences.

Many educators have taken Gardner's theory of multiple intelligences and translated it into classroom practices. Some of the best books out on the subject include:

Armstrong, T. (1994). *Multiple intelligences in the classroom*. Alexandria, VA: Association for Supervision and Curriculum Development.

Armstrong, T. (1993). *Seven kinds of smart: Identifying and developing your many intelligences*. New York City: Plume Books.

Haggerty, B. A. (1995). *Nurturing intelligences: A guide to multiple intelligences theory and teaching*. Menlo Park, CA: Addison-Wesley Publishing Company.

Lazear, D. (1991). *Seven ways of teaching: The artistry of teaching with multiple intelligences*. Palatine, IL: Skylight Publishing, Inc.

Socratic Seminar

Rigorous discussion guided by the teacher rests as the foundation of the Socratic Seminar. By asking thought-provoking questions, teachers engage students in a dialogue that centers around evaluating ideas and gaining a deep understanding of a particular piece of reading text drawn from literature, history, philosophy, science, the arts, or mathematics. The Socratic Seminar begins with an open-ended question designed to spark curiosity and encourage participants to delve more deeply into the text. Often this exploration raises more questions and, of course, more dialogue. The following Web site, maintained by the Los Angeles County Office of Education, includes an excellent overview, along with tips for implementing the Socratic Seminar teaching strategy:

http://www.lacoe.edu/pdc/professional/socratic.html

Teacher Advisory Programs

Many successful middle schools have implemented Teacher Advisory Programs as a way to meet the social and emotional needs of their students. These schools explicitly create within their curricula opportunities for teachers and students to explore issues relating to the emotional needs of students. Furthermore, teachers work to build student skills in such areas as interpersonal relations, decision-making, and conflict resolution. Finally, schools with a teacher advisory program, pair each student with a school adult who serves as the student's advisor throughout the middle school years. In implementing teacher advisory programs, some middle schools have transformed the conventional daily homeroom into time where teachers and students meet to discuss issues, build skills and create a "family."

Although written in 1986, Michael James' short book Adviser-Advisee Programs: Why, What and How published by the National Middle School Association, continues to provide useful ideas and advice on implementing a teacher advisory program. For more information on teacher advisory programs, visit the National Middle School Association's website at:

http://www.nmsa.org/

Click on the Resource Center and you'll find a button labeled "Advisory Programs," Click here and you'll go to a listing of books, including the one by James, that gives more ideas and advice.

Index

Q A   About the Authors

Brenda Guenther LeTendre began her career as an educator in 1971, teaching English at a large inner-city high school in Dallas. She has taught students at all grade levels from first to post-secondary and served as a central office administrator. In 1986, while pursuing a doctoral degree at Stanford University, she joined Henry M. Levin and his team to start the first Accelerated School in the nation. Since that time, she has helped launch and support Accelerated Schools across the nation, particularly those in her home state of Missouri. Currently, she teaches full-time at Pittsburg State University in southeast Kansas. Brenda lives in Joplin, Missouri, with her husband Dana, and daughter Danielle.

Richard Lipka is a Professor of Education at Pittsburg State University in Kansas. A graduate of the State University of New York College at Buffalo (B.S., M.S.) and the University of Illinois (Ph.D.), he taught sixth grade as a member of a four person team in Amherst, New York. His research interest is affective development with an emphasis on self-concept and self-esteem. To that end, he serves as a co-editor (with Tom Brinthaupt) of the *Studying the Self* book series for SUNY Press. In addition, he has written book chapters and articles for a variety of professional journals.